THE HISTORY OF MICHIGAN LAW

Ohio University Press Series on
Law, Society, and Politics in the Midwest

Series Editor: Paul Finkelman

THE HISTORY OF
MICHIGAN
LAW

Edited by Paul Finkelman
and Martin J. Hershock

*With a foreword by Hon. Clifford W. Taylor,
Chief Justice, Michigan Supreme Court*

Ohio University Press   Athens

Ohio University Press, Athens, Ohio 45701
www.ohio.edu / oupress
© 2006 by Ohio University Press

Printed in the United States of America

Ohio University Press books are printed on acid-free paper ⊗ ™

14 13 12 11 10 09 08 07 06   5 4 3 2 1

The views expressed herein do not necessarily represent
those of the Michigan State Bar Foundation.

Library of Congress Cataloging-in-Publication Data

The history of Michigan law / edited by Paul Finkelman and Martin J.
Hershock with a foreword by Clifford W. Taylor.
    p. cm. — (Ohio University Press series on law, society, and politics in the
Midwest)
    Includes bibliographical references and index.
    ISBN-13: 978-0-8214-1661-7 (cloth : alk. paper)
    ISBN-10: 0-8214-1661-8 (cloth : alk. paper)
    1. Law—Michigan—History. I. Finkelman, Paul, 1949– II. Hershock, Martin J.,
1962– III. Taylor, Clifford W. IV. Series.
    KFM4278.H57 2006
    349.77409—dc22

                                                                    2006009921

Publication of *The History of Michigan Law* has been made
possible by the generous financial support of the

 Michigan State Bar Foundation

To Gillian Berchowitz

a wonderful editor and even better friend

CONTENTS

FOREWORD

In William Shakespeare's *Tempest,* the character Antonio observes:

> [W]hat's past is prologue, what to come [is]
> In yours and my discharge.
>
> (Act 2, scene 1)

That past-as-prologue line came to mind when I read the manuscript for *The History of Michigan Law.* Antonio dismisses past events as insignificant when compared to his more important business of the moment. Similarly, we judges and lawyers who debate today's tempestuous legal and political issues often know too little about the people and events that shaped those issues.

In the letter that accompanied my copy of this manuscript, the editors promised:

> This collection of essays does not offer a traditional (and potentially dry) narrative history of law in Michigan, but rather aims to provide an introduction to the key themes and events that determined the evolution of law and justice in Michigan.

The editors and their contributors have delivered on that promise. I confess that I was not particularly eager to begin reading the manuscript; but once I started, I found it hard to put aside. Each chapter—indeed almost every page—serves up some new piece of information that helps to explain how and why Michigan's society and government evolved as they did. The city of Hamtramck and Woodward Avenue in Detroit are the namesakes of early Michigan leaders. Likewise, the small towns named Freesoil, Temperance, and Liberty honor important political movements.

As the editors promised, the essays in this book are not dry. To the contrary, I think that most who read this book will enjoy the experience. And, while being entertained, readers will come to know the people who shaped our state's history. Some possessed great intellect and courage; others were less distinguished, but still well worth knowing.

I am pleased to recommend *The History of Michigan Law* to all citizens of Michigan, especially to attorneys and to students of American government, civics, and related subjects.

Clifford W. Taylor
Chief Justice, Michigan Supreme Court

ACKNOWLEDGMENTS

Endeavors such as *The History of Michigan Law* are collaborative by their very nature. Although many scholars might openly lament the loss of direct control and the precarious interdependence inherent in such work, we have chosen rather to embrace it and have been amply rewarded for the effort. Our collective debt is enormous, and it would be impossible to thank individually all those who have contributed to this work. A number of people, however, have made particularly significant contributions to this project, and we would be remiss if we failed to acknowledge and thank them.

This book would not have been possible without the support and encouragement of the Honorable Avern Cohn. His vision and initiative were critical in breathing life into this project, and his keen mind and probing intellect have left an indelible mark on the final product. Judge Cohn's passion for the material has sustained us both throughout the entire project, and we consider it a tremendous privilege and honor to have had the opportunity to share our work with him.

Thanks go to the entire staff at the Ohio University Press. In particular, we'd like to thank Rick Huard for a fabulous edit of the collection and for riding herd over both the editors and the contributors (a thankless but necessary task). Gillian Berchowitz is much more than an editor to us (though an incredible editor she is); she is our sounding board, our confidante, our pick-me-up, and the most remarkable of friends. "Thank you" seems woefully inadequate to express our gratitude for all that Gill has done for us.

We also would like to acknowledge the generous financial support of the Michigan State Bar Foundation. Without assistance from Michigan's legal community this project would not have been possible. We also thank the Bentley Historical Library at the University of Michigan for individual research support for both of the editors in the form of two Mark C. Stevens Researcher Travel Fellowships.

Obviously, a big debt of gratitude is owed to our contributors. It has been a wonderful experience working with all of them, and we look forward to continuing our relationships (both professional and personal). The authors of these essays come from different fields—history, law teaching, political science, and law practice—and it has been a delight to learn from all of them. Each has brought a profound dedication to this book.

No work of this magnitude can succeed without the support and encouragement of family and friends. We are both especially grateful for the support and love of our spouses, Byrgen and Kathy, and our children, Abby, Isaac, and Kaysi, and Rebecca and Rachel. Thank you all.

Paul Finkelman
Martin J. Hershock

INTRODUCTION

In 1881, Oliver Wendell Holmes Jr., who was then serving on the highest court of Massachusetts, observed in his great book *The Common Law* that the "life of the law has not been logic; it has been experience." He asserted that the "felt necessities of the time, the prevalent moral and political theories, intuitions of public policy, avowed or unconscious, even the prejudices which judges share with their fellow-men, have had a good deal more to do than the syllogism in determining the rules by which men should be governed."[1] The essays in this volume on Michigan law underscore the wisdom of Holmes's insights.

At the same time, they also suggest how we must expand on Holmes's understanding of the forces that have led to legal development. Holmes wrote in New England some two centuries after settlement. He observed a mature industrial society expanding in the wake of the national and regional triumph of the Civil War. Nineteenth-century Michigan was a new place, just barely settled, and did not become a state until 1837. Michigan grew up along with an industrializing and expanding America. These facts alone make for a different kind of legal history. But the legal history of Michigan suggests that we must add at least two other categories to the forces shaping law: geography and the environment of a place and the people who settle and inhabit a place. In the Midwest, the environment profoundly affected economic growth, while the population grew dramatically through migration from other parts of the country and immigration from Europe and Canada. Three tiny midwestern settlements of the early nineteenth century—Chicago, Cleveland, and Detroit—had become three of the nation's greatest cities by the end of the century.

In Michigan, access to abundant water (especially the Great Lakes), trees, and furbearing animals has helped shape the economy and the law. Forests and fish spurred development; rapacious timber cutting and commercial fishing led to laws mandating conservation and protection of natural resources. Similarly, the natural resources and transportation routes helped make Michigan a manufacturing powerhouse and led to the creation of the automobile industry, which, in turn, led to a vibrant union movement.

Legal change—both case law and legislation—developed along with industrialization, unionization, and urbanization. The downturn in the industrial economy—the emergence of the Rust Belt—has led, not surprisingly, to other legal developments.

Of greater consequence still is the source of the population. The "felt necessities of the time" were felt differently by people whose social, political, and ethnic origins were different. Thus, in the end, the history of Michigan law is the history of people transporting ideas and beliefs to a new region and applying them to the circumstances of that new place.

Although squarely in the heart of the Midwest, Michigan, as historian George May notes, "is perhaps the least typical of all of the original forty-eight states in the Union" and, in point of fact, differs in many pronounced ways from the rest of the states in the region.[2] Unlike its primary midwestern peers, Michigan, located on the nation's northern frontier, developed without significant ties to the South. Rather, it was the influence of New England and upstate New York that most obviously shaped Michigan in the years after the United States took possession of the territory. Sometimes called the "Third New England" or the "Yankee West," Michigan was profoundly influenced by transplanted Yankee culture. Sagacious, cunning, and rationally acquisitive, this Yankee spirit also was notable for its strident moralism, reform-mindedness, activism, devotion to public education, and, oftentimes, conservatism. Collectively, these values permeated Michigan society during its formative period. Perhaps nothing else makes this more evident than Michigan's legal heritage, a heritage that undeniably reflects the legal environments of New York and New England. Indeed, much of Michigan's legal code was lifted wholesale from the New England states or from New York State, whose central and western counties served as the second home for Yankee culture and as the primary staging point for emigration to Michigan.

This continuity of traditions and values, especially with regard to the law, manifested itself in innumerable ways in Michigan. Yankee settlers brought to the state an abolitionist ideology and a Puritan heritage that led to some of the most progressive civil rights law in the Midwest, to an early opposition to the death penalty, and to what John Quist calls, with some irony, "An Occasionally Dry State Surrounded by Water." Thus, the most important aspect of Michigan's geography may not have been its location between four great lakes but its proximity to New York and New England. As people from those states moved into Michigan, the state became a Yankee enclave on the western edge of American settlement.

A brief look at race relations in Michigan and other midwestern states further illustrates how the people of the state shaped the laws. Unlike the states of the lower Midwest, early Michigan did not have a population that was a mixture of southerners and Yankees. Early Ohio, Indiana, and Illinois were, in many ways, far more southern than northern. Settlers from Virginia, Kentucky, and Tennessee dominated those states in their early years. These southerners brought with them attitudes about slavery and race that led to repressive black codes and a persistence of bondage in Illinois.[3] By 1849, an influx of settlers from the free states had led to a repeal of the black laws in Ohio.[4] However, there was no similar population shift in Indiana or Illinois, and race discrimination remained an integral part of the law in those states until well after the Civil War.

When the Michigan Territory was separated from the lower Northwest, it inherited these black codes but effectively abandoned them before statehood. As a state, Michigan never tried to restrict black migration and, in 1838, eliminated the old territorial law that had established such limits. Thus, Michigan became a safe haven for free blacks and fugitive slaves escaping the more repressive laws of the South and the lower Midwest. In the antebellum period, Michigan was without question the most egalitarian state in the Midwest.[5] Although not as liberal as Massachusetts or New York in matters of race, it was far closer to those states than it was to its neighbors to the south. Like New York, Pennsylvania, and the New England states (but unlike Ohio, Indiana, and Illinois), Michigan allowed blacks to testify in court on the same basis as whites. When Ohio repealed its black code in 1849, the Buckeye State managed to catch up to where Michigan had been since 1838. In the 1850s, Michigan moved past Ohio again, when it allowed black men to vote in school board elections. As Roy Finkenbine demonstrates in his essay, Michigan was a leader in protecting the liberty of free blacks and fugitive slaves. Similarly, Paul Finkelman's essay on race after the Civil War shows that Michigan's legislature and courts provided strong protections for the civil rights of African Americans.

These attitudes toward race were not a function of mere geography or economics. Like the state's early abolition of the death penalty—Michigan was the first jurisdiction in the English-speaking world to do so—its early admission of women to law schools, its modern commitment to gender equality, and its sometime support for prohibition, the state's legal heritage on race reflected the people of the state. The persistent commitment to racial equality in Michigan—illustrated by the state's abortive foray into the world of cross-district bussing in the 1970s and its successful defense of affirmative action in higher education in *Grutter v. Bollinger* in the twenty-first century—is also a reflection of how the law of the state grew out of the goals, attitudes, and beliefs of its people. This history is, of course, not entirely rosy. Unlike African Americans in Massachusetts or Vermont, for example, blacks in antebellum Michigan could not vote on the same basis as whites. Post–Civil War Michigan did not always live up to the promises of equality found in its own laws. Nevertheless, Michigan retained its progressive Yankee heritage in its legal culture, even as its implementation of these ideals proved incomplete.

Although its population and legal heritage differ from those of other midwestern states, Michigan's legal culture is still very much midwestern. Situated in the center of the continent, the Midwest and its inhabitants have long been represented as the most American of all the nation's regions and peoples. In this literal and figurative middle ground in the nation's heartland, Americans from diverse regions, possessing varied traditions and distinct regional cultures, joined together to create a unique identity. Indeed, the Midwest stands as perhaps the most iconic of all American regions. From the mid-nineteenth century to the first third of the twentieth century, the region was the cradle of the American presidency, sending a spate of its sons to the White House. Twentieth-century American politicians and advertising executives adhered to the adage "If it plays in Peoria." The sometimes ridiculed midwestern dialect has become the standard on the nation's airwaves. Moreover, the region has retained its resonance in more recent times as a political bellwether and as the battleground upon which presidential aspirants are made or broken.

As already noted, Michigan's legal heritage is both typically midwestern and, at the same time, distinctive. The state's legislation and jurisprudence on race are examples of this. So, too, is the importance of its highest court in the nineteenth century. Although one might be hard-pressed to think of a great court in Ohio, Indiana, or Illinois, the Cooley Court of late nineteenth-century Michigan is very much in the tradition of the noted Shaw Court in Massachusetts. Similarly, Cooley is the natural heir to the jurisprudential tradition of Joseph Story, of Massachusetts, and James Kent, of New York.

Michigan's law and its inherited legal culture were never stagnant and unchanging. Michigan (and the Cooley Court) also reflected the traditions of the dynamic jurisprudence of New England and New York. Michigan's history illuminates a legal culture that was flexible and adaptable in the face of new conditions and circumstances. Frontier living, the expansion of market capitalism, rapid industrialization on a grand scale, the diversification of the state's population, and a host of attendant social problems shattered and disrupted traditional life and sorely tested the host culture. Michigan's twentieth-century history set it further apart from its midwestern neighbors, as the state led the nation into the modern industrial age and became the center of America's most important industry. The dramatic expansion of the auto industry and the promise of relatively high wages in the aftermath of Henry Ford's fabled "five-dollar day" declaration made Michigan a magnet for native- and foreign-born migrants and immigrants alike. In spite of the furious pace of development and growth, however, the tradition of Yankee-influenced jurisprudence continued unabated. The state was among the first in the nation to embrace the concept of publicly funded legal counsel for criminal defendants, and it led the nation in the adoption of a modern rape law. Moreover, the state's unique water-bounded geography, abundant natural resources, and industrially blighted landscape compelled Michigan to become an innovator in environmental and conservation law.

More recently, Michigan has been the poster child for a postindustrial America. The auto industry, the heart and soul of the nation's manufacturing economy and the lifeblood of Michigan, was dealt a body blow by the 1973 oil embargo and foreign competition. Plant closures, layoffs, and an aggressive "Buy American" campaign failed to put the industry back on its feet. Anti-Asian resentment and hostility coursed through the state, rearing its head most famously in the 1982 murder of Vincent Chin by two unemployed auto workers. The collapse of the auto industry hit Detroit extremely hard. The city, once the nation's fourth largest with a population of roughly two million people, lost many of its residents to factory closures and white flight in the 1960s and 1970s. In the 1980s, it became the nation's largest city with a black majority—a great many of whom live mired in poverty. Today, the city is a tattered remnant of its glorious past, producing very few automobiles and losing population at an alarming rate. The future direction of Michigan law, like its history, may depend in large measure on the state's economic development.

Through it all, however, Michigan's Yankee heritage has stood up to the challenge and has served as a useful and flexible mechanism for dealing with change. Even as Michigan's legal culture adapted and evolved to meet changing circumstances, it remained true to its moral compass and the reforming spirit established by its originators. This powerful blend of judicious rationality and crusading fortitude propelled Michigan onto the national legal stage and resulted in a number of innovative and precedent-setting laws. The essays included in this volume examine some of these laws and other issues that highlight the unique character and evolution of the law in Michigan from its territorial phase to the present time. *The History of Michigan Law* is not intended to be an all-encompassing work. Rather, it offers a collection of essays on a number of topics that are central to Michigan's legal past. The book not only will educate people about Michigan law but also will serve as an invitation to delve more deeply into the legal history of the state. The varied perspectives and approaches of the lawyers, historians, policymakers, and legal scholars who have contributed their talents to this collection add richness and texture to the work and facilitate the focused exploration of these discrete legal subjects. At the same time, the essays prompt a multifaceted consideration of common themes and a clear delineation of the persistence of Yankee influences, in all of their permutations, on Michigan's legal environment. Indeed, this common thread informs, to varying degrees, all of the volume's essays.

The book's opening essay, "The Northwest Ordinance and Michigan's Territorial Heritage" by David Chardavoyne, explores the origins and maturation of Michigan's foundational legal structures. Historians often have depicted Michigan's earliest legal phase in almost utopian terms as an era of exuberant idealism, moral certitude, and burgeoning democracy. Chardavoyne reminds readers of the contested nature of the contemporary legal environment and of the obvious limits of the dominant historical paradigm, particularly with regard to slavery in the region and the autocratic nature of territorial governance. Nevertheless, Chardavoyne affirms, in spite of these very real obstacles and restrictions, the Yankee spirit that permeated Michigan fostered innovation and progressiveness, attributes that manifested themselves in, among other things, the successful crusade by Michigan reformers to abolish capital punishment.

Martin Hershock's "Blood on the Tracks: Law, Railroad Accidents, the Economy, and the Michigan Frontier" also examines the Yankee influence on early Michigan law. This essay, however, pays particular attention to the tension between the settlers who favored development and those who retained the more conservative characteristics of Yankee culture, a tension embodied in the antebellum struggle of Michigan's pioneer farmers to preserve open-range grazing in the face of an expansive market capitalism symbolized by the railroad. Michigan's first American settlers, fresh from the booming Empire State, borrowed extensively from their previous home and Yankee traditions to create a legal system that encouraged commercial development, highlighting Yankee acquisitiveness and entrepreneurship. But dogged independence, a commitment to the notion of community, and economic collapse brought forth a conservative desire to blunt and temper the power of the cash nexus and to preserve traditional self-provisioning farming. The resultant conflict, brought to a head by the expansion of the state's railroad network and the inadvertent slaughter of local livestock—a key component in subsistence agriculture—completely reordered Michigan's political climate and redefined the state's legal environment. The outcome of this conflict paved the way for the full-blown development of industrial capitalism in the state during the late nineteenth and early twentieth centuries.

Social reform and moral advocacy, trends long associated with Yankee culture, are highlighted in the essays by historians John Quist and Roy Finkenbine. In "An Occasionally Dry State Surrounded by Water," Quist outlines the social and legal crusade against alcohol in Michigan in the years before the Civil War. Because reformers continually shifted tactics between moral suasion and legal activism, Quist argues, the cyclical nature of the movement against alcohol in Michigan produced few tangible results in the 1830s and 1840s. In the following decade, however, aided by far-reaching social disruption and the enactment of the so-called Maine Law of 1852, supporters lobbied for and obtained prohibitory legislation designed to end "King Alcohol's" rule in the state. The victory, however, was a pyrrhic one, as Yankee moralism quickly gave way in the face of an increasingly diverse public and a hostile state judiciary controlled by the Democratic Party. These forces soon rendered the laws unenforceable.

Roy Finkenbine examines a strikingly similar disconnect between moral advocacy and reality in antebellum race relations in Michigan. A hotbed of antislavery fervor from its founding, Michigan remained in the forefront of the crusade against the peculiar institution and gave birth to the most successful antislavery political force in the nation's history, the Republican Party. In addition, many of the state's residents worked tirelessly to protect fugitive slaves who moved to Michigan or to assist those on their way to freedom in neighboring Canada. Michigan residents foiled efforts by slave catchers to return fugitives to bondage. Weak and relatively unenforced black laws in the territorial period—which were mostly repealed almost immediately after statehood—furthered the state's reputation as "a beacon of liberty" in the years before the Civil War. This reputation, Finkenbine hastens to add, although partially valid, is partially fabricated and masks a more complex reality: the state "was no racial utopia." Restrictive laws, a lack of political rights and privileges, and rampant racism were an undisputed reality in the state. In the end, Finkenbine contends, although Michigan fares very favorably in comparison to many of the antebellum northern states, especially its midwestern peers, in regard to its racial climate, it did not fully live up to its mythic image of "a beacon of liberty" on the Great Lakes.

Thomas Cooley was one of the giants of American legal history and the most eminent of the state's "Big Four" justices, a group that also included James V. Campbell, Isaac P. Christiancy, and Benjamin F. Graves. Cooley and his court are the subject of Paul Carrington's "Deference to Democracy." Steeped in "the equal rights doctrine embodied in the culture brought to Michigan from western New York," Cooley sought to establish order and the predictability of the law in the face of social change. Although committed to the notion of "plain meaning" in the law, Cooley, as Carrington notes, did not shy away from judicial interpretation. On the contrary, mirroring the Jacksonian spirit and presaging twentieth-century liberalism, he embraced democratic politics as the "appropriate source of the moral values informing his judgments." In nineteenth-century Michigan that meant, for all intents and purposes, Yankee values. This dedication to the vox populi culminated in a number of landmark cases promoting the Jacksonian ideals of equality (*People v. Board of Education of Detroit*), freedom of expression (*Atkinson v. Detroit Free Press*), and the existence of governmental power for public purposes (*People v. Salem*).

Commitment to democratic ideals and the general good, as Frank Ravitch demonstrates, has shaped Michigan's four state constitutions (1835, 1850, 1908, and 1963). In his survey of the construction and subsequent evolution of Michigan's constitutional framework, Ravitch focuses on the issues of legislative apportionment, the judiciary, and religion and religious freedom as written into the state constitutions. Through an analysis of these constitutions, he details the relationship between the people of Michigan and their government in response to changing social and economic circumstances and historical trends. In the judiciary, for instance, Michigan moved from a system in which most judges were appointed to one in which judges generally were elected. The apportionment debate, Ravitch contends, reflected a similar democratizing trend and shifted, in 1963, in important ways in response to civil rights concerns. Taken as a whole, Ravitch concludes, the constitution of the state of Michigan has broken important new ground while retaining its basic principles and remains "in many ways a cutting-edge document."

Michigan has been a leader in the field of environmental and conservation law, as well. In his essay "Ruin and Recovery: Conservation and Environmental Law in Michigan," Dave Dempsey, former director of the Michigan Environmental Council, graphically details the wanton destruction of Michigan's rich natural resources. Timber, game, fish, land, and water, at various times in the state's history, have been the targets of unregulated commercial exploitation. The result, Dempsey argues, was and continues to be an environment in peril. Urged forward by a conservation-minded and fiercely activist citizenry and resenting the rapid abandonment of the state by the lumber industry, Michigan's legislature overcame intense lobbying and began, in the late nineteenth century, to adopt laws to protect and restore the state's depleted resources. This environmental policy resulted in, among other things, the creation of the Michigan state forest system—one of the most extensive in the country. This sense of responsibility and stewardship, as Dempsey notes, inspired the modern environmental movement in the state and led to the passage, in 1969, of the Natural Resources and Environmental Protection Act, which authorized private citizens to bring suit to protect the environment. The tradition also has influenced contemporary efforts to curb urban sprawl and to safeguard Michigan's invaluable water resources.

Ronald Bretz's contribution, "170 Years of a Balancing Act: A Brief History of Criminal Justice in Michigan," surveys some of the most important trends in the area of Michigan criminal law (substantive criminal law, punishment, juvenile offenders, the criminal court system, the right to counsel, the exclusionary rule, and the rights of crime victims). Bretz's work once again reminds the reader of the Yankee imprint on Michigan law. The state's first penal code, drawn primarily from the English common law as supplemented by the Northwest Ordinance, was adopted in 1846, at the height of Yankee influence, and still serves as the basis for the state's criminal law. This substantive criminal law—in large part because of the poor definitions of the crimes codified—has been the subject of changing interpretations over time, including a marked conservative shift in the last quarter century. In the realm of punishment, Michigan was an early advocate of rehabilitation for criminals and constructed its first penitentiary in 1842. The state also was a pioneer in the use of a parole system and, early on, created a separate house of corrections for its juvenile offenders. Michigan is also notable as a leader in providing the right to counsel for those accused of crimes (an 1820 statute provided for counsel at public expense) and for being the first state in the nation to adopt voluntarily the exclusionary rule in the wake of the U.S. Supreme Court's 1914 decision in *United States v. Weeks.*

Michigan's leading role in the post–Civil War civil rights story is recounted by Paul Finkelman in "The Promise of Equality and the Limits of Law." In clear distinction to its southern counterparts, some of its northern peers, and the late nineteenth-century federal judiciary, Michigan readily embraced the concept of legal equality among the races and enacted a number of sweeping measures intended to erase the color line. Furthermore, in the late nineteenth century, the Michigan Supreme Court vigorously denounced segregation and racism. Indeed, in few other areas does the state's Yankee heritage show more distinctly than in the realm of civil rights law. From antebellum guarantees of civil liberties for blacks to its postbellum efforts to ensure equality and racial fairness, Michigan legislators and judges succeeded in creating a race-blind legal code for the state by the beginning of the twentieth century. Although the enforcement of these laws never matched the aspirations written into them, Finkelman nonetheless demonstrates that "the repeated attempts by the legislature to create equality in the state . . . led to greater equality and greater opportunity for African Americans than they had in most other states" and thus stand as "a significant legacy."

Michigan long has been recognized as a labor stronghold. In "'Methods of Mysticism' and the Industrial Order," labor historian Elizabeth Faue examines the evolution of labor law in Michigan from 1868 to 1940. Although much attention has been given to federal labor law and its role in either constraining or aiding the American labor movement, Faue urges readers to remember that it was "local and state laws [that] were more important than federal ones in determining the outcome of strikes and the efficacy of protective labor laws." State laws, legal decisions (such as the 1898 *Beck v. Railway Teamsters* case), and local ordinances limiting political expression and criminalizing disorderly conduct, trespass, vagrancy, and property damage were among the methods employed by local businesses and employer associations to restrict and bar labor organization in the pre–New Deal era. By the 1930s, Faue writes, increasing emphasis on federal laws and executive orders shifted the balance between workers and employers and unions and businesses, opening new arenas and strategies for labor action and restoring a sense of equity in the realm of labor law.

In "The Michigan Women's Commission and the Struggle against Sex Discrimination in the 1970s," Liette Gidlow examines the issue of equity. Established in 1961 as a parallel to John F. Kennedy's Presidential Commission on the Status of Women, the Michigan Women's Commission, housed within the state's Civil Rights Commission, was the first such state-level organization in the country. Over the next two decades, Gidlow shows, the commission evolved into a force for feminist legal reform and gender equity in Michigan law, thus ensuring that women were formally and consistently represented in state affairs. Although the commission met with mixed success in the areas of pay equity and abortion rights, it scored a tremendous victory in 1974 when it succeeded in convincing the state legislature to enact a new rape law. The new law modernized the definition of the crime, declaring it a crime of violence, not of passion, and revamped the legal process to be more sensitive to the victims of the crime. This law, Gidlow notes, initiated a national wave of reform culminating in the enactment of similar laws in every other state in the union.

The book's final essay, Byron D. Cooper's "Legal Education in Michigan," surveys the process of lawyer training in the state. At the time of statehood, access to the legal profession was limited by the apprenticeship system and formal rules that shut out both women and African Americans. Until 1949, Cooper notes, training for a legal career through an apprenticeship was permissible in Michigan. This system perpetuated the racial and sex bias of the bar because lawyers often were unwilling to accept clerks who were not like them—male and white. However, the devotion of Michigan's Yankee settlers to education quickly led to the creation of an alternative and more formalized system of academic and legal training—the university—a system that also became a tool for breaking down barriers to the profession. The state's first law school was established at the University of Michigan at its founding in 1817. Subsequently, five additional law schools (Detroit College of Law—now affiliated with Michigan State University, founded in 1891; the University of Detroit—now the University of Detroit Mercy, founded in 1912; Detroit City Law School—now a part of Wayne State University, founded in 1927; Thomas M. Cooley Law School, established in 1972; and Ave Maria School of Law, opened in 2000) were created throughout the state. Among the many notable accomplishments of the state's law schools, Cooper observes, was an early commitment to the principle of equality and equal access. The University of Michigan, the state's oldest law school, admitted its first African American student "apparently without comment" in 1868 and its first female law student two years later. The university's commitment to diversity in admissions has remained a strong one, resulting, in 2003, in the U.S. Supreme Court decision in *Grutter v. Bollinger.*

These essays contribute greatly to our understanding of the history of Michigan law and, taken as a whole, elucidate the many consistencies and changes in the evolution of the state's legal environment. These essays also attest to the power and persistence of Michigan's Yankee heritage and its imprint on every facet of state law, even as they also suggest how the Yankee heritage was changed and altered by the geography, history, and population of the Midwest. Most important, the stories in this volume demonstrate the powerful influence of law on Michigan's development and the importance of Michigan's legal developments to the nation as a whole. It is certain, if history is any indicator, that Michigan law will remain a vibrant and organic entity and that it will continue to shape and influence the legal landscape as it evolves and adapts to changing circumstances.

Notes

1. Oliver Wendell Holmes Jr., *The Common Law* (Boston: Little, Brown, 1881), 3.

2. Willis F. Dunbar and George S. May, preface to *Michigan: A History of the Wolverine State,* 3d rev. ed. (Grand Rapids: William B. Eerdmans, 1995), x.

3. See Paul Finkelman, *Slavery and the Founders: Race and Liberty in the Age of Jefferson* (Armonk, N.Y.: M. E. Sharpe, 2001), ch. 2 and 3.

4. Paul Finkelman, "Race, Slavery, and the Law in Antebellum Ohio," in *The History of Ohio Law,* ed. Michael Les Benedict and John F. Winkler (Athens: Ohio University Press, 2004), 2:748–81.

5. Wisconsin, which became a state in 1848, followed in Michigan's egalitarian footsteps, as did Minnesota, which achieved statehood in 1858.

ONE

David G. Chardavoyne

THE NORTHWEST ORDINANCE AND MICHIGAN'S TERRITORIAL HERITAGE

The Northwest Ordinance, passed by the Continental Congress in July 1787 to establish American government for "the Territory of the United States north-west of the river Ohio," was one of the most significant accomplishments of that short-lived body. Its provisions established a structure of government that encouraged settlement of that vast region and provided those settlers a startling set of civil rights that presaged the U.S. Constitution's Bill of Rights. But the Ordinance also imposed a system of unelected government that was resented by many inhabitants of the Northwest as an "accursed badge of despotism." In the Michigan Territory, the Ordinance meant decades of autocratic government by unelected officials, while many of its protections, particularly its ban on slavery, proved to be ephemeral. Nevertheless, because of the commitment of most of those officials to the development of the territory, Michigan's territorial experience under the Ordinance produced, in 1837, a self-governing state that was innovative, progressive, and confident.

The Northwest Ordinance

The Continental Congress enacted the Northwest Ordinance of 1787 to solve a problem and to secure an asset. In the Treaty of Paris of 1783, which ended the War of Independence, Great Britain recognized American claims to all former British lands between the Alleghenies and the Mississippi River that were south of a line drawn along the middle of the Great Lakes waterway from Niagara on Lake Erie, through Lakes Huron and Superior, to Lake of the Woods.[1] Those western lands included what Americans called the Northwest, 265,000 square miles north of the Ohio River that now make up Ohio, Indiana, Illinois, Michigan, Wisconsin, and eastern Minnesota.

Although the acquisition of the western lands presented the new nation with an enormous opportunity, it also brought into focus a serious dispute among the states. On the basis of their royal charters, some states claimed ownership of large parts of the lands west of the Alleghenies. Virginia, for example, claimed all of the Northwest, while Pennsylvania, Massachusetts, Connecticut, and New York asserted their own conflicting claims to large tracts in the region.[2] Other new states, fearing the loss of population and power, objected to all such claims. In 1780, after years of debate and negotiation, the states agreed that the western lands would be "settled and formed into distinct republican states which shall become members of the federal union, and have the same rights of sovereignty, freedom and independence, as the other states."[3] Left unanswered for the moment were questions of how these new states would be formed and governed.

Only after the Treaty of Paris did Congress turn to such practical issues. In 1784, a committee chaired by Thomas Jefferson submitted to Congress a document entitled *Plan for Government of the Western Territory,* which set out a formula for determining the boundaries of new states.[4] Congress was to buy land in each prospective state from the Indians and sell it to settlers, who would form a temporary state government based on the constitution and laws of one of the original states. When a new state had twenty thousand "free inhabitants," they could form a permanent state constitution and government. When the state's "free" population was equal to that of "the least numerous of the thirteen original states," the state would be admitted "into the Congress of the United States, on an equal footing with the said original states."

The Continental Congress accepted most of Jefferson's plan in April 1784 but never put it into effect.[5] Instead, in 1787, Congress approved a new scheme that was tailored to satisfy a land company. The Ohio Company proposed to buy and settle land at the confluence of the Ohio and Muskingum rivers but warned Congress that the region would attract few settlers without a strong government capable of protecting them from the dangers of the frontier. On July 13, 1787, Congress accommodated the

Ohio Company by enacting the Northwest Ordinance[6] under which the Northwest became a single district or territory of the United States governed by officers (a governor, a secretary, and three judges) appointed by Congress.[7] After Congress reenacted the Ordinance in 1789 to reflect the ratification of the Constitution in place of the Articles of Confederation, the president made those appointments with the advice and consent of the Senate.[8]

The Ordinance promised that, in due time, the Northwest would be divided into additional districts that would evolve, in stages, into no fewer than three and no more than five new states. During the first stage, the governor and judges, in addition to their executive and judicial duties, would constitute a legislative board, adopting (subject to veto by Congress) "such laws of the original states, criminal and civil, as may be necessary, and best suited to the circumstances of the district." When a district reached a population of "five thousand free male inhabitants of full age," the legislative duties would be transferred to a general assembly consisting of the governor, an elected house of representatives, and a five-man legislative council selected by the federal government from a list of ten candidates nominated by the representatives. To become law, statutes needed a majority in both the house and the council and the approval of the governor. When a district had sixty thousand "free inhabitants," it would become a state "on an equal footing with the original states, in all respects whatever."

Congress repeated this process across the continent to turn the forests, plains, and deserts into territories and then into states, but the Ordinance's significance resides equally in its "articles of compact" between the original states and the people and states of the Northwest that were to "forever remain unalterable, unless by common consent," many of which foreshadowed provisions of the Constitution and the Bill of Rights. The articles of compact guaranteed, inter alia, religious freedom; the protections of the common law, including habeas corpus, trial by jury, due process, and full compensation for any taking of an individual's liberty or property; bans on slavery and on cruel or unusual punishments; the encouragement of education; and good faith in dealings with the Indians of the Northwest.

Wandering Thro' Inhospitable Deserts

As Congress was well aware when it enacted the Northwest Ordinance, the United States still had not taken physical possession of all the lands accorded it under the Treaty of Paris. In order to protect its lucrative fur trade, Britain refused to abandon its military posts in what are now Michigan and northern Ohio. At the same time, the Indians living in Ohio were determined to oppose American settlement of their lands. It took the combined efforts of General Anthony Wayne and Chief Justice John Jay of the U.S. Supreme Court to extend American control throughout the Northwest. Wayne and his Legion of the West did their part by defeating the Ohio tribes at Fallen Timbers in August 1794. Three months later, news of that battle helped Jay convince King George III to agree, in what is popularly called the Jay Treaty, to "withdraw all his troops and garrisons from all posts and places within the boundary lines assigned by the treaty of peace to the United States" by June 1, 1796.[9] In August 1795, after learning of the terms of the treaty and of the approaching departure of their British mentors, the Ohio tribes signed the Treaty of Greenville, in which they sold to the United States most of southern Ohio and other strategic locations in the Northwest, including Detroit and Mackinac.[10] A year later, after the evacuation of its British garrison, Detroit witnessed the arrival of American soldiers and American government.

The wisdom of the Northwest Ordinance's scheme of appointed government, at least in the case of Detroit, was confirmed by the political situation that prevailed during the town's first years of American government. When troops under Colonel John Francis Hamtramck raised the American flag over Fort Detroit, there was only one American citizen in a civilian population of about five hundred people—Peter Audrain, an elderly immigrant from France by way of Pennsylvania. The French-speaking majority was made up of remnants of French Canada who lived by subsistence farming, hunting, and trapping and who had little interest in government. The small class of businessmen—landowners, merchants, and fur traders—was made up, for the most part, of British citizens of doubtful allegiance to the United States.[11] The Jay Treaty allowed French and British residents of Michigan to remain, with the proviso that they could not "be compelled to become citizens of the United States, or to take any oath of allegiance to the government thereof."[12] Many took advantage of that provision. Indeed, the commanders of the British militia and naval units in the area, John Askin and Alexander Grant, continued to live in their stately homes in Detroit and Grosse Pointe, from which they issued orders to their forces across the Detroit River.[13] In that environment, immediate self-government by the people, as envisioned by Jefferson in 1784, would have produced chaos. American control of the Great Lakes hung by a thread: among an indifferent or hostile population, territorial government by American officials of known ability and loyalty, appointed by the federal government, made eminent sense even if those officials were located on the Ohio River, two hundred miles away through roadless forests and swamps.[14]

By 1803, though, Detroit was tired of being ruled—and usually ignored—by distant governments. Although there were local courts conducted by merchants to deal with minor matters, most of the governmental business that affected Michigan took place in distant Chillicothe or Cincinnati. The territorial court traveled to Detroit only twice in six years, cases removed from local courts lingered undecided, and no territorial governor ever bothered to travel to Detroit to hear the residents' complaints.[15] But the final straw was the decision by Congress in 1802, when it created the new state of Ohio, to exclude the residents of Detroit, Mackinac, and Sault Ste. Marie from the benefits of statehood. Instead, Congress transferred them to the Indiana Territory, whose capital at Vincennes on the Wabash River was even farther away.[16] Only a month after they came under the jurisdiction of the Indiana government, 311 Detroiters petitioned Congress (in both English and French) to create "a Separate Territory" for the country north of an east-west line drawn "from the southwardly bend of Lake Michigan."[17] In careful, diplomatic phrases, the petitioners expressed their concern that Congress was not aware of "the immense distance from the settlements upon the waters of the Lakes" to Vincennes through a country full of hostile "Savages." More petitions followed, arguing that, based on geography alone, "the necessity of Erecting this part into a Separate Territory—will appear strikingly evident"[18] and that the failure of Congress to act would result in "all the horrors of outlary [sic], oppression, and anarchy,"[19] including murderers unpunished and creditors unpaid for lack of a competent government. The Jeffersonian faithful of Wayne County pleaded that their Democratic Republican brethren in Congress "compel us not to wander seven hundred miles thro' inhospitable deserts."[20]

On January 11, 1805, Congress answered those pleas and created a new territory, named after Lake Michigan and with a government "in all respects similar to that provided by" the Northwest Ordinance, including a governor, secretary, and three judges.[21] Several residents of Detroit, including attorney Solomon Sibley, postmaster Frederick Bates, and Indian agent Charles Jouett, campaigned to be governor or secretary of the new territory, but President Thomas Jefferson, like any other politician, took the opportunity to reward supporters who were closer to hand. In the end, only one Michigan resident, Bates, was appointed to a territorial office, although not the one he preferred.

President Jefferson appointed General William Hull, of Connecticut, to serve as governor and Stanley Griswold, of New Hampshire, to be the territorial secretary. Both men were veterans of the Revolution who had strong ties to the president. To the three-judge territorial court, Jefferson appointed Samuel Huntington of the Ohio Supreme Court (who declined), Augustus Brevoort Woodward, of Washington, D.C., and Bates.[22] Although snubbing local men may have caused initial resentment, the people of Detroit came to appreciate the energetic leadership of the appointed officials, especially that of Woodward and Hull. They both arrived in Detroit just three weeks after a fire had destroyed the entire civilian settlement and the old French citadel, and their efforts were crucial in raising a new Detroit from the ashes. Finally, the people of Detroit and the rest of the Territory of Michigan had what they had demanded: a territorial government that was local, visible, and active.

The First Supreme Court of Michigan

Read together, the Northwest Ordinance and the Michigan Territory Act provided the new territory with "a court to consist of three judges, any two of whom to form a court, who shall have a common law jurisdiction, and reside in the district, and have each therein a freehold estate in five hundred acres of land, while in the exercise of their offices; and their commissions shall continue in force during good behavior."[23] Another act of Congress passed two months after Michigan's creation granted all territorial courts the power to hear "all cases in which the United States are concerned" that otherwise would have been referred to a federal district or circuit court.[24]

On July 24, 1805, Judges Woodward and Bates joined with Governor Hull in their role as legislators to give the territorial court its official name, "the Supreme Court of the Territory of Michigan," and to provide that the court would hold one regular term each year, beginning on the third Monday in September, and such extra sessions as the court saw fit.[25] Woodward and Bates held the first session of the Supreme Court of the Territory of Michigan four days later on July 29 and the first regular term of the court from September 16 to 30.[26] In 1806, they were joined on the bench by John Griffin, a former judge on the Indiana territorial court, but the three judges did not serve together for long. At the end of 1806, Judge Bates left Detroit for St. Louis to become secretary of the Louisiana Territory. He was not replaced until 1808, when President Jefferson appointed to the court another veteran of the Revolution, James Witherell, of Vermont.[27]

Judges Woodward and Griffin were a congenial pair who, only thirty years old when appointed, served on the court long enough to be called derisively "the Old Bachelors" by their enemies in the territory. Born Elias Brevoort Woodward in New York City in 1774, Woodward was the son of a successful merchant. He attended Columbia College and then studied law in Virginia. By 1805, he had renamed himself Augustus and become a prominent lawyer and land speculator in Washington, D.C., where he served on the first city council. In addition to English, he was fluent in Greek, Latin, French, and Spanish, and, like his friend and idol Thomas Jefferson, he was deeply intelligent and well-read, with broad interests in the arts and sciences. Many of his constituents, though, saw him as eccentric, arrogant, and pedantic.

Griffin, born around 1774, was the scion of a prominent Virginia family, who had studied law after graduating from William and Mary College.[28] In 1800, President John Adams appointed Griffin to the Indiana territorial court, but he complained about the climate at Vincennes. His father, Cyrus Griffin, a member of the Continental Congress and later U.S. district judge for Virginia, prevailed on President Jefferson to transfer him to the Michigan Supreme Court. Judge Griffin was, as it turned out, "one of the most petulantly dissatisfied office-holders of all time."[29] Throughout his seventeen-year tenure in Michigan, Griffin conducted a ceaseless campaign to obtain a federal job elsewhere. In addition to being perpetually unhappy with his position, Griffin was also a timid and indecisive judge who quickly became dependent on the dynamic Woodward.

It was the fate of James Witherell to spend sixteen of his twenty-two years in the government of the Michigan Territory in conflict with Woodward and Griffin. Fifteen years older than his fellow judges, Witherell had been born in Massachusetts and had participated in many of the major battles of the War of Independence. After the war, he moved to Vermont, where he became active in politics as a Jeffersonian. He resigned his seat in Congress to become a judge in Michigan, where he served with distinction even though he was a physician, not a lawyer, by training.[30]

Slavery in Michigan

During the Michigan Supreme Court's 1807 term, Judge Griffin decided to be elsewhere looking for a better job. Because Witherell had not yet replaced Bates, Judge Woodward found himself alone on the bench when the supreme court became the forum for a debate on the most incendiary issue of the nineteenth century, slavery.

The question of the status of slaves in the Michigan Territory had simmered for years before boiling over in 1807. Article VI of the Northwest Ordinance, one of its articles of compact, promised that "[t]here shall be neither Slavery nor involuntary Servitude in the said territory, otherwise than in the punishment of crimes, whereof the party shall have been duly convicted."[31] On the other hand, slavery was an established and legal custom in Michigan during the British and French periods. Although it is not clear when the first slaves were brought to Detroit, a British census taken in 1782 counted 179 slaves among the 2,191 people living along both shores of the Detroit River.[32] In 1796, 31 adult black slaves and 16 black children, presumably the children of slaves, lived in the Township of Detroit among a "free white" population of 238.[33] The actual number of slaves was probably higher because many families in Michigan owned Indians as slaves, known locally as "panis," who, like other Indians, were not included in any census.[34]

The arrival of American rule and the enactment of the Northwest Ordinance did not emancipate any slaves in Michigan—on the contrary, for many black and panis slaves, the words of Article VI of the Ordinance were just words, seemingly incapable of freeing them. The cultural reasons for the impotence of Article VI were many, but the legal reason was Article II of the Jay Treaty. To induce Great Britain to evacuate its military forces from the Northwest, the United States had guaranteed that "settlers and trappers" who resided in the Northwest under British rule and who decided to remain there after the transfer of sovereignty to the United States would "continue to enjoy, unmolested, all their property of every kind, and shall be protected therein."[35] Slave owners argued that "property of every kind" included slaves and that the rights of property holders under the treaty took precedence over any provision to the contrary in the Northwest Ordinance. Opponents of slavery replied that slaves freed by the Northwest Ordinance in 1787 could not possibly still be property, under any definition of that word, in 1796 when the Jay Treaty went into effect. The debate remained theoretical until 1807, when Detroit attorney Elijah Brush asked the Michigan Supreme Court to free four slaves on the authority of the Northwest Ordinance.

In 1806, Brush had leased two slaves, Peter and Hannah Denison, from their owner, Catherine Tucker, on the condition that they would be freed from slavery after one year. Tucker also held as slaves the Denisons' four children, Elizabeth, Scipio, James, and Peter Jr. In September 1807, Brush, as attorney for the Denison children, obtained a writ of habeas corpus directing Tucker to appear before the Supreme Court and to justify the continued detention of the children in defiance of Article VI of the Ordinance.[36] Tucker and her attorney, Harris H. Hickman, son-in-law of Governor William Hull, appeared before Woodward and presented evidence that the Denison children had been owned as slaves by the Tucker family before the arrival of the Americans in July 1796. Hickman argued that the Denisons' children were, therefore, Tucker's property under the terms of the Jay Treaty.[37]

Although personally uncomfortable with slavery, Woodward construed legal issues regarding slavery as he did all others, in the most formal and narrow fashion. After hearing the arguments of counsel, Woodward stated his objection to slavery but then explained that he had to rule in favor of Tucker. He observed that slavery was legal in most of the United States and Upper Canada (although not in Great Britain itself) and that slaves were characterized as property wherever the institution existed. Therefore, he explained, because the Jay Treaty did not qualify or limit the types of property entitled to protection, slaves were indeed property for purposes of the treaty.[38] Woodward also reasoned that the laws of a government can apply only in regions over which that government has actual control. Consequently, the Northwest Ordinance, although enacted in 1787, did not apply in Detroit until July 1796, after Tucker's property interest in the Denison children had received the protection of the Jay Treaty.

Woodward did note that the property interest protected by the treaty was no greater than the interest allowed by Canadian law. In 1793, the provincial parliament of Upper Canada had passed a law for the gradual abolition of slavery, providing that any child born to a slave mother after May 31, 1793, would become free on his or her twenty-fifth birthday.[39] Therefore, Woodward opined, (1) all human beings born in the Michigan Territory on or after July 11, 1796, were free; and (2) all persons born to a slave mother in the Michigan Territory after May 31, 1793, but before July 11, 1796, remained slaves until their twenty-fifth birthday and were then free; whereas (3) all slaves born before May 31, 1793, remained slaves for life. Woodward remarked, defensively, that this result "brings the existence of Slavery in the territory of Michigan to as early and to as favorable a Close as perhaps the imperfections necessarily attached to all human measures will allow to be expected."[40]

That "close" did not become complete for many years. In 1811, there were still seventeen slaves in Detroit among a total of twenty-four in the entire Michigan Territory, which, at that time, included the Lower Peninsula and the stub of the Upper Peninsula east of Mackinac.[41] Twenty years later, the

1830 census found thirty-two slaves in a much larger Michigan Territory that included Wisconsin and eastern Minnesota, although only one of those slaves lived within the borders of present-day Michigan.[42] Elizabeth and Scipio Denison were not among the slaves enumerated after 1807. Shortly after Woodward's decision, they escaped across the river to Canada, the government of which, despite its own slavery laws, refused to return escaped American slaves. After several years in Canada, they returned to Detroit, where, although still legally slaves, they lived unmolested for the rest of their lives.[43]

The Accursed Badge of Despotism

It is unlikely that Congress anticipated that any part of the Northwest would remain in the first stage of government for almost two decades. The Northwest Territory achieved the second stage in 1798, just three years after the Treaty of Greenville opened large portions of Ohio and Indiana for settlement. When Congress split the Northwest Territory in 1800, the new Indiana Territory returned to the first stage but voted in September 1804 to advance to the second stage.[44] Michigan, which had returned once more to the first stage when it separated from the Indiana Territory in June 1805, did not reach the second stage until 1823, eighteen years later.[45] This delay was due, in part, to the conservatism of the French and British who remained in Detroit after 1796 and to the provisions in the Ordinance dealing with Indian lands. Settlers could acquire title to land in the Northwest only from the United States, and, under the Ordinance, the United States could survey and sell only land to which "the Indian title shall have been extinguished." Because Indian title could be "extinguished" only by treaties between the United States and the Indian tribes, settlement had to wait for treaties. The Treaty of Greenville opened up most of Ohio to settlement, but in Michigan it affected only small areas near Detroit and Mackinac. Further expansion of land available for sale was slow. Only after the 1807 Treaty of Detroit, the 1819 Treaty of Saginaw, and the 1821 Treaty of Chicago were the eastern and southwestern parts of the Lower Peninsula available for settlement.[46]

Whatever the reason, although government in the new Michigan Territory after June 1805 was no longer distant and faceless, for almost two decades power was concentrated in the hands of the governor, the secretary, and the three judges of the supreme court, all chosen in Washington, not in Michigan. The growing Anglophone population, most of which had roots in New England and its tradition of participatory democracy, was frustrated that its voice counted for little in territorial government, a condition attributed, rightly or wrongly, to the Northwest Ordinance. Their views were similar to those expressed in an Illinois newspaper in 1816: "The colonial and degraded status of this country under the government of the Ordinance, that accursed badge of despotism, which withholds from the people, the only true source of all power, a participation in those rights, guaranteed by the constitution of every state in the Union, seems to have the effect of chilling every spark of political disquisition, and to have sunk man beneath the dignity of his nature, a poor fallen creature from that proud station, the destiny of freemen."[47]

In the Michigan Territory, residents focused their unhappiness with the political status quo on Judge Woodward. Whereas in other parts of the Northwest power was shared among four appointees, in Michigan he was, de facto, the sole decision maker. The unquestioning support he received from Judge Griffin assured him a majority on the supreme court and no worse than a tie on the legislative board. Nothing happened without his approval, and he had little taste for compromise. Governor Hull grumbled that "[e]very thing in this Territory was perfectly tranquil, until his arrival—Since that time he has been doing all in his power to create parties and excit [sic] tumult."[48] Governor Lewis Cass, who replaced Hull in 1814, was hard to anger, but even he found Woodward intractable and his ideas perplexing: "His very singular opinion of things generally would baffle any little sagacity."[49] Territorial Secretary William Woodbridge remarked to a friend that "[o]ur chief Judge is a wild theorist, fitted principally for the 'extraction of sunbeams from cucumbers.'"[50] Nevertheless, Woodward retained support among the French and British traditionalists in the territory who turned to him for protection from the increasing number of "Bostonians" in the territory.

Although Woodward's reputation for pompous eccentricity may have been exaggerated by his enemies, it was not entirely inaccurate. Although it is sometimes difficult to sort fact from fiction in contemporary accounts (particularly those by his nemesis, John P. Sheldon, editor of the *Detroit Gazette*, the territory's first successful newspaper),[51] Woodward's own writings demonstrate a verbosity, pedantry, and love of showing off that no doubt irritated friends and enemies alike. In one 1818 case, for example, the issue was straightforward: the validity of the service of a summons on a Sunday.[52] In their arguments, the parties agreed that service of legal process on Sunday was valid at common law. They disagreed only as to whether a statute of the Northwest Territory barring Sunday service was still the law in Michigan after it became a separate territory. Instead of resolving that disagreement, Woodward investigated whether, in fact, the common law did allow Sunday service of process. He decided that it did not, a decision that he supported, in a frenzy of scholarship, with citations to, among a multitude of authorities, the apostles John, Luke, and Paul; Byzantine emperors Theodosius, Constantine, and Anastasius; Pope Gregory IX; sixth-century kings Childebert of France and Gontran of Burgundy; and English kings Edward I, III, and VI, William I, Henry II, VI, and VIII, James I, and Charles II.[53]

In January 1818, Governor Cass called an election to decide whether Michigan should apply to advance to the second stage of government, including an elected legislative council and a nonvoting delegate to Congress. Cass sincerely favored progress to the second stage as a step toward statehood, but he also hoped to reduce Woodward's power by eliminating his legislative duties. Cass's initiative was, however, premature. The traditionalists, who still had a majority, cared little about an elected legislature and a great deal about the cost of second-stage government. Whereas the costs of first-stage government, including the salaries and expenses of the governor, secretary, and judges, were paid by the federal government, the costs of a legislature and a delegate in Washington would fall on the taxpayers of the territory. That economic argument defeated the initiative.[54] A year later, Woodward supported Cass in obtaining a nonvoting delegate to Congress from Michigan,[55] both because it would save the territorial officials from having to travel to Washington so often and because he saw himself as the perfect man for the job.[56] He lost, however, to Cass's candidate, William Woodbridge.

Before his election as delegate, Woodbridge and Solomon Sibley, the U.S. attorney for Michigan, launched a lobbying effort to obtain a U.S. district court for the Michigan Territory. Such a court would take over the cases involving the United States, including many customs cases that the Supreme Court had allowed to languish for years, and would provide for the territory a court independent of Judge Woodward.[57] In January 1819, an Ohio senator sponsored a bill for a federal court in Michigan, but it died in committee, largely because Congress did not want to pay for federal courts in the territories.[58] Woodbridge tried to keep the idea alive, but without success.[59]

In December 1821, Woodbridge (who had returned from Washington to resume his duties as territorial secretary) and Sibley (who had succeeded him in Washington) hatched a devious plot to divest Woodward of his monopoly of power—or even to rid the territory of Woodward for good. Their conspiracy, which included lawyers from several counties, was inspired by complaints by litigants following the expansion of the Michigan Territory in 1818 to include the Upper Peninsula, Wisconsin, and the portion of Minnesota lying east of the Mississippi.[60] Although Governor Cass appointed county court judges and justices of the peace there to deal with minor legal matters, a litigant who was charged with a capital crime, or whose civil case exceeded one thousand dollars in value, or who was being sued by the United States had to travel to Detroit to attend the Michigan Supreme Court, which still held only one term each year, beginning in September. To reach Detroit in time for the court's term, a resident of Prairie du Chien on the Mississippi would have to leave home in July and might not return home until the following spring. Even for residents of Mackinac or Port Huron, attending court in Detroit was a burden.

Woodbridge and Sibley joined with other Detroit attorneys to convince colleagues in Pontiac, Mount Clemens, St. Clair, and Mackinac Island to obtain signatures for petitions asking Congress to add a fourth judge to the supreme court and to require all four judges to hold one-judge sessions of the supreme court in each county once every year, including in the counties west of Lake Michigan.[61] The conspirators expected a dual benefit from the plan: the fourth judge would "throw the balance with Cass and Witherell" on the legislative board,[62] and requiring the judges to hold court outside Detroit would certainly induce the already unhappy Griffin to resign and might cause Woodward to resign as well.[63] Even if Woodward remained, without Griffin he would be powerless to enforce his will on the court or the legislative board.

Governor Cass, however, already had put into motion a plan of his own. In the summer of 1821, he sent his protégé James Duane Doty to Mackinac to drum up support for an additional territorial judge who would hear all cases from Michilimackinac, Brown, and Crawford counties but who would have no vote on the legislative board.[64] One of Sibley's conspirators warned him that "Doty has the recommendation of those three counties—backed by the whole influence of the American Fur Company and the active support of the Govr to be judge."[65] As might be expected, Congress listened to Cass: in January 1823 it authorized a fourth judge on Cass's terms and in February 1823 named Doty as that additional judge.[66]

Thwarted in their attempts to outflank Woodward, his opponents were reduced, finally, to launching a frontal attack. The Northwest Ordinance provided that the commissions of the territorial judges "shall continue in force during good behavior," a phrase usually interpreted as meaning tenure for life unless impeached. Because the Michigan judges' positions had been created by Congress rather than by the Constitution, however, Congress had the power to change the rules under which the judges served. In November 1822, a "Memorial to Congress" signed by hundreds of residents of Wayne County demanded a law limiting the term of the territorial judges to four years.[67] A counterpetition submitted by other residents protested against any such change in "the permanency of the Judiciary, [which is] one of the noblest features in the science of Government,"[68] and petitions from outside Detroit favored limits to the tenure of the judges of the supreme court.[69] Meanwhile, from November 1822 to January 1823, the *Gazette* conducted a relentless attack on Woodward.[70] On March 3, 1823, Congress, with little or no floor debate, directed that the judges of the Michigan Supreme Court would be subject to reappointment every four years, effective February 1, 1824.[71]

Rather than seek reappointment, Judge Griffin resigned at the end of 1823 and left the territory. Judge Woodward informed President Monroe that he wanted another term. Woodward had the support of Michigan's new delegate to Congress, Father Gabriel Richard, and it appears that President Monroe intended to reappoint Woodward but was dissuaded, at the last moment, by more petitions from Michigan alleging that Woodward was intemperate and had vacated a judgment against Richard in order to obtain his support.[72] For whatever reason, Monroe did not reappoint Woodward; instead, Solomon Sibley and another of the Detroit conspirators, John Hunt, replaced Woodward and Griffin.[73] Monroe did appoint Woodward to a position on the territorial court of Florida, where he died in 1827 at the age of fifty-three.

A Territory Reaching Maturity

Structurally, the government of the Michigan Territory in 1825 did not look very different from that in 1805. The governor, the secretary, and the three supreme court judges were still federal appointees. It was true that Congress had authorized a legislative council to take over lawmaking for the territory, but its nine members were themselves appointed by the president, with the advice and consent of the Senate, from a slate of eighteen candidates elected by the voters of the territory, and their laws were subject to veto by the governor.[74] But this appearance of a government mired in status quo was deceptive.

The territorial officers brought Michigan much closer to the self-governed state that Thomas Jefferson had envisioned for the western lands in 1784. Although all of them—Governor Lewis Cass, Secretary William Wood-bridge, and Judges James Witherell, Solomon Sibley, and John Hunt—had been born and educated in New England, they had devoted many years to the service of the territory. Sibley arrived in Detroit in 1797, Witherell in 1808, Cass in 1813, Woodbridge in 1814, and Hunt in 1818. The public held all of them in high regard and would have elected them to their offices, if given the chance, because of their well-known affection for Michigan. They were not opportunistic office-seekers: instead; they were deeply in-volved in the political and social life of the territory. Later arrivals also be-came firmly embedded in the territory, such as Ross Wilkins, who left Pittsburgh to join Michigan's supreme court in 1832 and served as Michigan's U.S. district judge from 1836 until his retirement in 1870.

The legislative council, despite being appointed by Washington, was also a great advance over the old system because, for the first time in Michigan, the legislature was independent from the judiciary. Although democracies are more often concerned with the independence of the judiciary from the influence of the other branches of government, in Michigan the opposite had been true. The judges of the supreme court had used their dual roles to pass laws that ensured that they never had to work too hard and never had to hold court outside of Detroit. Soon after it was confirmed by the president, the legislative council began reorganizing the court system in order to increase the judicial work load and to bring justice closer to the thousands of immigrants who were settling the counties to the west and north of Detroit.

In April 1825, the council stripped the supreme court of its remaining trial jurisdiction, making it a purely appellate court. The council also created a new trial court, called the circuit court. Unlike the existing county courts, which had a limited jurisdiction and were held by justices of the peace, circuit courts were to be the workhorses of the judicial system, with the power to try civil cases in which the amount in controversy exceeded $1,000 and all criminal cases. The council also added a provision that Woodward and Griffin would never have agreed to—the judges of the supreme court were to hold the circuit courts, at least one judge holding a circuit court in each of five counties (Wayne, Macomb, Oakland, St. Clair, and Monroe) every year.[75] In July 1828, the council increased the judges' burden, decreeing that at least *two* of them had to attend every circuit court held in each of the ten counties east of Lake Michigan.[76]

This was, of course, very much like the plan by which Sibley and Wood-bridge had hoped to scare away Judges Woodward and Griffin in 1822. Be-cause they were now judges of the supreme court (Sibley was appointed to the court in 1824, and Woodbridge replaced Witherell in January 1828), they themselves were now faced with riding circuit from county to county, over bad roads and no roads, and in all seasons. Judge Woodbridge com-plained loudly and often that the judges had to ride through trackless forests across the territory to hold fifteen courts each year and that, as new counties were formed, the burden would become only heavier.[77] His com-plaints were ignored, however, in the enthusiasm of the population out-side Detroit for justice brought to their doorsteps.

The territory, although it would not become a state until 1837, had evolved beyond the limits and the cultivation of narrow interests inherent in the scheme decreed in the Northwest Ordinance. This more mature and stable society helped attract a wave of immigrants from New England and from western New York, where many New Englanders had moved in the years following the Revolution. Between 1830 and 1840, Michigan's popula-tion increased from twenty-eight thousand to two hundred thousand resi-dents, and "it seemed as though all New England was coming."[78] Those immigrants, adventurous young families seeking new homes, quickly set about reinforcing New England's progressive influence on the settlements they created throughout the southern Lower Peninsula.[79] This influence, particularly among the families that had spent a generation or two in west-ern New York, included an active and reformist approach to the social is-sues of the time, such as temperance, slavery, the property rights of married women, and, in particular, the abolition of capital punishment, a cause in which Michigan led the nation.

Abolishing a Relic of Barbarism

The story of Michigan's abolition of capital punishment begins in 1830 with one of the most notorious trials held in a circuit court during the ter-ritorial period: that of Stephen Gifford Simmons, who was tried and con-victed in Wayne County for the murder of his wife. In July 1830, supreme court judges William Woodbridge, Solomon Sibley, and Henry Chipman (who had replaced John Hunt after his death in 1827), sitting as the Wayne County Circuit Court, struggled through an exhaustive (and exhausting) three days of jury selection followed by little more than a day of proofs and closing arguments. There was no doubt that Simmons had killed his wife, Levana, in a drunken rage, and the jury took only a few hours to convict him of murder. He was hanged in front of the Wayne County Jail on September 24, 1830, the first person executed by the territorial government since 1821 and the last person ever executed by Michigan as a territory or a state. His death began a process that culminated in Michigan's becoming the first jurisdiction in the English-speaking world to abolish capital punishment.[80]

Still, capital punishment was very rare in Michigan—the territorial government had hanged only one other man since it was created in 1805, and the federal government had conducted only two executions in Michigan since 1796.[81] Some Detroiters, no doubt, opposed all capital punishment, but there does not seem to have been any public debate on the issue before Simmons's execution. The only overt protest before the event came from Wayne County Sheriff Thomas Knapp, who decided to forgo the last few months of his term of office rather than carry out his statutory duty to hang Simmons. The few people who did bother to record their thoughts found Simmons's death part of a larger tragedy that began long before Levana's death, when both spouses had jumped into the bottle. Attendance at the execution (reported to be two thousand people at a time when the population of Detroit was twenty-two hundred)[82] suggests that there was no lack of people living in and near Detroit who were entirely in favor of hanging Simmons.

Efforts to abolish capital punishment had a long pedigree, going back at least as far as seventeenth-century England, and reached a peak in New York and Pennsylvania in the 1790s. The first recorded opposition in Michigan to an execution came not from (relatively) sophisticated Detroit but from the remote outpost on Mackinac Island. In January 1830, nine months before Simmons's execution, island residents, led by the Reverend William Ferry, sent President Jackson a petition asking him to vacate the federal death sentence imposed on a private in the island's garrison, James Brown, for the murder of his corporal, Hugh Flinn. Ferry's petition was unsuccessful, as was a similar petition three years later, which tried to stop the federal execution of an Indian known at Mackinac as White Thunder for killing a trapper near Lake Superior.[83] Nevertheless, there were signs of increasing public concern in Michigan about the morality of capital punishment.

In January 1831, in his annual address to the territorial legislature, Governor Cass expressed regret that the Michigan Territory did not distinguish between first- and second-degree murder. He also deplored the fact that, although he could pardon a convict entirely, he could not reduce a capital sentence to a term of imprisonment.[84] During the next several years, the *Detroit Free Press* was an occasional but fervent voice against capital punishment. In 1833, for example, the newspaper printed extracts from Edward Livingston's proposed criminal code, which included a ban on capital punishment, and commented: "We are glad that the public mind has commenced a serious examination into this relic of barbarism, and we cannot doubt as to the conclusion of its enlightened and liberal spirit."[85]

Michigan's first practical step toward that conclusion came during the convention held in Detroit in May and June 1835 to draft a constitution that would fulfill statutory requirements to advance Michigan to statehood. Elijah F. Cook, a delegate from Farmington, asked that a committee investigate whether Michigan, by its constitution, should "abandon the practice of capital punishments." The committee, chaired by Cook, proposed that the constitution direct the legislature to abolish capital punishment because "the true design of all punishment [is] to reform, not to exterminate mankind." The convention, however, fearing that the proposal would divide delegates and detract from the goal of a constitution by consensus, rejected the committee's proposal.[86]

Undeterred, Cook renewed his campaign in 1838–39 when he served in the Michigan Senate. Although defeated once more on the issue of abolition, Cook and his allies were able to pass important reforms—distinguishing first-degree murder (punishable by death) from second-degree (punishable by imprisonment), banning the execution of the insane and of pregnant women, and prohibiting public executions. Emboldened by these successes, the enemies of capital punishment kept up the pressure. In February 1839, the *Free Press* printed a particularly graphic description of the physiology of a hanging:

> If the neck be not broken by the sudden lateral jerk, an appalling scene of human agony succeeds that is immeasurably beyond description. The heavings of the chest; the convulsions of the limbs; the darkened and distorted visage; the knotted veins upon the brow and temples; and the fiery, glaring eye, evince the agonizing struggle between life and death that now rages within the heart and brain . . . . [T]he face blackens; the eye-balls protrude; a convulsive shudder runs through the frame; the chin drops; life has been inhumanly taken and justice is satisfied. In the name of humanity in the name of heaven, we ask, shall such scenes be

repeated among people who boast of civilization and refinement?[87]

Although "such scenes" had been unknown in Michigan for nearly a decade, the *Free Press* and other Michigan papers kept their readers informed of executions elsewhere, particularly of the twenty-nine Americans and Canadians hanged by the British government in the winter of 1838–39 for attempting a revolution in Upper and Lower Canada. Six of the men executed were in a party of 150 "Patriots" who invaded Windsor from Detroit in December 1838.[88]

The legislative battle over capital punishment resumed in the Michigan House of Representatives on January 28, 1843, with a full day of debate on an abolition bill sponsored by Flavius Littlejohn, a Democrat from Allegan County. The Detroit newspapers, the *Democratic Free Press* and the *Detroit Daily Advertiser,* gave the debate unprecedented coverage, printing the speeches of a dozen legislators for and against the bill. Littlejohn began the debate, noting that capital punishment "is a question on which gentlemen might well differ." Speakers on both sides of the debate united in disagreeing with Littlejohn on that point. In the very room in which Simmons had been sentenced to death, each side appealed to history, morality, humanity, and religion to support its position.[89] When they were done debating, the Michigan House of Representatives became the first legislative body in the United States to vote to abolish capital punishment. The Senate, however, could not be convinced, and Littlejohn's bill died.

Three years later, Flavius Littlejohn was in a much stronger position to influence his fellow legislators. As president pro tempore of the Michigan Senate and chair of a committee charged with revising the state code, he proposed to change the mandatory penalty for first-degree murder from death to life imprisonment in solitary confinement. His bill passed in the Senate with a bipartisan majority. In the House, an identical proposal was defeated twice, but Austin Blair, Republican from Jackson County, refused to be beaten and finally achieved victory for the abolitionists by agreeing to amend the bill to provide that a convicted first-degree murderer's life imprisonment would be served "at hard labor."

When Michigan's Revised Code of 1846 became effective on March 1, 1847, Michigan became the first state, as well as the first English-speaking jurisdiction, to ban capital punishment for first-degree murder.[90] The impetus of that reform, the progressive spirit that was the legacy of Michigan's territorial period and of the men who governed the territory, drove

Michigan to the national forefront of other reform movements during the nineteenth century, including temperance, the abolition of slavery, and the reform of education. Although the decades of territorial government under the rules of that "accursed badge of despotism," the Northwest Ordinance, may have frustrated citizens who yearned for direct participation in local decision making, the collective efforts of the territorial officers, appointed in distant Washington, created an environment capable of giving birth to a politically active, mature, and progressive state.

Notes

1. Definitive Treaty of Peace between the United States of America and His Britannic Majesty, art. II, 8 Stat. 80 (1783).

2. See map of colonial land claims, Willis F. Dunbar and George S. May, *Michigan: A History of the Wolverine State,* rev. ed. (Grand Rapids, Mich.: William B. Eerdmans Publishing, 1980), 111.

3. *Journals of the Continental Congress, 1774–1789,* ed. Worthington C. Ford (Washington, D.C.: Government Printing Office, 1933), 18:915.

4. Dumas Malone, *Jefferson the Virginian* (Boston: Little, Brown, 1948), 412–14. Jefferson planned ten states in the Northwest alone, each with a pseudo-Greek or pseudo-Latin name. The area within the present-day borders of Michigan, for example, would have been shared by Metropotamia, Cherronesus, and Sylvania; Michigania would have occupied the western shore of Lake Michigan.

5. *Journals of the Continental Congress,* 26:275–79.

6. An Ordinance for the government of the territory of the United States North West of the river Ohio (Northwest Ordinance I), ibid., 32:343.

7. The Ordinance refers to the governmental unit as a "district," but later legislation and common usage replaced that term with "territory."

8. An Act to provide for the Government of the Territory North-west of the river Ohio (Northwest Ordinance II), 1 Stat. 50 (1789).

9. Treaty of amity, commerce and navigation, Between His Britannic Majesty and the United States of America, by their President, with the Advice and Consent of their Senate (Jay Treaty), art. II, 8 Stat. 116, 117 (1794).

10. A Treaty of Peace between the United States of America and the Tribes of Indians, called the Wyandots, Delawares, Shawanoes, Ottawas, Chipewas, Putawatimes, Miamis, Eel-river, Weea's, Kickapoos, Piankashaws, and Kaskaskias, 7 Stat. 49 (1795).

11. Frederick Clever Bald, *Detroit's First American Decade, 1796 to 1805* (Ann Arbor: University of Michigan Press, 1948), 29, 33.

12. Jay Treaty, 8 Stat. 116, 117 (1794).

13. Bald, *Detroit's First American Decade,* 120–21.

14. Ibid., 55–56. The governor did appoint justices of the peace and other local officials to handle day-to-day matters, but real power remained at the territorial level.

15. Ibid., 207–8.

16. In May 1800, Congress split the Northwest Territory, creating the Indiana Territory, which included western lower Michigan and the Upper Peninsula west of Mackinac. Indiana Territory Act, 2 Stat. 58 (1800). The border was a line running from the Ohio River, at a point opposite the mouth of the Kentucky River, north-northeast to Fort Recovery, then north to the Canadian border in Lake Superior. In April 1802, when Ohio became a state, Congress transferred the rest of present-day Michigan to the Indiana Territory, effective in February 1803. Ohio Enabling Act, 2 Stat. 173 (1802).

17. *The Territorial Papers of the United States,* comp. Clarence Edwin Carter (Washington, D.C.: Government Printing Office, 1934–), 7:99.

18. Ibid., 7:118.

19. Ibid., 7:227.

20. Ibid., 7:240, 241.

21. An Act to divide the Indiana Territory into two separate governments (Michigan Territory Act), 2 Stat. 309 (1805).

22. Robert Paul Fogerty, "An Institutional Study of the Territorial Courts of the Old Northwest, 1788–1848" (Ph.D. diss., University of Minnesota, 1942), 43. President Jefferson had difficulty filling the seats on the bench of the Michigan Supreme Court. In addition to Samuel Huntington, three other candidates declined a seat on the court: Ohio Supreme Court Justice William Sprigg (in June 1805), John Coburn, of Kentucky (in March 1807), and Ohio Supreme Court Justice Return Jonathan Meigs Jr. (in April 1807).

23. Northwest Ordinance II, § 4, 1 Stat. 50 (1789); Michigan Territory Act, § 2, 2 Stat. 309 (1805) ("[T]here shall be established within the said territory, a government in all respects similar to that provided by [the Northwest Ordinance I]").

24. An Act to extend jurisdiction in certain cases, to the Territorial Courts, 2 Stat. 338 (1805).

25. An Act concerning the supreme court of the territory of Michigan, *Laws of the Territory of Michigan* (Lansing: W. S. George and Co., 1871–84), hereafter LTM, 1:9 (July 24, 1805).

26. *Transactions of the Supreme Court of Michigan, 1805–1846,* ed. William Wirt Bloom (Ann Arbor: University of Michigan Press, 1935–40), hereafter TSCM, 1:345–53.

27. Fogerty, "Institutional Study," 43.

28. Alec R. Gilpin, *The Territory of Michigan [1805–1837]* (East Lansing: Michigan State University Press, 1970), 24; William L. Jenks, "Judge John Griffin," *Michigan History* 14 (Spring 1930): 221. Many other sources, including the usually authoritative *Michigan Biographies: Early History of Michigan with Biographies of State Officers, Members of Congress, Judges and Legislators* (Lansing: Thorp and Godfroy, 1888), 1:354, state that Griffin was born in 1799, obviously a mistake.

29. Fogerty, "Institutional Study," 111.

30. *Michigan Biographies,* 2:463–64.

31. Northwest Ordinance I, art. VI, *Journals of the Continental Congress,* 32:343. The first two drafts of the Ordinance did not include any reference to slavery. Ibid., 32:281–83, 314–20. The drafters of the final version adopted Article VI at the last possible moment, without any debate or discussion of its meaning. For a history of the

adoption of Article VI, see Paul Finkelman, *Slavery and the Founders: Race and Liberty in the Age of Jefferson,* 2d ed. (Armonk, N.Y.: M. E. Sharpe, 2001), ch. 2 and 3.

32. William Renwick Riddell, *The Life of William Dummer Powell: First Judge at Detroit and Fifth Chief Justice of Upper Canada* (Lansing: Michigan Historical Commission, 1924), 197; Donna V. Russell, *Michigan Censuses for 1710 to 1830* (Detroit: Detroit Society for Genealogical Research, 1982), 49–56.

33. Russell, *Michigan Censuses,* 59.

34. Bald, *Detroit's First American Decade,* 40–41; Milo M. Quaife, ed., *John Askin Papers* (Detroit: Detroit Library Commission, 1928), 1:98. Presumably, this name comes from the Plains Indian ethnic group known to Europeans as "Pawnee." Although excluded from territorial censuses, their presence is confirmed by contemporary letters and records, including the captions of cases filed in the Michigan Supreme Court such as *U.S. v. Josette Allard, a Panis Woman,* TSCM, 1:70.

35. Jay Treaty, 8 Stat. 116, 117 (1794).

36. In the Matter of Elizabeth Denison, James Denison, Scipio Denison, and Peter Denison, Jr., Case No. 60, TSCM, 1:86–88, 380–81, 385–95; 1:133–36.

37. Ibid., 2:134–36.

38. Ibid., 1:385–95.

39. An Act to Prevent the Further Introduction of Slaves and to Limit the Term of Enforced Servitude Within this Province, *Statutes of Upper Canada,* 1793, 33 George 3, c. 7.

40. TSCM, 2:395.

41. Ibid., 1:5.

42. Ibid., 5:liv. Most of the other slaves (twenty-three) lived in Iowa County, along the Mississippi River in what is now southwestern Wisconsin, where extensive lead mining created a demand for their labor.

43. Ibid., 1:87.

44. Governor William Henry Harrison proclaimed advancement to the second stage in December 1804. Proclamation of December 5, 1804, *Messages and Letters of William Henry Harrison,* ed. Logan Esarey (1922), 1:112–13.

45. An Act to amend the ordinance and acts of Congress for the government of the territory of Michigan, and for other purposes, 3 Stat. 769 (1823).

46. Treaty of Detroit, 7 Stat. 105 (1807); Treaty of Saginaw, 7 Stat. 203 (1819); Treaty of Chicago, 7 Stat. 218 (1821). For a map of the areas covered by these and other treaties opening Michigan lands to settlement, see Richard W. Welch, *County Evolution in Michigan* (Lansing: Michigan Department of Education, 1972), 16.

47. R. Carlyle Buley, *The Old Northwest: The Pioneer Period, 1815–1840* (Bloomington: Indiana University Press, 1950), 1:79, quoting the *Kaskaskia (Illinois) Western Intelligencer,* August 21, 1816.

48. Frank B. Woodford, *Mr. Jefferson's Disciple: A Life of Justice Woodward* (Lansing: Michigan State College Press, 1953), 59.

49. Ibid., 125–26.

50. William Woodbridge to Charles Lanman, December 12, 1822, in Charles Lanman, *The Life of William Woodbridge* (Washington, D.C.: Blanchard and Mohun, 1867), 32–34.

51. See, e.g., *Detroit Gazette,* October 18, 1822 to January 3, 1823, reprinted in TSCM, 3:479–96. Many of Sheldon's tales about Woodward's eccentricity are memorialized in Silas Farmer, *History of Detroit, Wayne County and Early Michigan: A Chronological Encyclopedia of the Past,* 3d ed. (Detroit: Silas Farmer, 1890), 178–86.

52. James Grant v. Thomas, the Earl of Selkirk, Case 581, TSCM, 3:431–51.

53. Ibid.

54. Gilpin, *Territory of Michigan,* 74.

55. An Act authorizing the election of a delegate from the Michigan territory to the Congress of the United States, and extending the right of suffrage to the citizens of said territory, 3 Stat. 482 (1819).

56. Woodford, *Mr. Jefferson's Disciple,* 166–67.

57. Solomon Sibley to Adam Stewart, November 14, 1818, *Territorial Papers of the United States,* 10:787–90; Solomon Sibley to William Woodbridge, December 5, 1818, ibid., 10:793–94.

58. *Debates and Proceedings in the Congress of the United States (1789–1824)* (Washington, D.C.: Gales and Seaton, 1834–56), 33:176.

59. TSCM, 5:xxix.

60. Illinois Enabling Act, 3 Stat. 428, 431 (1818).

61. John Hunt to Solomon Sibley, December 29, 1821, folder for December 1821, Solomon Sibley Papers, Burton Historical Collection, Detroit Public Library (Sibley Papers).

62. Andrew G. Whitney to Solomon Sibley, January 26, 1822, folder for January 16–31, 1822, Sibley Papers.

63. John Hunt, one of the conspirators and later a Supreme Court judge himself, reported to Sibley that Judge Griffin "trembles at the responsibility of *one* Judge holding a Court, & accuses the New England population, of faction & a disposition for revolution." John Hunt to Solomon Sibley, January 26, 1822, folder for January 16–31, 1822, Sibley Papers.

64. Andrew Whitney to Solomon Sibley, January 5, 1822, folder for January 1–15, 1822, Sibley Papers.

65. Andrew G. Whitney to Solomon Sibley, January 26, 1822, folder for January 16–31, 1822, Sibley Papers.

66. An Act to provide for the appointment of an additional judge for the Michigan territory, and for other purposes, 3 Stat. 722 (1823). See Patrick J. Jung, "The Additional Court of Michigan Territory," pts. 1 and 2, *Court Legacy* 7, no. 3 (December 1999): 1–5; 8, no. 1 (September 2000): 1–5.

67. Fogerty, "Institutional Study," 110–11.

68. Ibid.

69. *House Journal,* 17th Cong., 2d sess. (January 13, 1823), 123 (petition from Monroe County); ibid. (February 24, 1823), 251–52 (petition from Oakland County asking for "a form of government more congenial to the feelings of American citizens, than that under which they now live").

70. *Detroit Gazette,* October 18, 1822 to January 3, 1823, reprinted in TSCM, 3:479–96.

71. An Act to amend the ordinance and acts of Congress for the government of the Territory of Michigan, and for other purposes, § 3, 3 Stat. 769 (1823).

72. *Territorial Papers of the United States*, 11:494, 541; Woodford, *Mr. Jefferson's Disciple*, 176–77; Fogerty, "Institutional Study," 111.

73. *Journal of the Executive Proceedings of the Senate of the United States*, 18th Cong., 1st sess. (January 20, 1824), 357.

74. An Act to amend the ordinance and acts of Congress for the government of the territory of Michigan, and for other purposes, 3 Stat. 769 (1823).

75. LTM, 2:264.

76. Ibid., 2:692.

77. TSCM, 5:xxxiv–xxxv.

78. Farmer, *History of Detroit, Wayne County and Early Michigan*, 1:335.

79. J. Harold Stevens, "The Influence of New England in Michigan," *Michigan History* 19 (Autumn 1935): 321–53.

80. For a discussion of the Simmons case and its place in Michigan legal history, see David G. Chardavoyne, *A Hanging in Detroit: Stephen Gifford Simmons and the Last Execution under Michigan Law* (Detroit: Wayne State University Press, 2003).

81. In December 1821, two Indians, Ke-wa-bish-kim and Ka-ta-kah, were hanged in Detroit for separate murders committed near Green Bay. Ke-wa-bish-kim was indicted and tried under territorial law because the land on which he killed a trapper was under territorial jurisdiction. Ka-ta-kah killed an army officer on Indian lands within the boundaries of the United States over which the territory lacked jurisdiction and was, consequently, indicted and tried under federal law. TSCM, 2:244, 485; *Detroit Gazette*, December 28, 1821.

82. *North Western Journal*, September 29, 1830.

83. Keith R. Widder, "Justice at Mackinac," *Mackinac History* 2, no. 2 (1974): 1–12. There has been only one other execution in Michigan—in 1938, the United States hanged Anthony Chebatoris at Milan Prison for killing a man during a bank robbery. For accounts of the Chebatoris case, see Margaret A. Leaming, "An Occurrence at Milan—Michigan's Last Execution," *Court Legacy* [no vol. number] no. 3 (April 1994): 1–4; and Aaron J. Veselenak, "Making Legal History—The Execution of Anthony Chebatoris." *Court Legacy* 6, no. 2 (Fall 1998): 7–10.

84. George Newman Fuller, *Messages of the Governors of Michigan* (Lansing: Michigan Historical Commission, 1925–27), 1:64–65.

85. *Democratic Free Press*, August 21, 1833.

86. Harold McVicar Dorr, *The Michigan Constitutional Conventions of 1835–36: Debates and Proceedings* (Ann Arbor: University of Michigan Press, 1940), 85, 349, appendix A, roll call 53; *Democratic Free Press*, June 12, 1835.

87. *Democratic Free Press*, February 25, 1839.

88. Roger L. Rosentreter, "'To Free Upper Canada': Michigan and the Patriot War, 1837–1839" (Ph.D. diss., Michigan State University, 1983); Fred Landon, "Trial and Punishment of the Patriots Captured at Windsor in December 1838," *Michigan History* 18 (Winter 1934): 25–32.

89. *Democratic Free Press*, January 30 to February 10, 1843.

90. Revised Statutes of the State of Michigan, ch. 173, § 1 (1846).

—∞∞∞—

Martin J. Hershock

BLOOD ON THE TRACKS

Law, Railroad Accidents, the Economy, and the Michigan Frontier

In the summer of 1835, Nathaniel Hawthorne joined a band of westward migrants—many bound for Michigan—for a journey along New York's Erie Canal. As his packet boat crept through the flourishing New York countryside he imagined that

> De Witt Clinton was an enchanter, who had waved his magic wand from the Hudson to Lake Erie, and united them by a watery highway, crowded with the commerce of two worlds, till then inaccessible to each other. This simple and mighty conception had conferred inestimable value on spots which Nature seemed to have thrown carelessly into the great body of the earth, without foreseeing that they could ever attain importance. I pictured the surprise of the sleepy Dutchmen when the new river first glittered by their doors, bringing them hard cash or foreign commodities, in exchange for their hitherto unmarketable produce. Surely, the water of this canal must be the most fertilizing of all fluids; for it causes towns—with their masses of brick and stone, their churches and theaters, their business and hubbub, their luxury and refinement, their gay dames and polished citizens—to spring up, till, in time,

the wondrous stream may flow between two continuous lines of
buildings, through one thronged street, from Buffalo to Albany.

It was from these towns and their hinterlands that Michigan, now made
readily accessible by the canal, drew the bulk of its initial wave of settlers.
Not surprisingly, having benefited directly from the dramatic transformation wrought by the Erie Canal, many of Michigan's first white settlers
sought to replicate the Empire State's commercial success in the Rochesters,
Troys, Uticas, and Palmyras they created in their new western home.[1]

Riding a tide of national prosperity, Michigan lands sold quickly in the
late 1820s and early 1830s, and the territorial population swelled, quickly
surpassing the benchmark of sixty thousand free inhabitants required for
statehood under the Northwest Ordinance of 1787. The final step before
Michigan could formally apply to Congress for admission into the federal
union was the creation of a state constitution. In 1835, delegates, the majority of whom listed New York as their place of birth, gathered in the territorial capital, Detroit, to draft such a constitution. The document that
emerged from that convention borrowed shamelessly from New York
State's legal code, particularly as it related to economic and commercial
concerns, thus mirroring the predilection of the delegates for promoting
commercial development.[2]

Among the provisions written into the proposed state constitution were
those authorizing the chartering of banks via a two-thirds vote of both
houses of the state legislature (no other restrictions hindered the creation
of banknote credit) and one reading "internal improvements shall be encouraged by the government of this state; and it shall be the duty of the
legislature, as soon as may be, to make provisions by law for ascertaining
the proper objects of internal improvement, in relation to roads, canals,
and navigable waters." Michigan's infant legislative body wasted no time
in furthering that cause. In its sessions in 1835, 1836, and 1837, the body authorized the chartering of a spate of corporations: three canals, seventeen
railroads, and fourteen banks. In 1837, as well, the legislature passed a bill
authorizing the state to borrow $5 million to build a network of roads,
canals, and railroads to crisscross the state. During the same legislative
term, lawmakers endorsed a general incorporation bill for banks (also
known as a free banking law) to accelerate economic activity through the
expansion of credit.[3]

Unfortunately, however, these policies did not bear their intended fruit
as Michigan's economy plunged into depression on the heels of the panic

of 1837. By 1839, severe economic hardship paralyzed the state. Virtually overnight, Michigan's dizzying economic bubble had burst. Land prices plummeted, and property reverted to the state for nonpayment of taxes. Moreover, the state's banks closed their doors as quickly as they had opened them, leaving behind tens of thousands of dollars—millions in contemporary terms—in worthless, unredeemable banknotes. As currencies collapsed, farm prices fell, and banks foreclosed mortgages and called in loans, many Michiganians faced the very real threat of losing everything they had. To make matters worse, Michigan itself teetered on the brink of insolvency, unable to meet its loan obligations.[4]

Throughout most of the 1840s, Michigan's economy languished, and the state's financial situation remained uncertain. In the last few years of the decade, however, Michigan experienced a pronounced turnaround characterized by sustained growth and heightened economic activity. In part, this recovery was the result of the expansion of Michigan's rail lines, which offered residents direct rail connections to Chicago and the all-important eastern seaboard by 1852. Situated along one of the nation's main east-west trade arteries, southern Michigan rapidly was transformed into a center of market activity. Although many Michiganians welcomed the renewal of economic growth, others, conditioned by the recent panic to fear commercial entanglements and safely ensconced in a self-provisioning lifestyle, approached this new boom period with skepticism, ambivalence, and even outright hostility. This uncertainty assumed myriad forms in the state, manifesting itself most concretely in the political dominance of the Democratic Party (with its attendant ambivalence toward markets and hostility toward monopolies) and in a Democrat-engineered antimarket revision of the state's organic law in 1850. Among the changes made were provisions limiting state indebtedness, prohibiting state funding of internal improvements projects, establishing a homestead exemption clause to protect debtors, and regulating the activities of banks—which had been outlawed by state Democrats in 1844—should the people of the state ever decide to allow them in the future. The most dramatic expression of this uncertainty, however, was the struggle to maintain traditional open-range privileges in the face of an emerging capitalist order embodied most tangibly by the state's flourishing railroad corporations.[5]

The preservation of traditional communal rights in the form of range laws was a prominent concern for Michigan's family farmers in the years before the Civil War. *The Bark Covered House,* an 1876 memoir written by William Nowlin, a member of a Dearborn pioneer family, nicely illustrates the central role of the range in the lives of Michigan's early settlers. Shortly after the Nowlins arrived in Dearborn in 1834, John, William's father, purchased two oxen and one cow. Nowlin remembered that the family's free-ranging cattle fed on "cow-slips and leeks, which grew in abundance, also on little 'French-bogs'" that remained green all winter. These cattle, which young Nowlin tracked daily across miles of timbered and newly broken farmland, were for many years the family's "main dependence" and, in Nowlin's words, "our stand-by through thick and thin." As the family struggled to clear its land (employing the free-roaming oxen) and later as it worked to free the farm from a mortgage, potatoes and milk and "thickened milk" (rolled lumps of salted, dampened flour boiled in milk) remained staples of the Nowlin family diet well into the 1840s.[6]

Such subsistence practices had been adhered to for generations back East, and thus they made perfect sense to the tide of Yankee settlers flooding into Michigan in the middle decades of the nineteenth century. The daunting task of clearing heavily timbered land and the lack of a reliable transportation network throughout much of the era ensured that even the most commercially minded farmers spent a substantial number of years subsistence farming. Making use of unimproved open land for grazing, foraging, or hunting was a fundamental element of that precapitalist subsistence strategy.[7] The traditional rights and the legal foundation that supported them, however, quickly came under attack as the agents of the new capitalist order, particularly the railroads, sought to restructure state law in a manner compatible with commercial expansion and the protection of private property.

The railroads and the state of Michigan grew up together. Indeed, as mentioned earlier, one of the very first actions of the fledgling state legislature was to enact an overly optimistic public works bill that included plans for the construction of three parallel railroad lines across the three southernmost tiers of counties. Work began almost at once on the Michigan Southern and Michigan Central lines, originating in Monroe and Detroit, respectively. The panic of 1837, however, soon brought construction to a virtual halt. Miraculously, although they reached only a short distance into the western hinterlands (the Central reached Kalamazoo in early 1846, and the Southern ran as far as Hillsdale) and were hampered by antiquated technology, the state-run railroads consistently managed to wring out a small profit. As Michigan's financial problems mounted and the railroads began to deteriorate, however, the state legislature determined in March 1846 to sell the lines to private investors while they still had some value. In return for the railroads' assets and protection against competing parallel lines, the purchasers agreed to reconstruct the existing roadbeds and to extend the lines to the Lake Michigan shoreline within three years.[8]

True to their word, the railroads' new owners immediately embarked on initiatives to rebuild and extend their rail lines: old oak and iron strap rails were torn up and replaced with new "T" rails made entirely of iron, roadbeds were surveyed and cleared, new track was laid, new engines and freight and passenger cars were ordered, and, after an active lobbying effort in Lansing, the legislature issued variances enabling the two lines to build farther southwest and eventually to forge a rail link with the growing city of Chicago by 1852. The lengthening reach of the railroad radically transformed the state's farming practices and thrust Michigan's southern counties into the cash economy. Enticed by the opportunity provided by quick and reliable market connections, many farmers residing near the rail lines began shifting toward commercial farming. Wheat production in the counties contiguous to the Michigan Central soared from 500,000 bushels in 1837 to more than 1,618,000 bushels in 1850. In addition, the value of flour produced by these counties burgeoned from $303,000 to $1,038,000 during the same period. Between 1845 and 1850, the gross tonnage of goods passing over the Central's rails jumped 415 percent, from 26,000 tons to 134,000 tons. Ralph Waldo Emerson, a contemporary observer of this metamorphosis, marveled that a "clever fellow was acquainted with the expansive force of steam; he also saw the wealth of wheat and grass rotting in Michigan. Then he cunningly screws on the steam pipe to the wheat crop. Puff now, O Steam! The steam puffs and expands as before, but this time it is dragging all Michigan at its back to hungry New York and hungry England."[9]

Not everyone, however, shared Emerson's exuberance. Traveling at the unheard-of speed of thirty miles an hour, the Michigan Central's new engines were involved in a number of accidents with livestock that wandered onto the largely unfenced track. Historian James Ely notes that "lawsuits over injuries inflicted on livestock by railroads were ubiquitous" in the nineteenth century—and the reaction to these accidental deaths is revealing. When similar accidents had occurred during the period of state ownership of the railroads, state policy—partly dictated by political necessity and in keeping with local township and county ordinances that recognized livestock as free commoners—was to pay farmers the full amount claimed for their livestock. However, the Central's president, John W. Brooks, had no such electoral concerns and was responsible only to the company's directors and stockholders. He therefore determined to make the farmers face up to what he interpreted as their negligence by implementing a policy of paying only one-half the appraised value of any livestock killed by the railroad. Farmers, construing Brooks's offer to pay as an admission of guilt and bolstered by the state's open-range tradition, demanded instead that the company pay full restitution.[10]

Although it might be tempting to conclude that the farmers' insistence on receiving full value represented "a calculating state of mind characteristic of capitalism," the equation of concern for money with a full-blown capitalist mentality may be too strong. Participation in and cognizance of the market did not always mean complete acceptance of it. A strong argument can be made, in fact, that the Michigan farmers' insistence on full, even inflated, compensation was adopted as a survival tactic in the face of an expanding cash nexus. Because of the importance of livestock in their day-to-day lives, farmers could not help but be aware of the cost of replacing their animals. This interpretation is supported by the frequent claims made by the Michigan Central and its supporters that farmers inflated the value of their animals or that they intentionally drove sick and feeble animals onto the tracks. Some farmers certainly may have done so. Others, however, may have claimed what seemed exorbitant values for their livestock because, in their self-provisioning world, livestock often represented a farmer's most valuable asset outside of real estate.[11]

Moreover, the fact that these farmers continued to operate on the "fencing-out" principle is a strong indication that they were still, in many respects, precapitalist. Proponents of laws (often referred to as stock laws) requiring the "fencing-in" of animals advocated such measures as a means of securing property rights. Furthermore, supporters of these laws argued that such measures would foster improved stock breeding, renew the fertility of land through manuring, facilitate the intensification of agriculture, and free up capital and labor (required to maintain the extensive fences needed to enclose fields of crops) for more productive purposes—all trends closely associated with a capitalist sensibility. It is inconceivable that Michigan's farmers would have reacted with righteous rage to accidental railroad slaughter if they had already accepted the "fencing-in" notion that free-roaming stock threatened their market crops. Again, Nowlin's memoir offers a tangible illustration of this tension. After working diligently to clear a portion of his land and to construct "brush" fencing around his fields, Nowlin's father put in a small crop of wheat. The wheat "came up and looked beautiful," Nowlin recalled. "One day," however, "a neighbor's unruly ox broke into it." Young Nowlin was told by his father to retrieve the ox and take it home. When he arrived at his neighbor's house with the ox, Nowlin told the neighbor "that his ox had been in our wheat and that father wished him to keep his ox away." The neighbor replied that the Nowlins "must make the fence better and he [the ox] wouldn't get in." The senior Nowlin's desire to protect his market commodity from his neighbor's foraging ox and the neighbor's insistence upon traditional open-range privileges nicely illustrate a major tension spawned by encroaching capitalism—one that was brought to a head by the conflict between the Michigan Central Railroad and the farmers of Michigan.[12]

Up and down the Michigan Central line, the state's yeomanry reacted to the new challenge posed to their communities and to their way of life. Near Ann Arbor, a group of irate farmers tore up the track. West of Kalamazoo, angry farmers greased upgrades with lard rendered from their slaughtered livestock. In few places, however, did the level of anger match that expressed by the farmers of Jackson County, where a coterie of outspoken citizens, led by Abel Fitch, a Leoni Township farmer, and Benjamin Burnett, a Grass Lake attorney, whipped up local indignation. Letters and petitions to the railroad and local protest meetings produced no satisfactory resolution of the issue. In the face of corporate intransigence and a mounting death toll of livestock, farmers took matters into their own hands in the summer of 1849, placing obstructions on the rails, derailing engines, greasing or tearing up the tracks, burning woodpiles, and even stoning and shooting at passing trains. As one Calhoun County farmer explained in a letter to his local paper,

> The road has been for a long time, one gore of blood. No heathen altar ever smoked more continually with the blood of its victims. Horses and Oxen and cows and sheep and hogs—all free commoners by law—the road not fenced, and yet we are told that the owners [of the livestock] are the trespassers. They [the company] force their way through our farms, leaving our fields and meadows and pastures all open as commons, and yet we are the trespassers if our stock pass over the road of their high-mightiness, and liable to them for damages. . . . The road must be fenced, in the meantime, something near the value of the property destroyed must be paid.[13]

The Michigan Central, faced with diminished revenues and timetables in disarray, quickly stepped up its efforts to snuff out the revolt, flooding the region with undercover operatives. After fire destroyed the Michigan Central's freight depot in Detroit late in 1850, agents investigated the suspected arsonist, whom they later linked to the Leoni Township protesters. Warrants were issued, and nearly fifty of the railroad insurgents were arrested and brought to trial. Who were these open-range activists, and what did they hope to achieve? A brief statistical profile of the Jackson County conspirators who were arrested offers some interesting insights. From the names provided by various arrest lists published by state newspapers, forty-two of the men have been located in the 1850 federal census.[14]

Among the first things that are evident about the members of this group are their relative maturity and overwhelmingly Yankee origins. Of those arrested, 71 percent were younger than forty. Most of these men (70 percent of the sample group and 50 percent of the overall total) were between the ages of twenty-five and forty, and 40 percent were between the ages of thirty and thirty-nine. Moreover, almost 79 percent of these men had been born in New England or New York, and another 12 percent listed Pennsylvania or New Jersey as their state of origin. These individuals had had significant exposure to the emerging market economy, having matured during its rapid expansion before the panic of 1837 and witnessed the market's transformation of the eastern United States. At the same time, these men also were well acquainted with the tradition of open-range grazing. They came from states where, in many cases, such practices were still protected by law as late as 1860 (New York being the most relevant example). The protesters' economic awareness must have been further enhanced by the fact that they had come of age politically at the height of the Jacksonian debates over banking, internal improvements, federal land policy, tariffs, and other economic concerns. Finally, it is likely that this same group also felt the full effects of the panic of 1837 and thus may have found it difficult to assert manly independence in the face of economic downturn. In other words, these men belonged to a generation of Americans that was intimately acquainted with the positive and, perhaps more important, the negative ramifications of socioeconomic change.[15]

The movement drew the bulk of its support from tradition-based segments of Michigan society. Of those arrested, twenty-seven (64 percent) were farmers, and another ten (24 percent) were artisans, figures in line with the state's overall occupational profile (farmers made up 60 percent of the state profile, and artisans 16 percent).[16]

A comparison of the mean value of real estate held by the sample group to the mean value figure for the state population as a whole also yields some suggestive results. The mean value for the sample group is $1,063, roughly comparable to the state figure of $1,048 but a bit below the $1,300 mean value in Leoni Township, where most of the men lived. A good many of those arrested owned little or no real estate: seventeen of them (40 percent) worked as hired hands, rented farms from others, or resided on their parents' farms as dependents. As a group, these men had not fared quite as well as their immediate neighbors.[17]

Further indications that these farmers, though connected to the markets, were somewhat less prosperous than many of their peers can be derived from the agricultural census of 1850. The mean value of farms owned by the accused, $1,331, was 11 percent less than the $1,488 mean value for farms throughout the state and 15 percent less than the Jackson County mean of $1,565—a difference even more notable when one considers the direct access to markets available to these men by virtue of their farms' prime location near the track of the Michigan Central. Furthermore, the alleged conspirators had farms with a slightly lower mean number of improved acres (44) than did the rest of the state's farmers, whose average stood at 55 acres. More to the point, this figure fell 33 percent short of the Jackson County mean of 66 acres. These same farmers tended to produce less marketable grain (wheat, corn, and oats) than did their statewide peer group (228 bushels compared to 357), or 5.1 bushels per improved acre—20 percent less than the statewide figure of 6.4 bushels. Similarly, the mean value of the farmers' herds, $147, fell considerably short of the statewide mean of $225, a possible indicator of the minimal market value placed on their inferior-quality free-ranging stock. Finally, the average value of agricultural implements owned by the accused stood at $44, as opposed to the state average of $79.[18]

The evidence from this small sample, though not conclusive, is suggestive. It implies that those individuals involved in the effort to preserve the open range in Michigan, though frequently connected to the market, shied away from a complete immersion in and acceptance of the emerging capitalist order. One can only speculate about why this was true. Perhaps these men resented their loss of economic autonomy to impersonal market forces and seemingly tyrannical corporate power, a loss driven home by their inability to preserve their traditional way of life and established rights against the incursion of the railroad. (This frame of mind was consistent with the Democratic proclivities of many of the arrested.) For others, such as Abel Fitch—the largest landowner among the group—and John D. Pierce—a Calhoun County minister and farmer, Michigan's first superintendent of public instruction, and one of the movement's most out-spoken supporters—traumatic experiences in the marketplace and, per-haps, a degree of incompetence may have led them to reevaluate their priorities. Fitch endured losses as the result of bad investments and the panic of 1837, and Pierce suffered a number of severe economic setbacks, including the loss of a farm, in commercial ventures. Younger activists and those who were not yet established as independent producers may have felt insecure about their prospects in the emerging capitalist order, or they may have lacked access to the capital necessary to make a go of things. Others may have seen the issue as a simple matter of preserving the na-tion's republican heritage and traditional property rights. Whatever the reason for their activism, these men felt buffeted and threatened by the shift-ing world around them; thus, they reacted by attacking those forces most closely identified with commercial expansion.[19]

Many of those involved in the reaction against the Michigan Central resorted to violence to vent their frustrations. Indeed, the use of such vio-lence, even against inanimate objects like railroad engines, further reflected these farmers' traditional ideal of personal, face-to-face relationships. By and large, free-range activists ignored the courts and the organized structures of the state at this early stage. In the main, Michigan's self-provisioning farmers remained suspicious of the legislature and courts, believing that powerful corporate entities like the Michigan Central could manipulate and control the structures of government (indeed, the powerful Michigan Central lobby had already blocked a prior effort to introduce new regula-tory measures). Accordingly, open-range activists fell back upon tradi-tional community-based modes of direct action.[20]

Curiously, another of the prime movers in the movement to defend tra-dition, Edward Williams, who lost a number of horses to a Michigan Cen-tral locomotive on a bridge near the town of Dearborn in the summer of 1849, did not adhere to this pattern. In most respects, Williams was typical of his fellow defenders of traditional rights. Born in New York State in 1794, Williams migrated to Michigan with his wife Rebecka (b. 1804) and his son William (b. 1832) sometime between 1832 and 1836. Two additional children, a daughter Saphara (b. 1836) and a son Barney (b. 1839), com-pleted the Williams household. Together the family worked an eighty-acre farm, valued at a mere $252 in the 1850 census, in Wayne County's Romulus Township. The Williams family fell far short of the mean wealth ($1,048) attributed to state farmers as a whole and even further behind its Wayne County peers, whose farm values averaged $1,851. The family seems either to have missed out on or to have opted out of the state's expanding commercial system. The 1850 census provides further evidence of the family's failure to adopt the modernizing trends of the day—although 70 percent of Michigan's children between the ages of five and nineteen were reported to have attended school (where skills necessary to succeed in an emerging commercial world were taught) the previous year, none of the Williams children did so. Nonetheless, rather than responding in a personal manner to the loss of his property and the affront to traditional rights posed by the Michigan Central's refusal to compensate him fully for his dead livestock, Williams turned to the courts.[21]

It seems unlikely, given the above description of his life, that Edward Williams was entirely comfortable with emerging market forces and legal institutions, although on at least one other occasion he did resort to the court system as a remedy for a perceived wrong. Perhaps Williams's close proximity to the state's main legal and commercial hub—Detroit—and thus his and his neighbors' long-term exposure to legal institutions, explains his choice. Although Williams and his neighbors participated in Michigan's cash economy, one cannot therefore infer that they were untroubled by their connections to it or by the potential loss of their autonomy to this system over which they had little control. On the contrary, Williams apparently valued his independence very highly and took aggressive steps to protect it. That Williams employed legal means rather than personal ones to do so may merely reflect the fact that the community in which he lived already had been transformed by an emerging capitalism that had rendered the world of personal interaction largely irrelevant and had begun to use law as an alternative to personal confrontation. Conditioned to operate in the impersonal world of the market, Williams responded to his loss by resorting to the impersonal courts.[22]

The Williams suit and the trial of the so-called Jackson County conspirators brought to the fore an ongoing debate that until then had been waged quietly along Michigan's country lanes, in isolated frontier clearings (such as the one farmed by the Nowlins), in village taverns and country stores, and beside the hearths of the state's numerous family farms. In these two highly publicized and symbolic cases, the emerging capitalist order had its day in court.

Although no transcripts or court filings exist for the Williams suit, the published decision in the case enables one to reconstruct the basic argument put forth on behalf of the plaintiff. Williams's Detroit-based attorneys, Henry T. Backus and David S. Harbaugh, argued that he was due compensation under the state's 1847 session laws, which provided that "no person shall recover for damages done upon lands by beasts unless in cases where, by the by-laws of the township, such beasts are prohibited from running at large, except where such lands are enclosed by a fence." Because the relevant Dearborn Township law deemed cattle and horses "free commoners" and thus able to graze on any unfenced land, this argument maintained that it was incumbent upon the Michigan Central to fence its property or face the risk of litigation for damages done to legally grazing livestock.[23]

Concurrently, in a jam-packed court just a short distance away, the alleged Jackson County conspirators and their lawyers waged a similar battle on behalf of traditional rights. Painting Fitch, Burnett, and the other alleged conspirators as righteous victims of a tyrannical corporation, defense attorneys, led by New York's William Seward, denounced the "monetary power" of the Michigan Central: "a power behind and above the government—a power that is seldom regulated by humane and just sentiments; [a power] that always seeks to crush those it cannot cajole." "It is well known," intoned the Reverend G. L. Foster in his August eulogy for the martyred Fitch, who had died in jail awaiting his day in court, "that heavy, moneyed corporations are not apt to be distinguished for their tender mercies, nor for their regard for justice, except it can contribute to pecuniary gain. *Corporations become corporate for the sake of the dollar.* Everything else is apt to be made subservient to its attainment. Somebody has recently said, 'Corporations have no souls.' How true! And no conscience—and no regard for God nor man—except so far as both God and man will subserve the interests for which they became corporate." As one state paper saw it, the conflict was between "the power and pretensions of a mighty corporation, aided by the use of an immense capital," and "the high prerogatives of the people and the just attributes of sovereignty . . . a war between the *creature* and the *creator*."[24]

Prosecuting attorney James Van Dyke vehemently disagreed with these hostile characterizations of the railroad. The railroad and the broader changes that it represented, he professed, had done nothing but good in Michigan: "Where heaven's light was once shut out by dense forests, it [now] shines over fertile fields and rich luxuriant harvests . . . ; hope and energy sprung from their lethargic sleep, labor clapped her glad hands and shouted for joy. . . . A detestable monopoly! These railroads built by united energies and capital are the great instruments in the hand of God to hasten onward the glorious mission of Religion and Civilization." Van Dyke continued, asking, "Who shall stop this glorious work which is spreading blessings and prosperity around us? Who shall dare to say 'thus far shalt thou go and no farther?'" The question facing the state supreme court, the Detroit jury, and the residents of Michigan was clear: Which of these competing social visions should prevail? Traditional open-range community norms or the common-law principle of unhindered personal property rights?[25]

The Michigan Supreme Court offered the first response in July 1851, affirming Brooks's assertion of an owner's culpability for livestock killed on the tracks of the Michigan Central. "The idea that because horses and cattle are free commoners, they have therefore the lawful right of trespassing on private property, is absurd—preposterous in the extreme," Justice Abner Pratt asserted unequivocally in his majority opinion. "What are free commoners? Where may they run?" Pratt continued. "Surely not on individual property." Should railroad corporations, Pratt asked, "be compelled to assume the guardianship of all the stray cattle, horses, and swine . . . found strolling along the track on their Railroad?" "Most certainly not," the justice chided. "The owners are the only persons to look after them; and if they do not, it is but just that they . . . should suffer the consequences of their own negligence . . . of their own want of care, in the protection . . . of their own property."[26]

On September 25, 1851, the Detroit jury determined the fate of the Jackson County conspirators: twenty defendants were acquitted, and twelve were convicted and sentenced to prison terms varying from five to ten years. These two related decisions marked the end of Michigan's longstanding open-range tradition and dealt a devastating blow to the state's self-provisioning family farms. They also, in light of historian James Ely's recent work on railroads and the evolution of American law, set Michigan apart from its peer states, where, "in most areas of law, courts were broadly supportive of the legislative lead."[27]

These court decisions did not, however, mean the end of the struggle to preserve traditional rights. On the contrary, the furor in defense of the open-range and precapitalist values continued. Writing shortly after the decisions were handed down, the editor of the *Jonesville Telegraph* asked the legislature to intervene and warned that "we are only in our infancy, and if we allow supinneness [sic] and inactivity to control us, we shall never, as a state arrive at manhood." In January 1853, one of the acquitted conspirators, Benjamin Burnett, began publication of the *Grass Lake Public Sentiment.* Convinced that justice had been "sacrificed under the iron heel of R.R. [*sic*] power," Burnett pledged to keep the cause of the Jackson County conspirators, and thus of the defenders of traditional rights, before the people. "Does '*Tuebor, si quaeris peninsulam amoenam circumspice,*' mean 'I swear to defend our beautiful peninsula,'" he asked in a subsequent edition, "or does it mean to defend the Michigan Central Railroad Company?" Declaring railroad tyranny his uncompromising enemy, Burnett swore to "take open ground on all questions involving the rights or liberties of freemen." Continuing this theme, he charged in 1854 that "an iron armoured slave-holding giant without any soul, is the owner and possessor of Michigan, and has the keeping of her fetters." He lamented further: "How often has this tyrant of a slave dealer sought the destruction of freemen?" The antirailroad hostility generated by the open-range debate persisted throughout Michigan between late 1851 and 1855 and joined with a host of other emergent issues (local school control, temperance, nativism, and, most famously, opposition to the extension of slavery) to create a volatile political environment.[28]

The growing antipathy toward the Michigan Central attracted the attention of Michigan's languishing Free Soil activists. Weakened by the temporary abatement of the slavery controversy as a result of the Compromise of 1850 and faced with a unified and seemingly perpetually dominant Democratic Party, Michigan's Free Soil Whigs saw the rapidly swelling antirailroad movement as an opportunity to make political capital with the state's Democratic yeomanry. Disregarding their own party's well-established tradition of support for the market economy and the agents of commerce, Free Soil Whigs such as Charles V. DeLand, the editor of the Jackson-based *American Citizen,* declared "a war as lasting as life . . . against [the Michigan Central's] despotism." In so doing, they linked the interests of the Michigan Central with the political fortunes of the state's Democratic Party, which had granted the railroad its original charter and had handled the prosecution of the conspirators. Both the ease with which Free Soil Whigs adopted such traditionally Democratic antimonopoly rhetoric and the ability of Whigs and Democrats (most of the defendants were Democrats) to unite and cooperate in the fight against the Michigan Central suggest that the defense of open-range privileges had a profound political impact in Michigan, blurring partisan lines in the state well before the traditional 1854 date emphasized by historians of party realignment. In short, the Free Soil Whig position regarding the Michigan Central foreshadowed the more thorough partisan melding that created the Republican Party in 1854.[29]

The Free Soil Whig decision to embrace the animus directed against the Michigan Central immediately paid political dividends. In 1851, antirailroad hostility became entwined with state politics in Jackson County during the campaign for governor. This enabled the Whig candidate, Townsend E. Gidley, to win Jackson County for his party for the first time in twelve years, even though he lost the election statewide to his Democratic rival, Robert McClelland.[30]

The following year, hatred of the Michigan Central again flared up during the congressional contest in the first district, which encompassed Wayne, Washtenaw, Jackson, and Livingston counties, pitting Democrat David A. Stuart, the Wayne County prosecutor who oversaw the conspiracy case, against William A. Howard, one of the defense attorneys in the case and a noted Free Soil Whig. For many district voters, the election undoubtedly represented an opportunity to voice their opinions about the trial's outcome. Not surprisingly, Stuart's candidacy faced widespread hostility in Jackson County. In a letter to one of David's siblings, Stuart's mother Elizabeth wrote, "Dave is having hard times—Jackson, from where he expected a large majority, sware [sic] vengeance against him. This is the home, or nest, of the R.R. Conspirators. They say their comrades are suffering imprisonment unjustly—that they were put there on false oaths &c."[31]

Cognizant of his weak position in Jackson County, Stuart set to work to overcome his handicap, allegedly offering large sums of money "to conciliate the opposition of certain prominent democrats in this county" to his candidacy. In addition, Stuart, along with several prominent Jackson County residents, petitioned Governor McClelland to pardon some of the incarcerated conspirators. To placate his opponents further, Stuart met privately with Benjamin F. Gleason, who afterward publicly claimed that Stuart had taken personal credit for the acquittal of some of the "conspirators" and emphasized that he now sought pardons for the rest. In return for his support, Gleason alleged, Stuart had promised him a job, if elected. "After being rode and made a cripple by his lies," Gleason asserted, "I cant [sic] vote for him." In the end, despite such intense opposition, Stuart won the election because of his strength in Wayne and Livingston counties. To no one's surprise, Jackson County went to Whig candidate William A. Howard, even though the county gave Democratic presidential candidate Franklin Pierce a majority over the Whigs' Winfield Scott.[32]

As 1853 dawned, opponents of the Michigan Central, alarmed by the rapidly expanding power of the railroad, which had reached Chicago in the spring of 1852, launched an all-out assault. They took their fight to the state legislature when it reconvened in January. Awaiting the newly seated legislators were numerous petitions, including those bearing the signatures of nearly one thousand legal voters from Oakland and Jackson counties, demanding the pardon of the imprisoned conspirators. A great many Michiganians, including Governor McClelland, seem to have concluded that pardoning the conspirators was the correct course. To deal with the onslaught of petitions, the state House of Representatives appointed a special committee. The committee, apparently controlled by friends of the rival Michigan Southern and enemies of the Michigan Central, issued a report attacking the entire prosecution of the conspiracy trial and recommended that all the conspirators be pardoned. A motion to adopt the report and the resolution passed the House, 39 votes to 23 votes. After further debate by the representatives and active lobbying by the Michigan Central, however, the House reversed itself and tabled the matter. Finally, on March 4, 1853, Governor McClelland issued a pardon for three of the Jackson County farmers, prior to resigning his office to become the U.S. secretary of the interior.[33]

Other supporters of the cause worked tirelessly throughout the session in an unsuccessful bid to convince state legislators to enact a general railroad law. One such law had been proposed in 1850 by Michael Shoemaker, a Free Soil Democratic senator from Jackson County and a neighbor of many of the conspirators. Such a law would have, among other things, regulated the activities of railroad companies and required that such corporations build fences along their tracks. These measures, the *Grand Rapids Enquirer* insisted, would ensure that railroad corporations were not "'booted and spurred' to ride over . . . the people." Despite the difficulties it encountered during the legislative session, the general-railroad-law crusade snowballed. Addressing a throng of two thousand citizens gathered at the Jackson County courthouse on August 23, 1853, W. T. Howell urged state residents to stay the course:

> Build your road across this wall—batter it down—improve the heritage you have—watch this company. They boast their millions—watch their money. Let it not barter away your rights. To save these, lay aside political differences and all things else. This is called an age of progress—if that means sin and corruption, it is true. In railroad progress it is true, for they progress over all our rights and on the most sacred privileges of our people. . . . By keeping this corporation where it belongs it will be a great blessing—such let us make it.[34]

Growing outrage across the state spawned three large meetings in December at Adrian, Detroit, and Jackson. The aim of these meetings was to pressure Governor Andrew Parsons (who was completing McClelland's term) into calling a special session of the state legislature to enact the desired railroad law. The general railroad law, DeLand's *Jackson American Citizen* asserted, is a measure "of the people; politicians have nothing to do with [it]; party should be eschewed. . . . If monopolies or individuals undertake to ride down the people, and deprive them of their rights, the people must oppose; and thus we should act as regards a special session. *We all want it,—let us all unite in calling for it."* In the end, Parsons resisted the mounting pressure. But as these well-attended meetings made clear, the antirailroad movement was at high tide and no longer could be restrained. Or, as the *American Citizen* put it, "The [Jackson] Convention settled one fact—that hereafter the will of the people must be respected by our Legislature. The days of Corporation Monopoly bearing sway over the rights of citizens is [*sic*] at an end. Politicians and 'traders in stock' will find soon, like Othello, their 'Vocations gone'—that there is a race of men inhabiting this Peninsula, and they demand rights and attention." DeLand's prophecy proved accurate; attention was quick in coming. The railroad issue, arising as it did out of the defense of traditional open-range rights, had truly become, "one of the ingredients in the bubbling political cauldron in the state."[35]

In short order, that "political cauldron" boiled over, and Michigan's Jacksonian party structure crumbled. A great many political undercurrents, such as temperance, nativism, and the Free Soil movement—all of which have been examined in other works—played a role in eroding the old party foundations. Frequently overlooked, however, is the critical role played by hostility to the state's railroads (especially the Michigan Central), a hostility that was created in good measure by the attempt to preserve a vanishing lifestyle in the face of sweeping social and economic transformation. Similarly ignored is the central role of this issue in the formation of the new Republican organization in Jackson, Michigan, in July 1854. Although the bulk of the new party's platform focused on the alleged machinations of the "Slave Power" and the need to prevent the spread of slavery into the western territories, delegates to the Jackson meeting also adopted a plank pertaining to state affairs. At the heart of this plank was the following resolution put forth by Jackson County's prosecutor (and Free Soil Whig), Austin Blair: "Resolved, That in our opinion the commercial wants require the enactment of a general railroad law, which, while it shall secure the investment and encourage the enterprise of stockholders, shall also guard and protect the rights of the public and of individuals, and that the preparation of such a measure requires the first talents of the State." Convention president David Walbridge, considered by many to be a shill for the Michigan Central Railroad, refused to put the resolution to a vote and unceremoniously left his chair. A number of angry delegates pursued Walbridge and forced him to return and put the question before the delegates. Given the opportunity to speak their minds, convention delegates voted for inclusion by a large majority.[36]

The new party's surprising victory in the 1854 state election enabled the fledgling organization to act upon this plank. The Republican administration immediately moved to placate anxious state residents by pardoning the remaining conspirators. Moreover, consideration of a general railroad law became a top priority for the new Republican legislature. In a revealing letter to Governor Kinsley Bingham, Isaac Christiancy, one of the chief architects of the new party, presented the importance of such a measure plainly: "What contributed to the unpopularity of the last legislature more than anything else was the impression among the people that they had been too much influenced by Railroad companies and neglected matters of general interest to the people. . . . Now unless our legislators set their faces like flint against all these special favors to incorporated companies our Republican triumph . . . is at once blown to the winds. . . . The lobbies ought to be made to understand that the best thing they can do for their employers is to go home on the shortest possible route." Other less-renowned Republicans echoed Christiancy's plea. Referring to problems with the Michigan Southern Railroad, a resident of Jonesville wrote, "We want some legislation to make them behave right. A law ought to be passed preventing trains going through the village at a greater speed than 5 miles an hour." This correspondent continued, "Another great cause of complaint, is because a Rail Road Co never settles any damages. . . . If you have any claim against the Co you must go to the head office in NY, Toledo or Chicago to get it settled. A law should be passed making it imperative to settle it where the property is deliverable to the consignee."[37]

Austin Blair, the Jackson lawyer who was serving as majority leader, eagerly assumed the management of the general railroad bill. He introduced the bill early in the legislative session. As anticipated, the Michigan Central lobby, headed by James Van Dyke, immediately swung into action against the bill. In a memorial presented to the Senate, Van Dyke argued that the proposed law (which established general rules of organization for future railroad companies) violated the company's charter by allowing competing railroads to be built. The Michigan Central, he maintained, had paid two million dollars to the state for what it believed to be monopoly privileges. If the state was dissatisfied with the contract into which it had entered, it could simply repurchase the railroad according to the terms laid out in the charter. Such a law, another employee of the Michigan Central wrote in a letter to Governor Bingham, "is so manifestly unjust, inequitable and I think illegal and unconstitutional . . . that I think such an act would make the Republican party a stench in the nostrils of all honorable men." As it had in the past, the Michigan Central lobby prevailed, smothering the proposed bill.[38]

In late January, however, the Central lobby reversed course, clearing the way for the law's passage. The Central's sudden turnabout did not signify a surrender. In fact, the Michigan Central and the Michigan Southern had reached a tentative understanding that, two years later, resulted in a pooling agreement—legal in Michigan at the time—that minimized the threat of competition between the two lines. In addition, the nature of the proposed law helped alleviate the Central's fears because "the only substantial limitation on railroads" in terms of their corporate structure was "a prohibition of mergers between parallel lines within the state." On the other hand, the law encouraged the merger of other railroads to form trunk lines. Although the law opened the door for the creation of new railroad corporations (and thus placated antimonopoly activists), it also contained many prohibitions that addressed the concerns of a very different group of Republican voters—those who viewed the party as a means of preserving an older and rapidly waning lifestyle. Accordingly, all new railroads organized under the act, as well as those already operating in the state, were required to install upon their locomotives bells and steam whistles to be sounded before all grade crossings, to post warning signs at crossings, to fence the right-of-way, and to install special farm crossings with cattle guards where needed. The law also fixed maximum passenger rates and gave the legislature the power to reduce those rates in the future. The legislature could not, however, lower rates below a sum required to provide a 15 percent annual return on capital stock paid in. By passing the law, the Republicans had lived up to a very important political promise and had reassured tradition-bound Michiganians that their rights once again were safe.[39]

Such a limited victory, however, did not and, of course, could not change the fact that the tradition of self-sufficient farming was in decline. One of the main elements of the state yeomanry's self-provisioning lifestyle had been circumscribed. The encroachment of market capitalism would continue unabated, and soon the John Nowlins of the state no longer would be free to loose their livestock to forage upon the unfenced lands of their neighbors. No longer could they reflexively look upon open land that they did not own as a resource available for communal use. A symbolic shift had occurred in Michigan law, and the culture of capitalism had gained the upper hand.

Notes

The author wishes to thank the editors of the *Michigan Historical Review* for permission to reprint the portions of this work that appeared in a slightly different form as "Free Commoners by Law: Tradition, Transition and the Closing of the Range in Antebellum Michigan," *Michigan Historical Review* 29 (Fall 2003): 97–123.

1. Nathaniel Hawthorne, "The Canal Boat," *New England Magazine* 9 (December 1835): 398. The northeastern origins of Michigan's early settlers are documented in Kenneth E. Lewis, *West to Far Michigan: Settling the Lower Peninsula, 1815–1860* (East Lansing: Michigan State University Press, 2002), 134.

2. Harold M. Dorr, ed., *The Michigan Constitutional Conventions of 1835–36: Debates and Proceedings* (Ann Arbor: University of Michigan Press, 1940), 16–17. An excellent study of the parallels between Michigan's first state constitution and New York law is Ronald Seavoy, "Borrowed Laws to Speed Development: Michigan, 1835–1863," *Michigan History* 59 (Spring–Summer 1975): 38–68.

3. Mich. const. of 1835, art. XII, § 2, reprinted in Dorr, *Michigan Constitutional Conventions*, 336–37, 392; Seavoy, "Borrowed Laws," 42–53. To skirt around the 1835 constitution's requirement for two-thirds approval of proposed banking charters, banks organized under the new free banking law were reclassified as "associations," not corporations. For a broader treatment of the constitutional convention of 1835, see Alec R. Gilpin, *The Territory of Michigan, 1805–1837* (East Lansing: Michigan State University Press, 1970), 154–58.

4. On the effects of the panic of 1837, see Martin J. Hershock, *The Paradox of Progress: Economic Change, Individual Enterprise, and Political Culture in Michigan, 1837–1878* (Athens: Ohio University Press, 2003), 2.

5. For a fuller account of Michigan's antebellum history, see Willis F. Dunbar, *Michigan: A History of the Wolverine State* (Grand Rapids: W. B. Eerdmans, 1970); Richard J. Hathaway, ed., *Michigan: Visions of Our Past* (East Lansing: Michigan State University Press, 1989); and Hershock, *Paradox of Progress*. Many historical works outline the Democratic constituency's trepidation about the emerging market. Among the most insightful is Harry L. Watson, *Liberty and Power: The Politics of Jacksonian America* (New York: Hill and Wang, 1990). On the Michigan constitutional convention of 1850, see Martin J. Hershock, "To Shield a Bleeding Humanity: Conflict and Consensus in Mid-Nineteenth Century Michigan Political Culture," *Mid-America* 77 (Winter 1995): 33–50b. The commonly held perception that the railroad and economic progress were synonymous is well established in

James W. Ely Jr., *Railroads and American Law* (Lawrence: University Press of Kansas, 2001).

6. William Nowlin, *The Bark Covered House; or, Back in the Woods Again* (Ann Arbor: University Microfilms, 1966), 31–34, 60–66, 110. Caroline Kirkland, in her thinly fictionalized portrayal of life in frontier Pinckney, Michigan, noted the annual spring burning of local marshes to facilitate the growth of new grass for local ranging livestock. Caroline M. Kirkland, *A New Home, Who'll Follow? or, Glimpses of Western Life* (New Brunswick, N.J.: Rutgers University Press, 1990), 112. Cattle were known to be hardy animals requiring little direct attention, able, as Alan Taylor describes them, to "endure the cold and find sustenance in the forests." Moreover, because of their size, cattle could defend themselves against marauding carnivores better than other livestock. Equally important, cattle, when tended by a few men, could walk long distances over primitive roads to get to market. On the advantages of cattle for pioneering families, see Alan Taylor, *William Cooper's Town: Power and Persuasion on the Frontier of the Early American Republic* (New York: Vintage Books, 1995), 105–6.

7. Richard W. Judd, *Common Lands, Common People: The Origins of Conservation in Northern New England* (Cambridge, Mass.: Harvard University Press, 1997).

8. Robert J. Parks, *Democracy's Railroads: Public Enterprise in Jacksonian Michigan* (Port Washington, N.Y.: Kennikat Press, 1972).

9. Martin J. Hershock, "Liberty and Power in the Old Northwest: Michigan, 1850–1867" (Ph.D. diss., University of Michigan, 1996), 85; James A. Van Dyke, *Argument in the Railroad Conspiracy Case; Entitled the People of the State of Michigan vs. Abel F. Fitch and Others* (Detroit: Duncklee, Wales, 1851), 13; Ralph Waldo Emerson, *The Conduct of Life, Nature and Other Essays* (New York: E. P. Dutton, 1908), 192.

10. Charles Hirschfeld, *The Great Railroad Conspiracy: The Social History of a Railroad War* (East Lansing: Michigan State College Press, 1953), 4; Ely, *Railroads and American Law,* 120.

11. Shawn E. Kantor, and J. Morgan Kousser, "Common Sense or Commonwealth? The Fence Law and Institutional Change in the Postbellum South," *Journal of Southern History* 59 (May 1993): 212–13. Accusations regarding the intentional slaughter of debilitated animals were frequent. See Charles Hirschfeld, "The Great Railroad Conspiracy," *Michigan History* 36 (June 1952): 100.

12. Nowlin, *Bark Covered House,* 44. A good discussion of the promarket orientation of stock-law proponents can be found in Steven Hahn, *The Roots of Southern Populism: Yeoman Farmers and the Transformation of the Georgia Upcountry, 1850–1890* (New York: Oxford University Press, 1985), 249–51. See also Jane Adams, "'How Can a Poor Man Live?' Resistance to Capitalist Development in Southern Illinois, 1870–1890," *Rural History: Economy, Society, Culture* 3 (Spring 1992): 97–98; Charles E. Brooks, *Frontier Settlement and Market Revolution: The Holland Land Purchase* (Ithaca, N.Y.: Cornell University Press, 1996), 99; Charles H. Danhof, "The Fencing Problem in the Eighteen-Fifties," *Agricultural History* 19 (October 1944): 169–70; and Judd, *Common Lands, Common People,* 40–47. Caroline Kirkland also alluded to the tensions surrounding the fencing controversy when she wrote that "bad fences, missing dogs, unruly cattle, pigs ears [a reference to the notches carved into pigs' ears to denote ownership of free-ranging hogs], and women's tongues, are among

the most prolific sources of litigation" in her town of Pinckney. Kirkland, *New Home,* 176.

13. *Marshall Democratic Expounder,* June 25, 1849. A perceptive discussion of "out-state" hostility to the Michigan Central Railroad can be found in Hirschfeld, *Great Railroad Conspiracy.*

14. The model used for the following statistical analysis was derived from John W. Quist, "'The Great Majority of Our Subscribers Are Farmers': The Michigan Abolitionist Constituency of the 1840s," *Journal of the Early Republic* 14 (Fall 1994): 325–58.

15. J. D. B. DeBow, comp., *The Seventh Census of the United States, 1850: Embracing a Statistical View of Each of the States and Territories* (Washington, D.C.: R. Armstrong, 1853), Jackson County; Quist, "Great Majority," 342–54. By 1860, as historian Ben Brown notes, only seven states had "unequivocally" closed the range: Massachusetts, New Hampshire, Rhode Island, Vermont, New Jersey, Wisconsin, and, of course, Michigan. R. Ben Brown, "The Southern Range: A Study in Nineteenth Century Law and Society" (Ph.D. diss., University of Michigan, 1993), 98. Noticeably absent from this list is New York (from which twenty-four of the accused men came), the state that, more than any other, served as a model for Michigan's economic development and legal code. The standard work on the evolution of American railroad law erroneously minimizes this tradition and argues instead that many northeastern jurisdictions adhered to a common-law "fencing-in" ideal. See Ely, *Railroads and American Law,* 118.

16. Of the remaining five men, three were professionals (one physician, one dentist, and one lawyer). The other two men were younger than nineteen years old and had no occupation listed. For a highly readable and persuasive discussion of the economic connotations of Jacksonian politics, see Watson, *Liberty and Power.*

17. DeBow, *Seventh Census of the United States,* Jackson County; Quist, "Great Majority," 342–54. Leoni Township had 191 households and a population of 1,290 in 1850.

18. DeBow, *Seventh Census of the United States,* Jackson County.

19. It is likely that the market activities of some of these farmers, Ammi Filley for example, have been exaggerated by historians such as Charles Hirschfeld. Though Filley did possess a great deal of property ($4,500) and produced 420 bushels of grain on his 280-acre farm, his main connection to the market seems to have been supplying fresh game and fish to Detroit. This reliance on extracted resources rather than the products of commercial farming suggests a more tenuous connection to the cash nexus than one might otherwise assume. It also helps to account for Filley's devotion to the cause of the open range. An end to communal range rights undoubtedly would have hindered Filley's ability to continue trading. William Nowlin also killed and dressed game (mainly deer) near his Dearborn home for the Detroit market, where they brought between $2.50 and $5.00 apiece. His participation, however, was not designed to increase his personal wealth. Rather it was part of the family's effort to pay off a mortgage, which, Nowlin wrote, "was like a cancer eating up your substance." Nowlin, *Bark Covered House,* 156. On Fitch's early exposure to the market, see Hirschfeld, "Great Railroad Con-

spiracy," III. Pierce's economic misfortunes are outlined in Hershock, "To Shield a Bleeding Humanity," 45.

20. Wayne K. Durrill, "Producing Poverty: Local Government and Economic Development in a New South County, 1874–1884," *Journal of American History* 71 (March 1985): 764–81; Hershock, *Paradox of Progress*, 47, 92.

21. DeBow, *Seventh Census of the United States*, Jackson County; Edward Williams Papers, 1838–1878 (hereafter cited as Williams Papers), Michigan Historical Collections, Bentley Historical Library, University of Michigan, Ann Arbor; Quist, "Great Majority," 355.

22. Williams resorted to the courts again in 1860 to challenge his 1859 drain-tax levy. The event is described in a petition written by Williams to the Wayne County Board of Supervisors dated October 22, 1872. Williams Papers.

23. Williams v. Michigan Cent. R.R. Co., 2 Mich. 259 (1851).

24. Closing argument of William Seward, quoted in Hirschfeld, "Great Railroad Conspiracy," 185; *Jackson American Citizen*, August 27 (first quotation), September 3, 1851; *Jonesville Telegraph*, October 15, 1851 (second quotation). All emphases in original.

25. Van Dyke, *Argument in the Railroad Conspiracy Case*, 13, 130; Brown, "Southern Range," 164.

26. Williams v. Michigan Cent. R.R. Co., 2 Mich. 259, 266–67 (1851).

27. Hirschfeld, "Great Railroad Conspiracy," 197. Charges were dismissed for some, and at least one defendant (Fitch) died in prison. Ely asserts that state legislators, responding to public sentiment, "consistently took the initiative in crafting [American] railroad law." Michigan's experience suggests that this pattern did not always hold true. It was the state court system that initially promoted the cause of the new economic order. See Ely, preface to *Railroads and American Law*, ix.

28. *Jonesville Telegraph*, October 15, 1851; *Grass Lake Public Sentiment*, February 1, June 1, 1853; March 15, 1854. Burnett actually conflated two separate phrases that appear on the Michigan state seal. The first, "tuebor," does mean "I shall defend." The second, however, actually translates as, "If you seek a pleasant peninsula, look about you." Michigan politics in the 1850s are described in detail in Ronald P. Formisano, *The Birth of Mass Political Parties: Michigan, 1827–1861* (Princeton, N.J.: Princeton University Press, 1971); Hershock, *Paradox of Progress;* and Benjamin F. Streeter, *Political Parties in Michigan, 1837–1860: An Historical Study of Political Issues and Parties in Michigan from the Admission of the State to the Civil War* (Lansing: Michigan Historical Commission, 1918).

29. *Jackson American Citizen*, August 27, 1851. The Free Soil Whig response to the conspiracy trial is detailed in Dale R. Prentiss, "Economic Progress and Social Dissent in Michigan and Mississippi, 1837–1860" (Ph.D. diss., Stanford University, 1990), 60; and Hershock, *Paradox of Progress*, 83–84.

30. *Jackson American Citizen*, November 12, 1851; Isaac P. Christiancy to Thomas M. Cooley, October 23, 1851, "Correspondence, 1851," box 1, Thomas M. Cooley Papers, 1850–1898, Bentley Historical Library, University of Michigan, Ann Arbor. In this letter, Christiancy noted (in reference to the railroad issue) that "it will be an evil day for Michigan when such matters are brought into politics and control elections."

31. Elizabeth Stuart to her son, September 6, 1852, in Helen Stuart Mackay-Smith Marlatt, ed., *Stuart Letters of Robert and Elizabeth Sullivan Stuart and Their Children, 1819–1864* (n.p.: privately printed, 1961), 402.

32. *Jackson American Citizen,* October 6, 1852. Stuart addressed a letter to Governor McClelland requesting the pardon of Erastus Champlin. An excellent account of the campaign in Jackson County can be found in Hirschfeld, "Great Railroad Conspiracy," 203–4.

33. Hirschfeld, "Great Railroad Conspiracy," 203–7; *Jackson American Citizen,* March 9, 1853. In defense of the pardons, McClelland cited the favorable recommendations of James F. Joy (the Michigan Central's chief attorney), David Stuart, and prominent citizens of Jackson County; the petitions of more than twenty-five hundred citizens; and the prisoners' good behavior.

34. Hirschfeld, "Great Railroad Conspiracy," 125–26; *Grand Rapids Enquirer,* January 8 (first quotation), 12, 1853; *Jackson American Citizen,* August 24, 1853 (second quotation). A very good discussion of the railroad fence law controversy can be found in Ely, *Railroads and American Law,* 117–20.

35. *Jackson American Citizen,* December 14, 1853 (emphasis in original). Further coverage of the meetings can be found in the *Detroit Free Press,* December 30, 1853; *Grand Rapids Enquirer,* January 4, 1854; and *Jackson American Citizen,* January 4, 1854. See also Hirschfeld, "Great Railroad Conspiracy," 214.

36. Hirschfeld, "Great Railroad Conspiracy," 215. See also Prentiss, "Economic Progress," 64–66. Prentiss astutely notes that advocacy of a general railroad law was necessary for Republicans to win over Michigan's small farmers and laborers.

37. Isaac P. Christiancy to Kinsley Bingham, folder 8, box 141; George A. Coe to Kinsley Bingham, December 4, 1854, folder 9, box 134; William [illegible] to Kinsley Bingham, December 16, 1854 (second quotation), folder 8, box 141, all in RG 44, State Archives, Lansing, Michigan.

38. Hirschfeld, "Great Railroad Conspiracy," 216–17; W. Tracy Howe to Kinsley Bingham, February 1, 1855, folder 16, box 191, Executive Department, State Archives, Lansing, Michigan.

39. Seavoy, "Borrowed Laws to Speed Development," 65; Hirschfeld, "Great Railroad Conspiracy," 217. State-level legislative activism of this sort, spurred by public opinion, was central to the evolution of railroad law in the United States. Ely, *Railroads and American Law,* 2.

∽✺∽

THREE

John W. Quist

AN OCCASIONALLY DRY STATE SURROUNDED BY WATER

Temperance and Prohibition in Antebellum Michigan

Temperance in antebellum Michigan followed a cyclical pattern. Emerging in the late 1820s, it was initially an elite-dominated movement that tolerated the use of wine but fervently condemned hard liquor. In the mid-1830s, it moved gradually—but not without dissension and loss of adherents—toward total abstinence and prohibition. The cause suffered setbacks, however, when legislators refused to ban liquor sales. During the early 1840s, temperance activists retreated to the tactic of moral suasion but, later in the decade, pursued local-option legislation. Agitation peaked during the 1850s as enthusiasts sought prohibitory legislation patterned after the so-called Maine Law. Michigan lawmakers enacted general prohibition statutes in 1853 and 1855, but neither succeeded: the Michigan Supreme Court and public opinion proved unreceptive to their enforcement.

Early nineteenth-century Americans drank heavily: modern scholarship indicates that the country's per capita consumption peaked in 1830. Michigan fit the norm. L. D. Norris recalled in 1874 that, fifty years earlier, Ypsilanti inhabitants had deemed whiskey a "necessity" that "cured rattlesnake bites, and alleviated 'fever and fatigue.'" Cooperation was essential on the frontier, and those who aided their neighbors expected whiskey as reciprocation.[1]

Beginning in late 1829, Michigan temperance societies experienced phenomenal growth: as many as nine local bodies quickly sprang into existence. Although both men and women joined these early temperance organizations, men filled all the leadership positions and recorded little about women's contributions, save the necessity of women's encouraging men to be sober. By 1833, advocates had formed the Michigan State Temperance Society and convened their first two annual meetings in Ann Arbor.[2]

A half century later, one Michiganian recalled how "a grand wave of temperance swept over the whole land" at this time: "In every city, village and hamlet the enthusiasm was caught." The pious, particularly evangelical Protestants, dominated the ranks of temperance organizations. The Reverend William Jones, of Ypsilanti, offered a typical description when he noted that members of his Presbyterian Church had formed "themselves into a temperance Society," adding that revivals succeeded best "in the very neighborhood & with the same persons" who initially embraced temperance. During the movement's early years, in particular, temperance societies usually exhibited a decidedly religious tone. Meetings generally assembled at evangelical Protestant churches, where they always opened with prayer and often featured clerical addresses. Evangelicals' attraction to temperance is not surprising: consciously accepting Christ required a commitment, along with a mental concentration, that evangelicals believed eluded the grasp of liquor-enslaved drunkards. Alcohol thus blocked inebriates from salvation. But the elites who dominated the early movement made little effort to adapt their message to working-class culture. The solution to working-class intemperance, Israel Branch explained in January 1832, was to "effect a change in those who give tone to fashions[.] Let those who lead the fashions propose one . . . no matter how absurd & multitudes are surely to follow their tracks."[3]

Scholars have noted that antebellum temperance participants typically welcomed the era's modernizing economy and celebrated abstemiousness as essential to worldly success. Nevertheless, by the mid-1830s, factionalism regarding the best means of establishing a temperate society overwhelmed the cause: some continued to favor persuasion—or "moral suasion" as contemporaries worded it—and others endorsed prohibition, or "legal suasion." George Corselius, of Ann Arbor, adhered to the former position in 1833 when he championed a "moral force" to govern human behavior. The "more our actions are controlled by this power, and the less by human laws, the better," he argued. Only the proper cultivation of public opinion could rid America of intemperance.[4] By the time Corselius spoke, however, New England's temperance vanguard was already pressing for prohibition. Many New England temperance enthusiasts—and, before long, their Michigan counterparts—concluded that moral suasion alone would not convince everyone to lead abstemious lives. Accordingly, many turned to the law for assistance. During the 1830s, prohibitionists experimented with several approaches. In Michigan, their favorite proposals were abolishing liquor licenses, raising license fees, increasing the minimum quantity of liquor that retailers could sell, and outright prohibition.

Public authorities had used liquor licenses to raise revenue and to regulate alcohol sales long before widespread temperance activity commenced. But the temperance movement's advent motivated some to urge using the license system to control the liquor trade further. Perhaps because of temperance's rapid rise in Ypsilanti—where, by January 1834, some 450 residents had pledged abstinence—prohibitory license laws quickly emerged there. According to Ira M. Wead, a recently enacted municipal statute enraged Ypsilanti's grocers because it prohibited the sale of liquor in volumes of less than a quart and had as its aim precluding alcohol sales at groceries, inns, bars, and other public places renowned for immoderate drinking.[5] Taking a different tack, the *Michigan Emigrant* proposed in February 1834 that temperance devotees launch a petition campaign "to increase the tax on taverns retailing ardent spirits."[6]

Later that year, some writers denounced the alcohol licensing system and advocated curtailing what they regarded to be the government sponsorship of vice. One denounced the liquor traffic as an "immorality" and the license system as having "no public benefit," while another wondered how "our laws" can "countenance a practice so destructive of the highest ends of society?" In February 1835, the Washtenaw County Temperance Society resolved that "laws licensing the sale of ardent spirits are morally wrong, and ought to be abandoned." The Washtenaw body, though, proved to be ahead of the Michigan State Temperance Society, which continued to support persuasion as the best means of effecting a temperance revolution.[7]

Yet sentiment against the license system was clearly growing. The "Ann Arbor Young People" announced in May 1835 that a county convention would explore "the propriety of petitioning" the territorial legislature "to abolish the Law granting Licenses for the sale of Ardent Spirits." The convention delegates unanimously adopted several resolutions decrying retailers, the licensing system, the revenue collected from liquor licenses, and the scarcity of grain occasioned by its conversion into whiskey; they also favored a law empowering local communities to regulate the granting of liquor licenses. Significantly, George Corselius, who but two years earlier had defended moral suasion as the only feasible way to achieve temperance objectives, coauthored these resolutions. His conversion to strict liquor license regulation—a soft prohibition in this instance—points to the fundamental changes in temperance thinking: obviously the intemperate had proved unresponsive to the temperance forces' glaring disapproval. Moral suasionists seldom spoke publicly during the half dozen years following this convention.[8]

The growth of legal suasion accompanied a shift in temperance doctrine, as abstinence from hard liquor alone gave way to teetotalism. Early devotees of temperance had attacked principally the sale and consumption of whiskey, and, during the early 1830s, even their leaders, such as Corselius, drank beer and hard cider. It was at this time, Lorenzo Davis recalled, that he "took the ground that no one could be a thorough temperance advocate in theory or practice who drank wine." Soon he formed a total abstinence society that forswore all intoxicants. Detroiters heard their first teetotal speech in 1831, and the Monroe County Temperance Society reorganized itself as a teetotal body in March 1834. Other groups soon followed. Some activists, though, refused to endorse teetotalism. Ypsilanti's Ira Wead lamented in April that "our old Temperance Soc. during the year has been rather inefficient and still remains so, except in its opposition to TeeTotalism." Three months later, he rejoiced that temperance statewide enjoyed a new impulse, as "Teetotalism is the doctrine that prevails"—a point affirmed by several other observers.[9]

Teetotal opponents, however, were plentiful at the statewide Young Men's Temperance Association meeting in Ann Arbor in January 1836. After prolonged debate, teetotalers and moderates reached a compromise by which both groups would continue to affiliate. Cooperation ended in March, when state teetotalers, reassembling in Ann Arbor to form the Michigan Total Abstinence Temperance Society, condemned all who rejected complete abstinence. According to the *State Journal,* one speaker insisted that old temperance hands refusing to adopt a total abstinence pledge were "nothing but a dead weight to the cause of Temperance" and "had only joined at all because it was popular to do so." "All such friends could be profitably spared," he added, they being "more injurious to the cause than open enemies." When another speaker tried to challenge total abstinence, teetotalers responded "by low scurrility, black guardism and ridicule." The

State Journal editor, himself a temperance moderate, argued that this counterproductive meeting impeded both teetotalism and temperance.[10]

This assessment proved accurate throughout most of 1837 and 1838, when temperance notices virtually disappeared from Michigan's newspapers. After the November 1838 gubernatorial election, though, Washtenaw County temperance devotees—pursuant to a directive from the Michigan State Temperance Society—launched a drive to petition state legislators to abolish intoxicant sales. "The most active Temperance men in each town" were to collect the signatures of sympathetic men and women. Praising this effort, the state body's executive committee recommended "the holding of county temperance meetings throughout the state, immediately, to take speedy measures to follow the noble example of Washtenaw County." Despite believing that prohibition would "promote the welfare of all classes," the *State Journal*'s editor doubted that Michiganians were "prepared for such a law. We are less enlightened, and less moral than the people of Massachusetts," whose legislature recently had enacted a statewide prohibitory liquor law. Instead, the editor favored empowering local citizens to determine whether "spirituous liquors [should] be retailed within their town."[11]

Because petitioners embraced several prohibition methods, this statewide campaign lacked focus. It also proved disappointing: petitioners garnered only 1,450 signatures. Although they predictably praised the activists' objectives, legislators questioned whether prohibition would create a temperate society. Instead, the House Temperance Committee, chaired by Justus Goodwin, a Democrat, and the Senate committee, chaired by Whig William Woodbridge, encouraged temperance workers to continue their labors through moral suasion. Outraged temperance devotees threatened to vote only for prohibitionists. Nevertheless, the issue played little part in the 1839 state electoral campaigns. Although the Whigs captured the governorship and both legislative houses, they proved unwilling to act on the wishes of their prohibitionist supporters. Whatever temperance fervor remained in 1840 was quickly doused by that year's Whig hard-cider presidential campaign.[12]

Following the teetotalist victory over the moderates, the antebellum movement never again debated teetotalism. The struggle between moral and legal suasionists, however, remained unresolved. The failed petition drives disheartened prohibitionists for a season and invigorated moral suasionists, whose arguments prevailed during the early 1840s. The Ann Arbor Total Abstinence Society exemplified these trends. Emerging in 1841, the

group firmly advocated total abstinence. In its endeavor to halt the manufacture of all intoxicants, the society emphasized moral suasion and proclaimed that the abolition of alcohol would occur only "when the whole
community, acting upon total abstinence principles, shall cease to drink."
The members also recognized that the radicalism of the late 1830s had
offended some people and had earned temperance champions a reputation as imperious zealots. The Ann Arbor Total Abstinence Society la-
bored to counteract this perception, and its members assured the community that they would not denounce "as unchristian" those failing to unite
with them.[13]

Not all of Michigan's temperance enthusiasts retreated from legal suasion. Most abolitionists, slavery's fiercest opponents, remained committed
prohibitionists and constituted a disproportionate share of the temperance
rank and file. Certainly, each individual's decision to espouse temperance
or abolitionism sprang from a complex mix of motivations. At bottom,
both temperance and abolition focused upon freedom—either from the
overseer's lash or from an inveterate addiction to alcohol. Most antebellum reformers would have categorized both slavery and alcohol consumption as sins—but might have been as hard-pressed as modern historians to
explain why so many of their evangelical contemporaries, as well as the
pious of previous ages, had failed to draw the same conclusions. Historians generally agree that revivalism, religious perfectionism, and market expansion coalesced to transform the moral compass of many in the Atlantic
world. During the antebellum years, these influences also fostered temperance, abolition, and other causes, often generating crusades. Although
some contemporaries embraced a broad reformist vision, others ignored
these efforts or endorsed them only selectively. Despite the broad backing
that temperance won from abolitionists, temperance did not depend
solely upon abolitionists for its support, for it enjoyed a healthy life in the
slaveholding South, where whites ruthlessly suppressed abolitionism.[14]

During the 1840s, the Liberty Party directed most of Michigan's antislavery activism, and its members advocated prohibition. Theodore Foster,
editor of the state's Liberty paper, denounced both the Whigs' and the
Democrats' unreliability regarding prohibition. He urged voters to consider
the temperance credentials of the Liberty Party: "The Abolitionists in this
State are strenuous temperance men, with but few, if any exceptions."
Michigan abolitionists favored "carrying the principle of temperance to
the ballot box" with the aim of abolishing the license system. Temperance
and abolition intertwined at the 1842 Michigan State Anti-Slavery Society's

annual meeting, where delegates, "with very little exception," were the "same persons" who, the day previous, had attended the yearly gathering of the Michigan State Temperance Society. Indeed, until the Michigan State Anti-Slavery Society's collapse in 1849, the annual meetings of the state temperance and abolition societies invariably convened on consecutive days in the same locale.

Foster derided moral suasion as ineffective. Claiming that most temperance energy had "but little influence" on drinkers and liquor merchants, Foster asserted that "so long as the law licenses the sale of intoxicating drink . . . *moral suasion cannot remove the evil, and* DRUNKENNESS WILL SURELY CONTINUE." But he also recognized that petitioning the legislature for legal sanctions would come to naught. Because the majority of legislators "use intoxicating drinks, and are opposed to the suppression of the traffic," no one expected them to act as agents of prohibition.[15]

With the onset of the Washingtonian temperance movement, enthusiasts continued waving the banner of moral suasion and generally ignored Foster's prohibitionist pleas. Washingtonianism began in Baltimore in May 1840, when six drunkards committed themselves to total abstinence after attending a temperance lecture. The Washingtonians—named after the first president—were more secular than earlier temperance reformers and were less likely to seek ties with churches. Moreover, they did not attempt to advance temperance from above through self-appointed executives who envisioned themselves as society's moral vanguard. Instead, the Washingtonians were, in most locales, an explicitly working-class movement that sought to convert inebriates to sobriety. Like the Sons of Temperance— who subsequently adopted a number of their techniques—the Washingtonians undertook to re-create the barroom's conviviality. Inasmuch as bars constituted a masculine sphere, the Washingtonians excluded women—in stark contrast to previous organizations. The Washingtonians offered new roles for women with the creation of Martha Washingtonian Temperance Societies—organizations staffed by female officers who worked in conjunction with men. Like their male counterparts, Martha Washingtonians directed most of their energies toward reforming men.[16]

Within two months of its establishment in late 1841, the Detroit Washingtonian Tee Total Society quickly organized eight local bodies throughout Michigan that collectively numbered nearly two thousand members. Ann Arbor's Washingtonian body alone generated 436 total abstinence pledges within a week of its founding. Of these new adherents, "large numbers" were "accustomed to moderate drinking and not a few . . . were confirmed inebriates." Washingtonian organizations persisted in Michigan for over four years, until another widespread appeal to prohibition undermined their moral suasion tactics.[17]

Although the Washingtonians' secular approach alienated those longtime activists who envisioned temperance as inseparable from Protestantism, one can easily overstate the movement's secularism. Washingtonians often convened in churches, and local Sabbath-school organizations sometimes joined Washingtonians to host Independence Day celebrations. Yet some evangelicals questioned whether the Washingtonians merited the praise sometimes showered upon them. In Jackson County, the Reverend George Barnum noted in late 1844 that a self-professed temperance landlord had "induced" several Washingtonians "to drink a little beer" until drinking had become "the order of the day." As Samuel Chipman informed the Michigan State Temperance Society's executive committee, Washingtonianism had "worked wonders in reclaiming the drunkard" but had done so only where it and the older temperance organizations had cooperated. In those places where they had "discarded all religion" and prohibited the use of prayer to open their meetings, Washingtonians had "returned to their 'wallowing in the mire.'"[18]

During the heyday of Washingtonianism, prohibitionist demands emanated mostly from antislavery activists, but, by 1844, Michigan's temperance leadership had recognized the limits of moral suasion. In January of that year, the Michigan State Temperance Society's executive committee praised moral suasion's achievements but lamented that some people never remained sober long enough to hear a reasoned argument. These inebriates, the committee claimed, clearly needed help, for they constituted the majority of poorhouse inmates and caused the suffering of many women and children. Believing that licensing liquor retailers gave alcohol consumption moral legitimacy, the executive committee advanced a local-option law authorizing communities to vote directly on licensing liquor sales. Prohibitionists were convinced that abolishing the licensed liquor trade—a course designated by contemporaries as "no license," in contrast to the "license" position of permitting regulated liquor sales—would destroy the liquor traffic and accomplish "what moral suasion cannot." The Michigan State Temperance Society's annual convention endorsed this proposal, and, of their "fifteen or twenty" speakers, only two opposed this shift in strategy. Those questioning the usefulness of a local-option law argued that "Washingtonians had done well, and all we needed was to keep on in the same track, only with more diligence." Such sentiments rang hollow for many Washingtonians, who increasingly recognized the limits of moral suasion. The Washingtonian Temperance Society of Medina, for example, instructed its delegates to favor the local-option law at the 1844 state meeting.[19]

Despite their failure to achieve statewide prohibition during the late 1830s, temperance activists throughout Michigan now urged the legislature to enact a local-option law. In March 1845, the legislators empowered communities to deny licenses for intoxicant sales in volumes under twenty-eight gallons, thereby aiming to inhibit alcohol retailing to consumers. In local elections held during the subsequent four months, roughly half of Michigan's communities selected no license. Nevertheless, many localities recorded fewer ballots for the license measure than for municipal races, suggesting either apathy or confusion among voters. It is possible, too, that this referendum produced a smaller response because voters had to cast separate ballots on the license question and to place them in special boxes.[20]

Of course, no license supporters anticipated that the 1845 law would eliminate the sale of spirits. Their opponents feared that liquor would indeed be suppressed, for a few Wets in Ann Arbor and Plymouth retaliated by vandalizing prohibitionists' property with intimidating graffiti. No license, however, failed to eliminate the liquor traffic. Because violators were tried as civil offenders, and because legal authorities lacked power to impose any penalty beyond a fine, liquor retailers usually regarded such intrusions as another cost of doing business. But some citizens charged the authorities with shirking their duty. In September 1845, an Ann Arbor writer complained of "rowdies made drunk with liquor sold without license, amid yells and shrieks worthy of Milton's Pandemonium." In February 1846, Halmer H. Emmons, of Detroit, lamented that, statewide, the no-license law was unenforced save "in very few instances." Despite modest dissent at the February 1846 state temperance convention—a member of the state society's executive committee from Jackson remained ardently committed to moral suasion and opposed to any legal action—the society continued to support the local-option law. Meanwhile, Michigan's women integrated both approaches. Ann Arbor's Martha Washingtonian Society, which sought to "prevent the manufacture, sale, and use, of intoxicating drinks," also pleaded with the village's liquor retailers to comply with the local no-license ordinance and to cease alcohol sales. Women in Dexter used similar tactics and reported gleefully that liquor had lost all respectability there, forcing retailers to sell spirits clandestinely.[21]

Voter participation on the ballot proposal ebbed and flowed in the local elections of most communities. Uncertainty regarding the placement of the no-license ballot box in relation to the one for local officers was part of the problem. Continued liquor sales in most communities doubtless generated voter cynicism about using this method to halt the traffic. Most polities eventually ignored the state law mandating such referenda, and, even when they were held, many voters no longer bothered to cast their ballots on this question.[22]

Local votes on the license question continued until 1851. Voters in some communities would favor issuing licenses one year but oppose them the next. Extant primary sources provide few clues regarding voters' changing positions on no license. The constant shifting of votes and the failure of numerous citizens to respond to this question suggest that many Michiganians were internally conflicted with regard to the best method to halt widespread alcoholism and its attendant social problems. They found that none of their efforts—license, no license, licensing only responsible citizens to sell liquor, or prohibiting liquor sales to chronic inebriates—eliminated alcohol's ill effects. Nevertheless, such failures did not dissuade people from seeking to remedy these problems, nor did the public cease demanding that politicians take some action. Frustration with the failure of local-option laws, as well as an openness to experimentation, eventually culminated in Michiganians' embrace of statewide prohibition.

Throughout the 1840s and early 1850s, Michigan's temperance stalwarts remained committed to no license, believing that continued vigilance eventually would bring success. In February 1847, the Michigan State Temperance Society renewed its endorsement of the local-option law, disavowed efforts to repeal it, and urged temperance adherents to attend their respective parties' conventions and to nominate candidates who, if elected, would enforce the existing no-license mandates. The Jackson-based *Michigan Temperance Journal and Washingtonian* praised the local-option law because it had "taken away the sanction of law to the unholy traffic, [shown] . . . the hostility of a great majority of the people to the sale of intoxicating drinks in their midst," and improved communities' morals. Any shortcomings of no license arose from "the apathy of temperance men."[23]

Along with weak penalties for violators and voters' vacillating responses to license referenda, politics prevented temperance advocates from improving the implementation of the local-option law. Although both parties' newspapers supported no license with occasional words of encouragement, neither party devoted itself to prohibition because party leaders feared offending voters who still enjoyed their alcohol. Nevertheless, Whigs favored prohibition more often than Democrats, and, in some townships, Whigs and Libertyites occasionally united behind a single ticket to elect a prohibitionist supervisor or town council. The *Signal of Liberty* discouraged such actions, claiming that their objective was the Liberty Party's destruction. Notwithstanding the importance of temperance to most abolitionist voters, that cause was, for the majority, secondary to that of combating slavery.[24] Adherents of the major parties were no different because few voters regarded temperance as the paramount issue.

Concurrent with the fight over the local licensing of liquor retailers, a new national temperance organization emerged. Concerned about the recurrent cycles of temperance activism and about the numerous Washingtonians who relapsed into inebriety, sixteen Washingtonians gathered in New York City in September 1842 to form the Sons of Temperance. A fraternal organization offering membership solely to men, the Sons of Temperance featured a hierarchy of officers and societies (called divisions) on the local, state, and national levels. Aside from its commitment to total abstinence, the brotherhood resembled the Masons and the Odd Fellows, incorporating secret handshakes, sickness and death benefits, rituals, and ornate regalia. Local divisions met often, and their sessions explicitly aimed at replacing the camaraderie of the tavern. Members focused on converting drunkards to total abstinence and drawing them into the order. The Sons of Temperance grew rapidly. By 1845, most northern states hosted divisions, and, by 1847, they had spread throughout the Deep South. The national body peaked in 1850 with 238,000 contributing members, but it continued operating through the Civil War.

First appearing in Michigan in 1847, the Sons of Temperance encountered a considerably cooler reception there than elsewhere. This lesser enthusiasm probably resulted from Michigan's strong residual Antimasonic sentiment, as Antimasons in the Wolverine State had once constituted the Democrats' major opposition. Despite Antimasonry's disappearance as a political force by the mid-1830s, hostility toward secret societies persisted, particularly among evangelicals. Yet one can overstate Michiganians' opposition to the Sons. The Sons of Temperance appealed to a less-affluent constituency that was far less likely to be connected to a church or a political party than were Michigan's other temperance cohorts. The sizable Michigan membership—exceeding five thousand—attests that the group's message resonated well in some quarters. After some initial outbursts, the antagonism subsided, and, by 1849, some churches ceased expelling members associated with the Sons. But, as enmity toward the order diminished, its novelty faded. Attendance at meetings dwindled, divisions collapsed, and, by early 1851, Michigan's Sons of Temperance had become moribund. Before its disappearance, however, some divisions had embraced prohibition. A Dexter division resolved to "watch the liquor sellers if possible to obtain evidence for prosecution" of those violating local license laws—thereby operating, in part, as a standing vigilance committee for temperance and prohibition.[25]

The inadequacies of the local-option law neither caused the proponents of legal measures to retreat nor encouraged moral suasionists to take control of the movement, as had happened in the late 1830s and early 1840s. In 1848, the *Detroit Michigan Christian Herald* urged temperance forces to stand firm against repeal of the local-option law until securing a law that would abolish the liquor licensing authority. In January 1849, the Michigan State Temperance Society endorsed submitting prohibitionist petitions to the legislature. On a number of occasions in the next two years, a Sons of Temperance division in Dexter circulated petitions and passed resolutions toward the same end. Yet the prospect of statewide prohibition failed to energize temperance partisans until Maine launched its landmark prohibitory law in 1851.

At that time, the Michigan State Temperance Society's activity had reached its nadir. The delegates to its October 1851 meeting in Ann Arbor represented only six of the state's counties and had to revise the society's constitution because the previous one "could not be found." Yet public concern over alcohol control continued to assert itself, independent of the state temperance organization. The preceding June, the Michigan legislature enacted the "Wisconsin Law." This law, a response to the ambiguous way Michigan's 1850 constitutional convention had abolished the license system, still left people uncertain whether state law recognized either total prohibition or unregulated liquor transactions. Michigan's 1851 Wisconsin Law permitted liquor retailers to continue selling spirits in volumes of less than twenty-eight gallons as long as they posted a bond of between $500 and $1,000 with two sureties, either biennially or annually at the option of local officials. Anyone sustaining damages resulting from liquor sales could file a lawsuit against the bond's principal and sureties.[26]

Delegates to the Michigan State Temperance Society's meeting in October 1851 endorsed the "Temperance law of the State of Maine," but they did not push for its passage in Michigan. Instead, they praised the existing

Wisconsin Law and urged its continued enforcement. In February 1852, however, the state's remaining Sons of Temperance embraced the prohibitionist Maine Law and pressed for enactment of a similar law in Michigan.[27] The tide had turned by the following June, when the Michigan State Temperance Society called for a Detroit meeting to consider "more stringent" legal measures. By this time, Michigan's Presbyterians were espousing prohibition and the state's Baptists shortly followed suit. Rallies throughout Michigan demanded the adoption of the Maine Law. At one Ann Arbor gathering, organizers specifically invited women, indicating that they recognized female participation as crucial to prohibition's success.

As support for the Maine Law's passage in Michigan swelled, politicians took note. Many of Michigan's Whigs and Democrats advocated temperance and prohibition, but neither party took a position on these issues, fearing the loss of drinkers' votes. Furthermore, their failed venture during the late 1830s had left temperance partisans leery of politics. Widespread ardor for the Maine Law, though, thrust the issue into the 1852 gubernatorial campaign. Both Democrat Robert M. McClelland and Whig Zachariah Chandler responded to the Michigan State Temperance Society's entreaties by pledging to sign a Maine Law bill should it pass the legislature, while Free Democrat Isaac P. Christiancy vowed not only to sign such a bill but also to pressure the solons to enact one.[28]

After the November election, enthusiasm for the Maine Law remained unabated. Late-December reports that Michiganians were eagerly signing prohibitionist petitions proved true: by the end of the legislative session, prohibitionists had gathered the signatures of more than one hundred thousand men, women, and children—one-fifth of the state's population. On February 12, 1853, Governor McClelland signed the prohibitionist law, a virtual clone of Maine's 1851 statute. Voters were to determine its final status in a June referendum. If approved, the law would take effect in December 1853; if rejected by the voters, it would become binding nevertheless in 1870.[29]

Prohibitionists continued their well-organized campaign in preparation for the June referendum. Throughout Michigan, Maine Law proponents met to construct the political machinery to ensure that temperance voters made it to the polls. Most newspapers, both Whig and Democratic, favored passage of the law. The Democratic *Detroit Free Press* was the principal dissenter in this emerging consensus. The *Ypsilanti Sentinel* accused the *Free Press* of endeavoring to give prohibition "a party character, hoping thereby to rally the democratic majority against it." Despite continually carrying editorials and letters opposing passage of the referendum, the *Free Press* denied the *Sentinel's* charges and labeled prohibition a "moral question" that would "retard rather than advance the cause of temperance." On June 20, 1853, Michigan voters overwhelmingly approved the Maine Law, 40,449 to 23,054 (63.7 percent). Although turnout fell short of the state's tally in the November 1852 presidential contest, it surpassed that in the 1851 gubernatorial election. Statewide, the measure did best in large towns and in highly developed agricultural areas.[30]

Determined not to have another prohibitory law rendered ineffective and, undoubtedly, expecting municipal governmental reluctance to prosecute violators, temperance activists throughout the state mobilized prior to the new law's December 1, 1853, implementation date to form the Carson League. Each local Carson League created a common fund to help finance the prosecution of manufacturers and sellers of alcoholic beverages. Within weeks, the Carson League was pursuing violators. This course of action, however, stalled on February 1, 1854, when, in *People v. Collins*, the Michigan Supreme Court split 4 to 4 on the Maine Law's constitutionality. The justices divided on the issues of whether the legislature could delegate power to voters in a referendum and whether prohibition amounted to an unconstitutional confiscation of private property. On the same day, the court issued two other decisions, *People v. Hawley* and *People v. Hoffman*, that sustained, each by a 4-to-3 vote, other aspects of the prohibition act (Justice Joseph Copeland, absent during these cases' arguments, abstained from voting in the decisions). In *Hawley*, the court held that Michigan's Maine Law prohibited beer and ale as well as hard liquor, and, in *Hoffman*, the court upheld the act's provision that defendants were not entitled to jury trials unless they paid jury fees.[31]

Drys celebrated *Hawley* and *Hoffman* as victories and argued that *Collins* sustained Michigan's Maine Law. Wets countered that state law rendered nonbinding both split decisions and decisions from a partially seated bench. This confusion effectively gutted Michigan's Maine Law. Had *Collins* reached the supreme court through appeal, writ of certiorari, or writ of error, a deadlock on the high court would have validated the lower court's judgment. Because *Collins* had arrived at the court on reservation, the judges remanded the case to the Wayne Circuit Court. There, Justice Samuel T. Douglass (the presiding judges of Michigan's eight circuit courts sat together to form the state Supreme Court) ruled the prohibition law unconstitutional and declared the defendant not liable for violating state liquor laws. This decision, however, pertained only to the Wayne Circuit.

Commenting on *Collins*, the *Washtenaw Whig* recognized that this "anomalous state of affairs" would place the Maine Law "in quiescence" until the legislature reconvened. Events of the following week confirmed the *Whig*'s prescience: prosecutions in Ann Arbor effectively ceased after liquor sellers sued the constables who had seized their alcohol. In Ypsilanti, confusion regarding the issue prompted retailers and local officials to reach a compromise: prosecutions would halt, provided that those trafficking in liquor would cease selling it and that each side would be responsible for its previously incurred legal expenses.[32]

Township elections in early April revealed a changed sentiment toward prohibition. According to the *Argus,* the Maine Law was the principal issue in the elections, and "in a large majority" of places "the opponents of the law have triumphed." For the *Argus,* the most striking election was in Kalamazoo, where Maine Law opponents, who had lost the referendum the previous June, won by a hundred votes. A few weeks later, the *Argus,* which claimed that Whigs and Free Soilers had been endeavoring to politicize the Maine Law, asserted that these parties' newspapers—in particular the Whigs'—were retreating because of the perceived repudiation of the law. Recognizing by late April that the new law was gutted beyond repair, the Michigan State Temperance Society urged prohibitionists to interrogate every political candidate on this issue and to vote only for those who would "publicly pledge" to support "the passage and enforcement of [another] law."[33]

Michigan's most significant political development in 1854, however, was not the evisceration of its Maine Law but the demise of the Whig and Free Soil parties and the creation of a fusion movement that became the Republican Party. Riding upon opposition to the Kansas-Nebraska Act, hostility to the South, nativism, anger toward monopolies, and widespread dissatisfaction with the Democrats—who since the 1841 elections had controlled the governorship and both legislative houses—Republicans swept into office in November 1854. Although their platform did not explicitly endorse the passage of another Maine Law—reckoning, undoubtedly, that the year's township elections had revealed voters' shallow commitment to prohibition—the large number of temperance partisans in the Republican Party nonetheless caused many to perceive the fusionists as the "Maine Law Party" and the Democrats as the "Whiskey Party."[34] Consequently, many anticipated the enactment of a new law.

Both the Republican and Democratic parties, of course, were broad-based coalitions, each containing Wets and Drys. One Democratic prohibitionist,

Elihu Pond, editor of the Ann Arbor *Michigan Argus,* urged Michiganians to petition the legislature for a new Maine Law. "Legislative bodies," Pond argued, "are not in the habit of conferring favors unsolicited. We believe there is no trouble in passing a constitutional effective liquor law, one that will restrain the traffic in Alcoholic preparations as a beverage and yet not prevent their free sale for medicinal and mechanical purposes." Pond's Republican counterpart, Stephen B. McCracken of the *Washtenaw Whig,* had some second thoughts. Following the Republican victory in November 1854, McCracken—a former Sons of Temperance officer and an early supporter of the 1853 Maine Law—explained that, given the state's other pressing needs, the "precious time of the Legislature will be wasted in useless debate" if prohibition occupied the lawmakers' attention. "In our opinion, the least said about the 'Maine Liquor Law,' the better," particularly because McCracken expected that any law passed by the legislature would have "some useless provision engrafted upon it which will render it valueless." In February 1855, the legislature passed a new prohibitory act outlawing the sale of distilled liquor while permitting the manufacture of alcohol for industrial use and allowing bonded druggists to sell it for medicinal purposes. It exempted the production of wine and cider, provided that they be sold in volumes of more than one gallon and ten gallons, respectively.[35]

According to some initial reports, Michiganians generally obeyed the 1855 statute. Antiprohibitionist sentiment flared, however, following an incident of shocking violence in Portland, Maine, in June 1855. Mayor Neal Dow, father of the Maine Law, ordered the city's militia to fire upon a crowd angered by his illicit purchase of liquor intended for medicinal and industrial purposes. Antiprohibitionists in Michigan flaunted the Portland riot as evidence that the Maine Law would lead to a police state. Throughout the Wolverine State, this allegation alone resulted in diminished support for prohibition. Especially opprobrious were the 1855 law's search and seizure provisions that broadened public officials' authority.[36]

Not unexpectedly, committed prohibitionists remained steadfast. Acknowledging that the 1855 Maine Law was "not fully enforced," Elihu Pond asserted that it was "accomplishing much good," as "the open traffic is done away with, and liquor rows and public drunkenness are numbered among the things that were." Nevertheless, violations increased throughout Michigan in the months following the Portland riot, and, by the end of 1855, the law was widely ignored. In March 1856, in *People v. Gallagher,* the Michigan Supreme Court sustained, by a 6-to-1 vote, the legislature's authority to prohibit liquor manufacture and sales. Yet, on the same day, the court undermined prohibition by unanimously striking down the Maine Law's search and seizure provisions in *Hibbard v. People*. *Hibbard* did not console angry Democrats in Dexter Township, Washtenaw County: they quickly denounced *Gallagher* as both a "full endorsement of the fusion Legislature Liquor Law" and an affirmation that the legislature "may exercise any power, however despotic, tyrannical, oppressive, and unjust, which the Constitution does not in express terms prohibit to them."[37]

Other local Democratic caucuses throughout Michigan soon followed Dexter Township's lead. At its August statewide convention, the divided party took an ambiguous position on the Maine Law, allowing Democrats to campaign on either side of the issue. This was the first time that the platform of one of the state's major political parties had addressed temperance. Yet Republicans, whose resolutions had ignored liquor control, captured more than 57 percent of Michigan's 1856 presidential vote and handed state Democrats their worst political defeat of the antebellum era. The following year, the Republican-led legislature, recognizing the erosion of public support for the Maine Law, further enfeebled it by repealing the 1855 law's search and seizure provisions—which *Hibbard* already had struck down—and by permitting the unlimited sale and production of wine, cider, and beer. Although spirits remained prohibited, the new measure represented a major setback for legal suasionists. Among those mourning its passage was the Reverend J. S. Smart of Ypsilanti, who recorded his sentiments in his pamphlet *Funeral Sermon of the Maine Law and Its Offspring in Michigan*. Smart proved perceptive. Despite banning the hard liquor trade, the amended law likewise proved unenforceable, and sober-minded Michiganians soon complained of "drunken frolicks," Sabbath liquor traffic, and illegal barrooms that "habitually sell to or harbor drunkards." Nevertheless, the 1855 law—with its 1857 amendments—remained on the books until 1875.[38]

Other temperance regulars remained ardently committed to the 1855 Maine Law. Speaking in May 1858, Donald McIntyre, soon-to-be president of the Michigan State Temperance Society, set forth "in an elaborate speech . . . the superior advantages of the law of 1855 over that of 1857 to suppress drunkenness." The *Ann Arbor Journal* agreed with McIntyre, arguing that allowing traffic in wine, cider, and beer was counterproductive: "The fact is there is no middle ground upon this subject. Total abstinence is the true ground, and whatever effort may be made by friends of the law . . . must be made upon this principle or it will fail of success." A year later, the Michigan State Temperance Society proclaimed its continued support of the 1855 Maine Law and called for "restoring that clause in relation to wine, beer and cider, which was stricken out by the Legislature of 1857."[39]

Except for some municipal attempts at liquor control, temperance atrophied following the passage of the 1857 law. One easily can imagine that many rank-and-file temperance activists considered their work completed following the Maine Law's implementation and reasoned that responsibility for enforcement fell upon municipal authorities. Their spirits certainly flagged in the wake of the Portland riot, the successful legal challenges to the 1855 Maine Law, and the passage of the watered-down 1857 law. These cumulative defeats resulted in the most serious downturn of Michigan's antebellum temperance movement. This statewide decline coincided with waning enthusiasm for temperance throughout the United States during the late 1850s. Such timing has prompted some scholars to attribute this national decline to the increased preoccupation with sectionalism. But in Michigan and across the nation, prohibitionists either faced defeat when they tried to enact their proposals or found them to be unenforceable once passed into law. Like Michigan's temperance promoters, devotees in other states faced discouragement following the failure of their most concerted effort to date. Their cause continued to wane during the Civil War, but reemerged as a vital issue shortly after the war's end.[40]

Their failures notwithstanding, Michigan's antebellum temperance partisans could cite significant political victories. The most notable included the Michigan legislature's passage of a local-option law in 1845, the enactment of the Wisconsin Law in 1851, and the statewide implementation of prohibitory statutes in 1853 and 1855—each aimed at offsetting the shortcomings of the preceding act. Although temperance men generally relegated antialcohol women to a supporting role, during the 1840s women formed and operated their own societies. Unfortunately, the documentary record of these women's organizations is scanty.

Public opinion propelled prohibitionist acts through the legislature, aided prohibitionists in local-option referenda, and secured the Maine Law's implementation. Yet the public proved unwilling to back prohibition enforcement, never demanding that the state's police powers be marshaled against violators. The Michigan Supreme Court's split in the Collins decision exemplified the public's schizophrenic mind-set regarding prohibition. Two years later, the court sustained prohibition in Gallagher yet repudiated it on the same day by denying authorities the powers of search and confiscation in Hibbard.

These defeats notwithstanding, Michigan's temperance enthusiasts could celebrate the state's diminished alcohol consumption. In 1848, the *Primitive Expounder* pointed to the state's remarkable progress, noting that the extensive public drinking that had been so widespread thirty years earlier had subsided and that, as a consequence of the temperance movement's successes, imbibers were now on the defensive.[41] After the mid-1830s, opponents of legal suasion rarely argued that drinking was a personal decision. Instead, the opponents of statewide and local prohibition insisted that such legal measures were the wrong strategy and that a temperate society would be achieved only through persuasion. Undoubtedly, antiprohibitionists sometimes uttered these arguments disingenuously. Although temperance principles gained widespread acceptance, temperance activists' ultimate goal—permanently banning the liquor traffic and eliminating alcoholic consumption—remained elusive.

Notes

1. W. J. Rorabaugh, *The Alcoholic Republic: An American Tradition* (New York: Oxford University Press, 1979), 232–33; *History of Washtenaw County, Michigan* (Chicago: Chas. G. Chapman, 1881), 338–40, 524, 679, 692, 955–56. Regarding the antebellum temperance movement, see also Norman H. Clark, *Deliver Us from Evil: An Interpretation of American Prohibition* (New York: W. W. Norton, 1976); Ian R. Tyrrell, *Sobering Up: From Temperance to Prohibition in Antebellum America, 1800–1860* (Westport, Conn.: Greenwood, 1979); Jed Dannenbaum, *Drink and Disorder: Temperance Reform in Cincinnati from the Washingtonian Revival to the WCTU* (Urbana: University of Illinois Press, 1984); Jack S. Blocker, *American Temperance Movements: Cycles of Reform* (Boston: Twayne, 1988); and Thomas R. Pegram, *Battling Demon Rum: The Struggle for a Dry America, 1800–1933* (Chicago: Ivan R. Dee, 1998). For the movement in Michigan, see Peter Donald Slavcheff, "The Temperate Republic: Liquor Control in Michigan, 1800–1860" (Ph.D. diss., Wayne State University, 1987); Bruce Tap, "'The Evils of Intemperance Are Universally Conceded': The Temperance Debate in Early Grand Rapids," *Michigan Historical Review* 19 (Spring 1993): 17–45; and John W. Quist, *Restless Visionaries: The Social Roots of Antebellum Reform in Alabama and Michigan* (Baton Rouge: Louisiana State University Press, 1998), 235–302.

2. Slavcheff, "Temperate Republic," 57; *Western Emigrant*, December 30, 1829, January 27, 1830; John Beach to American Home Missionary Society (hereafter AHMS), January 31, 1833, American Home Missionary Society Papers (hereafter AHMS Papers), Bentley Historical Library, University of Michigan, Ann Arbor.

3. *History of Washtenaw County*, 954, 1113–14; William Jones to AHMS, May 24, 1830, AHMS Papers; minutes of the Ann Arbor Temperance Society, March 9, 1832, Bentley Historical Library, University of Michigan, Ann Arbor. Regarding the elite characteristics of Michigan's early temperance reformers, see Quist, *Restless Visionaries*, 284–85.

4. Tyrrell, *Sobering Up*, 87–115, 226–27; Rorabaugh, *Alcoholic Republic*, 202–5; Quist, *Restless Visionaries*, 155–302; *Michigan Emigrant*, March 6, 1833.

5. *History of Washtenaw County*, 220–24; Ira M. Wead to AHMS, January 7, 1834, AHMS Papers. Detroit enacted a similar ordinance in 1834, but a judicial challenge made it ineffectual. Slavcheff, "Temperate Republic," 91–92. The Ypsilanti statute's absence from subsequent records suggests that it, too, was soon abandoned.

6. *Michigan Emigrant*, cited in Detroit *Journal and Courier*, December 15, 1834, as quoted by Slavcheff, "Temperate Republic," 82.

7. *Michigan Emigrant*, July 24, October 23, December 25, 1834; *Michigan Whig*, January 15, February 12, 1835.

8. *Michigan Whig and Washtenaw Democrat*, May 7, June 11, July 16, 1835.

9. Jonathan Marwil, *A History of Ann Arbor* (Ann Arbor: Ann Arbor Observer, 1987), 11; Lorenzo Davis, "History of the Temperance Movement in Washtenaw County," undated [c. 1885], Lorenzo Davis Papers, Bentley Historical Library, University of Michigan, Ann Arbor, 9–10; Slavcheff, "Temperate Republic," 88, 328; *Detroit Courier*, December 24, 1834, cited in Slavcheff, "Temperate Republic," 97; I. M. Wead to AHMS, April 11, July 20, 1836, Edward B. Emerson to AHMS, December 23, 1836, April 4, June 28, 1837, John G. Kanouse to AHMS, March 16, 1837, AHMS Papers.

10. *The Proceedings of the Young Men's State Temperance Convention, Held at Ann Arbor, January 20, 1836*, pamphlet in Burton Historical Collection, Detroit Public Library; *State Journal*, March 17, 1836; *Michigan Argus*, February 4, 1836.

11. *State Journal*, August 16, November 11, December 6, 1838; *Journal of the American Temperance Union* 2 (December 1838): 188.

12. *Michigan Times*, June 16, 1840; Slavcheff, "Temperate Republic," 108–20, 332.

13. *Michigan State Journal*, June 22, 1841.

14. Thomas Bender, ed., *The Antislavery Debate: Capitalism and Abolitionism as a Problem in Historical Interpretation* (Berkeley: University of California Press, 1992); Ronald G. Walters, *American Reformers, 1815–1860*, rev. ed. (New York: Hill and Wang, 1997); Steven Mintz, *Moralists and Modernizers: America's Pre–Civil War Reformers* (Baltimore: Johns Hopkins University Press, 1995); Quist, *Restless Visionaries*, 1–7, 155–234, 297.

15. *Signal of Liberty*, August 4, September 1, September 29, October 20, 1841, March 16, 1842, January 23, November 6, 1843, December 16, 1844, February 17, 1845, February 6, 1847, January 8, 1848; Quist, *Restless Visionaries*, 294–98.

16. Dannenbaum, *Drink and Disorder*, 32–42; Tyrrell, *Sobering Up*, 159–209; Blocker, *American Temperance Movements*, 39–47.

17. *Michigan State Journal*, November 30, 1841, January 25, 1842; Slavcheff, "Temperate Republic," 126–27.

18. George Barnum to AHMS, December 2, 1844, AHMS Papers; *Signal of Liberty* August 7, 1843.

19. *Michigan Argus*, February 14, February 28, 1844; *Signal of Liberty*, March 25, 1844.

20. *Michigan Argus*, March 19, 1845; Slavcheff, "Temperate Republic," 157, 342–43.

21. *Signal of Liberty*, August 11, August 18, 1845, February 9, February 16, May 4, May 23, 1846; *Michigan Argus*, September 9, 1845; *True Democrat*, June 4, 1846; *Michigan Temperance Journal and Washingtonian* 1 (July 1846): 53.

22. *Acts of the Legislature of Michigan Passed at the Annual Session of 1845* (Detroit, 1845), 56; *Acts of the Legislature of the State of Michigan Passed at the Annual Session of 1849* (Lansing, 1849), 295–96; *The Revised Statutes of the State of Michigan, Passed and Approved May 18, 1846* (Detroit, 1846), 187–88. As of April 2, 1849, all local-option elections in Michigan were reversed. Liquor sales in the state were prohibited thereafter except in those communities where liquor license supporters placed the local-option question on the ballot. Slavcheff, "Temperate Republic," 183–84.

23. *Michigan Temperance Journal and Washingtonian* 2 (February 1847): 12, 14–15; ibid., 2 (March 1847): 21.

24. *Signal of Liberty*, March 13, 1847.

25. William Preston Vaughn, *The Antimasonic Party in the United States, 1826–1843* (Lexington: University Press of Kentucky, 1983), 54; Records of the First Baptist Church, Ann Arbor, February 8, 1849, Bentley Historical Library, University of Michigan, Ann Arbor; *Washtenaw Whig*, December 5, 1849; Records of the Phoenix Division of the Sons of Temperance, August 20, 1849, February 27, 1851, Bentley Historical Library, University of Michigan, Ann Arbor; Slavcheff, "Temperate Republic," 184.

26. *Michigan Christian Herald*, January 28, 1848, March 16, 1849; Records of the Phoenix Division of the Sons of Temperance, January 8, January 29, December 17, 1849, January 27, 1851; *Washtenaw Whig*, November 19, 1851; Slavcheff, "Temperate Republic," 200–207.

27. *Washtenaw Whig*, November 19, 1851; *Michigan Argus*, February 25, 1852; Slavcheff, "Temperate Republic," 210.

28. *Washtenaw Whig*, June 2, June 16, August 11, October 20, 1852; *Michigan Argus*, October 27, 1852; *Michigan Free Democrat*, September 7, 1852; Slavcheff, "Temperate Republic," 210–16.

29. *Michigan Free Democrat*, December 29, 1852; *Michigan Argus*, January 26, 1853; Slavcheff, "Temperate Republic," 218, 223.

30. *Ypsilanti Sentinel*, quoted in *Detroit Free Press*, June 15, 1853; Slavcheff, "Temperate Republic," 223–30; John W. Quist, "Social and Moral Reform in the Old North and the Old South: Washtenaw County, Michigan, and Tuscaloosa County, Alabama, 1820–1860" (Ph.D. diss., University of Michigan, 1992), 567–68.

31. People v. Collins, 3 Mich. 343 (1854); People v. Hawley, 3 Mich. 248 (1854); People v. Hoffman, 3 Mich. 330 (1854); Clark F. Norton, "Early Michigan Supreme Court Decisions on the Liquor Question," *Michigan History* 28 (January–March 1944): 46–60; Slavcheff, "Temperate Republic," 235–50; Tyrrell, *Sobering Up*, 293–95.

32. *Washtenaw Whig*, November 16, 1853, February 8, February 15, March 22, 1854; Norton, "Early Michigan Supreme Court Decisions," 48–60.

33. *Michigan Argus*, April 13, April 27, May 4, 1854.

34. Martin J. Hershock, *The Paradox of Progress: Economic Change, Individual Enterprise, and Political Culture in Michigan, 1837–1878* (Athens: Ohio University Press, 2003), 76–135; Ronald P. Formisano, *The Birth of Mass Political Parties: Michigan, 1827–1861* (Princeton, N.J.: Princeton University Press, 1971), 239–53; Slavcheff, "Temperate Republic," 254–58.

35. *Michigan Argus*, December 22, 1854; *Washtenaw Whig*, November 29, 1854, December 13, December 20, 1854, February 14, 1855; Slavcheff, "Temperate Republic," 258.

36. *Michigan Argus,* May 18, 1855; *Washtenaw Whig,* June 13, 1855; Tyrrell, *Sobering Up,* 295–96; Tap, "Temperance in Grand Rapids," 39; Slavcheff, "Temperate Republic," 261–63.

37. *Michigan Argus,* June 22, July 27, 1855, April 4, 1856; *Ann Arbor Journal and Washtenaw Whig,* September 12, 1855; *Ann Arbor Journal,* October 31, 1855; Slavcheff, "Temperate Republic," 266, 364n109; People v. Gallagher, 4 Mich. 244 (1856); Hibbard v. People, 4 Mich. 125 (1856).

38. Slavcheff, "Temperate Republic," 267–68, 364n110; *Michigan Argus,* May 14, 1858, July 22, 1859; *Ann Arbor Journal,* June 1, 1859; John Fitzgibbon, "King Alcohol: His Rise, Reign, and Fall in Michigan," *Michigan History* 2 (October 1918): 749; Floyd B. Streeter, "History of Prohibition Legislation in Michigan," *Michigan History* 2 (April 1918): 298–301.

39. *Ann Arbor Journal,* May 26, 1858; *Michigan Argus,* May 14, 1858, July 1, 1859.

40. Quist, *Restless Visionaries,* 277–78n; Fitzgibbon, "King Alcohol," 748–49, 760–61; Blocker, *American Temperance Movements,* 71–73.

41. *Primitive Expounder,* August 10, 1848, 288.

FOUR

⸺ ⚬⚬⚬ ⸺

Roy E. Finkenbine

A BEACON OF LIBERTY
ON THE GREAT LAKES

Race, Slavery, and the Law in Antebellum Michigan

Michigan acquired a reputation among antebellum Americans—black and white, slave and free—as a beacon of liberty on the Great Lakes. Several factors favored the construction of this image. Foremost among them was the opposition of its citizens and their political and legal institutions to the practice of slavery, which was outlawed in Michigan's founding documents. Furthermore, free blacks, Quakers, and other white allies, as well as the legislature and the courts, usually protected fugitive slaves who reached the state and prevented their return to bondage. Eventually, Michigan became a hotbed of antislavery organizing and political opposition to the extension of slavery into the new territories of the American West. The relative mildness of the state's black laws and their limited enforcement also played a major role.[1] Other factors included Michigan's distance from the slave states, its proximity to Canada, and the promise of land and economic opportunity along its fertile frontier.

Even so, the Wolverine State was no racial utopia before the Civil War. Michigan's population expanded rapidly after the War of 1812, especially after the opening of the Erie Canal in 1825 as a conduit for the movement of raw materials and agricultural products from the Great Lakes. During the 1820s and 1830s, migration into the territory was so dominated by settlers from New England and Yankee-influenced areas of upstate New York that Michigan became known as "the third New England." This Yankee character began to change after 1840, as thousands of immigrants from Germany, Ireland, and Canada took up residence in the state. These broader waves of settlement were supplemented by the arrival of thousands of antislavery Quakers from the South.[2] As smaller numbers of free blacks and fugitive slaves joined this movement, many white settlers became ambivalent about the prospect of African Americans living in their midst, and this ambivalence was reflected in the actions of Michigan officials. In 1827, for example, the territorial council passed an "Act to Regulate Blacks and Mulattoes, and to Punish the Kidnapping of Such Persons." On the one hand, the act provided free blacks with some protections against kidnapping and required that even fugitive slaves be returned to slavery only through the due process of the courts. On the other hand, African Americans were denied the right to reside in the territory unless they registered with the clerk of courts in the county in which they lived and provided a certificate indicating their free status and a $500 surety bond guaranteeing their good behavior. As was typical for the territories at this time, the act borrowed from the laws of another jurisdiction, in this case, Ohio. Indeed, much of the act came directly from Ohio's infamous black laws of 1804 and 1807.[3]

In the territorial period, the restrictions on African American residency went virtually unenforced. Some officials, however, called for stricter enforcement. In 1828, the sheriff of Wayne County published a notice in newspapers throughout the territory warning black residents of the law, and, in that same year, the territorial council amended the act to urge the judiciary to "diligently inquire if the said act is duly executed." But many residents in the territory disagreed. In 1830, jurors in Wayne County Circuit Court registered their disapproval, finding that "no such law ought to exist or be enforced in a free republican country." They went on to state: "We do not believe that a human being, who is a freeman, although possessing a black or yellow complexion, or being one or more shades darker than is common to white freemen, should be deprived of those rights and privileges, which are the common heritage of this happy and republican country. Attempts have been made to carry into execution said law. But owing to public opinion to the contrary, on account of its unconstitutionality, it cannot be effected." The law may have been enforced only once. In 1837, a black man in the village of Scio Township near Ann Arbor was banished from the state on the warrant of two white neighbors, who protested his inability to provide the surety bond required by law. Even that stirred some protest. The editor of the *Adrian Constitutionalist* pleaded, "[H]ow long shall this abominable law continue to disgrace our state?" In fact, the legislature debated repeal of the registration and bond requirements of the act several times during the 1830s.[4] The state never explicitly repealed the act, but it was not included in the first revised code of Michigan, authorized in 1838. In addition to this *sub silentio* repeal, the revised statutes also contained a new antikidnapping law. Thus, after 1838, blacks could migrate to the state without legal impediments and could expect some legal protection from kidnappers. Slave catchers still could capture fugitive slaves under the federal law of 1793, but they could expect little help from the state and, if they mistakenly seized a free black, could face a ten-year jail sentence for kidnapping.[5]

Because of the lack of enforcement of the 1827 act and its subsequent repeal in 1838, African American settlers arrived in the territory and then the state in ever-increasing numbers. Michigan's black population grew from 293 in the 1830 census, to 707 in 1840, to 2,583 in 1850, and to 6,799 in the year before the Civil War. Among the migrants were free blacks from elsewhere in the North or the upper South, as well as fugitive slaves fresh from bondage. They came alone, as families, or as part of extended families. On at least one occasion, all of the slaves from a single plantation came as a group, having been manumitted in the will of their Virginia master, Sampson Sanders. The migrants concentrated in a few places. Many flocked to existing African American communities in the cities. Others sought out the protection and assistance of the several Quaker settlements in rural southern Michigan. By 1850, nearly half lived in just two counties—Wayne (primarily in the city of Detroit) in the southeast part of the state and rural Cass in the southwest part of the state. Significant numbers also clustered in secondary cities like Kalamazoo, Battle Creek, Marshall, Jackson, and Ann Arbor and in their surrounding hinterlands along the Territorial Road (now I-94), a major thoroughfare for people and goods and an Underground Railroad route running due east from Lake Michigan to Detroit. Eight of every ten Michigan blacks lived in the two lower tiers of counties in the state, within fifty miles of the border with Indiana and Ohio. Only a few hardy souls ventured farther north into the remainder of Michigan's Lower Peninsula; even fewer made their way to the Upper Peninsula.[6]

That this growing African American presence merely reinforced white ambivalence is clear from the debates over black suffrage in Michigan's 1835 constitutional convention as the territory headed toward statehood.

Darius Comstock, a Quaker delegate from Lenawee County, called for striking the word "white" out of voting provisions in the new constitution, arguing that black settlers should be given "a chance to raise [*sic*] in the world and make themselves respectable." Other delegates fought for the prohibition against black suffrage on the ground that "the negro belonged to a degraded caste of mankind." They claimed that both society and nature had "marked the distinction [and] . . . recognized and sanctioned it." In the end, a majority of delegates voted to keep the prohibition, fearing that "if the blacks are to be admitted to all the rights of citizens, they will be encouraged to come and fix up their residence in the new State." This continuing fear of African American settlement impelled white citizens occasionally to petition the legislature to ban African American migration into Michigan. It also provoked some to call for removing blacks from the state. The editor of the *Detroit Journal and Michigan Advertiser* pushed in the early 1830s for sending all Michigan blacks to the new West African settlement of Liberia. A second wave of sentiment in favor of African colonization swept through Michigan in the late 1840s and early 1850s. According to the *Detroit Free Press*, "whites did not want the Negroes as residents." The Michigan legislature offered a rationale in 1846, when it rejected requests from blacks and white allies to extend the vote to blacks and to strike down an 1838 act prohibiting interracial marriage. Speaking for the majority, one legislator observed that "the two races [could] never live in a state of freedom under the same government."[7] At the same time, ironically, many white Michiganians increasingly worked to prevent the kidnapping of free blacks and recapture of fugitive slaves in their midst.

The laws of Michigan continued to reflect white ambivalence about African Americans throughout the antebellum period. Anthony Glessner has explained this ambivalence, noting that, despite having laws limiting black rights, "the state also had churches, politicians, newspapers, abolition societies, and black and white activists battling to improve the lot of black people in Michigan, none of which would have been tolerated" further south. Occasional efforts to limit African American rights in the legislature and the courts notwithstanding, the work of these activists and the rather weak enforcement of the black laws ensured that in Michigan these rights were "usually more advanced than those [in the states] of the lower Midwest."[8] Fugitive slaves in Michigan felt safer than did those in the states of Ohio, Indiana, and Illinois. All of these factors enhanced Michigan's reputation among Americans as a beacon of liberty on the Great Lakes and allowed the image to remain strong, even amid so much white ambivalence.

The Reputation Emerges

Michigan's reputation emerged during the territorial period and was amplified between 1837 and 1861—the era of antebellum statehood. The growing opposition of Michigan's citizens to slavery and their increasing willingness to protect fugitive slaves, even if only passing through to Canada, shaped this developing image. The Northwest Ordinance, which established territorial government in the area north of the Ohio River in 1787, prohibited slavery in the region; most Michigan officials, however, interpreted this act as outlawing only the importation of new slaves into the territory, so small numbers of local African Americans continued to be enslaved. In the early years of the territorial period, slaves escaped in both directions across the Detroit River—runaways from Michigan, motivated by the continuing existence of slavery in the territory, fled to Canada; fugitives from Canada, reacting to the refusal of the territorial courts to return Canadian slaves, absconded to Michigan. When slavery ended in Canada in 1833, this became a one-way traffic. But slavery was dying in Michigan as well. Over the first third of the nineteenth century, the number of slaves dwindled from a few dozen to three. The 1835 state constitutional convention finally ended bondage in the territory. Eventually, however, fear of the federal Fugitive Slave Act of 1793, which established procedures for the capture and return of runaway blacks, brought thousands of fugitive slaves from the South to Michigan, where they could more easily continue on to Canada if slave catchers pursued them.[9]

Fugitive slaves from the southern states began to make their way to Michigan after the War of 1812. From the beginning, slave hunters coming to the territory met with difficulty. In 1827, H. V. Somerville, of Baltimore, tracked his runaway bondsman, Hamlet, to Detroit. Convinced that locals were sheltering the fugitive, he ran an advertisement in the *Detroit Gazette* for more than four months, promising a reward of $200 for Hamlet's arrest and confinement in the city jail. The fugitive was never recovered. In 1833, slave catchers tracked Kentucky fugitives Thornton and Lucie Blackburn to Detroit, where they found them living respectably in the local African American community; they had the couple arrested and incarcerated in the city jail. When the Blackburns were unable to offer any evidence of being legally free, the federal court ordered them returned to their Kentucky master. This order was foiled, however, by local blacks who spirited Lucie off to Canada after she exchanged clothes with a visitor to her cell. When authorities attempted to transfer Thornton to a waiting vessel the following day, an armed mob of local blacks freed him by force, mortally wounding the sheriff, and spirited him away in a waiting horse cart. Thornton also turned up in Canada. Recognizing the state's emerging reputation as a haven for fugitives, settlers in both St. Joseph County and Washtenaw County established villages named Freedom near the border with Ohio and Indiana in the 1830s.[10]

An organized Underground Railroad network took shape in Michigan in the 1830s. Across southern Michigan, major activists could be found in Quaker settlements and African American communities. Laura Haviland, of Adrian, assisted runaways passing through the city, frequently escorted them north from Cincinnati, and even made several forays into Kentucky to help slaves escape. Erastus Hussey aided more than a thousand fugitives going through Battle Creek. In Detroit, the Colored Vigilant Committee, which was led by free blacks George DeBaptiste and William Lambert, helped thousands of fugitive slaves after its founding in 1840. Often, the committee cooperated with local white activists like Seymour Finney, who frequently hid runaways in his livery stable. Most of these runaways came from Kentucky, although some came from other states in the upper South. Fugitives generally entered the state by one of three routes: through western Ohio to Adrian and Detroit; through eastern Indiana, to Coldwater, Marshall, and Battle Creek; or through central Indiana to Niles and Cassiopolis. Most of those who came through Indiana then followed the Territorial Road east to Detroit. A smaller number were sent northeast from Battle Creek toward Port Huron. Fewer still were forwarded to Canada via vessels on Lake Michigan or overland toward the Upper Peninsula. Along the way, Underground Railroad activists could be counted on to provide runaways with food, clothing, medical care, hiding places, protection from slave catchers, transportation if they chose to go on, and assistance settling into local communities in southern Michigan if they chose to remain. By the early 1840s, the Michigan underground was a bustling concern. One historian has estimated that, between 1842 and the Civil War, some thirty thousand fugitive slaves escaped through Michigan to Canada, making it a primary site on the Underground Railroad.[11]

At the same time that the Underground Railroad network was emerging in Michigan, an antislavery movement also was developing, even during territorial days. The first antislavery society, the Logan Female Anti-Slavery Society, was founded in 1832 in Lenawee County (in what is now Adrian). Over the next four years, nine other local societies were established. In November 1836, these societies came together at Ann Arbor and formed the

Michigan State Anti-Slavery Society. During its first decade, it organized dozens of other local societies, sponsored tours of southern Michigan by antislavery lecturers, and frequently petitioned the legislature. At first, abolitionists were not well received in Michigan. There were threats and reports of mob violence against antislavery speakers and meetings. One Detroit antiabolitionist argued that "lynching was the only way to treat abolitionists." In spite of such opposition, both the statewide and local societies grew. One of the major successes of the statewide society was the establishment of a newspaper of its own. Although names, editors, and locations varied, this organ continued for over a decade as the *American Freeman* (1839), *Michigan Freeman* (1839–41), *Signal of Liberty* (1841–48), and *Michigan Liberty Press* (1848–49). This vehicle disappeared when antiabolitionists, in their own version of the Elijah Lovejoy incident,[12] destroyed Erastus Hussey's press by throwing it into Battle Creek in June 1849. Even so, the various manifestations of this organ brought many additional Michiganians to the movement. Most of the subscribers to the *Signal of Liberty,* for example, were ordinary farmers across the southern part of the state. Michigan abolitionists transformed their moral crusade into a political movement in the 1840s. The Liberty Party, a strictly antislavery party, competed in elections throughout the state from 1840 to 1848. James G. Birney, a prominent abolitionist who lived near Saginaw, was the presidential standard-bearer for the national Liberty ticket in 1840 and 1844. The Free Soil Party was organized in the state in 1848 by Liberty Party men, radical Democrats (who opposed slavery), and antislavery Whigs. It garnered nearly one-sixth of the ballots cast in Michigan that fall.[13] Yet, even as the antislavery movement competed in the political realm, Underground Railroad activists continued their work.

Four incidents in the late 1840s solidified Michigan's reputation as a bastion of freedom, angering slaveholders in Kentucky and across the South. In 1847, abolitionists in Battle Creek openly fed, sheltered, and paraded through the city a party of forty-five fugitives. According to Quaker Underground Railroad activist Erastus Hussey, "everybody heard of their coming and every man, woman and child in town was out to see them. . . . It looked like a circus." This was an overt attempt to flout enforcement of the federal fugitive slave act. Even more troubling to southerners were three attempts by Kentucky slave hunters to capture and return fugitive slaves from southern Michigan, all thwarted by local citizens. In January 1847, slave catcher Francis Troutman and three other Kentuckians attempted to take into custody the runaways Adam and Sarah Crosswhite and their five children—the property of Francis Giltner, of Carroll County, Kentucky—in Marshall. An interracial crowd of some three hundred neighbors, however, surrounded them before they could leave the Crosswhites' cabin. Led by local banker Charles T. Gorham, the crowd confined the Kentuckians for hours until authorities could arrest them for housebreaking and assault and battery. Gorham told Troutman and the members of the party that the crowd's action served "as a warning to others and a lesson to you." Meanwhile, the Crosswhites were smuggled to Canada on the Underground Railroad. The Kentuckians eventually were fined and released, but Giltner successfully sued Gorham in federal circuit court for the loss of his slave property and was awarded $4,500.[14]

In August of that same year, a company of thirteen slave catchers from Bourbon County, Kentucky, attempted to capture and return dozens of fugitives living in Cass County. Again, alarms were sounded, and two to three hundred free blacks and white Quakers responded to protect their neighbors. The crowd surrounded the Kentuckians and herded them to the county courthouse, where they were tried before a judge for kidnapping and assault and battery but were released. Meanwhile, sixty fugitive slaves from Cass County escaped to Canada for safety. The slave owners brought suit against the judge and the leaders of the crowd. When the case came to trial in 1851, the plaintiffs received $3,800 in damages for the loss of their slave property, a judgment that impoverished several Cass County abolitionists.[15]

In September 1849, a group of nine slave hunters from Boone County, Kentucky, led by John Norris, invaded the home of a family of runaways from Cass County. Norris and his men seized Lucy Powell and her three sons and headed south. Some of Norris's party remained in the Powell cabin to prevent a visiting white neighbor and the free black wife of one of the Powell men from sounding an alarm. Norris and the rest of his party got as far as South Bend, Indiana, where the local sheriff detained them after receiving a telegram about the "kidnapping" from people in Cass County. Within a day, huge crowds of blacks, estimated to number as many as four hundred, had arrived in South Bend, many from Cass County. After listening to all parties, the judge released the runaways, who were escorted back to Michigan by several hundred blacks. The slave owners sued in federal circuit court for the loss of their slave property and were awarded $2,850 in damages, plus various court costs. These three cases intimidated some slave catchers and led them to refrain from "invading" southern Michigan. The rumor spread that it was nearly impossible to return fugitives from some communities in southern Michigan. But the cases also generated howls of protest in the South. Kentuckians responded to all three of the thwarted slave returns by generating legislative petitions for redress and pressing the U.S. Congress for a tougher federal fugitive slave law.[16]

Passage of the Fugitive Slave Act of 1850, which created a federal apparatus of marshals and commissioners to assist in the capture and return of runaway slaves and prohibited obstruction of the process, met with immediate resistance from the citizens of Michigan. Protest meetings were held across the southern part of the state. One female fugitive was arrested at New Buffalo in southwestern Michigan and returned to bondage in Kentucky under the law. More typical, however, was the case of Giles Rose, of Detroit. Slave hunters from Kentucky arrived in the city in October 1850, located Rose, and had him arrested and confined in the city jail. Massive protest by angry citizens, both blacks and whites, forced a wary federal fugitive slave commissioner to adjourn Rose's hearing until the alleged fugitive could produce some proof of his free status; he was never returned to slavery. The act largely became a dead letter in Michigan during the 1850s. In addition to the resistance of the citizenry, there were official efforts to hamstring the activities of slave catchers or others attempting to enforce the federal law. The Michigan legislature passed a tough personal liberty law in 1855 that prohibited the use of state officials and facilities in arresting, detaining, or returning fugitive slaves; guaranteed alleged fugitives a jury trial and legal counsel; and required the testimony of at least two witnesses to a runaway's slave status.[17]

Fugitive slaves flowed through Michigan into Canada in ever-increasing numbers in the 1850s. DeBaptiste reported in 1854 that Detroit's Colored Vigilant Committee was "doing a very large business at this time." During one eight-month period, from May 1855 to January 1856, the organization assisted 1,043 fugitives. On the eve of the Civil War, the flow had become a veritable flood—in April 1861, just before the fall of Fort Sumter, the *Detroit Daily Advertiser* reported that 300 fugitives had passed through the city on their way to Canada in the few days before—190 of them in one day alone. Underground Railroad activists in Michigan were becoming bolder. On several occasions, they eschewed the usual secrecy, carrying fugitives across the state on trains, especially those of the Michigan Central Railroad. The most famous example came in March 1859, when radical abolitionist John Brown escorted a band of twelve runaways from a Missouri plantation by rail from Iowa to Detroit, then saw them to safety in Canada aboard a Windsor-bound ferry. Detroit blacks applauded Brown's daring, met with him about his proposed raid at Harpers Ferry, Virginia, and memorialized him after he was executed for his part in the failed attack.[18]

The fugitive slave issue, and the related matter of the expansion of slavery into the federal territories in the West, dominated Michigan politics in the 1850s, eventually turning the entire state in an antislavery direction. As early as 1846, there had been considerable opposition in Michigan to the Mexican War, largely out of fear that it would lead to the creation of new slave territories. After passage of the Fugitive Slave Act of 1850, Free Soilers, radical Democrats, and antislavery Whigs did very well in that year's fall elections. When passage of the Kansas-Nebraska Act reopened all federal territories in the West to slavery in 1854, Michigan politics were completely reoriented by the issue. In July 1854, Free Soilers, radical Democrats, and antislavery Whigs met at Jackson and created a statewide Republican Party concerned about the new federal fugitive slave law and devoted to opposing the expansion of slavery into the western territories. It won the fall elections and dominated Michigan politics through the Civil War. Many of the new Republican leaders, such as Zachariah Chandler and Jacob M. Howard, of Detroit, had been active in the antislavery movement and the Underground Railroad for years. By the time that Michigan voted overwhelmingly for Abraham Lincoln for president in 1860—88,445 votes for Lincoln to 66,136 votes for the other three candidates—southerners fully accepted the state's reputation as a beacon of liberty.[19]

The Reputation Compromised—Michigan's Black Laws

The existence of a series of black laws in antebellum Michigan compromised the state's emerging reputation as a stronghold of freedom on the Great Lakes. Among these—in addition to the 1827 restrictions on black residency in the state, which disappeared in 1838—were statutes or constitutional provisions prohibiting black suffrage and militia service, outlawing interracial marriage, and permitting segregated education by local option. In addition, Michigan blacks faced a range of extralegal forms of discrimination, including de facto segregation in public facilities and on common carriers. Although these laws were far less extensive and sometimes less stringently enforced than in Ohio, Indiana, and Illinois to the south, they nevertheless limited the rights of African Americans and challenged their claims to citizenship. As a result, black activists and their white allies fought to overturn these laws throughout the antebellum period. They were not successful until after the Civil War.

Foremost among Michigan's black laws, especially in the minds of African Americans, was the prohibition against black suffrage. In spite of extensive debate, the delegates to the 1835 state constitutional convention excluded African Americans from the franchise in Michigan's founding document. Because only electors could serve on juries, blacks were excluded from that privilege of citizenship. Blacks and some whites, especially Quakers, objected to the racial qualification for voting from the very beginning. The Michigan State Anti-Slavery Society began petitioning the legislature to extend the suffrage to blacks in the late 1830s. Local antislavery societies and churches flooded the legislature with such petitions in the 1840s. As early as 1841, blacks in Detroit and elsewhere began organizing to protest their exclusion from the vote and to petition the legislature on the subject. In addition to aiding fugitive slaves, suffrage was one of the foremost concerns of Detroit's Colored Vigilant Committee. Committee members argued that this fight was their responsibility, claiming that "the long lost rights and liberties of our people . . . could only be regained by our own exertions." The fight for the vote prompted the committee to organize a black state convention in 1843; meeting in Detroit, the delegates reminded white citizens of Michigan that, like Americans at the time of the Revolution, they were being subjected to "taxation without representation . . . by shutting us out from the elective franchise." Calling their cause the same one as that which animated the Founders in 1776, they declared that efforts to deprive them of the vote were violations of the Declaration of Independence, the U.S. Constitution, republican principles, and Michigan law. Laying claim to the "name and rights of American citizens," they reminded the legislature that suffrage was the first leg of an "unshackled citizenship." Michigan blacks held similar state conventions in 1850 and 1860 to protest their disfranchisement and to petition the legislature for redress.[20]

Petition campaigns against disfranchisement were regular features of Michigan politics in the 1840s and 1850s. Hundreds of such petitions reached the legislature, especially from 1843 to 1846, and sparked widespread political debate. Most opponents of black suffrage argued that it would encourage further African American immigration into the state—an opinion that marked white ambivalence toward the blacks already in their midst. John S. Bagg, the editor of the *Detroit Free Press*, claimed that "if they let Africans vote the whole state would be peopled by these dark bipeds." A series of petitions also reached the 1850 state constitutional convention. In both cases, the prohibition against suffrage continued, even though the 1850 constitution permitted detribalized Native Americans to vote. The constitutional convention submitted the issue of black suffrage to the voters, and it was overwhelmingly defeated. The dominance of the Republican Party in Michigan politics after 1854 brought some improvement. In 1855, the legislature allowed blacks to vote in local school elections. But other efforts failed, including an 1859 Republican proposal to permit blacks holding $200 or more in property to vote, and disfranchisement remained the norm in Michigan politics until ratification of the Fifteenth Amendment to the U.S. Constitution in 1870.[21]

In spite of the prohibition on black suffrage, a few African Americans still succeeded in voting at certain times and in certain places. Because the determination of who was "black" was left to local elections boards, some were permitted to vote by local preference. There are reports of blacks voting in local and county elections in certain parts of the state, especially Washtenaw County and Cass County. Blacks apparently voted for the Liberty ticket in Detroit in 1844. It was not unusual for black men to be allowed to vote in the frontier setting of northern Michigan. Light-skinned blacks sometimes voted by passing for white. This act could be tricky. In 1844, a light-skinned black named Gordon, who was of one-quarter African ancestry, was denied the right to vote by elections inspectors because of his race. A circuit court awarded him limited damages because "the Saxon blood in him greatly predominates over the African." In 1847, the Michigan Supreme Court reversed the ruling in the case of *Gordon v. Farrar* and held that only elections inspectors had the authority to determine a voter's race.[22]

For Michigan's African American citizens, the second leg of an "unshackled citizenship" was equal access to the educational opportunities offered in the state. Although the 1835 state constitutional convention provided for a system of common schools, blacks at first seem to have been excluded from public education in Michigan. The Public Primary Schools Act of 1846 mandated partially tax-supported common schools across the state and racially segregated education by local option. As the state's public education system took shape in the late antebellum decades, African American schoolchildren generally gained access to at least rudimentary schooling, although that access took a variety of forms. In Ann Arbor, Cass County, and throughout most of rural southwest Michigan, blacks attended integrated public schools. The Crosswhite children, for example, attended an integrated public school in Marshall in the 1840s. Segregated schools were the norm, however, in Detroit, Ypsilanti, Kalamazoo, and Jackson until after the Civil War. A few isolated communities of rural Michigan continued to exclude black children from public schools or consigned them to a lonely corner of a one-room schoolhouse.[23]

Public schools were not the only educational avenue open to black schoolchildren. Detroit's black community operated several private schools in the years leading up to the Civil War. Black educator Prior Foster incorporated the Woodstock Manual Labor Institute, one of the first such schools in the nation, in 1848 near Adrian. It attracted both black and white students and continued to operate for nearly two decades. But even private schools generated conflict over the question of racially integrated education. In 1837, Laura Haviland established the integrated Raisin Institute near Adrian as a private academy for area children. Even some local abolitionists criticized the arrangement, claiming that "freedom for the Negro was one thing but . . . sharing a desk with their children was quite another." Several white parents eventually removed their children from the school.[24]

Michigan lagged behind most other northern states in providing free public education until after the Civil War. Not until 1869 did the legislature mandate that the common schools of the state be supported entirely by taxation. Even so, African Americans made tremendous strides in gaining access to education for their children, whether in public or private schools. The percentage of black children (ages six through twenty) who attended school in Michigan far exceeded the average of all free states—46 percent to 35 percent—by 1860. In Cass County, one of the two major concentrations of African American population in the state, a majority of black children attended school. A major reason for these educational successes was the willingness of Michigan's black citizenry to press for equal educational access. The Colored Vigilant Committee of Detroit spoke for most Michigan blacks when it argued in its 1843 annual report that "education is the principal means by which an enslaved and degraded people can be elevated." But in many parts of Michigan, blacks found—as the 1843 black state convention reported—that they were provided "a scanty and inadequate participation in the privileges of education." They listed this among their foremost grievances.[25]

The struggle of Detroit's black community to educate its children illustrates the nature of the problem. Not until 1836, long after schools had been established for whites in the city, were even private schools made available to black schoolchildren. In that year, a private school was opened in the black Second Baptist Church. The black community assumed most of the cost of operating the school, even though its members paid taxes to support public education. This burden became doubly difficult after the Panic of 1837 forced several white benefactors to withdraw their aid. In 1839, white friends petitioned the legislature to establish a black public school in the city. After a false start, the legislature passed an 1842 act authorizing free public schools in the city and permitting them to be segregated. The schools were organized into eight districts—seven geographically based districts for whites and a separate district for blacks. Detroit's black community allowed the private school to now become the new public school—Colored School Number One. When the Detroit Board of Education fired Rev. William C. Monroe, however, and replaced him with a white teacher, black parents protested. They eventually reestablished a black private school in the Second Baptist Church and rehired the reverend. Over the next two decades, the public school had a tenuous existence, operating out of a series of black and white churches and leased buildings. Black parents regularly complained of inadequate facilities, funding, and supplies and of incompetent teachers. The school nearly closed in 1856 because so many parents had withdrawn their children. Finally, in 1860 the board moved the school to a permanent location and hired an experienced administrator and several capable teachers. Within a year, the school was thriving, having grown to nearly two hundred students. The black community also continued to support two small private schools. Five years later, Colored School Number Two was established, and trained black teachers began to be hired.[26]

Excluded from the ballot box and often segregated within the public schools, Michigan blacks faced still other legal inequalities. In 1838, as part of the state's first revised legal code, the Michigan legislature prohibited interracial marriage between whites and those of full or partial African ancestry. Such unions were declared null and void, and their issue was deemed to be illegitimate. By this action, Michigan copied the practice of nearly all states at the time. Ironically, the law permitted whites and Native Americans to wed, and, in an act of comity, it also appeared to recognize interracial marriages performed out of state. At first, enforcement provisions were limited. But the legislature later added such provisions, making ministers and justices of the peace who performed such marriages liable for up to a $500 fine. Couples married in violation of this act were deemed guilty of a misdemeanor punishable by imprisonment in a county jail for up to one year, a fine of $50 to $500, or both.[27]

In spite of this legislation, a limited number of interracial marriages took place in Michigan, and the law against racial intermarriage went largely unenforced for its first two decades. In Detroit, for example, four such unions were listed in the 1850 census; eleven appeared in the 1860 census. Nearly all of these unions were between black or mulatto working-class males and white working-class females living in the city's African American neighborhoods. Although such marriages were few, there was a growing public perception by the late 1850s that both the frequency and number of such unions were rising dramatically. Commenting on the practice, the *New York Journal of Commerce* noted in 1859 that "these amalgamation matches have been very frequent in Detroit and vicinity of late." Among the events fueling this perception was the highly publicized elopement of a black farmhand and the daughter of a leading Republican in Oakland County earlier in the year. Sensationalizing the affair, the *Pontiac Jacksonian* asked readers to contemplate their "own daughter . . . clasped in the embrace of a greasy black nigger, willing and ready, and even enthusiastically reciprocal, in the secret game of dalliance which lovers (?) delight to celebrate their union."[28]

The sole antebellum effort to enforce the law prohibiting interracial marriage came in the wake of the Oakland County case and the national excitement caused by John Brown's 1859 raid at Harpers Ferry, Virginia. On December 1, the front page of the *Detroit Daily Advertiser* warned residents of a "Clear Case of Amalgamation." One week earlier, Rev. Samuel V. Berry, a black Episcopal priest who had recently arrived in the city, married Thomas Slaughter, a black saloon keeper and musician, to Eliza Watson, a sixteen-year-old white Canadian of Scottish ancestry. Her parents brought a complaint before the police court, which ordered Slaughter and Watson to appear. When confronted, Berry admitted to having performed the ceremony, and a warrant issued for his arrest. He was found guilty of violating the law against interracial marriage and fined $50 by the police court. Because of the particulars of the case, local officials, the press, and ordinary citizens initially were scandalized. Foremost was the racial issue. The *Daily Advertiser* observed that "thus has another woman made herself a Desdemona for a rascally Othello." Watson's youth and beauty also heightened the sensational quality of the case and fed negative public perceptions of the "jet-black" Slaughter. There were fears that Berry, having recently given a public lecture vindicating the African race, was a radical amalgamationist. Fervor to prosecute Slaughter and Berry diminished, however, after it was found that both Slaughter and Watson previously had been married but had not been divorced. Because of the preexisting marriages, weaknesses in the testimony, and questions about the jurisdiction of the police court, charges eventually were dropped against all parties. The attention brought by the case diminished the willingness of interracial couples to challenge the law. But, at the same time, there were no more attempts at enforcement of the statute until after the Civil War.[29]

The last of the black laws to be fashioned in Michigan was one that disqualified African American men from militia service. Prior to 1850, neither the legislature nor the state constitutional conventions had said anything about the role of race in militia enlistment. Ostensibly, African Americans could have served. Although there seems to be no evidence that they did, or even attempted to, the state constitutional convention closed the loophole in that year. Mirroring the language of the federal militia law, the new constitution provided that "the militia shall be composed of all able-bodied white male citizens between the ages of eighteen and forty-five years." This provision remained in force until the middle of the Civil War.[30]

There seem to have been few challenges to the provision during the 1850s. In May 1860, however, Detroit blacks formed an independent military organization called the Detroit Liberty Guards. Over the year that followed, the thirty-five-member unit, which was captained by Obadiah C. Wood, a local black abolitionist, regularly drilled, studied military tactics, obtained equipment and uniforms, created a unit flag, and assembled an accompanying military band. Within a few days of the fall of Fort Sumter in April 1861, the unit offered its services to the government of Michigan, hoping to become part of a state regiment in the Union army. They were refused, but black abolitionist William J. Watkins, then visiting the city, urged them to remain ready, saying, "perhaps before the war is over, *they will be needed.*" The unit continued to drill. Michigan blacks soon came to understand that the Civil War offered a means of helping to bring freedom to the southern slaves and equality to themselves. Members of the Detroit Liberty Guards pledged to fight and die for the Union, if given the chance, "relying on the magnanimity of the American people to render us those rights, privileges, and protections which the Declaration of Independence, the Constitution, and the laws of the government extend to, and should be *extended* to all men!"[31] Nevertheless, another two years passed before the state of Michigan allowed black men to get into the fight.

In January 1863, the Union army allowed and began to encourage the northern states to recruit black troops and to form them into all-black units, but Michigan lagged behind other states in organizing black regiments. A black state convention, meeting in Ypsilanti during that month, called on the state legislature to overturn the militia law and to enlist black soldiers. Delegates pledged that they "feel willing and stand ready to obey our country's call, in a summons to arms in her defence," but they also appealed to white citizens to erase racial distinctions from the state's constitution, noting that "we cannot feel willing to serve a State, while it . . . denies us much if not the most that is due to us." Many blacks left Michigan to join regiments being organized in other northern states. More than two hundred enlisted in the famous Massachusetts Fifty-fourth Colored Infantry. Michigan finally permitted the enlistment of black troops in August, when Henry Barns, the editor of the *Detroit Advertiser & Tribune,* received approval from both the War Department and the state to organize a black regiment. Assisted by local black abolitionists George DeBaptiste and John Richards, Barns informed Michigan blacks that enlistment would "give the colored people of this section an opportunity to vindicate their patriotism and bravery." At first, enlistment proceeded slowly but steadily; it grew dramatically after the Detroit Board of Aldermen began to offer signing bounties in November. At the end of 1863, about 250 enlistees in the unit made a successful recruitment tour of African American communities throughout southern Michigan. In February 1864, having reached its full strength of 895 men, the First Michigan Colored Infantry was formally mustered into the Union army. Over the remaining year of the war, continuing enlistment brought the unit to 1,555 soldiers. Renamed the 102d U.S. Colored Troops in April, it saw action in limited fighting in South Carolina and Florida, demonstrating loyalty and courage. For many in the regiment, this was a vehicle for obtaining their "unshackled citizenship" in Michigan and the nation.[32]

In addition to these legal inequalities, blacks in antebellum Michigan faced a range of extralegal discrimination, from de facto segregation to racial violence. Although such discrimination could be found across the state, it was most overt and systematic in areas where blacks were most heavily concentrated, as in Detroit. Blacks in that city were denied service at many restaurants and hotels, confined to a separate gallery or balcony in many theaters and churches, forced into crowded and substandard housing on the city's east side (near the Detroit River), segregated on common carriers, and threatened with racial violence from rowdies on the street. In March 1863, racial tensions exploded into a major race riot in which working-class whites—mainly Irish immigrants—nearly destroyed Detroit's African American neighborhoods in a frenzy of vandalism and bloodshed. Although race hate did not rise to this level of virulence across the rest of the state, blacks were denigrated and stereotyped in the popular press and discomfited enough by religious racism that they withdrew from white churches and formed their own. But they could never fully escape racial discrimination in their daily lives.[33]

Although many blacks refused to respond to discrimination, and some struck back in isolated individual incidents, others challenged this mistreatment in organized ways. In Cass County in 1859, for example, three young black men refused to accept second-class treatment at a local hotel. After staying the night, they were seated by the proprietor at a separate table in the dining room, far away from the white guests. When they balked and insisted on integrated seating, the proprietor refused, and they left without being served. The three spread the word about their treatment, however, and local blacks and their white friends organized a boycott of the establishment.[34]

In response to one of these challenges, the Michigan Supreme Court upheld the practice of de facto segregation in public facilities and on common carriers. In 1855, black abolitionist William Howard Day and his wife Lucy were denied cabin accommodations on the steamer *Arrow* on its Detroit-to-Toledo route. Although offered the opportunity to travel on deck, the Days refused, choosing instead to go by land. They decided, however, to sue John Owen, the owner of the steamer, for violating the state law governing common carriers. The case took two years—at considerable expense—to reach the Michigan Supreme Court. Detroit blacks raised part of the funds to finance the suit, and William Day wrote wealthy New York abolitionist Gerrit Smith for the remaining funds. When the case reached the high court, the Days' attorney argued that Owen had denied them their right to accommodations. The defendant's lawyers countered that carrying a black person in a cabin would have violated the customs of vessels on Lake Erie, would have inconvenienced white passengers, and would have damaged Owen's business. The court found for Owen, deciding that the Days had a right to be carried under the Michigan law governing common carriers but not to cabin accommodations if that violated custom and impaired business. As a result of the ruling in *Day v. Owen*, de facto segregation in public facilities and on common carriers in Michigan continued to be practiced without further legal challenge until after the Civil War.[35] De facto segregation and racial violence, along with Michigan's black laws, compromised the state's reputation, especially among African Americans, throughout the antebellum period.

The Reputation Grows

After the Civil War, when slavery and the threat of the slave catcher were gone, the citizens of Michigan enhanced the state's image as a beacon of liberty on the Great Lakes. They did this in a variety of ways—they mythologized the state's involvement in the Underground Railroad, they publicized sites of racial harmony within the state, and they overturned the black laws that had existed within the state during the antebellum period.

Throughout the late nineteenth century, former activists, publishing houses and the press, local communities, and scholars cooperated to construct a public memory of Michigan's involvement in the Underground Railroad. The war had barely ended before newspapers began to spin tales of secret handshakes, coded messages, nighttime pursuits, and hairbreadth escapes in the Wolverine State. Community figures throughout Michigan pointed to buildings believed to have played a role in the effort—whether true or not. Before long, more formal efforts to memorialize local contributions to the Underground Railroad emerged. In 1870, George DeBaptiste posted a sign on the famous Finney Barn in Detroit, identifying its importance as a place to hide runaway slaves before the war. It read:

NOTICE TO ALL STOCKHOLDERS IN THE UNDERGROUND RAILROAD

THIS OFFICE IS CLOSED

HEREAFTER ALL STOCKHOLDERS WILL RECEIVE DIVIDENDS
ACCORDING TO THEIR MERITS

The death of Laura Haviland in 1898 prompted the citizens of Adrian to erect a statue honoring her Underground Railroad work there. Participants also wrote about their experiences or recounted them to journalists or scholars. Haviland's *A Woman's Life-Work* (1882), the most popular memoir penned by a Michigan Underground Railroad activist, told at great length of the fugitives assisted and of rescues from bondage in Kentucky. DeBaptiste and William Lambert, of Detroit, regaled local newspapers with tales of a mysterious and highly ritualized secret order of African Americans involved in assisting thousands of runaway slaves. Wilbur H. Siebert, professor of history at Ohio State University interviewed and corresponded with dozens of Michigan workers on the Underground Railroad and incorporated their memories into his pioneering *Underground Railroad from Slavery to Freedom* (1898). All of these conveyed an image of the railroad as a widely embraced, highly organized, and completely covert network across the southern half of the Lower Peninsula.[36]

In a few localities in Michigan, especially in the southwestern part of the state, "pockets of freedom" emerged—such as Covert in Van Buren County and Calvin Township in Cass County—in which blacks and whites interacted on terms of complete equality. These examples of racial harmony were publicized in African American magazines and in the state and national press. In 1896, for example, the *Detroit Journal* noted that, in the "dusky little republic" of Calvin Township, "Negroes have filled the township offices, ran [sic] the schools, handed out letters and papers from post offices to their white neighbors, and carried out the public improvements."[37]

Most important for Michigan blacks, the legislature and the courts eliminated legal inequalities based on race in the quarter century following the Civil War. In 1867, the legislature amended the Public Primary Schools Act to do away with segregation in public education. Detroit's Board of Education initially ignored the rule, however, and black parents challenged the continuation of the practice. Michigan's supreme court upheld the legislature's mandate in the case of *People ex rel. Workman v. Board of Education of Detroit* (1869), and, within two years, even the schools of that city came into compliance. In 1869, the legislature approved the Fifteenth Amendment, which prohibited racial inequalities in voting, and submitted it to the voters, who narrowly approved the measure five months before it became national law. Thus, by obtaining the right to vote and to educate their children in integrated schools, Michigan blacks had finally gained the "unshackled citizenship" for which they had fought for decades. But other changes were on the horizon. In 1883, the legislature repealed the ban on interracial marriage. Two years later, it approved the Civil Rights Act of 1885, guaranteeing "full and equal privileges of inns, restaurants, eating houses, barber shops, public conveyances, and theatres" without regard to race. Detroit blacks challenged the efforts of individual businessmen to circumvent this law, and it was upheld by the state supreme court in *Ferguson v. Gies* (1890). At the very time that southern states—and the nation as a whole—increasingly upheld segregationist practices and other legal inequalities, Michigan moved in the opposite direction.[38]

In 1900, D. Augustus Straker—a prominent black attorney who had represented the plaintiff in *Ferguson v. Gies*—was asked by William Maybury, the mayor of Detroit, to pen a letter surveying the substantial improvements that African Americans had witnessed in Michigan over the previous century. This was to be sealed with other letters in a time capsule to be opened at Detroit's tercentennial in 2001. Focusing on changes in the law, Straker's letter recounted the progress of black Michiganians from slavery to second-class citizenship to legal equality by the end of the century. He observed that

> the 19th century found the colored people . . . a race of slaves. . . .
> The incoming of the 20th century finds every man, and woman,
> and child of the colored race enjoying complete freedom under
> the law. . . . The 19th century found laws upon the statute books of
> our state, which deprived the colored man and woman of the en-
> joyment of every civil and social privilege, participated in by our
> white fellow citizen—the 20th century finds the colored citizen . . .
> in the enjoyment, and right to go, and enter every public place es-
> tablished for public accommodation.

All that remained, he suggested, was to eliminate the social prejudice that still denied blacks "the full enjoyment of those rights and privileges." Looking ahead optimistically to the next hundred years, he predicted that those remaining distinctions would disappear before the twentieth century was gone.[39]

In hindsight, Straker appears to have been a bit too optimistic. Although legal equality had been achieved in the late nineteenth century, Michigan's white citizens were still ambivalent toward the African American citizens in their midst. In the twentieth century, the state continued to be the site of considerable racial conflict, race riots, and de facto residential segrega-tion—as widely circulated and award-winning books such as *The Origins of the Urban Crisis* (1996), by Thomas Sugrue; *The Other Side of the River* (1998), by Alex Kotlowitz; and *Arc of Justice* (2004), by Kevin Boyle, recently have demonstrated. Perhaps, in the twenty-first century, the citizens of Michigan will completely realize Straker's dream, one shared by antebellum Michigan blacks and their white allies. Then the state will fully deserve to be known as a beacon of liberty on the Great Lakes.

Notes

1. In the works of modern scholars, the term "black laws" has at least two differ-ent meanings. Some, particularly those studying the history of the law, have used the term narrowly to refer to specific codes directed at African Americans, espe-cially those aimed at prohibiting or limiting black settlement within a state. Others, especially those studying the antebellum African American experience from a social

history or social movements perspective, have used the term more broadly to refer to the body of scattered state statutes and constitutional provisions that discriminated against blacks. Both uses existed even in the antebellum period. I have adopted the broader meaning of "black laws" in this chapter.

2. Kenneth E. Lewis, *West to Far Michigan: Settling the Lower Peninsula, 1815–1860* (East Lansing: Michigan State University Press, 2001), 103–52, 220–27.

3. Stephen Middleton, *The Black Laws in the Old Northwest: A Documentary History* (Westport, Conn.: Greenwood Press, 1993), 353–57; Paul Finkelman, "Race, Slavery, and Law in Antebellum Ohio," in *The History of Ohio Law,* ed. Michael Les Benedict and John F. Winkler (Athens: Ohio University Press, 2004), 2:748–81. Other scholars have noted this ambivalence on the part of whites in antebellum Michigan, including Paul Finkelman, "Prelude to the Fourteenth Amendment: Black Legal Rights in the Antebellum North," *Rutgers Law Journal* 17 (Spring–Summer 1986): 434n116; and Marilynn Hall Mitchell, "From Slavery to Shelley—Michigan's Ambivalent Response to Civil Rights," *Wayne Law Review* 26 (November 1979): 1–30.

4. David Katzman, *Before the Ghetto: Black Detroit in the Nineteenth Century* (Urbana: University of Illinois Press, 1973), 7; Middleton, *Black Laws,* 353–56; *North-Western Journal,* April 7, 1830, quoted in Arthur Raymond Kooker, "The Antislavery Movement in Michigan, 1796–1840" (Ph.D. diss., University of Michigan, 1941), 59; *Boston Emancipator,* June 7, 1839; Kooker, "Antislavery Movement in Michigan," 60–61.

5. *The Revised Statutes of the State of Michigan* (Detroit: John S. Bagg, 1838), 621–24.

6. Bureau of the Census, *Negro Population, 1790–1915* (Washington, D.C.: Government Printing Office, 1918), 57; Lewis Walker, Benjamin C. Wilson, and Linwood H. Cousins, *African Americans in Michigan* (East Lansing: Michigan State University Press, 2001), 4–15; Lewis, *West to Far Michigan,* 133–36, 201–6; "Colored People of Michigan," *Voice of the Fugitive* (Windsor, Canada West), April 23, 1851; *Statistics of the State of Michigan, Collected for the Ninth Census of the United States, June 1, 1870* (Lansing: n.p., 1873), 104–57; Betty DeRamus, "Black Pioneers Tackle Northern Wilderness, *Detroit News,* February 15, 2000.

7. Kooker, "Antislavery Movement in Michigan," 98–99, 110–11; Eugene H. Berwanger, *The Frontier against Slavery: Western Anti-Negro Prejudice and the Slavery Extension Controversy* (Urbana: University of Illinois Press, 1967), 33, 38, 53; Benjamin C. Wilson, *The Rural Black Heritage between Chicago and Detroit, 1850–1929* (Kalamazoo: New Issues Press, 1985), 74; "Justice Denied: Michigan Legislature (1846)," in *The Making of Michigan, 1820–1860: An Anthology,* ed. Justin L. Kestenbaum (Detroit: Wayne State University Press, 1990), 310–17.

8. Anthony Patrick Glessner, "Laura Haviland: Neglected Heroine of the Underground Railroad," *Michigan Historical Review* 21 (Spring 1995): 31n40; V. Jacque Voegeli, *Free but Not Equal: The Midwest and the Negro during the Civil War* (Chicago: University of Chicago Press, 1967), 170.

9. Reginald Larrie, *Black Experiences in Michigan History* (Lansing: Michigan Department of State, 1975), 2–4; Hall, "From Slavery to Shelley," 2–3. On the refusal of the courts to return Canadian fugitives, see, e.g., Pattison v. Whitaker, 1 Blume 414 (1807).

10. Maurice Dickson Ndukwu, "Antislavery in Michigan: A Study of Its Origin, Development, and Expression from Territorial Period to 1860" (Ph.D. diss., University

of Michigan, 1979), 111; Katzman, *Before the Ghetto,* 8–12; Walter Romig, *Michigan Place Names* (Detroit: Wayne State University Press, 1986), 211. The story of the Blackburn affair is wonderfully told in a forthcoming book; see K. S. Frost, *I've Got a Home in Glory Land: The True Story of Two Runaway Slaves Whose Flight to Freedom Changed History* (New York: Farrar, Straus and Giroux, 2006).

11. Blanche Coggan, "The Underground Railroad in Michigan," *Negro History Bulletin* 27 (February 1964): 122–26; Wilbur H. Siebert, *The Underground Railroad from Slavery to Freedom* (New York: Macmillan, 1898), 135–44; Glessner, "Laura Haviland," 19–48; Yvonne Tuchalski, "Erastus Hussey: Battle Creek Antislavery Activist," *Michigan History* 56 (January–February 1972): 1–18; Colored Vigilant Committee, "Annual Report of the Colored Vigilant Committee of Detroit" (1843), in *The Black Abolitionist Papers, 1830–1865,* ed. C. Peter Ripley et al. (Chapel Hill: University of North Carolina Press, 1991), 3:397–402; Benjamin Quarles, *Black Abolitionists* (London: Oxford University Press, 1969), 153–57; Larrie, *Black Experiences in Michigan History,* 12.

12. In 1837, a proslavery mob in Alton, Illinois, killed abolitionist Elijah Lovejoy and destroyed his press.

13. Ndukwu, "Antislavery in Michigan," 16–204; John W. Quist, "'The Great Majority of Our Subscribers Are Farmers': The Michigan Abolitionist Constituency of the 1840s," *Journal of the Early Republic* 14 (Fall 1994): 325–58.

14. Fergus M. Bordewich, *Bound for Canaan: The Underground Railroad and the War for the Soul of America* (New York: Amistad, 2005), 312; John C. Sherwood, "One Flame in the Inferno: The Legend of Marshall's Crosswhite Affair," *Michigan History* 73 (March 1989): 40–47; John H. Yzenbaard, "The Crosswhite Case," *Michigan History* 53 (Summer 1969): 131–43; Giltner v. Gorham, 10 Fed. Cas. 424 (C.C.D. Mich.1848) (No. 5,453).

15. Benjamin C. Wilson, "Kentucky Kidnappers, Fugitives, and Abolitionists in Antebellum Cass County, Michigan," *Michigan History* 60 (Winter 1976): 434–52.

16. Paul Finkelman, "Fugitive Slaves, Midwestern Racial Tolerance, and the Value of 'Justice Delayed,'" *Iowa Law Journal* 78 (October 1992): 89–141; Norris v. Newton, 18 Fed. Cas. 322 (C.C.D. Ind.1850) (No. 10,307); Norris v. Crocker, 54 U.S. (13 How.) 429 (1851); Wilson, "Kentucky Kidnappers," 352–53, 356–58; Sherwood, "One Flame in the Inferno," 43–44, 47.

17. Ndukwu, "Antislavery in Michigan," 202; *Voice of the Fugitive,* December 17, 1851; Thomas D. Morris, *Free Men All: The Personal Liberty Laws of the North, 1780–1861* (Baltimore: Johns Hopkins University Press, 1974), 222; Norman L. Rosenberg, "Personal Liberty Laws and the Sectional Crisis, 1850–1861," *Civil War History* 17 (March 1971): 32.

18. *Frederick Douglass' Paper,* November 17, 1854; *Provincial Freeman* (Toronto), May 31, 1856; Bordewich, *Bound for Canaan,* 429; Siebert, *Underground Railroad,* 79; John Chavis, "Freedom via Detroit, " *Negro History Bulletin* 26 (October 1962): 30, 49; Benjamin Quarles, *Allies for Freedom: Blacks and John Brown* (New York: Oxford University Press, 1974), 44–47, 58–60; *New York Weekly Anglo-African,* February 11, March 31, 1860.

19. Jeffrey G. Charnley, "'Swords into Ploughshares' a Hope Unfulfilled: Michigan Opposition to the Mexican War, 1846–1848," *Old Northwest* 8 (Fall 1982): 199–222;

Ndukwu, "Antislavery in Michigan," 202; Willis F. Dunbar and George E. May, *Michigan: A History of the Wolverine State,* 3d rev. ed. (Grand Rapids: Eerdmans, 1995), 297–318.

20. Ronald P. Formisano, "The Edge of Caste: Colored Suffrage in Michigan, 1827–1861," *Michigan History* 56 (Spring 1972): 20–24; Ripley et al., *Black Abolitionist Papers,* 3:397–400; Philip S. Foner and George E. Walker, eds., *Proceedings of the Black State Conventions, 1840–1865* (Philadelphia: Temple University Press, 1979), 1:186; *New York Colored American,* March 20, 1841; *Detroit Free Press,* June 10, 1850; Francis Warren, comp., *Michigan Manual of Freedmen's Progress* (Detroit: n.p., 1915), 35.

21. Formisano, "Edge of Caste," 24–41.

22. Ibid., 27–28; Katzman, *Before the Ghetto,* 33; Gordon v. Farrar, 2 Doug. 411 (1847).

23. Caroline W. Thrun, "School Segregation in Michigan," *Michigan History* 38 (March 1954): 4–8; Jonathan Marwil, *A History of Ann Arbor* (Ann Arbor: University of Michigan Press, 1987), 42; Ernestine K. Enomoto and David L. Angus, "African American School Attendance in the Nineteenth Century: Education in a Rural Northern Community, 1850–1880," *Journal of Negro Education* 64 (Winter 1995): 44; Wilson, *Black Rural Heritage,* 119, 121; Mitchell, "From Slavery to Shelley," 12; Katzman, *Before the Ghetto,* 84.

24. Katzman, *Before the Ghetto,* 22–23; William J. Watkins, "A Few Notes by the Way," *Pine and Palm,* October 5, 1861; Blanche J. Coggan, *Prior Foster: Pioneer Negro Educator* (Lansing: John Kaechele, 1969), 1–27; Norman C. McRae, *Negroes in Michigan during the Civil War* (Lansing: Michigan Civil War Centennial Observance Commission, 1966), 7–8.

25. Thrun, "School Segregation in Michigan," 4–8; Finkelman, "Prelude to the Fourteenth Amendment," 471–75; Enomoto and Angus, "African American School Attendance," 46–50; Ripley, *Black Abolitionist Papers,* 3:398; Foner and Walker, *Black State Conventions,* 1:186.

26. Katzman, *Before the Ghetto,* 22–25; Thrun, "School Segregation in Michigan," 6, 8; William Stephenson, "Integration of the Detroit Public Schools, 1839–1869," *Negro History Bulletin* 26 (October 1962): 23–28; *Pine and Palm,* October 5, 1861.

27. David H. Fowler, *Northern Attitudes towards Interracial Marriage: Legislation and Public Opinion in the Middle Atlantic and the States of the Old Northwest, 1780–1930* (New York: Garland, 1987), 183–85; Peter Wallenstein, *Tell the Court I Love My Wife: Race, Marriage, and Law—An American History* (New York: Palgrave, 2002), 49–50; Thomas M. Cooley, comp., *The Compiled Laws of Michigan* (Lansing: Hosmer and Kerr, 1857), 2:950–51.

28. Raymond Leashore Bogart, "Interracial Households in 1850–1880 Detroit, Michigan" (Ph.D. diss., University of Michigan, 1979), 61, 74, 145–51; Katzman, *Before the Ghetto,* 92; *New York Journal of Commerce,* quoted in *Detroit Daily Advertiser,* December 12, 1859; *Weekly Anglo-African,* December 31, 1859; *Pontiac Jacksonian,* January 6, February 3, 1859.

29. *Detroit Daily Advertiser,* December 6, 7, 13, 19, 31, 1859, January 10, 1860; George Freeman Bragg, *History of the Afro-American Group of the Episcopal Church* (Baltimore: Church Advocate Press, 1922), 191; *Weekly Anglo-African,* October 7, 1859; In re

Berry, 7 Mich. 467 (1859); Leashore, "Interracial Households," 151; Katzman, *Before the Ghetto,* 92.

30. Mich. const. of 1850, art. XVII, § 1.

31. Watkins, "Notes by the Way"; Michael O. Smith, "Raising a Black Regiment in Michigan: Adversity and Triumph," *Michigan Historical Review* 16 (Fall 1990): 25–26. All emphases in original.

32. "Appeal of the State Central Committee of Colored Men," in *Liberator,* March 6, 1863; Smith, "Raising a Black Regiment," 22–41; Hondon Hargrove, "Their Greatest Battle Was Getting into the Fight: The 1st Colored Infantry Goes to War," *Michigan History Magazine* 75 (January–February 1991): 24–30.

33. Katzman, *Before the Ghetto,* 17, 19, 26–29, 44–47, 93–98, 100–101; Wilson, *Rural Black Heritage,* 82, 129.

34. Wilson, *Rural Black Heritage,* 129–30.

35. R. J. M. Blackett, *Beating against the Barriers: Biographical Essays in Nineteenth-Century Afro-American History* (Baton Rouge: Louisiana State University Press, 1986), 312; William Howard Day to Gerrit Smith, March 27, 1856, Gerrit Smith Papers, George Arents Research Library, Syracuse University; Day v. Owen, 5 Mich. 20 (1858); Katzman, *Before the Ghetto,* 93–98.

36. Larry Gara, *The Liberty Line: The Legend of the Underground Railroad* (Lexington: University Press of Kentucky, 1961), 1–18, 168; Coggan, "Underground Railroad in Michigan," 122–26; Glessner, "Laura Haviland," 47; Laura Haviland, *A Woman's Life-Work: Labor and Experiences of Laura S. Haviland* (Cincinnati: Walden and Stowe, 1882), 111–244; *Detroit Daily Post,* February 7, 1870; *Detroit Tribune,* January 17, 1886; Katherine DuPre Lumpkin, "'The General Plan Was Freedom': A Negro Secret Order on the Underground Railroad," *Phylon* 28 (Spring 1967): 63–77; Siebert, *Underground Railroad,* 31, 79, 88, 106, 116, 135–39, 141, 144, 203, 236, 246, 250, 412–13.

37. Anna-Lisa Cox, "A Pocket of Freedom: Blacks in Covert, Michigan, in the Nineteenth Century," *Michigan Historical Review* 21 (Spring 1995): 1–18; George K. Hesslink, *Black Neighbors: Negroes in a Northern Rural Community* (Indianapolis: Bobbs-Merrill, 1968), 53–62.

38. Lewis G. Vander Velde, "The Michigan Supreme Court Defines Negro Rights, 1866–1869," in *Michigan Perspectives: People, Events, Issues,* ed. Alan S. Brown, John T. Hudek, and John H. Yzenbaard (Dubuque, Iowa: Kendall-Hunt, 1974), 121–25; People ex rel. Workman v. Bd. of Educ. of Detroit, 18 Mich. 400 (1869); Willis F. Dunbar with William G. Shade, "The Black Man Gains the Vote: The Centennial of 'Impartial Suffrage' in Michigan," *Michigan History* 56 (Spring 1972): 47–55; Mitchell, "From Slavery to Shelley," 1–14, 16–20; Katzman, *Before the Ghetto,* 84–97; Ferguson v. Gies, 82 Mich. 358, 46 N.W. 718 (1890).

39. D. Augustus Straker to Hon. William Maybury, December 31, 1900, Century Box Letters, Detroit Historical Museum, at http://www.detroithistorical.org/exhibits/index.asp?MID=1&EID=186&ID=220. For Straker's role in *Ferguson v. Gies,* see Katzman, *Before the Ghetto,* 95–97.

FIVE

Paul D. Carrington

DEFERENCE TO DEMOCRACY

Thomas Cooley and His Barnburning Court

When Thomas Cooley left the Supreme Court of Michigan in 1886, he left a two-decade legacy of Jacksonian politics and jurisprudence. What remains of Cooley's unpublished papers does not illuminate his judicial decisions, but his many judicial opinions reveal that the "common thoughts" he celebrated were conventional in the Jacksonian social order. He employed his power with cautious regard for the prerogatives and responsibilities of those elected to legislate. Only once in his twenty years on the bench did he render a decision that could reasonably be regarded as idiosyncratic and intrusive, and even it was much admired by many fellow Jacksonians.

Frederick Grimké suggested as one reason for the election of judges that elected judges are more courteous than appointed ones.[1] So it may be. Soon after his election to the court in 1865, Cooley became known to the Michigan bar as an exceptionally attentive listener, one who, in his opinions, responded forthrightly to the arguments advanced by losing counsel.[2] He was reelected in 1869 and 1877, but failed to be reelected in 1885.[3]

Cooley's twenty years on the bench occurred in a time denoted by Robert Wiebe as a "search for order."[4] America was responding to the destabilizing effects of an epic war in which a million young men, constituting at least a fifth of those of military age, had been killed or maimed. The

popular hope for restored stability in the social order was reflected in a desire, widely shared among lawyers, for predictability in the law.[5] Cooley understood and shared in this anxiety, and it was likely a factor in his preference
for "safe" judges. Several years after his defeat at the polls and retirement
as a judge, Cooley found occasion to reassure the electorate and the bar
that the legal process in his time on the bench had been predictable in its
results.[6]

Nevertheless, Cooley was always conscious that his judicial office was a
political one and did not recoil from giving political reasons for judicial decisions.[7] When he expressed political values, they were often those of the
Equal Rights doctrine embodied in the culture brought to Michigan from
western New York, values that he shared with most of the people of Michigan. His behavior was controlled by a professional discipline requiring
scrupulous attention to the mandates of legislation and to the text of the
1850 Michigan constitution, as understood by his political constituents.
Cooley read both constitutional and statutory texts in light of the cultural
context from which they arose and viewed their ratification or enactment
as events in the social history of Michigan. He did not deny the possibility
that constitutional language might over time experience a change of meaning, but his historicism and professional self-restraint dictated that such
constitutional changes originate in cultural change already reflected in the
values and moral aspirations of the people. Genuine cultural change, in
this view, ought to be reflected in the understandings of a broadly representative legal profession, not merely in a change in the personnel of the
court or the personal ambitions of judges to effect cultural change reflec-
tive of their idiosyncratic, subcultural, or class preferences.

One of Cooley's first judicial opinions in 1865 seemed admirably professional to his constituents. He held the state's election laws to be in violation of the Michigan constitution's requirement that voters be resident in
the state.[8] The law that his court invalidated had been enacted to permit
voting by soldiers on military duty outside the state, a purpose warmly approved by the people of Michigan as well as by Cooley and the other
members of his court, all of whom were committed to the Union cause.
Because the absentee soldiers were predominantly Republicans, the decision was especially unwelcome to those who had supported Cooley's election to the court. As a result of the decision, some Republican legislators
lost offices to which they had been elected by votes cast by servicemen.

Cooley, a Republican himself, explained that the text of the constitution was clear and that to disobey it "in times like these" would loosen "the

anchor of our safety." The judiciary, he said, should do nothing to "bend the meaning of words to meet unexpected exigencies."[9] "Plain meanings" of constitutional dictates must be obeyed. "Times like these" required the court to give no one occasion to question its fidelity to law.[10]

Cooley did not add that he was constrained not to bend the meaning of words to advance his own interests or the obvious interests of his political allies, for that was the difficulty he faced. His political adversaries, not without reason, would have identified a holding for the military voters as a self-serving manipulation. He was aware that, in the past, many Americans had been offended by seemingly partisan judicial decisions, such as *McCulloch, Dartmouth College,* and *Dred Scott.*[11] There could be no Michigan judges wholly disinterested in the outcome of the case, because all had political allegiances of one stripe or another. Possibly an appointed judge having no political constituents might have reached a different result, because he could have done so without fear that his decision would be regarded as self-serving. Although the constitution limited the franchise to those in residence in Michigan, a disinterested judge might well have concluded that soldiers performing their public duty to the state of Michigan by serving in its militia were "present" in Michigan within the "plain meaning" of the constitutional text.

Cooley's strict fidelity to text in this circumstance proved to be good politics. The decision led the Democrats to give serious consideration to supporting his reelection in 1869, even though it caused Republicans to complain that while they did the electing, the Democrats got the decisions. Many may have taken special pride in the integrity of their court.[12]

Although the voting rights decision exemplified Justice Cooley's obedience to "plain meaning" even when it yielded personally unwelcome results, he was not committed to strict adherence to "original intent" as the source of constitutional meaning.[13] He was quite willing to project the constitutional purpose of 1850 onto circumstances unforeseen by its drafters and thus to accommodate the constitutional text to discernible contemporary mores, when in his judgment the text admitted of such accommodation, at least in circumstances different from those bearing on the voting rights case.

For example, the 1850 Michigan constitution had authorized the state to provide for "primary schools." In 1874, the question was presented whether a school district created by the legislature was authorized to collect taxes to support a high school teaching adolescents nonelementary subjects, such as Latin. Cooley held that it was. In his opinion for the court, he reviewed the history of public education in Michigan and praised the fore-

sight of the founders of 1850 in authorizing the state to furnish "the poor-
est boy of the state" with instruction as good "as the rich man can furnish
for his children with all his wealth."[14] He found in the constitution no re-
striction on "primary schools" with respect to "the branches of knowledge
which their officers may cause to be taught, or the grade of instruction
[that] may be given, if their voters consent in regular form to bear the expense and raise the taxes for the purposes."[15] It was pertinent that the constitution required the legislature to create and support a public university;
the founders of 1850 would have been irrational to authorize and even to
require elementary and higher education while forbidding the use of public revenue to support interconnecting secondary education.

Although this case contrasts with the voting rights case in its method of
interpreting constitutional texts, an important difference lies in the fact
that Cooley and his political allies had no stake in the secondary schools
case. There being no risk that his decision would be seen as self-dealing or
self-indulgent, Cooley was more free to interpret the text without artificial
formal rigidity. This was, indeed, an easy case; it is hard to imagine an
American court reaching a contrary result. The two cases together serve
as a good example of the inadequacy of either "plain meaning" or "original intent" as an overriding principle of interpretation.

Other examples of Cooley's interpretative art exhibit his commitment
to democratic politics as the appropriate source of the moral values informing his judgments. He believed in local government as the best outlet for
the expression of popular morality. He explained this preference to an au-
dience at Johns Hopkins University in 1878, advancing the idea of constitutional home rule to protect local government as Burkean conservatism.
His proposal was then an idea of some novelty and ran contrary to the dictum of Chief Justice John Marshall in *Dartmouth College* but reflected
thought expressed by Francis Lieber in 1852.[16] The idea became an article
of faith for twentieth-century Progressives.[17] In presenting it, Cooley was
"in advance of his age," but his aim was, as he put it, to "conserve democracy" and the institutions of popular self-government.[18]

As a judge, Cooley assumed that the Michigan legislature shared his
predisposition favoring local self-government. Although this supposition
may have been unwarranted, he was careful not to insist on his position but
left it open to the legislature to reject it. An illustrative case is *People ex rel.
Leroy v. Hurlbut.*[19] The 1850 constitution in pertinent part provided that
"[j]udicial officers of cities and villages shall be elected; and all other officers
shall be elected or appointed as the legislature may direct."[20] The Common

Council of Detroit had designated sewer and water commissioners, of whom Hurlbut was one. The legislature had thereafter created a board of public works for Detroit, with powers formerly exercised by Hurlbut, and it designated other persons to serve on that board. Pursuant to that enactment, an action was brought by the attorney general of Michigan to remove Hurlbut from his now disabled office. Cooley's court held for the attorney general and removed Hurlbut but interpreted the statute in question as one making only provisional appointments to the board of public works, thus leaving the common council free to make permanent appointments to that board, perhaps even of Hurlbut himself.

This decision embodied an aggressive interpretation of the controlling legislation, one that could be said to have twisted its apparent meaning. The statutory text expressed rather clearly a legislative purpose to displace the officers appointed by the common council. What the Cooley court did was to return the issue to the legislature, with a cautionary expression of concern that the legislature had perhaps overlooked public values of constitutional import.[21] If the legislature were to revise the board of public works legislation to make it explicit that the responsibility for appointment of its members had been taken away from the common council, then the court, Cooley noted, would be forced to decide an issue that it had evaded by its strained interpretation of the statute.

If forced by explicit legislative reenactment to reconsider the issue, the later court might defer to the superior political station of two legislatures. It then could rely on the most obvious meaning of the constitutional text quoted above, that is, that the mode of selection of the members of the board is a matter for unfettered legislative choice. But Cooley's opinion also left open the possibility of a different decision by a later court that might give force to a different principle.

This technique may be usefully contrasted to a technique sometimes employed by judges who are less deferential to the legislature. I refer to the "constitutional flare."[22] A flare is dictum not necessary to decide a case before a court that utters it and may appear in a concurring opinion. It is a caution to the legislature that, although the present case does not require judicial intervention, there is something amiss in a statute to which the legislature's attention is called. This device, although not without its utility, is not one to be employed by a deferential court seeking to perform its judicial role with minimum intrusion on the legislative role.

The different principle that Cooley had found in the interstices of the constitution of 1850 and that he was calling to the legislature's attention in the *Hurlbut* case was a general constitutional preference for local government. He reasoned that it was implicit in the constitutional language quoted that the officers of a local board of public works should be either elected or appointed, as the legislature might choose, but only by local voters or their locally elected representatives. They could not, he suggested, be appointed by a potentate in distant Lansing or elected by the voters of some larger region such as the state as a whole.[23] It might thus be unconstitutional for the voters of the state to presume to elect a mayor of Detroit.

In justifying this inference, Cooley relied not on case law but on the whole range of literature asserting self-government to be an essential element of the English and especially the American legal tradition. In particular, he relied upon Jefferson, de Tocqueville, and Lieber. Lieber, no Jacksonian, had emphasized in his work on comparative constitutional law the importance to republican government of decentralization facilitating participation by citizens in public decisions most affecting their own interests.[24] The right to jury trial was viewed as part of the same fabric woven to assure every man an equal voice in government. Cooley wrote in Lieber's terms:

> When the state reaches out and draws to itself and appropriates the powers which from time immemorial have been locally possessed and exercised, and introduces into its legislation the centralizing ideas of continental Europe, . . . we seem forced back upon and compelled to take up and defend the plainest and most primary axioms of free government, as if even in Anglican liberty, which has been gained step by step, through extorted charters and bills of rights, the punishment of kings and the overthrow of dynasties, nothing was settled and nothing established.[25]

"Some things," Cooley said, weakening in his resistance to natural law, "are too plain to be written." Breathlessly, he elaborated:

> If this charter of state government we call a constitution were all there was of constitutional command; if the usages, the customs, the maxims, that have sprung from the habits of life, modes of thought, methods of trying facts by the neighborhood, and mutual responsibility in neighborhood interests, the precepts which have come from the revolutions which overturned tyrannies, the

sentiments of manly independence and self-control which impelled our ancestors to summon the local community to redress local evils, instead of relying upon King or legislature at a distance to do so, if a recognition of all these were to be stricken from the body of our constitutional law, a lifeless skeleton might remain, but the living spirit, that which gives force and attraction, which makes it valuable and draws it to the affections of the people, that which distinguishes it from the numberless constitutions, so called, which in Europe have been set up and thrown down in the last one hundred years, many of which in their expressions have seemed equally fair and to possess equal promise with ours, and have only been wanting in support and vitality which these alone can give, this living and breathing spirit, which supplies the interpretation of the words of the written charter, would be utterly lost and gone.[26]

One might guess from the shrill tone of this opinion that the judge was on thin legal ice, as indeed he was. The conventional view, expressed by Marshall in *Dartmouth College* and acknowledged by Cooley in his treatise, was that local government is the mere creature of the state having no status independent of the legislature in the absence of explicit constitutional provisions conferring home rule powers.[27] Nevertheless, the Michigan legislature was persuaded by the court; it revised the statute to provide that members of the board of public works should be appointed by the Detroit Common Council.[28]

Cooley performed a similar interpretation of another statute imposing state control on local matters. The legislature had created a park commission for Detroit as part of the state government. The commission identified land suitable for an urban park and sought to compel the common council elected by the people of Detroit to buy and improve it at local expense.[29] The Supreme Court of Michigan upheld the common council's right of refusal, interpreting the statute narrowly to avoid conflict with the constitutional value of local self-government. The same principle of construction later was invoked to shield local communities from the efforts of a state-appointed regional drain commissioner to require them to build drains at local expense to serve neighboring communities.[30] In none of these cases was there a conflict between local government and an office of state government having statewide jurisdiction and thus the full political backing of the legislature. Justice Cooley, for the court, reasoned that, in such matters, "the motive for outside interference [by the state] will very likely be something besides a desire to do good to a community in which the parties interfering have no personal interest."[31] The legislature, he concluded, should be presumed (in the absence of the most explicit language expressing a statewide policy or establishing a statewide program) to respect the right of a local community to control local affairs.

In these matters of local self-government, Cooley likely succeeded in expressing the prevailing values of the people of Michigan and perhaps those of the legal profession of Michigan, although this is less clear. Cooley and his court were anticipating, by only a few years, the Home Rule movement that inserted into many state constitutions explicit provisions limiting the powers of state legislatures to regulate or burden local communities. That movement first surfaced in Missouri in 1875 and was fostered in the early years of the twentieth century by Progressives.[32] The Supreme Court of the United States would hold that institutions of local government are not protected from the state by the federal Constitution,[33] but the Court would recognize local self-government as having constitutional value bearing in other respects on the application of the Fourteenth Amendment.[34]

Cooley also employed his interpretative art to protect other values favored by the radical Jacksonians' principle of Equal Rights that he found embedded in the interstices of the Michigan constitution. For example, he used the technique of interpreting legislation to avoid a constitutional issue in an early school segregation case. In 1869, Cooley's court ordered the elected Detroit Board of Education to reverse its decision and admit African American children to schools previously restricted to white children.

Public schools in Detroit had been segregated from an early time, when African American children first began to appear in the community. The legislation creating the Detroit schools and governing their operation was silent on matters of attendance. There was, however, an 1867 amendment to the laws generally governing schools in the state that provided, somewhat enigmatically, that local schools should be open "to residents of any district therein." For other purposes, the general school laws had been regarded as inapplicable to the Detroit schools because those schools were the subject of a separate body of legislation. Justice James V. Campbell wrote that the clause quoted was (like the rest of the general school code) inapplicable to Detroit schools and, in any case, did not address issues of racial assignment. But the majority, led by Cooley, rejected Campbell's interpretation of the statutes and held that the Detroit practice violated the new state law.[35]

Cooley also slyly noted that, inasmuch as the statute applied, "it does not become important to consider what would otherwise have been the law,"[36] thus implying the possibility that the practice of the Detroit schools was constitutionally proscribed. He refrained from quoting his own recently published text elaborating on his statement of a general doctrine of state constitutional law that "[e]quality of rights, privileges, and capacities unquestionably should be the aim of the law."[37] Nor did he refer to the equal protection clause of the recently adopted Fourteenth Amendment to the Constitution of the United States. Had he, even in dicta, pursued the avoided constitutional issue, his court's decision could have been a precedent of some weight favoring the dissent in the 1896 decision of the Supreme Court of the United States in *Plessy v. Ferguson*.[38] And he might thus have enshrined his name in the history of the civil rights movement.

The constitutional issue that Cooley avoided in deciding the school segregation case was not raised by any explicit provision of the Michigan constitution. Cooley had, however, in his treatise stated it to be settled law under diverse state constitutions that legislatures cannot lawfully enact "unequal or partial" legislation. "Equality of rights, privileges, and legal capacities should be the aim of the law," he wrote. And, "[t]he State, it is to be presumed, has no favors to bestow, and designs to inflict no arbitrary deprivation of rights."[39] These are among the few statements in the treatise that are not heavily documented. Perhaps this gloss was warranted, but Cooley's opinion confirms that he was not always a close textualist.

Another Cooley interpretation favored freedom of expression, Barnburner icon. Perhaps most prescient of Cooley's constitutional opinions was his dissent in *Atkinson v. Detroit Free Press*.[40] Atkinson had been a member of the Detroit Board of Trade. The *Free Press* reported that Atkinson, as a member of the board, was engaged in activity that it not unreasonably deemed fraudulent. Atkinson sued the publisher and recovered a judgment for libel that was affirmed by the Supreme Court of Michigan in an opinion by Justice Campbell. Cooley filed a long dissent, arguing that a newspaper commenting on the conduct of a public figure should be held liable for defamation only on proof of malice. His position was supported by an inference from provisions of the Michigan constitution protecting freedom of expression but prefigured the 1964 decision of the Supreme Court of the United States in *New York Times v. Sullivan*.[41] He emphasized the need for integrity on the board of trade and the duty of the press to expose moral shortfalls in the performance of duty by its members.[42] He concluded:

> If such a discussion of a matter of public interest were prima facie an
> unlawful act, and the author were obliged to justify every statement

by evidence of its literal truth, the liberty of public discussion would be unworthy of being named a privilege of value. It would be better to restore the censorship of a despotism than to assume to give a liberty which can only be accepted under a responsibility that is always threatening and may at any time be ruinous. [E]very man of common discernment who observes what is taking place around him and what influences public opinion, cannot fail to know that reputation is best protected when the press is free.[43]

Although prescient, Cooley's reasoning in *Atkinson* is open to question. His suggestion that prior restraint might be less objectionable than the imposition of tort liability for defamation has been roundly rejected by the Supreme Court of the United States.[44] And one "who observes what is taking place around him and what influences public opinion" today might possibly fail to recognize that "reputation is best protected when the press is free of any accountability for purveying falsehoods about participants in our public life." Had Cooley encountered modern media and the transmogrification of our politics by their means, he might have wondered whether media free of the restraint imposed by defamation law are the best protection either of honest reputation or of public discussion. When politics are conducted through false and misleading advertisements ornamented with professional art and music, which then are inserted into spots within commercial entertainment when large and inadvertent audiences can be filled with disinformation, Cooley's dictum seems out of touch with reality. Perhaps had he decided *Atkinson* a century later, he would have led the way in an opposite, or at least a different, direction. His court (and the Supreme Court in *Sullivan*) could have imposed liability for proven special damages on publishers who cannot show a sound basis for their allegations, limiting only the liability for general or punitive damages. This would have afforded public officials a forum in which to challenge statements made about them without the severe chilling effect that concerned Cooley. In any case, Cooley's decision again reflected his willingness to interpret the constitutional text as an expression of Jacksonian Barnburner values.

Only once did Cooley's court frontally challenge the Michigan legislature in a way that provoked serious controversy. This was yet another occasion when his Jacksonian premises were detected in the interstices of the constitutional text. The case involved public financial assistance to privately owned railroads. Cooley's decision was widely heralded by the people of Michigan, even as it deeply distressed railroads and investment bankers. The decision was perhaps more quaint than prescient, although a postmodern generation chafing over the expenditure of hundreds of billions of tax dollars in corporate welfare might see the issue in a light favorable to Cooley.[45] So might those who have lost their jobs as a result of plant closings caused by subsidies paid by distant state and local governments to employers as inducements to relocate, or taxpayers whose taxes are used for the benefit of private profit-seekers such as the operators of major league franchises, or fans whose teams are moved to secure the benefits of a public subsidy provided in a different venue.[46]

The signal case involved the town of Salem, Michigan, which had pledged its credit to aid construction of the Detroit & Howell Railroad in consideration of a promise by the railroad to provide service to the town; the railroad was constructed in reliance upon that and other such pledges. Many towns in Michigan, indeed thousands in the United States, had made such pledges under the duress that their failure to make the commitment would result in a denial of rail service and the almost certain atrophy of the local economy. In 1864, the legislature, at the insistence of the railroads and after a sustained dispute signaling widespread popular opposition, had authorized municipalities such as Salem to levy taxes to aid railroads.[47] In 1870, the Detroit & Howell Railroad sued the town of Salem to compel it to honor its promise of support by issuing bonds to be retired from the town's future tax revenues. The Supreme Court of Michigan denied relief, holding the 1864 legislation unconstitutional because any payment of interest or principal on such bonds would entail the use of public revenue for a private purpose; because the municipalities were unable to pay interest or principal, it would be fraudulent to issue bonds as demanded by the railroad.[48]

The opinion of the court first distinguished public subsidies from the exercise of the power of eminent domain. "It is true," Justice Cooley wrote,

> that a railroad in the hands of a private corporation is often spoken of as a public highway, and that it has been recognized as so far a public object as to justify the appropriation of private property for its construction; but this fact does not conclusively determine the right to employ taxation in aid of the road in the like case. Reasoning by analogy from one of the sovereign powers of the government to another, is exceedingly liable to deceive and mislead. An object may be *public* in one sense and for one purpose, when in a general sense and for other purposes, it would be idle and misleading to apply the same term. All governmental powers

exist for public purposes, but they are not necessarily to be exercised under the same conditions of public interest. . . .

[The railroads'] resemblance to the highways which belong to
the public, which the people make and keep in repair, and which are
open to the whole public to be used at will, and with such means of
locomotion as taste, pleasure, or convenience may dictate, is rather
fanciful. . . . [Railroads] are not, when in private hands, the *people's
highways;* but they are private property, whose owners make it their
business to transport persons and merchandise in their own carriages,
over their own land, for such pecuniary compensation as may be
stipulated. . . . [Their] business . . . has indeed its public aspect inasmuch as it accommodates a public want. . . . But it is not such a purpose [so different from] the opening of a hotel, the establishment of
a line of stages, or the putting into operation of a grist mill.[49]

The court then proceeded, with restraint, to give expression to the received
doctrine of Equal Rights embodied in the Michigan constitution of 1850:

We concede . . . that religion is essential . . . yet we prohibit the state
from burdening the citizen with its support. . . . Certain professions
and occupations in life are also essential, but we have no authority
to employ the public moneys to induce persons to enter them. . . . [50]

However great the need in the direction of any particular calling, the interference of the Government is not tolerated because,
though it may be supplying a public want, it is considered as invad-
ing the domain that belongs exclusively to private inclination and
enterprise. . . . [51]

[T]itle discrimination between different classes or occupations,
and the favoring of one at the expense of the rest, whether that
one be farming, or banking, or merchandising, or milling, or printing, or railroading is not legitimate legislation, and is a violation of
that equality of right which is a maxim of state government. . . .
[W]hen the state once enters upon the business of subsidies, we
shall not fail to discover that the strong and the powerful interests
are those most likely to control the legislation, and that the
weaker will be taxed to enhance the profits of the stronger.[52]

This decision was "the great news of the summer" of 1870.[53] The governor heatedly reported that it destroyed the value of millions of dollars of

bonds already issued by Michigan towns other than Salem, some of them in the hands of third parties, and asked the legislature to do something to protect the innocent investors. Railroad men were apoplectic. The decision was criticized as contrary to the great weight of precedent,[54] which it was, and lacking footing in any explicit constitutional text,[55] which it was, but defended as a prudent application of established principle to restrain the savaging of the public fisc by titans of industry extorting payments of public money as a precondition to the provision of a private service to private citizens. The decision proved to be popular among Michigan voters, and every member of the court rendering it was considered a candidate for higher public office.[56]

There is no reason to doubt that Cooley knew precisely how shocking the decision would be and that he intended it as a rallying cry against what he regarded as widespread knavery. The *New York World* crowed:

> [I]t is a pleasing reflection that, mocked and disregarded as it has been as effete, illiberal, and unprogressive, [the old doctrine's] sound sense and old fashioned honesty are bringing it once more into prominence, approved and vindicated. . . . [I]f now reaffirmed in other courts . . . and maintained in the press and in the ballot box, many spoliations may be averted.[57]

But too few rallied to the cry for it to have its intended consequence. Although the railroads never succeeded in effecting any change in the Michigan law to reverse the holding of the Cooley court, they did succeed in preventing the spread of the doctrine so damaging to their interests.[58] Had Cooley's doctrine been federal law in the 1980s, the U.S. Supreme Court might have forbidden the use of federal tax revenues to bail out failed savings banks and their depositors, and state supreme courts might have forbidden cities and states to compete in giving public funds to private investors in the expectation of creating new jobs stimulating to their local economies, or of attracting major-league franchises away from other cities.

That the *Salem* case was singular merits emphasis. More characteristic was Cooley's dictum in *State v. Iron Cliffs Co.*[59] Iron Cliffs in that case challenged the powers of the tax commission established by the legislature in 1882; Cooley responded for the court:

> If the demurrer is sustained the law will be defeated, and we shall have decided that the Legislature has assumed to exercise authority

which does not belong to it. In cases heretofore presented for our examination we have indicated certain rules of propriety and caution which should be observed by us when thus invited to declare void the action of a coordinate department of the government, and to those rules we should be inexcusable if we did not strictly adhere. One of these is that we must enter upon an examination of a constitutional question like this assuming that the Legislature has been guilty of no usurpation. We are to remember also that we have no supervisory power in respect to legislation; that the law-making power is not responsible to the judiciary for the wisdom of its acts, and that however unwise or impolitic their acts may appear, they must stand as law unless the Legislature has plainly overstepped its constitutional authority, or lost jurisdiction in the attempt to exercise it, by failing to observe some express constitutional direction. And the case must be clear: a mere doubt on our part of the validity of what the lawmaking department of the government has undertaken to enact is no ground for annulling it. These are commonplaces in constitutional law; they have often been declared by us, and still more often by other courts. . . . [I]t is to be feared that courts sometimes, without perhaps being conscious of the fact, proceed in the examination of questions concerning the constitutionality of legislation as if they were at liberty to consider the questions as questions of policy merely.

But every such case is mischievous in its tendency, for it shows that courts lay down proper rules for the government of their own conduct, and then fail to observe them. It is not less important that a court keep carefully within its proper jurisdiction than that the Legislature should observe the limits set by the Constitution to its powers.[60]

Whether Cooley was faithful to his own dictum in all the cases described above is a question the reader may well consider. Perhaps *Salem* merely confirms that even Cooley was imperfect in his own self-restraint. To the extent that Cooley imparted his own personal values to constitutional texts, he exhibited the failing against which he protested in *Iron Cliffs*. On the other hand, it is not unlikely that Cooley was right in believing that his Jacksonian premises were the "common thoughts of men" in Michigan in his time.

How did a judge so solicitous of "the common thoughts of men" fail in his bid for reelection in 1885? His defeat seems to have had little to do with public reaction to his professional work. Some of his court's decisions on employer liability for work-related injuries had drawn criticism from the labor movement. It was likely more significant that in his nonjudicial writings he had been critical of Republican presidents Grant[61] and Hayes;[62] but this was a better explanation for his failure to be appointed to the Supreme Court of the United States than for the weakness of Republican support for his reelection. Moreover, it was known that he had supported Grover Cleveland, a Democrat, for president in 1884 against the candidacy of James Gillespie Blaine, a Republican senator widely known for his elastic public morals.[63] Indeed, Cleveland's campaign slogan, "A public office is a public trust," was known to be Cooley's expression. He lacked the support of Detroit newspapers for more personal reasons. The owner of the *Free Press* had been an aggressive member of the board of regents who had attacked the president of the university, whom Cooley had defended publicly and effectively. The other major paper, the *Evening News,* was one against whom Cooley's court had recently rendered an unfavorable decision in a libel case,[64] leading its editorialist to describe him as an "ingenious sophist" who "covered up with the ermine of the highest tribunal in the commonwealth the shameful record of fraud and corruption" that it had sought to reveal.[65] It might have been a factor that he also accepted the nomination of the Prohibition Party; temperance, it may be recalled, was another Barnburner tradition but did not attract universal support among Michiganians. All these causes of his political weakness may have been inconsequential, because the voters recorded a "Democratic Deluge"[66] in which all Michigan Republican candidates lost.

For Cooley, the event was the signal for another career. He became for a time a political scientist as well as a lawyer and in 1887 became the founding chair of the Interstate Commerce Commission. His appointment to that office was widely celebrated at the time for he had become the most respected lawyer or judge in the land.[67]

Notes

The Barnburners were antislavery Democrats, so called for their willingness to burn down the barn (i.e., the party) to rid it of rats (proslavery politicians).

1. Frederick Grimké, *The Nature and Tendencies of Free Institutions,* ed. John William Ward (Cambridge, Mass.: Harvard University Press, Belknap Press, 1968), 457. Previously published as *Considerations upon the Nature and Tendency of Free Institutions,* 2d ed. (Cincinnati: H. W. Derby, 1856).

2. Harry Burns Hutchins, "Thomas McIntyre Cooley," in *Great American Lawyers,* ed. William D. Lewis (Philadelphia: John C. Winston, 1909), 7:458.

3. The story is told in George Edwards, "Why Justice Cooley Left the Bench: A Missing Page of History," *Wayne Law Review* 33, no. 5 (1987): 1563.

4. Robert H. Wiebe, *The Search for Order, 1877–1920* (New York: Hill and Wang, 1967). Wiebe begins his account with the recovery from the depression of 1873 and the aftermath of the Grant administration.

5. G. Edward White, *The American Legal Tradition: Profiles of Leading American Judges* (New York: Oxford University Press, 1976), 114.

6. Thomas M. Cooley, "The Uncertainty of Law," *American Law Review* 22 (May–June 1888): 347. To this reader, the reassurance was not especially convincing. This was one of Cooley's more pedestrian works. The theme, however, is also that of Karl N. Llewellyn, *The Common Law Tradition: Deciding Appeals* (Boston: Little, Brown, 1960).

7. This was not so extraordinary as some twentieth-century observers may have supposed. See Harry N. Scheiber, "Instrumentalism and Property Rights: A Reconsideration of American 'Styles of Legal Reasoning' in the Nineteenth Century," *Wisconsin Law Review* 1975, no. 1 (1975): 1.

8. People v. Blodgett, 13 Mich. 163 (1865).

9. Ibid., 173.

10. Cf. Abraham Lincoln, "The Perpetuation of Our Political Institutions," in *Collected Works of Abraham Lincoln,* ed. Roy Basler (New Brunswick, N.J.: Rutgers University Press, 1953), 1:108. G. Edward White, *The Marshall Court and Cultural Change, 1815–35* (New York: Macmillan, 1988), 927–64.

11. White, *Marshall Court,* 927–64.

12. Alan R. Jones, *The Constitutional Conservatism of Thomas McIntyre Cooley: A Study in the History of Ideas* (New York: Garland, 1987), 172.

13. Cf. Antonin Scalia, "Originalism: The Lesser Evil," *University of Cincinnati Law Review* 57, no. 3 (1989): 851–52.

14. Stuart v. Sch. Dist. No. 1 of Kalamazoo, 30 Mich. 69, 80 (1874).

15. Ibid., 85.

16. David J. Barron, "The Promise of Cooley's City: Traces of Local Constitutionalism," *University of Pennsylvania Law Review* 147, no. 3 (1999): 489.

17. Cooley's position on home rule is examined in Joan C. Williams, "The Constitutional Vulnerability of American Local Government: The Politics of City Status in American Law," *Wisconsin Law Review* 1986, no. 1 (1986): 83; and Edwin A. Gere, "Dillon's Rule and Cooley's Doctrine," *Journal of Urban History* 8 (1982): 271.

18. Thomas M. Cooley, lecture I, "Equality in American Politics," Johns Hopkins University (1878), unpublished manuscript, box 1, Cooley Papers, Bentley Historical Library, University of Michigan, Ann Arbor.

19. People ex rel. Leroy v. Hurlbut, 24 Mich. 44 (1871). For background, see Alan R. Jones, "Thomas M. Cooley and the Michigan Supreme Court, 1865–1885," *American Journal of Legal History* 10, no. 2 (1966): 115–17.

20. Mich. const. of 1850, art. XV, § 14.

21. Cf. Alexander M. Bickel and Harry Wellington, "Legislative Purpose and the Judicial Process: The Lincoln Mills Case," *Harvard Law Review* 71, no. 1 (November 1957): 34, 38.

22. See Ronald J. Krotoszynski Jr., "Constitutional Flares: On Judges, Legislatures, and Dialogue," *Minnesota Law Review* 83, no. 1 (November 1998): 1.

23. Hurlbut, 24 Mich. at 44, 109.

24. Francis Lieber, *On Civil Liberty and Self-Government,* 3d ed., ed. Theodore J. Woolsey (Philadelphia: J. B. Lippincott, 1874).

25. Hurlbut, 24 Mich. at 108.

26. Ibid., 107.

27. Thomas M. Cooley, *A Treatise on the Constitutional Limitations Which Rest upon the Legislative Power of the States of the American Union* (Boston: Little, Brown, 1868), 192.

28. Act No. 392, 1873 Mich. Pub. Acts 175.

29. People ex rel. Bd. of Park Comm'rs v. Mayor of Detroit, 29 Mich. 343 (1874).

30. Robertson v. Dexter, 57 Mich. 127, 23 N.W. 711 (1885). See also Allor v. Wayne County Comm'rs, 43 Mich. 76, 4 N.W. 492 (1880).

31. Bd. of Park Comm'rs v. Common Council of Detroit, 28 Mich. 227, 241 (1873).

32. For the present status of home rule provisions, see David L. Callies, "Home Rule," in *Local Government Law,* ed. C. Dallas Sands and Michael E. Libonati (Wilmette, Ill.: Callaghan, 1994), 1:ch. 4. For an analysis of the judicial role in enforcing such provisions, see Terrance Sandalow, "The Limits of Municipal Powers under Home Rule: A Role for the Courts," *Minnesota Law Review* 48, no. 3 (1964): 643.

33. Hunter v. City of Pittsburgh, 207 U.S. 161 (1907).

34. See, e.g., San Antonio Indep. Sch. Dist. v. Rodriguez, 411 U.S. 1 (1973); cf. Milliken v. Bradley, 418 U.S. 717 (1974).

35. People v. Bd. of Educ. of Detroit, 18 Mich. 400 (1869).

36. Ibid., 414.

37. Cooley, *Treatise on Constitutional Limitations,* 393. He did, however, acknowledge the force of a state constitutional provision limiting the elective franchise to whites. Ibid., 394. The Fifteenth Amendment to the Constitution of the United States trumped this Michigan constitutional provision, but not until 1870.

38. Plessy v. Ferguson, 163 U.S. 537, 557 (1896) (Harlan, J., dissenting). Cf. Strauder v. West Virginia, 100 U.S. 303 (1880) (holding that the equal protection clause precludes states from restricting jury service to white persons).

39. Cooley, *Treatise on Constitutional Limitations,* 393.

40. Atkinson v. Detroit Free Press, 46 Mich. 341, 9 N.W. 501 (1881).

41. New York Times v. Sullivan, 349 U.S. 254 (1964).

42. The next year, the court upheld a privilege of the press against a claim by a judge whom the newspaper had accused of confining a man without charge and setting excessive bail. Miner v. Detroit Post and Tribune, 49 Mich. 358, 13 N.W. 773 (1882).

43. Atkinson, 46 Mich. at 383, 9 N.W. at 523 (Cooley, J., dissenting). Compare Harry Kalven Jr., *A Worthy Tradition: Freedom of Speech in America,* ed. Jamie Kalven (New York: Harper and Row, 1988), 205. In Maclean v. Scripps, 52 Mich. 214, 17 N.W. 815 (1883), Cooley joined in affirming a judgment in favor of a professor of medicine accused by the press of adultery.

44. See, e.g., Near v. Minnesota, 283 U.S. 439 (1911).

45. Jones, "Cooley and the Court," 101–6.

46. See Matthew Schaefer, "State Investment Attraction Subsidy Wars Resulting from a Prisoner's Dilemma: The Inadequacy of State Constitutional Solutions and

the Appropriateness of a Federal Legislative Response," *New Mexico Law Review* 28, no. 2 (Spring 1998): 303.

47. A Republican governor had vetoed such legislation in 1866 and 1867. Constitutional revision was proposed in 1868 to authorize such aid, and the revision was defeated by vote of the people. Jones, *Constitutional Conservatism,* 174.

48. People ex rel. Detroit & Howell R.R. Co. v. Twp. Bd. of Salem, 20 Mich. 452 (1870).

49. Ibid., 477–79 (emphases in original).

50. Ibid., 483–84.

51. Ibid., 485.

52. Ibid., 486–87.

53. Jones, *Constitutional Conservatism,* 181n41.

54. There was a somewhat similar holding in *Hansen v. Iowa,* 27 Iowa 18 (1869).

55. See, e.g., Charles Kent, "Municipal Subscription in Aid of Railroads," *American Law Register,* n.s., 9, no. 11 (November 1870): 649. The Supreme Judicial Court of Maine reached a similar result relying upon the explicit language of the Maine constitution forbidding takings without compensation. Allen v. Jay, 60 Me. 124 (1872).

56. Jones, *Constitutional Conservatism,* 183.

57. Quoted ibid., 180.

58. See, e.g., Twp. of Pine Grove v. Talcott, 86 U. S. 666 (1874) (holding that state subsidization of railroad construction is not a violation of the Fourteenth Amendment).

59. State v. Iron Cliffs Co., 54 Mich. 350, 20 N.W. 43 (1884) (also cited as the *State Tax-Law Cases*).

60. Ibid., 360–61, 20 N.W. at 498–99.

61. E.g., Thomas M. Cooley, "The Administration of President Grant," *International Law Review* 4 (1877): 170.

62. E.g., Thomas M. Cooley, "The Method of Electing the President," *International Law Review* 5 (1878): 198.

63. "Blaine, Blaine, James G. Blaine, continental liar from the state of Maine!" was a popular cry. Mark D. Hirsch, "Election of 1884," in *History of American Presidential Elections, 1789–1968,* ed. Arthur M. Schlesinger Jr. (New York: Chelsea House, 1971), 2:1561. For a contemporaneous account of the Blaine-Cleveland campaign, see Frederick E. Goodrich, *The Life and Public Services of Grover Cleveland* (Portland, Me.: H. Hallett, 1888), 386–87.

64. The case was Maclean v. Scripps, 52 Mich. 214, 17 N.W. 815 (1883). The attack of the paper on Cooley is described in Edwards, "Why Cooley Left."

65. Edwards, "Why Cooley Left," 1568 (quoting *Evening News,* March 16, 1885, 2). When he lost the election, the *Evening News* crowed that he had been "unmercifully slaughtered" by twenty thousand votes, "[j]ust the number of dollars that were given in a celebrated judgment." Ibid., 1572 (quoting *Evening News,* April 6, 1885, 2).

66. Lewis G. Van der Velde, "Thomas McIntyre Cooley," in *Michigan and the Cleveland Era,* ed. E. Babst and L. Van der Velde (Ann Arbor: University of Michigan Press, 1948), 92.

67. Paul D. Carrington, *Stewards of Democracy: Law as a Public Profession* (Boulder, Colo.: Westview, 1999).

THE FOUR MICHIGAN CONSTITUTIONS

Michigan's first constitution was drafted in 1835, well before Michigan was admitted to the Union on January 26, 1837.[1] Territorial leaders anticipated admission prior to that date, however, and applied the 1835 constitution internally even before Michigan became a state.[2] Two primary issues delayed Michigan's bid for statehood. First, the Michigan Territory was involved in an ongoing dispute with Ohio, which had become a state in 1803, over the area including and around Toledo.[3] Second, and just as important as the "Toledo War," was the issue of sectionalism and slavery. Southern states objected to the admission of Michigan, which would enter as a free state, until Arkansas could be admitted as a slave state, thus maintaining the balance of free and slave states in the Senate.[4]

As one might expect, the 1835 Michigan constitution derives quite a bit from the Northwest Ordinance of 1787, which was in force in the Michigan Territory prior to statehood.[5] Still, the 1835 constitution is a remarkable document that included a number of interesting provisions, including a bill of rights.[6] There was, however, some disenchantment with the 1835 constitution as time went on—especially with its Jacksonian-inspired promotion of spending for internal improvements. The voters of the state approved, by a wide margin, a constitutional convention in 1850 and ratified a new constitution drafted by the delegates.[7]

The 1850 constitution made a number of significant changes to the 1835 constitution, some of which will be discussed below. By the turn of the century, however, problems with the 1850 constitution led to voter approval in 1906 for a second constitutional convention, which ultimately produced the 1908 Michigan constitution.[8] Until 1960, a majority of voters in a given election had to vote to hold a constitutional convention. Thus, even if a majority of voters who voted on the *question* of a constitutional convention supported calling a convention, it was not enough to actually call the convention.[9] In fact, in 1892, 1898, and 1904, a majority of voters who voted on the question supported a constitutional convention, but, because a majority of voters who voted in those elections did not vote for a convention— many voters simply did not vote on the question at all—no constitutional convention was called until 1906, when a majority of the voters voting in that election did call for a convention.[10] The 1908 constitution is considered by many to be an excellent document, and many of its additions—including direct democracy provisions, such as the referendum and the initiative— reflected the progressive, populist mood of the period.[11]

Ultimately, however, issues such as apportionment and other civil rights concerns led to a fourth constitutional convention in 1961, which drafted the 1963 Michigan constitution.[12] The 1963 Michigan constitution was rather advanced for its time,[13] and even today it is regarded as one of the better state constitutions on account of its structure and a number of its substantive provisions that will be discussed below. The 1963 Michigan constitution is the current constitution in the state, although it has been amended several times.[14]

This chapter will address selected issues that were important to the evolution of Michigan constitutions, especially the 1963 constitution. These issues are apportionment, the judiciary, and the question of religion and religious freedom. It would be impossible to provide a comprehensive history of the Michigan constitution in this short chapter, and there is little discussion here of many important issues that drove the various incarnations of the constitution, such as municipal home rule, spending, the civil service, and a variety of political and social issues.

Apportionment

The question of apportionment in the state Senate was a driving force behind the 1963 constitution. Republicans in the state legislature favored an apportionment system based on area plus population, and the Democrats favored a system based solely on population.[15] The House already was apportioned on a population basis under the then existing constitution.[16] During the constitutional convention, the U.S. Supreme Court decided *Baker v. Carr*,[17] which recognized an equal protection claim for legislative districting and alleviated some of the tension over the Senate apportionment issue.[18] Still, the apportionment question is an interesting facet of Michigan constitutional history. This section will look at the apportionment provisions for both the state House and state Senate in each of the four Michigan constitutions and the debate over Senate apportionment in the 1963 constitution.

The 1835 Constitution

The 1835 constitution had an apportionment scheme that was mostly population based in both the House and Senate.[19] Of course, apportionment at that time was not "population based" in the same sense that it is today because of the racism that was built into the constitutional system, even in a free state like Michigan. Apportionment was based on the number of "white inhabitants."[20]

Nonetheless, apportionment was based on population for both the state House and Senate. Article IV, section 3, of the 1835 constitution included the following language regarding apportionment:

> The Legislature shall provide by law for an enumeration of the inhabitants of this state in the years [1837 and 1845], and every ten years after the said last mentioned time. . . . [T]he legislature shall apportion . . . the representatives and senators among the several counties and districts, according to the number of white inhabitants.

There was a provision in article IV, section 6, requiring that counties not be divided in setting up senatorial districts, but with the caveat that districts were to be based on population as nearly as possible. The 1835 constitution was, ironically, quite similar to the current constitution regarding apportionment, although there are differences that will be discussed below— and of course the racism inherent in the 1835 constitution is no longer part of the Michigan constitution.

The 1850 Constitution

The 1850 constitution changed the number of members of the House and Senate, and made several significant changes regarding the method of apportionment in the state House.[21] These changes centered on the number of voters necessary for a county that does not have its own representative to get its own representative. Read literally, the language in the 1850 constitution suggests that when a new county (a "county hereafter organized") reaches a moiety (half) of the ratio of representation, it is entitled to a representative.[22] Two problems arose from this system of apportionment. First, the constitution placed a cap of one hundred on the total number of possible seats in the state House of Representatives. Between the decennial reapportionments mandated by the constitution, districts having only a slightly higher population than their neighbors might get a representative, and larger population centers might have fewer representatives per capita than a county that had just reached a moiety of the ratio of representation. Second, there arose the question whether it was possible to divide counties in order to gain proportionality.

The Michigan Supreme Court clearly answered the second question and pointed out the first in an 1892 case, *Board of Supervisors of the County of Houghton v. Blacker*.[23] In *Blacker*, the court held that the 1850 constitution did not allow division of a county for purposes of maintaining proportionality (if a city or county was entitled to more than one representative based on population, an at-large election system was used). In refusing to remedy the problem created by the legislature's division of Houghton County by assigning the county another representative, the court pointed out that to do so would deprive another district of a representative because the constitution did not allow more than one hundred representatives.[24] Thus, the court held that the 1891 apportionment act that had divided the county was unconstitutional.[25]

The 1850 constitution contained highly biased language aimed at Native Americans who were not mainstreamed into the general society.[26] Still, although the 1850 constitution altered some aspects of the apportionment scheme of the 1835 constitution, the apportionment of legislators continued primarily on a population basis, albeit one with much less direct proportionality. However, the story of apportionment under the Michigan constitution was not over yet.

The 1908 Constitution

The 1908 constitution was quite similar to the 1850 constitution regarding the apportionment of representatives. It did, however, delete the "hereafter organized" language, thus clearly making the moiety provision applicable to all counties, whether new or established, consistent with the *Blacker* decision. Moreover, in another case, *Stevens v. Martindale*,[27] the Michigan

Supreme Court held that counties having a moiety of the ratio of representation are entitled to their representative and cannot be merged with counties that already have a representative. The only exception was for counties having less than a moiety that were entirely surrounded by counties having more than a moiety.[28]

The most important apportionment questions under the 1908 constitution did not arise under its original provisions but under a 1952 amendment. The 1952 amendment had several effects. It allowed up to 110 representatives.[29] Districts still needed to be divided "as nearly as may be" based on population, and they still needed to "consist of convenient and contiguous territory."[30] The moiety provision for counties gaining a representative remained, although the language was made clearer. The amended provision clearly stated, however, that counties entitled to more than one representative would gain an additional representative only for each "full ratio of representation."[31] The 1908 provision, as amended, maintained the requirements that townships and cities not be divided and that, when they are entitled to more than one representative, an at-large system be used to elect the representatives. It did, however, provide for the division of townships and cities when the number of representatives allowed them under this system exceeded five.[32] There were also some changes regarding the board of supervisors and the board of state canvassers (when the legislature did not reapportion if required to do so) that are beyond the scope of this chapter.[33]

The 1908 constitution as amended in 1952 set the number of senatorial districts at thirty-four and specifically apportioned them among the counties, Wayne County receiving more districts than any other county.[34] Counties with more than one senator were to divide into districts based on a roughly equal population distribution as well as convenient and contiguous boundaries.[35] The allotment of senators among the counties resulted, however, in significant distortions in the per capita distributions of senators: rural counties received disproportionate Senate representation. Population trends reflecting growth in the cities and suburbs and declines in rural areas only worsened the situation.[36] Thus, apportionment was a major focus of the convention that gave rise to the 1963 constitution.

The 1963 Constitution

The 1963 constitution made sweeping changes to article IV. These included a new formula for apportioning Senate seats, some changes to the provisions governing members of the House, and the creation of a commission on legislative apportionment.[37] The battle over apportionment was a controversial issue in the 1961–62 constitutional convention.[38] In 1962, the U.S. Supreme Court decided *Baker v. Carr*,[39] effectively requiring that the populations of state legislative districts be equal under the principle of "one person, one vote."[40] This decision helped pave the way for a compromise on the apportionment provisions of the 1963 constitution.[41]

In the time leading up to the 1963 constitution, there was great debate over whether state Senate apportionment should be based on population or on geographic area.[42] Democrats favored the former, and Republicans the latter.[43] Under the 1952 amendment to the 1908 constitution, urban areas were disproportionately underrepresented in the state Senate based on population.[44] This favored the Republicans, and, until *Baker v. Carr* was decided, it did not seem that the issue would be easily resolved.[45] The courts, too, became involved in the Senate apportionment issue. In 1960, the Michigan Supreme Court decided *Scholle v. Hare*, upholding the 1952 apportionment amendment against an equal protection challenge under the U.S. Constitution.[46] The case was appealed to the U.S. Supreme Court, which vacated the judgment and remanded the case in light of *Baker v. Carr*.[47] On remand, the Michigan Supreme Court held, over a strong dissent, that article V, § 2 and § 4, as amended in 1952, were unconstitutional.[48] During the evolution of this case, the legislative wrangling became more intense, and justices were being threatened with impeachment if they found the 1952 amendments unconstitutional.[49] This did not stop the court from holding the Senate apportionment provisions unconstitutional under the equal protection clause of the Fourteenth Amendment to the U.S. Constitution.[50] The court also noted that the decision was consistent with earlier Michigan Supreme Court decisions holding that disproportionate representation was unconstitutional.[51] The court was well aware that the opinion would be considered by the constitutional convention,[52] and in fact the decision may have forced the Republicans to compromise, thus facilitating the Senate apportionment provisions in the 1963 constitution. The court held that a more than two-to-one population ratio among districts is unconstitutional and that even a less than two-to-one ratio may be problematic.[53] Moreover, the court postponed the 1962 state Senate elections until the apportionment problem was rectified and declared the then current Senate a de facto legislature.[54]

After *Baker v. Carr* and, more importantly, *Scholle v. Hare*, advocates of a population-based Senate apportionment procedure were able to win some major concessions. At the same time, Republicans who preferred a geography-based apportionment were able to preserve a geographic factor in the overall formula within the boundaries laid out by the courts.[55] As a result, a new version of article IV, section 2, was approved by the convention and added to the 1963 constitution.[56] The compromise ultimately reached by the 1961–62 constitutional convention was based heavily on population factors, as demanded by the U.S. Constitution, but also factored in geographic area within constitutional limits.

The 1963 constitution also made several changes to the provisions for apportioning the state House of Representatives, although House apportionment remained population based. One major change was that any county having at least seven-tenths of 1 percent of the state's population is entitled to a representative. Other changes dealt with the methods for dividing representatives after the initial distribution under the seven-tenths rule. Much of the apportionment scheme for the House, however, remained unchanged.[57]

One of the most important changes to the legislative apportionment provisions of the constitution added by the 1961–62 constitutional convention was the addition of a commission on legislative apportionment.[58] The commission is bipartisan and is responsible for developing and recommending apportionment plans at ten-year intervals.[59] The commission is a creative approach to reapportionment that allows for bipartisan communication on apportionment by people with expertise regarding the constitutional requirements for apportionment and, most important, by people who are not eligible for office: members of the commission are constitutionally ineligible "for election to the legislature for two years after the apportionment they participated in becomes effective" and may not be "officers or employees of the federal, state or local governments."[60]

The Judiciary

There have been a number of changes to the constitutional provisions governing the judiciary over the years. Most notably, the state has moved from a system under which many judges were appointed to one under which judges generally are elected. Moreover, the structure of the judicial system has changed over the years: some courts have been done away with, and others have been added.

The 1835 Constitution

Under the 1835 constitution, the governor appointed justices to the Michigan Supreme Court with the advice and consent of the state Senate.[61] The constitution did not specify the number of justices. The judicial power was vested in the supreme court and the lower courts, which the legislature was authorized to establish.[62] The constitution specifically established courts of probate in each county.[63] The constitution also recognized county courts and circuit courts.[64] Judges on the probate, county, and circuit courts were elected by voters in the counties over which they had jurisdiction.[65] Moreover, the constitution authorized townships to "elect four justices of the peace."[66]

The 1850 Constitution

The 1850 constitution made sweeping changes to the court system that took some power away from both the legislature and the supreme court for a period of time. Article VI, section 1, of the 1850 constitution specified those courts in addition to the supreme court in which the judicial power is "vested," listing the circuit courts, probate courts, and justices of the peace. The legislature also was empowered to create municipal courts in the cities. The 1850 constitution eliminated the distinction between law and equity in the courts and formally prohibited the "office of master in chancery."[67] The 1850 constitution spread the bill of rights provisions that had been contained in article I of the 1835 constitution throughout the new constitution. Thus, article VI included provisions addressing searches and seizures, right to jury, rights of the accused, due process, and competency of witnesses based on religious beliefs.[68]

One of the most important changes in the 1850 constitution was the provision specifying the makeup of the supreme court and the terms of the justices. The new provision made judges of the circuit courts "judges of the supreme court" for a period of six years.[69] After that, the legislature was free to organize the supreme court with one chief justice and three associate justices, to be elected by the voters for staggered eight-year terms.[70] If the legislature did not do so, the circuit judges would continue to fill the role of supreme court judges. The legislature also had the power to change or discontinue the court after the initial eight-year period ended.[71] The supreme court was given "superintending control" over the lower courts, the power to issue writs, and broad appellate jurisdiction.[72] In an unusual, perhaps unique provision, the constitution required that justices provide written opinions, including written dissenting opinions, when deciding cases.[73]

The 1850 constitution also set up more formal judicial circuits.[74] Circuit judges were elected by the voters within their respective circuits, and specific provision was made for the legislature to "provide for the election of more than one circuit judge" for areas with greater populations, such as Detroit.[75] The legislature was given broad power to add circuits or "alter the limits of circuits."[76] The 1850 constitution gave the circuit courts jurisdiction "in all matters civil and criminal, not excepted in this constitution, and not prohibited by law; and appellate jurisdiction from all inferior courts and tribunals and a supervisory control of the same. They shall also have the power to issue writs."[77]

Judges of the probate courts remained under the 1850 constitution and were elected by the voters to four-year terms.[78] Justices of the peace also continued under the 1850 constitution and were elected by the voters in their respective townships to four-year terms.[79] They had exclusive jurisdiction over matters valued at up to $100 and "concurrent jurisdiction" over matters valued between $100 and $300 (a provision allowed this amount to be increased to $500).[80] The legislature was also authorized to create "courts of conciliation."[81]

The 1908 Constitution

The 1908 constitution made several changes that affected the judicial branch. One of the most significant mandated that elections for judicial office be nonpartisan.[82] Additionally, the 1908 constitution reverted to the format of the 1835 constitution regarding a bill of rights. Article II of the 1908 constitution contained the "declaration of rights," that is, the rights provisions that had been included in the article on the judiciary in the 1850 constitution.[83] Another key change in the 1908 constitution was the requirement that the legislature may establish inferior courts only by a two-thirds vote of the members of each house.[84] This supermajority provision is unusual among the state constitutions.[85]

The jurisdiction of the supreme court remained roughly the same as under the 1850 constitution, but the 1908 constitution specifically mandated that the supreme court consist of a chief justice and an unspecified number of associated justices to be elected by the voters of the state.[86] In a rather cryptic clause, the drafters of the constitution stated that the term of the justices "shall be prescribed by law."[87] Most of the other provisions of the 1850 constitution relating to the supreme court remained in the same or similar form.

The provisions relating to circuit court judges remained virtually unchanged from the 1850 constitution, although some were moved. The one major exception was the legislature's power to authorize more than one circuit judge in *any* county rather than only in specified counties, as under the 1850 constitution.[88] The provisions relating to the probate courts also remained roughly the same from the 1850 constitution, except that the probate courts were given "original jurisdiction in all cases of juvenile delinquents and dependents."[89] Additionally, the legislature could authorize the election of more than one probate judge for counties having more than one hundred thousand "inhabitants."[90] The provisions for justices of the peace remained unchanged, except that the language relating to the legislature's authority to provide for justices of the peace in cities was altered from allowing the legislature to provide for "additional" justices of the peace in the cities to "[t]he legislature may provide by law for justices in the cities," a slight expansion of legislative authority.[91]

The 1963 Constitution

The 1963 constitution made several significant changes to the article governing the judicial branch, including the establishment of an intermediate appellate court,[92] the vesting of power in "one court of justice which shall be divided into one supreme court" and the various lower courts,[93] and the abolition of justices of the peace.[94] Moreover, the number of justices of the supreme court was set at seven, to be elected to eight-year terms, no more than two of which may end at the same time.[95] The chief justice is selected from among the justices under court rules rather than being elected to the position by the voters.[96] The jurisdictional provision governing the supreme court remained similar but was far more streamlined and specifically excluded the power to remove a judge. The constitution provided that the jurisdictional rules of the supreme court would also apply to the newly created intermediate appellate court.[97]

As noted above, one of the biggest changes in the structure of the judicial branch under the 1963 constitution was the establishment of an intermediate appellate court. This court, the court of appeals, initially consisted of nine judges elected in nonpartisan elections from districts drawn along county lines but based on population.[98] The constitution allowed the supreme court to create divisions of the court of appeals consisting of at least three judges.[99] The constitution also provided for an increase in the number of judges on the court of appeals and for changes in the districts of the court of appeals.[100] The judges of the court of appeals are elected to staggered six-year terms.[101]

The provisions relating to circuit judges remained substantively similar to those in the 1908 constitution, except that the supreme court was given greater authority to recommend changes to the structure of the circuit courts and to the number of judges sitting on them.[102] The legislature was given increased power to alter the structure of the probate courts with the approval of the voters within affected counties, but the jurisdiction of the probate courts remained the same as under the 1908 constitution.[103] The 1963 constitution also provided for removal of judges by the governor with the support of two-thirds of the members of each house of the legislature in cases in which there are "insufficient grounds for impeachment."[104]

As noted above, the 1963 constitution abolished the office of justice of the peace. It also required the legislature to "establish a court or courts of limited jurisdiction with powers and jurisdiction defined by law."[105] The legislature did so.[106] The 1963 constitution preserved preexisting statutory courts, "except as provided by law, until they are abolished by law"—a somewhat odd way of saying that the legislature still retains control over their creation and abolition.[107] The 1963 constitution also provided for judicial review of administrative agency judicial or quasi-judicial proceedings.[108] Finally, the 1963 constitution created a judicial tenure commission to review allegations of judicial misconduct and to recommend sanctions to the supreme court.[109]

Religion and Religious Freedom

From the start, the Michigan constitution has maintained a commitment to religious freedom that is, at least in theory, even broader than the protections provided under the federal Constitution. The courts, however, often have interpreted the religious freedom provisions of the Michigan constitution in a manner that tracks the interpretation of the U.S. Constitution, even though the language of the two documents is different.[110] Additionally, Michigan has a constitutional provision that prohibits the expenditure of public funds for private education,[111] a provision that has a significant impact on the state's relationship with religious entities, at least with regard to education. Michigan's prohibition on private school funding also applies to secular private schools and thus is not a "Blaine Amendment."[112]

The 1835 Constitution

The bill of rights in the 1835 constitution had three provisions dealing with religious freedom. Additionally, the official state oath prescribed in Article XII of the 1835 constitution is relevant to religion because of what it didn't say. It is a completely secular oath, and no other oaths of office, declarations, or tests are allowed for any office or public trust.[113] As a practical matter, this section is similar to the religious tests clause of Article VI of the U.S. Constitution but demonstrates quite a bit more tolerance than some other state constitutions of that era. What follows is a discussion of the religious freedom provisions in the bill of rights in the 1835 constitution.

Taken together, the three religious freedom clauses of the 1835 constitution suggest broad free exercise rights and a strong distaste for government financial aid to religious institutions.[114] It is obvious that the Northwest Ordinance of 1787, which had a major impact on the 1835 constitution, also had an impact on the religious freedom provisions of that constitution (article I, sections 4–6), which read as follows:

RELIGIOUS WORSHIP

4. Every person has a right to worship Almighty God according to the dictates of his own conscience; and no person can of right be compelled to attend, erect, or support, against his will, any place of religious worship, or pay any tithes, taxes, or other rates, for the support of any minister of the gospel or teacher of religion.

SUPPORT OF RELIGIOUS SOCIETIES BY STATE TREASURY PROHIBITED

5. No money shall be drawn from the treasury for the benefit of religious societies, or theological or religious seminaries.

RIGHTS OF CONSCIENCE

6. The civil and religious rights, privileges and capacities of no individual shall be diminished or enlarged on account of his opinions or belief concerning matters of religion.

The three themes that run through these provisions are freedom of religious belief and conscience, a deep concern about compelled religious practices, and a disdain for government support—especially financial support—of religious institutions, positions that were quite progressive for the early 1830s. This progressive approach to religious freedom remains today, although the state supreme court rarely has interpreted the religious freedom provisions of the state constitution in recent years.

The 1850 Constitution

The 1850 constitution moved the religious freedom provisions to article IV, which dealt with the legislature. This was consistent with the reorganization of other provisions of the 1835 bill of rights into other articles in the 1850 constitution, but it did have a substantive impact, as discussed below; both the 1908 and 1963 constitutions followed the model of the 1835 constitution by having a bill or declaration of rights early in the constitution that included religious freedom provisions. The oath provision of the 1850 constitution was the same as that of the 1835 constitution.[115] The 1850 constitution did, however, add a provision allowing the legislature to authorize a paid chaplain for the state prison but prohibiting paid chaplains for either house of the legislature.[116] The latter provision underscores the state's commitment to separation of church and state, because many state legislatures as well as Congress had, and still have, paid chaplains.[117]

When the religious freedom provisions that had been in the bill of rights were transferred to the legislative article, this move had several substantive effects. Although the general language of article I, sections 4–6, in the 1835 constitution was moved verbatim to the 1850 constitution, section 39 (which had been article I, section 4) now began with "The legislature shall pass no law," and section 41 (which had been article I, section 6) began with "The legislature shall not diminish." These two changes seemed to limit the application of the relevant religious freedom provisions to the actions of the legislature, which, of course, had the power to originate any state laws, taxes, or spending. Yet there were no corresponding provisions in articles V and VI, which dealt with the executive and the judiciary, respectively. Moreover, articles X and XI (counties and townships, respectively), did not contain corresponding provisions. Similarly, section 40 (which had been article I, section 5) added the words "appropriated or" before "drawn from the treasury," also seeming to connect the section more closely with legislative action.[118]

All of this suggests that the primary focus of the religion provisions was the legislature. This may have been, however, an unintended result of the reorganization of provisions in the 1850 constitution. At any rate, the potential confusion was removed by the return to the 1835 format in the 1908 and 1963 constitutions.

The 1908 Constitution

The 1908 constitution is an odd document with regard to its provisions relating to religion. It is both more protective of religious freedoms and, in its embrace of what one might call "ceremonial deism," more overtly "religious" than its predecessors.[119] The most notable examples are additions to the preamble and section 1 of the education article. The preamble to the 1908 constitution reads as follows:

> We, the people of the state of Michigan, grateful to Almighty God
> for the blessings of freedom, and earnestly desiring to secure these
> blessings undiminished to ourselves and our posterity, do ordain
> and establish this constitution.

Neither the preamble to the 1835 constitution nor the preamble to the 1850
constitution made any reference to a deity or any other religious principle.
Similarly, article XI, section 1, of the 1908 constitution reads as follows:

ENCOURAGEMENT OF EDUCATION

1. Religion, morality and knowledge being necessary to good government and the happiness of mankind, schools and the means
   of education shall forever be encouraged.

This language is taken verbatim from the first sentence of article III of the
Northwest Ordinance of 1787. Neither the 1835 constitution, which derived
a great deal from the Northwest Ordinance, nor its 1850 successor contained this language, although both had an education article.[120]

The remaining provisions dealing with religion in the 1908 constitution
are virtually identical to those of the 1835 constitution. Article II, section
3, contains all of the elements of article I, sections 4–6, of the 1835 constitution plus the amended language from the 1850 constitution prohibiting the appropriation of state property for religious use.[121] In fact, the
1908 constitution returned these provisions to a bill-of-rights format in article II.[122] Both the chaplaincy and oath provisions remained the same, but
were renumbered as a result of other changes in the 1908 constitution.[123]

The 1963 Constitution

The 1963 constitution was similar to the 1908 constitution but with a few
significant changes. Several new civil rights provisions protected citizens
against discrimination, including religious discrimination;[124] a 1970 amendment prohibited funding to private schools, including religious schools;[125]
and a new provision was added giving tax exemptions to religious and other
charitable institutions.[126]

The preamble and religious freedom section in the declaration of rights
remained unchanged.[127] The oath of office section also remained unchanged.[128] As noted above, however, a new equal protection provision
was added to the declaration of rights:

No person shall be denied the equal protection of the laws; nor
shall any person be denied the enjoyment of his civil or political
rights or be discriminated against in the exercise thereof because
of religion, race, color or national origin. The legislature shall implement this section by appropriate legislation.[129]

This provision ultimately led to the passage of the Elliott-Larson Civil
Rights Act, which prohibited discrimination on the basis of religion or other
protected classifications.[130]

The section relating to prison chaplains remained substantively unchanged, but the provision relating to legislative chaplains was deleted.[131] Yet
no provision in the 1963 constitution authorized such chaplains, and the prohibition on tax dollars going to support legislative chaplains may have been
implicit in the religious freedom provision in the declaration of rights.[132]

As noted above, two of the most significant changes in the 1963 constitution relating to religion were the addition of a charitable tax exemption
and the prohibition of funding for private education. The latter was added
by a 1970 amendment. The tax provision exempts "[p]roperty owned and
occupied by non-profit religious or educational organizations and used exclusively for religious or educational purposes . . . from real and personal
property taxes."[133] The tax exemption is not, however, an indication of a
constitutional willingness to provide broader aid to religious entities. This
is clearly demonstrated by the language of article I, section 4 (the religious
freedom provision in the declaration of rights), and by the 1970 constitutional amendment that provided as follows:

NONPUBLIC SCHOOLS, PROHIBITED AID

No public monies or property shall be appropriated or paid or any
public credit utilized, by the legislature or any other political sub-
division or agency of the state directly or indirectly to aid or maintain any private, denominational or other nonpublic, pre-elementary,
elementary, or secondary school. No payment, credit, tax benefit,
exemption or deductions, tuition voucher, subsidy, grant or loan
of public monies or property shall be provided, directly or indirectly, to support the attendance of any student or the employment
of any person at any such nonpublic school or at any location or
institution where instruction is offered in whole or in part to such
nonpublic school students. The legislature may provide for the
transportation of students to and from any school.

This amendment was added to article VIII, section 2, which provided that the "legislature shall maintain and support a system of free public elementary and secondary schools" and that "every school district" must provide education that does not discriminate on the basis of a number of protected classifications, including religion. It is not a Blaine Amendment, both because of the date it was passed and because it does not discriminate between secular and sectarian private schools.[134] The amendment clearly prohibits state aid to parochial schools and explicitly prohibits tuition vouchers, which have become a significant issue in recent years.[135] Finally, the encouragement of education section added in the 1908 constitution remained unchanged.[136]

Each of the four Michigan constitutions has been inventive in its own way. This chapter reaches only the tip of the iceberg in analyzing these fascinating documents. Although the chapter touches on only three issues that have evolved through the four constitutions—apportionment, the judicial branch, and religious freedom—these issues provide a good window into the complex and often novel nature of the four Michigan constitutions. The constitutions have not remained static historical anomalies, but rather have adapted to changed circumstances in localities, the state, the nation, and the world. The citizens of the state of Michigan can be truly proud of their constitution, despite its warts. It remains, in many ways, a cutting-edge document.

Notes

1. Robert L. Maddex, *State Constitutions of the United States* (Washington, D.C.: Congressional Quarterly, 1998), 185; John Higgins, *History of Michigan Constitution* (Lansing: Citizens Research Council of Michigan, 1960), 1.

2. Higgins, *History of Michigan Constitution*, 1.

3. Ultimately, the Toledo area was given to Ohio, and Michigan was given the Upper Peninsula as compensation. Ibid.

4. Ibid.; Maddex, *State Constitutions*, 185.

5. Maddex, *State Constitutions*, 185–86.

6. Ibid., 185; Mich. const. of 1835, art. I.

7. Higgins, *History of Michigan Constitution*, 1–2; James K. Pollock, *Making Michigan's New Constitution, 1961–1962* (Ann Arbor, Mich.: George Wahr, 1962), 2.

8. Higgins, *History of Michigan Constitution*, 2–3; Pollock, *Making Michigan's New Constitution*, 3–4.

9. Pollock, *Making Michigan's New Constitution*, 3–6.

10. Ibid., 3; Higgins, *History of Michigan Constitution*, 2; Citizens Research Council of Michigan, *Michigan Constitutional Issues*, report no. 313-02 (July 1994), 3.

11. Higgins, *History of Michigan Constitution*, 2–3.

12. Harold Norris, "A Perspective on the History of Civil Rights Law in Michigan," *Detroit College of Law Review* 1996 (Fall 1996): 567, 579–82.

13. Maddex, *State Constitutions*, 186.

14. Amendments are incorporated into the general provisions of the Michigan constitution rather than being placed at the end, so readers can find the amended provisions in the general text of the constitution with notes stating the date and form (e.g., referendum) of the amendment. The easiest place to get this information is in the Michigan Compiled Laws Annotated (Thomson/West 2003), which has several volumes devoted to the state constitution.

15. Norris, "Perspective on the History of Civil Rights Law," 581–82; cf. Norman C. Thomas, "The Legislative Apportionment Provisions of the Proposed Michigan Constitution," in *The Proposed Michigan Constitution: Analysis and Interpretations* (Ann Arbor: Inter-University Faculty Committee on Constitutional Revisions March 1963), 30.

16. Mich. const. of 1908, art. V, §§ 3–4, as amended Nov. 4, 1952.

17. Baker v. Carr, 369 U.S. 186 (1962).

18. Ibid.

19. Mich. const. of 1835, art. 4, §§ 3–6.

20. Ibid., art. 4, § 3 ("the legislature shall apportion anew the representatives and senators among the several counties and districts, according to the number of white inhabitants").

21. Ibid., art. 4, §§ 2–3.

22. Ibid., art. 4, § 3. The ratio of representation is the population of the state divided by the total number of seats in the House.

23. Bd. of Supervisors of the County of Houghton v. Blacker, 92 Mich. 638, 52 N.W. 951 (1892).

24. Ibid., 647, 52 N.W. at 955.

25. Ibid.

26. Mich. const. of 1850, art. IV, § 3 (each district should contain a roughly equal number of people, "exclusive of persons of Indian descent, who are not civilized, or are members of any tribe").

27. Stevens v. Martindale, 181 Mich. 199, 203, 148 N.W. 97, 98 (1914).

28. Ibid.

29. Mich. const. of 1908, art. V, § 3, as amended by initiative petition ratified (1952).

30. Ibid.

31. Ibid.

32. Ibid.

33. Ibid., § 4.

34. Ibid., § 2.

35. Ibid.

36. Norris, "Perspective on the History of Civil Rights Law," 567, 582.

37. Mich. const. of 1963, art. IV, §§ 2–6.

38. Pollock, *Making Michigan's New Constitution*, 57–61.

39. Baker v. Carr, 369 U.S. 186 (1962).

40. Ibid.

41. Pollock, *Making Michigan's New Constitution,* 57–61.

42. Ibid.; Norris, "Perspective on the History of Civil Rights Law," 582–83.

43. Norris, "Perspective on the History of Civil Rights Law," 582.

44. Pollock, *Making Michigan's New Constitution,* 57–61.

45. Ibid., 57–61; Norris, "Perspective on the History of Civil Rights Law," 582–83.

46. Scholle v. Hare, 360 Mich. 1, 104 N.W.2d 63 (1960).

47. Scholle v. Hare, 369 U.S. 429 (1962).

48. Scholle v. Hare, 367 Mich. 176, 116 N.W.2d 350 (1962).

49. Ibid., 367 Mich. at 180–81, 116 N.W.2d at 351.

50. Ibid., 367 Mich. at 186–93, 116 N.W.2d at 353–57.

51. Ibid., 367 Mich. at 186–88, 116 N.W.2d at 354–55.

52. Ibid., 367 Mich. at 188, 116 N.W.2d at 355.

53. Ibid., 367 Mich. at 188–89, 116 N.W.2d at 355.

54. Ibid., 367 Mich. at 190–92, 116 N.W.2d at 356–57.

55. Pollock, *Making Michigan's New Constitution,* 57–61.

56. Ibid.

§ 2. Senators, number, term Sec. 2. The senate shall consist of 38 members to be elected from single member districts at the same election as the governor for four-year terms concurrent with the term of office of the governor.

SENATORIAL DISTRICTS, APPORTIONMENT FACTORS

In districting the state for the purpose of electing senators after the official publication of the total population count of each federal decennial census, each county shall be assigned apportionment factors equal to the sum of its percentage of the state's population as shown by the last regular federal decennial census computed to the nearest one-one hundredth of one percent multiplied by four and its percentage of the state's land area computed to the nearest one-one hundredth of one percent.

APPORTIONMENT RULES

In arranging the state into senatorial districts, the apportionment commission shall be governed by the following rules:

(1) Counties with 13 or more apportionment factors shall be entitled as a class to senators in the proportion that the total apportionment factors of such counties bear to the total apportionment factors of the state computed to the nearest whole number. After each such county has been allocated one senator, the remaining senators to which this class of counties is entitled shall be distributed among such counties by the method of equal proportions applied to the apportionment factors.

(2) Counties having less than 13 apportionment factors shall be entitled as a class to senators in the proportion that the total apportionment factors of such counties bear to the total apportionment factors of the state computed to the nearest whole number. Such counties shall thereafter be arranged into senatorial districts that are compact, convenient, and contiguous by land, as rectangular in shape as possible, and having as nearly as possible 13 apportionment factors, but in no event less than 10 or more than 16. Insofar as possible, existing senatorial districts at the time of reapportionment shall not be altered unless there is a failure to comply with the above standards.

(3) Counties entitled to two or more senators shall be divided into single member districts. The population of such districts shall be as nearly equal as possible but shall not be less than 75 percent nor more than 125 percent of a number determined by dividing the population of the county by the number of senators to which it is entitled. Each such district shall follow incorporated city or township boundary lines to the extent possible and shall be compact, contiguous, and as nearly uniform in shape as possible.

57. Specifically, article IV, section 3, of the 1963 constitution provides:

§ 3. Representatives, number, term; contiguity of districts
Sec. 3. The house of representatives shall consist of 110 members elected for two-year terms from single member districts apportioned on a basis of population as provided in this article. The districts shall consist of compact and convenient territory contiguous by land.

REPRESENTATIVE AREAS, SINGLE AND MULTIPLE COUNTY

Each county which has a population of not less than seven-tenths of one percent of the population of the state shall constitute a separate representative area. Each county having less than seven-tenths of one percent of the population of the state shall be combined with another county or counties to form a representative area of not less than seven-tenths of one percent of the population of the state. Any county which is isolated under the initial allocation as provided in this section shall be joined with that contiguous representative area having the smallest percentage of the state's population. Each such representative area shall be entitled initially to one representative.

APPORTIONMENT OF REPRESENTATIVES TO AREAS

After the assignment of one representative to each of the representative areas, the remaining house seats shall be apportioned among the representative areas on the basis of population by the method of equal proportions.

DISTRICTING OF SINGLE COUNTY AREA ENTITLED TO
2 OR MORE REPRESENTATIVES

Any county comprising a representative area entitled to two or more representatives shall be divided into single member representative districts as follows:

(1) The population of such districts shall be as nearly equal as possible but shall not be less than 75 percent nor more than 125 percent of a number determined by dividing the population of the representative area by the number of representatives to which it is entitled.

(2) Such single member districts shall follow city and township boundaries where applicable and shall be composed of compact and contiguous territory as nearly square in shape as possible.

DISTRICTING OF MULTIPLE COUNTY REPRESENTATIVE AREAS

Any representative area consisting of more than one county, entitled to more than one representative, shall be divided into single member districts as equal as possible in population, adhering to county lines.

58. Mich. const. of 1963, art. IV, § 6.
59. Ibid.
60. Ibid.
61. Mich. const. of 1835, art. VI, § 2.
62. Ibid., art. VI, § 1.
63. Ibid., art. VI, § 3.
64. Ibid., art. VI, § 4.
65. Ibid.
66. Ibid., art. VI, § 6.
67. Mich. const. of 1850, art. VI, § 5.
68. Ibid., art. VI, §§ 25–34.
69. Ibid., art. VI, § 2.
70. Ibid.
71. Ibid.
72. Ibid., art. VI, § 3.
73. Ibid., art. VI, § 10.
74. Ibid., art. VI, § 6.
75. Ibid.
76. Ibid., art. VI, § 7.
77. Ibid., art. VI, § 8.
78. Ibid., art. VI, § 13.
79. Ibid., art. VI, § 17.
80. Ibid., art. VI, § 18.

81. Ibid, art. VI, § 23. For a detailed discussion of the purpose of courts of conciliation and the Michigan legislature's experiments with such courts, see *Renaud v. State Court of Mediation and Arbitration,* 124 Mich. 648, 650–53, 83 N.W. 620, 621–23 (1900).

82. Mich. const. of 1908, art. VII, § 23.

83. Ibid., art. II, § 10–21.

84. Ibid., art. VII, § 1.

85. Maddex, *State Constitutions,* 191.

86. Mich. const. of 1908, art. VII, § 2.

87. Ibid.

88. Compare ibid., art. VII § 8, with Mich. const. of 1850, art. VII, § 6.

89. Mich. const. of 1908, art. VII, § 13.

90. Ibid., art. VII, § 14.

91. Ibid., art. VII, § 15.

92. Ibid., art. VII, § 8.

93. Mich. const. of 1963, art. VI, § 1.

94. Ibid., art. VI, § 26.

95. Ibid., art. VI, § 2.

96. Ibid., art. VI, § 3.

97. Ibid., art. VI, § 4.

98. Ibid., art. VI, § 8.

99. Ibid.

100. Ibid.

101. Ibid., art. VI, § 9.

102. Ibid., art. VI, § 14.

103. Ibid., art. VI, § 15.

104. Ibid., art. VI, § 25.

105. Ibid., art. VI, § 26.

106. See Mich. Comp. Laws § 600.6501 et seq.

107. Mich. const. of 1963, art. VI, § 26.

108. Ibid., art. VI, § 28.

109. Ibid., art. VI, § 30.

110. Aaron Gauthier, "Free Exercise Jurisprudence under the Michigan Constitution: Will the Michigan Courts Protect Religious Liberty?" *Thomas M. Cooley Journal of Practical and Clinical Law* 3 (August 1999): 55, 67–74.

111. Mich. const. of 1963, art. VIII, § 2, as amended 1970.

112. Blaine Amendments are state constitutional provisions modeled after a failed amendment to the U.S. Constitution proposed by Senator James G. Blaine that would have banned funding to religious schools. There is no doubt that the movement behind these amendments was highly influenced by anti-Catholic, and to a lesser extent, antiecclesiastical sentiment. The Blaine Amendments were designed to discourage the growth of the Catholic school movement, which evolved in part as a response to the Protestant domination of the common schools and ultimately the early public schools. See Philip Hamburger, *Separation of Church and State* (Cambridge, Mass.: Harvard University Press, 2002), 321–28, 335–42 (explaining that, both

before and after Senator Blaine's failed attempt to amend the U.S. Constitution to prohibit any government funding of religious schools, there was a strong movement that agreed with Senator Blaine's proposal, and that this movement was heavily influenced by anti-Catholic animus).

113. Mich. const. of 1835, art. XII, § 1.

114. Ibid., art. I, §§ 4–6.

115. Mich. const. of 1850, art. XVIII, § 1.

116. Ibid., art. IV, § 24.

117. See, generally, Marsh v. Chambers, 463 U.S. 783 (1983) (upholding Nebraska legislature's practice of having a paid chaplain and pointing out that Congress has paid chaplains as well).

118. This section did, however, add a provision prohibiting the legislature from appropriating property belonging to the state (in addition to money) "for the benefit of [any] religious societ[y], or theological or religious seminar[y]." Mich. const. of 1850, art. IV, § 40.

119. A broad discussion of ceremonial deism is beyond the scope of this chapter. For a basic definition of ceremonial deism and a discussion of that topic, including some sources that suggest that some of the additions to the 1908 constitution go beyond ceremonial deism, see Frank S. Ravitch, *Law and Religion, A Reader: Cases, Concepts, and Theory* (St. Paul, Minn.: Thomson/West 2004), 155–86 and sources cited therein.

120. Mich. const. of 1835, art. X; Mich. const. of 1850, art. XIII.

121. See Mich. const. of 1908, art. II, § 3.

122. Ibid.

123. Ibid., art. V, § 26 (chaplaincy); art. XVI, § 2 (oath of office).

124. Mich. const. of 1963, art. I, § 2; art. VIII, § 2.

125. Ibid., art. VIII, § 2, as amended 1970.

126. Ibid., art. IX, § 4.

127. Ibid., preamble and art. I, §4.

128. Ibid, art. XI, § 1.

129. Ibid., art. I, § 2.

130. Mich. Comp. Laws Ann. § 37.2102 (West 2001).

131. Mich. const. of 1963, art. IV, § 47.

132. Ibid., art. I, § 4.

133. Ibid., art. IX, § 4.

134. See note 103 and accompanying text.

135. See Zelman v. Simmons-Harris, 536 U.S. 639 (2002).

136. Mich. const. of 1963, art. VIII, § 1.

SEVEN

David Dempsey

RUIN AND RECOVERY

Conservation and Environmental Law in Michigan

To some residents of twenty-first-century Michigan, the lush state-owned forests of the northern two-thirds of the state appear a cherished remnant of the state's forest primeval. The approximately 3.9 million acres of state forest land—the largest state system of its kind in the country—is not in fact a wilderness, but a landscape managed for timber harvest, recreation, and environmental amenities. But it is even more remarkable in that it in no way represents, and in many ways does not resemble, the forest primeval that Europeans found on their arrival in the state in the seventeenth century. Instead, this sizable public resource is a second-growth forest that replaced the devastated, cutover, and burned landscape left by the rapacious timber harvest of Michigan's logging era. In that way, the forests are emblematic of much conservation and environmental law in Michigan. An attempt to correct the excesses of industrial, agricultural, municipal, and other development and to overcome the lobbies that fostered those excesses, the laws have sought to heal scars on the state's lands and waters. The state forests, envisioned and brought into being by a relative handful of academics, civic leaders, and professional foresters, also represent the state's tradition of fierce citizen activism on natural resources matters. These two characteristics of the state's conservation and environmental law history continue down to the present day, as citizens and lawmakers struggle with the rapid development of millions of acres of private land and its effect on the water, air, and, other natural resources of the state.

The conservation impulse did not accompany nineteenth-century European settlers into Michigan. The imperative of the pioneers was to subdue and tame the land, not to protect it. Yet, even in the earliest days of Michigan's official life as a territory and state, sometimes prosaic observers turned lyrical upon examining the landscape.

One of the best early nineteenth-century descriptions of Michigan is Henry Rowe Schoolcraft's *Narrative Journey*, recounting an 1820 trip organized by territorial governor Lewis Cass to explore the southern shore of Lake Superior and the headwaters of the Mississippi River.[1] Traveling up the St. Clair River in canoes, Schoolcraft describes the adjacent lands as "rich, and handsomely exposed to the sun . . . Indeed, the succession of interesting views, has afforded us a continued theme or admiration, and we can fully unite in the remark of Baron LaHontan, who passed this strait in 1688, 'that it is difficult to imagine a more delightful prospect, than is presented by this strait, and the little Lake St. Clair.'"

Mackinac Island prompted Schoolcraft to rhapsodize, "There is no previous elevation of coast to prepare us for encountering the view of an island elevated more than three hundred feet above the water, and towering into broken peaks which would even present attractions to the eye of the solitary traveller, among the romantic and sublime scenes of the wilderness of Arkansaw."[2]

If the land excited attention, the wildlife that thrived on it received even greater note. "Game of almost all descriptions was very plenty in the rivers and marshes," George Clark, of Ecorse, said when describing the land adjacent to Grosse Ile, along the Detroit River.[3] "The creeks and swamps teemed with fishes, snakes, frogs, etc. Wolves were very numerous; they would give chase to the deer, and to escape them the deer would run into the river, and when the river was frozen they would slip down, and thus become an easy prey to the wolves all ready to catch and eat them."

Settlers as well as speculators considered land first as an economic resource. It is difficult not to sympathize with them. Back-breaking labor characterized their daily lives; the risk of crop failure threatened their security; and quick-acting, lethal, and poorly understood diseases jeopardized their survival. The first imperative of the settler was to turn the land into something profitable. That meant clearing it as quickly as possible. But the treatment of land as a commodity planted the seeds of the serious land abuses of a later day, long after mere survival had ceased to be the prime motivation.

Robert C. Kedzie, who later joined the first faculty of Michigan Agriculture College and became one of the state's most distinguished citizens, traveled as a child with his family up the Raisin River in October 1826 to a new farmstead in eastern Lenawee County. The new home was deep in the forest. Kedzie's father cut spaces for doors and windows in the log walls, but there was nothing to fill the spaces. The family piled boxes and chests across the openings and hung blankets to bar intruders. "To call the region wild where we had settled was to state the facts tamely. Wild beasts roamed the forests, and wild Indians dominated all, the trees shut out the light of the sky and the murmur of the winds, as they swept through their interlaced branches, was like the moan of far off seas. The mystery and terror of the forest were heart crushing."[4]

The forest was not only a physical obstacle to development and success but also a dark symbol of the frightening wild. Later an outspoken advocate of tree planting, Kedzie recalled how his father axed a white oak four feet in diameter and invited the children outside to "see how it let the sky in." He wrote: "An enemy destroyed! No wonder we came to hate a tree. . . . These forest monarchs with coronals of green and majesty of form appealed in vain to our sense of beauty."

Of all the natural resources evident to the eye, Michigan's fisheries were the first to be ruinously exploited. Fish were so plentiful that they seemed limitless. In the 1870s, commercial fisherman George Clark remembered, "In the Detroit River, about a mile below Woodward Avenue, in the month of May 1829, and a number of years after, S. Gilliot caught and packed five hundred barrels yearly of wall-eyed pickerel, besides what were used and sold fresh." Clark also remembered it was common to catch from one thousand to five thousand whitefish with a single sweep of a seine off Grosse Ile in the lower Detroit River. By the time of his elegy in 1874, Clark said, "[N]ow there are but few points, compared with former fishing, where White Fish can be caught at any amount, and it requires the best of seines and fixtures to catch them."[5]

Commercial fishing was in place in Lake Superior by 1833 and began on Lake Huron in 1835.[6] The tasty Great Lakes whitefish swiftly became the basis for a profitable industry. Between 1830 and 1840, the total commercial fish catch in Michigan more than tripled, to 7 million pounds.[7] On the eve of the Civil War in 1860, the catch climbed to 17.5 million pounds. The industry employed 620 workers in the Lower Peninsula and accounted for $109,838 in value added.

In the second half of the nineteenth century, new technologies and the revaluing of once-discarded species like the lake sturgeon began to undermine the fishery. In the 1870s, the smoking of sturgeon brought the species into commercial demand. The development of sturgeon caviar, the use of sturgeon hides for leather, increased use of sturgeon oil, and the production of carriage glass (isinglass) from a gelatin derived from the swim bladders of sturgeon increased appreciation for the fish. By 1888, a state agency observed, "[t]he once despised sturgeon has become one of the most valuable, commercially, of the many fish that are caught in the great lakes and deep rivers of this state. . . . Nearly every part of it is utilized in some way."[8] The newly discovered commercial uses of the sturgeon increased its slaughter and undermined reproduction. From an 1880 catch of 4.3 million pounds, sturgeon harvests fell in the next twenty years to 140,000 pounds. More than a century later, the species has not recovered.

Whitefish suffered a fate similar to that of the sturgeon, although their more robust rates of reproduction made for a slower decline. Whitefish catches in Lakes Superior, Michigan, and Huron plummeted from 8.1 million pounds in 1885 to 5.3 million pounds in 1893. Catch per net showed an even more marked decline, from 315 pounds per net to 127 pounds per net in the same period, indicating that fishing effort was increasing at the same time catch was declining. In 1885, 58 steamers and 733 smaller boats trolled for whitefish; in 1891, 70 steamers and 1,423 other boats crowded the lakes.[9]

Ignorance was only one factor in the decline of fisheries and other resources. Powerful political lobbies were another. In the late nineteenth century, commercial fishermen exerted considerable muscle in the Michigan legislature, thwarting regulatory efforts. In its first report, on December 1, 1874, Michigan's fish commissioners observed that the catch of whitefish "is very appreciably diminishing, to the evident alarm of the States that border on the lakes, and of the country at large. The causes of this decrease are too transparent for enumeration or designation. The simple mention of the naked fact opens a volume replete with bitter recollections and reproof. Avarice, human greed, regard neither the times nor the modes of capture, and ignorance is their stupid associate and ally. Decay and famine have ever followed, and ever will follow in the footsteps of such a copartnership." Although the commissioners concentrated most of their early efforts on hatching whitefish to replenish the lakes, before long their reports called for stricter regulation as a method of assuring natural reproduction. But their call for legislation requiring the licensing of commercial fishermen met fierce resistance. In 1895, the board blamed the commercial industry for killing its legislative proposal after a favorable report by a joint House-Senate committee on the bill.

In the late 1890s, the frustration of the agency was evident. Noting that the legislature had found it worthwhile to enact strict laws to protect peach orchards from disease, the commissioners said that, in contrast, "the great commercial fisheries of the State are constantly subjected to the most destructive methods of fishing, with the certain prospect that in a short time they will become absolutely extinct."

The 1897 session of the legislature debated the commissioners' proposals for regulations on the number of commercial fishermen and controls on the amount of gear or catch—and defeated them. Punishing the agency for its advocacy, the legislature also slashed the commission's budget by almost 50 percent. For many years, the board of fish commissioners and its successor agencies would stay away from the prickly political issue of Great Lakes fisheries regulation and often from the Lakes themselves, concentrating instead on stocking Michigan's streams with sport fish. Meanwhile, the fisheries of the open Lakes declined to critically low levels.

Wildlife suffered a similar fate. The *Emmet County Democrat* observed on March 29, 1878, that "[g]reat flocks of [passenger] pigeons are seen flying in all directions recently, and almost every man and boy is seen with musket marching towards the woods, and by the way, Will Smith, L.C. and O.N. Watkins went out one day last week on a pigeon hunt and succeeded in capturing about 400 of these beauties." Once the word got out about the sheer number of birds, sportsmen and market hunters from around the Great Lakes region hastened to the area to get their share.[10] One sportsman estimated that of the five thousand "men who pursue pigeons year after year as a business" in the United States, four hundred to five hundred had rushed to the Petoskey area.[11] The passenger pigeon was bringing an unimagined economic boom to the area.

Local folk could find gainful employment hauling pigeons from the nesting area in their wagons, wringing the heads off the birds, and packing the pigeons in barrels. Local entrepreneurs had their hands full supplying the eager hunters with the barrels, providing the ice to keep pigeons fresh, and sending the meat to its destination. In early April 1878, an average of forty barrels of pigeons a day, or about eighteen thousand birds, shipped out from Petoskey.

The passenger pigeon never returned in abundance, and, before long, sightings were so rare that they excited considerable talk. Sportsman W. B. Mershon collected scattered reports in his 1907 book about the passenger pigeon, including a flock of about sixty in Kent County in 1890, one male and two females in Washtenaw County in 1893, and two near Saginaw Bay in 1905, although these may have been Carolina doves. By 1914, the passenger pigeon was globally extinct, likely a victim of the destruction of its habitat by lumbering as well as of the guns of greedy market hunters.

It was the astonishing harvest of timber, however, that awakened the citizenry to the need for reform. Government policies fostered the industry and made many rich. In the 1830s and 1840s, the generosity of Congress reduced the standard government price for land in undeveloped regions to $1.25 an acre and made enormous grants of "swamp lands." Michigan was one of fifteen states that benefited from an 1850 federal act that directed the secretary of the interior to compile lists and plats of swamplands and send them to the governors of the participating states. If the majority of a section was swampland, the state received it.[12] But much of the land classified as swampland from imperfect maps turned out to be productive pine land.

Michigan's state government was equally lavish. The state transferred 750,000 acres of land received from the federal government to the Sault Ste. Marie Canal Company in exchange for the construction of locks. Another act gave liberal land grants to railroad companies as an incentive to extend their lines to undeveloped areas.[13]

Although a large area of Michigan contained marketable stands of pine and other species such as oak, maple, beech, cherry, elm, hemlock, cedar, and balsam, the early speculators and lumbermen had eyes chiefly for the so-called cork pine. Often found on ridges and uplands, these choice trees were the kings of the forest, anywhere from one hundred to three hundred years old and between 120 and 170 feet tall. Trunks were as big as five feet in diameter. Lightweight and featuring creamy-white wood, these trees were of the greatest commercial value.

Although largely untouched into the 1850s, the north woods became the fodder for amazing industrial growth in the next decade. The number of lumber firms in the Lower Peninsula rose from 926 to 1,641 between 1860 and 1870. Employment in the industry jumped from 6,394 workers to

20,575. And the value added to the economy by lumber rose from $1,820,971 to $11,390,940.[14]

The coming of the logging railroads in the late 1870s quickly accelerated the pace of harvest. A Michigan log jobber named Winfield Scott Gerrish, visiting the Centennial Exposition at Philadelphia in 1876, saw a small locomotive and was inspired to build a steam railroad to connect holdings in the Lake George area with the Muskegon River, six miles away.[15] In 1877, while others struggled to haul logs to rivers in poor sleighing conditions, the new Lake George Railroad was able to get its logs to the Muskegon River. Quick to see the benefits of rail over the vagaries of uncertain snow conditions, logging firms constructed thirty-two narrow-guage railroads by 1882, and eighty-nine by 1889.[16]

At the same time, standard-guage railroads also spread across the northern Lower Peninsula and Upper Peninsula. The Pere Marquette reached from Saginaw to Ludington in 1874. The Michigan Central Railroad developed from Detroit to Bay City and along the Lake Huron shore all the way to Mackinaw City. It also ranged from Jackson through Lansing to Saginaw and through West Branch, Grayling, and Gaylord to the Straits of Mackinac in 1882. The Pennsylvania Railroad ran from Grand Rapids through Cadillac to the Straits the same year.[17]

The combination of more efficient transportation and cutting methods boosted harvests dramatically, and "firms formerly cutting three to five million feet a season . . . [were] now cutting thirty to fifty million during a full season." Markets were hungry for Michigan pine as well as other lumber. In the 1870s, more than a hundred mills ran full tilt, around the clock, on the Saginaw River between Saginaw and the river mouth below Bay City.[18] The west shore counties of the Lower Peninsula and Menominee County in the Upper Peninsula sent enormous amounts of wood to Chicago, which in turn passed the lumber on "to inhabitants in a broad fan-shaped swath of land reaching to the Great Plains and beyond."[19] Residents of Nebraska, Kansas, and even Colorado and Wyoming bought wood from the Chicago market to build houses and other buildings. In 1867, the west shore of Lower Michigan produced for these markets 492 million feet of lumber, 84.4 million laths, and 26.8 million shingles with a total value of $7.9 million.[20]

An industry journal pointed out that, although the absolute number of board feet reaped from Michigan forests was still climbing, it took more logs to produce the same amount of timber. Between 1870 and 1879, the length of the average log run down the Tittabawassee River fell from 229 feet to 143 feet. Grand Rapids logs shrank to less than 204 feet. The article noted that, in the previous decade, "clean cutting"—the practice of taking only the high-grade timber and leaving other trees standing—had been succeeded by the practice of taking everything off the land that could produce saw logs. The *Michigan Lumberman* commented: "It stands the lumbermen in hand at this time to hew to the line, and save all their chips, for the time of their harvest in Michigan is drawing to a close and there will soon be but stumps in the field to show where great bodies of valuable pine have been gathered into the storehouse of a nation's need."[21]

After claiming the best pine, the logging industry briefly found wealth in the state's hardwoods, including birch, beech, maple, cedar, and hemlock. The Upper Peninsula, last to be exploited, saluted the end of the white pine era in 1906 but looked forward to a "very big timber cut" nevertheless. The *Houghton-Calumet Sunday Mining Gazette* reported in October 1906 that "[f]or a region in which the white pine is no longer king, and which not so many years ago led all districts as a source of lumber supply, the cut of timber in the upper peninsula of Michigan will foot up a very considerable total during the season now opening, but it will be much less than were the supply of labor adequate to meet demands. . . . [A] far greater number of operators are devoting their attention to hemlock, cedar, mining timber, cordwood, and pulpwood."[22]

The move to hardwoods only postponed the inevitable decline. Before long, absolute timber volume began to fall. In 1870, Michigan ranked first among the states in production of lumber, turning out an amazing 2.25 billion board feet. The state maintained its lead in 1880 and in 1890, hitting a peak of 4.25 billion board feet in the latter year. Then production shrank. In 1899, Michigan fell back to second behind Wisconsin, producing 3.01 billion board feet. In the next five years, production shrank to just more than 2 billion board feet, putting the state in fourth place. By 1920 Michigan was sixteenth in timber production among states, turning out just less than 750 million board feet.[23] The lumber barons who had reaped profit from the forest harvest in many cases now moved on to new fields of plenty, including the still largely unexploited forests of the Deep South and Pacific Northwest. The lumberjacks either followed them or stayed behind and lamented the loss of the good old days.

Angered about the gross waste of a valuable resource, and the consequent impoverishment of large sections of northern Michigan, a citizen reforestation movement arose. A. A. Crozier described the grim scene in Michigan's north. While traveling to farmers' institutes in the region the past two winters, he said, "I think some of you will be as surprised as I was when I say that in traveling nearly two thousand miles through some forty counties in the lumber regions of the State, I cannot now recall having seen in any one place as much as a single standing acre of white pine in good condition." Riding from Manistee on the Lake Michigan shore to Saginaw, he added, he had seen an almost continuous succession of "abandoned lumber fields, miles upon miles of stumps as far as the eye can see."[24]

Such scenes, and the swift abandonment of the north by the lumber in-dustry, fostered a new political consensus that the state had been exploited and cheated. The rage deepened after the failure of a series of attempts to convert the waste lands to farms. In 1899, the legislature created a forestry commission, the forerunner of today's state Department of Natural Re-sources. Charles Garfield, of Grand Rapids, was named president of the three-man panel.[25] Although the commission's work was limited largely to collecting information and launching public education efforts, the legisla-ture also gave it tentative permission to move ahead with the experiment that Garfield and sportsmen had proposed in the 1880s—the first step to-ward the creation of a state forest preserve. The law authorized the com-mission to withdraw from sale up to two hundred thousand acres of state swamplands and tax-reverted lands for this purpose.[26] Working with the state land office, the commission set aside from homestead sales more than a hundred thousand acres in Roscommon and Crawford counties later that year and early in 1900. In May 1901, at the next session of the leg-islature, lawmakers approved a reserve of approximately thirty-five thou-sand acres—the genesis of the modern state forest system.[27]

After ruinous wildfires on the cutover lands of the north, particularly one near Metz that killed dozens in the fall of 1908, citizen advocates re-newed their push for a large system of state ownership and management of the former and future forest lands that would protect them for all time. Their work resulted in the establishment by the legislature of a state Pub-lic Domain Commission that would have "power and jurisdiction" over all public lands and forest reserves and interests, including stream protection and control, forest fire protection, and other matters previously under the autonomous commissioner of the land office, auditor general, and game, fish, and forestry warden. The commission was charged with appraising tax-reverted lands prior to sale. It could take actions to prevent forest fires and to "cause such lands as are unfit for agricultural purposes to be used for forestry reserve purposes," with a *minimum* reserve of two hundred thousand acres. This seed resulted in the flowering of the modern state forestry system.[28]

Meanwhile, citizen advocates had been busy for years trying to rationalize the state's approach to fish and game management. The state's game and fish conservation efforts gained new momentum and significance when citizens united in 1875. Ten clubs from the southern part of the state, including representatives from Allegan County, Battle Creek, Kent County, and the Lake St. Clair Fishing and Shooting Club, met in Detroit on April 28 to form the Michigan Sportsman's Association.

The purpose of the new group was expressly political, although not partisan: "securing the enactment of judicious and effective laws for the protection, at proper time, of wild game of fur, fin and feather, whose flesh affords nutritious food, and the pursuit of which furnishes a healthful recreation, and also all birds that assist the agriculturist and horticulturist in the production of their crops, by the destruction of noxious animals and insects, and the enforcement of all laws for such purposes."[29]

Market hunting was an early target of the association. Seeking to stop the massacre of deer and other game for out-of-state commercial markets, the sportsmen drafted a measure in 1877 banning the transport of most Michigan game across state lines. They modeled the proposed law after statutes enacted in several other states, including Illinois. To win its passage, the association retained an attorney, John L. Burleigh—in less genteel terms, a lobbyist. The state Senate deadlocked on the measure, defeating it on a tie vote. In 1879, the bill cleared the legislature but was vetoed by Governor Charles M. Croswell on grounds that it ran afoul of the interstate commerce clause of the U.S. Constitution.[30]

The Sportsman's Association's next major crusade was for the passage of a law creating a state game and fish warden. The legislation was bitterly disputed for years. After its defeat in 1883, William B. Mershon suggested sarcastically in a letter to the editor of Forest and Stream magazine that association members should come to the next meeting in Jackson and "bring along your member of the legislature and let [him] hear what a fine thing [he] . . . did by defeating our 'Game Warden Bill.'"[31]

The association didn't quit. Elaborating upon the original proposal, association president E. S. Holmes suggested in 1885 that the warden should be independent of politics. If appointed by the state Board of Fish Commissioners, as Holmes proposed, the warden would be immune from the pressures faced by elected officials and by the governor. Nearly fifty years later, the idea finally prevailed: legislation removed the appointment of the director of the state Department of Conservation from the governor's control and vested it in an independent commission.[32] But the legislature of the 1880s was not ready for such a bold step. In its fourth incarnation, a bill establishing the office of state game warden won legislative approval and took effect March 15, 1887. The governor was given power to appoint the warden for a four-year term at a salary of $1,200 per year, plus expenses. Although it was not everything the association had wished, the law made Michigan the first state in the nation to establish a paid state game warden.[33] By the end of the twentieth century, the state was fielding more than two hundred conservation officers, direct descendants of the 1887 game warden, more necessary than ever to fish and wildlife protection. A direct result of citizen organizing, the warden was a national landmark and a monument to the power of persistence.

During ensuing decades, even as the state's public forests rebounded and its and fish and game populations increased, degradation caused by private economic activities, particularly manufacturing, rendered much of southern Michigan ugly and unhealthy. In its report for 1935–36, the state Stream Control Commission stated:

> Uncontrolled sewage discharges and detrimental industrial wastes overload several public water supplies today, and threaten the development of future ones; many natural bathing places are rendered definitely dangerous, while the quality of water at others is periodically questionable; miles of inland streams, as well as the American side of the Detroit River, are so polluted as to offer no suitable habitat for fish, while other stretches of river become the occasional death bed of fish within those limits. At times pollution so taints the flesh of fish so as to render it inedible. Some shoreline resort properties suffer heavy depreciation in value. Hundreds of agricultural interests sustain health hazards and riparian losses while here and there throughout the state inadequate pollution control is evidenced by objectionable odor nuisance, both public and private.[34]

But, in tune with the generally laissez-faire attitude of the governments of its day, the commission pursued a policy of encouragement and voluntary compliance—with legal action only as a last resort. Air and water pollution continued to worsen, particularly after World War II.

The tradition of activism by Michigan sportsmen was more than eighty years old when the 1960s began. A dawning public awareness of the toll inflicted on air, water, and land by industrial pollution fostered a movement for a cleaner environment that resulted in profound changes in Michigan law. Like the sportsmen who had preceded them, the new activists enjoyed the outdoors but were more likely to hike, backpack, or watch birds with binoculars. Many were educated women raised in a tradition of community concern and action. Some spent little time relaxing or vacationing in rural areas but saw evidence in their own urban backyards of intolerable air and water pollution. A growing number were young men and women drawn into the fray by a surge of college campus activism. Some wearing fashionable long hair, others clean-cut, some politely organizing river cleanups, others staging mock executions of automobiles, the young activists added an irreverence and energy to conservation and environmental advocacy—but sometimes annoyed their fishing and hunting allies. As the nation was convulsed by protests against the Vietnam War and stirred by social movements for racial and sexual equality, the new environmental activists were neither hesitant to speak their minds nor patient with policies that many saw as excuses for intolerable conditions. During the 1960s, this movement found new strength, successfully promoting the passage of an air pollution act in 1965 and a $335 million clean water bond approved by voters in 1968.[35]

In early 1970, Joan Wolfe, a citizen leader who founded the West Michigan Environmental Action Council (WMEAC), the state's first major environmental group, joined a statewide coalition of conservationists, unions, legal experts, and citizens passionately aroused by worry about the future of the earth and delivered to Governor William G. Milliken a bill that set the tone for conservation and environmental protection for the rest of the decade. The WMEAC had begun work on the proposed Natural Resources and Environmental Protection Act early in 1969. Writing to Joseph L. Sax, an environmental law professor at the University of Michigan Law School, the group asked for "a new tool to protect the environment" but left most of the details to him.[36] Wolfe asked Representative Peter Kok, of the Grand Rapids area, a Republican, to sponsor the bill. But, although he was sympathetic, Kok suggested that a member of the majority Democratic Party should introduce it. Thus Representative Thomas Anderson, of Southgate, chairperson of the House Conservation and Recreation Committee, agreed to sponsor the bill. Anderson was a wise choice. A five-year veteran of the House and a former engineer at Ford Motor Company, the fifty-one-year-old Anderson was well liked by his colleagues. An active hunter and angler, he was also sensitive to pollution issues. His outdoor credentials and generous manner prevented colleagues from thinking of him as a revolutionary. He played an influential role in most Michigan conservation and environmental legislation until 1982.

Offered in the spring of 1969, House Bill 3055 was a "bombshell," said Wolfe. It authorized any citizen of the state to bring suit to stop the pollution, impairment, or destruction of Michigan's natural resources. Citizens angry with either governmental or private actions that harmed the environment traditionally had little recourse. Unless they were injured directly by the actions—something difficult to prove in most cases—and could resort to common-law remedies, such as nuisance or trespass, they had to rely on the attorney general or local prosecutors to file litigation. In many cases, these officials had political reasons not to sue polluters—or a simple lack of interest. House Bill 3055 in effect deputized any citizen willing to go to court to become a defender of the state's environment. Industries soon began to mobilize against the bill.[37]

George D. Moffett, chairman of the legislative committee of the Michigan Professional Industrial Development Association, wrote Anderson: "As sympathetic as the Association is toward efforts for environmental improvement, those efforts must be carried on without, in turn, destroying the economy of the state. If the bill, as written, ever became law, there'd be no need for anyone, anymore, to feel the slightest concern for further plant development. There wouldn't be any. We believe the machinery already fashioned to control environmental problems has the capabilities of doing it, and doing it well enough without introducing the rights of individuals whose zeal might well surpass their knowledge, or whose motives might not always be quite the purest, to supplement that machinery."[38]

But an unprecedented burst of citizen action outperformed the industrial lobbyists. Hundreds of citizens turned out for field hearings on the bill, impressing legislators. Newspaper editorial opinion heavily favored the legislation. On June 26, the last day of legislative work before the summer adjournment, the Senate took up the bill. Despite rumors of behind-the-scenes attempts by industry representatives to weaken the bill, the Senate briskly struck damaging committee amendments and passed the bill with only three dissenting votes. The House approved the Senate version later the same day. The governor signed into law on July 27, 1970, what has been known ever since as the Michigan Environmental Protection Act, or MEPA.[39]

The effects of the law turned out to be less dramatic than either its supporters or opponents had predicted. It was, instead, a helpful tool for citizens

seeking to hold government accountable for potentially harmful environmental plans. In the first three years after its enactment, author Joe Sax reported, citizens initiated seventy-four MEPA cases: twenty-six were resolved
in favor of the plaintiffs, sixteen in favor of the defendants, and the rest
were still pending. The most frequent subjects of this litigation were industrial air pollution and land development disputes.[40]

MEPA was merely a foretaste of the decade's sweeping environmental
reforms. Before the legislature finished work in 1970, it passed three more
significant environmental measures, including the "truth-in-pollution" law
requested by Milliken after the mercury crisis, an act protecting rivers
whose shorelines were still largely undeveloped, and a law giving the state
power to regulate development along the Great Lakes shoreline.[41]

The rest of the decade saw further impressive advances. Responding to
pressure from WMEAC and other citizen groups, the legislature enacted
the Inland Lakes and Streams Act, regulating development along inland
shorelines in 1972. In 1976, after the legislature balked at approving a deposit
on sales of soda and beer containers to curb roadside litter and promote
recycling, the Michigan United Conservation Clubs organized a petition
drive, placed the issue on the ballot by initiative, and won by an overwhelming two-to-one margin. In 1979, on a narrow vote, the environmental
movement persuaded the legislature to enact one of the nation's toughest
wetland protection statutes.[42]

The trend did not continue through the next two decades. As environmental law matured, critics began questioning the effectiveness of the control statutes, and the state's recurrent economic downturns undermined
funding and staffing of the agencies that implemented and enforced the
laws. A more conservative political climate, which began with the election
of Governor John Engler in 1990, did not favor new environmental laws.
Still, the state's third wave of runaway resource consumption—the rapid
development of private land in southern Michigan—fostered new legislative action whose ultimate significance is, as of this writing, unclear.

A panel appointed by Governor Engler to rank the state's greatest environmental risks reported in 1992 that "the absence of land use planning that
considers resources and the integrity of ecosystems" was at the top of the
list. The report recommended that the state develop a land use plan "to
demonstrate that good land-use design and management can be both
good ecologically and economically."[43]

William Rustem, who had served as Governor William Milliken's environmental policy advisor and had played a part in the debate of the 1970s,

coordinated the study and pressed the Engler administration to follow up on it. But the issue did not rank high on the administration's action list, despite the importance assigned it by the expert panel. The twin issues of urban sprawl and appropriate land use—especially if a state plan was involved—raised ticklish questions with key constituencies of the governor's, associations that represented home builders and realtors. Land use was not yet an issue with tangible public appeal, one for which a governor could marshal broad support.

Urban sprawl entered the Engler lexicon for the first time only when the governor sought to repeal the "polluter pay" law of 1990. The fear instilled in developers and property owners by the law's liability provisions on contaminated sites steered industrial, commercial, and residential projects away from brownfields in older cities and toward greenfields at the urban fringe, Engler argued. Urban mayors and the legislature agreed with him. After passing these changes to the contamination law in 1995, however, the governor and the legislature did little on land use for several years.[44]

State associations and the private sector, however, continued to build awareness of the issue. A September 1995 report by the Michigan Society of Planning Officials (MSPO) attracted considerable attention.[45] Summarizing an assortment of studies prepared by the MSPO and others, the report painted a dire picture of the recent past and the imminent future. The state had lost 7.8 percent of its farmland to development between 1982 and 1992, or an average of ten acres per hour during the decade. In northern Michigan, the rapid division of forest lands into both primary homes and cottages was threatening the physical and biological integrity of forests. In one township in Grand Traverse County that contained extensive state forest land, the number of lots between one and nine acres increased by more than 1,400 percent between 1964 and 1981.

Between 1990 and 2020, the report predicted, the population of Michigan would grow approximately 11.8 percent, but the amount of land consumed by new development would grow between 63 and 87 percent, or an area equal to that of 4.0 to 5.4 average-sized counties. Sprawling development was the reason: large-lot homes in rural areas and large commercial projects in expanding suburbs would alter disproportionate amounts of land. "This report will have succeeded if it alerts the Michigan public to the immense implications of current land use trends and what is at stake. Sprawl, if it is allowed to continue, will inevitably present society with lost opportunities, a variety of social and environmental problems and immense monetary costs," the MSPO concluded.[46]

Whereas the threatened loss of forests, wetlands, and open space moved some citizens, it was the disappearance of farmland that began to stir the legislature. Before that could happen, politicians had to be convinced there was a farmland problem. The Michigan Association of Home Builders argued there was not. The association pointed out that, although the total area of farmland was shrinking, the amount of land in active crop production actually had increased between 1982 and 1992. The association taunted newspapers that had deplored "demonic, rapacious home builders [who] are forcing farmers to sell their family farms for hundreds of thousands and sometimes upwards of a million dollars."

The concerns of farmers themselves finally stimulated legislators to consider the issue seriously. In Macomb County, northeast of Detroit, farmland had dwindled from ninety thousand acres in 1980 to sixty thousand in 2000, with a forecast for twenty-eight thousand for 2020. "My family has been farming in Macomb County for 100 years, and I don't know who thinks it's going to make another 100," said Matthew Pruehs.[47] In 2000, metropolitan Detroit had swollen to more than twelve hundred square miles containing more than five million people. "In fringe townships once dominated by farms, roads are being widened and sewer lines expanded in an attempt to meet the needs of thousands of new homes. Meanwhile in Detroit, open spaces are reappearing amid abandoned homes in the heart of a city that has lost half its population in five decades," the *Detroit News* reported.[48]

Appointed by Governor Jennifer Granholm upon her assumption of office in early 2003, a Land Use Leadership Council cochaired by former governor Milliken and former attorney general Frank Kelley and consisting of interest groups ranging from developers and realtors to local government associations, conservationists, and environmentalists produced a lengthy report in August of that year. Its many recommendations included reforms to the state's land division act and new incentives for the redevelopment of cities, lessening development pressure on outlying areas that include farmland, wetlands, and other open space.[49]

Momentum was building for changes in state policy to preserve farmland and to redesign suburban growth to consume less land. But few predicted that the state would move swiftly to check the breathtaking spread of roads, residential developments, stores, factories, and office buildings into areas characterized for most of the twentieth century by cornstalks, cattails, and trees.

Notes

1. Henry R. Schoolcraft, *Narrative Journal of Travels through the Northwestern Regions of the United States, Extending from Detroit through the Great Chain of American Lakes to the Sources of the Mississippi River, in the Year 1820,* ed. Mentor L. Williams (East Lansing: Michigan State College Press, 1953).

2. Schoolcraft had visited the Arkansas Ozarks in 1818–19.

3. George Clark, "Recollections," *Pioneer Collections,* Report of the Pioneer Society of the State of Michigan, 1876, 501.

4. Robert C. Kedzie, Historical Collections, Michigan Pioneer and Historical Society, 1901, 528.

5. *First Report of the State Commissioners and Superintendent on State Fisheries for 1873–4, Ending December 1, 1874,* appendix, 1875.

6. Frederick Willis Dunbar, *Michigan: A History of the Wolverine State,* 3d rev. ed. (Grand Rapids: W. B. Eerdmans, 1995), 263.

7. Michigan Department of Natural Resources, Fisheries Division, *Michigan Fisheries Centennial Report, 1873–1973,* Fisheries Management Report No. 6, 1973, 49.

8. Michigan State Board of Fish Commissioners, *Ninth Report of State Fish Commissioners,* Michigan State Board of Fish Commissioners, 1888.

9. *Michigan Fisheries Centennial Report, 1873–1973,* 59.

10. Reginald Sharkey, *The Blue Meteor: The Tragic Story of the Passenger Pigeon,* (Petoskey, Mich.: Little Traverse Historical Society, 1997), 5.

11. Henry B. Roney, *American Field,* January 11, 1879, reprinted in W. B. Mershon, *The Passenger Pigeon* (New York: Outing Publishing, 1907), 89.

12. An Act to enable the State of Arkansas and other States to reclaim the "Swamp Lands" within their limits, 9 Stat. 519 (1850).

13. An Act granting to the State of Michigan a Right of Way, and a Donation of Public Land for the Construction of a Ship Canal around the Falls at St. Mary's, in that State, 10 Stat. 35 (1852). For the state acts relating to the transfers, see Dave Dempsey, *Ruin and Recovery: Michigan's Rise as a Conservation Leader* (Ann Arbor: University of Michigan Press, 2001), 27.

14. Barbara E. Benson, *Logs and Lumber: The Development of the Lumber Industry in Michigan's Lower Peninsula, 1837–1870* (Mt. Pleasant, Mich.: Clarke Historical Library, 1989), 100.

15. Rolland H. Maybee, *Michigan's White Pine Era* ([Lansing]: Bureau of History, Michigan Department of State, 1988), 418.

16. Benson, *Logs and Lumber,* 100.

17. Ibid.

18. Irene M. Hargreaves and Harold M. Foehl, *The Story of Logging the White Pine in the Saginaw Valley* (Bay City, Mich.: Red Keg Press, 1964), 43.

19. William Cronon, *Nature's Metropolis: Chicago and the Great West* (New York: W. W. Norton, 1990), 180.

20. "The Lumber Region of Michigan," *North American Review* (July 1868): 94.

21. *Michigan Lumberman* 2, no. 2 (February 1873). See also Dempsey, *Ruin and Recovery*, 34.

22. "Very Big Timber Cut Is Expected," *Sunday Mining Gazette,* October 7, 1906.

23. R. V. Reynolds and Albert H. Pierson, Lumber Cut of the United States, 1870–1920 (Washington, D.C.: Government Printing Office, 1923) 30–33.

24. Michigan Bureau of Labor and Industrial Statistics, "Arbor Day at the Michigan Agricultural College," Fourteenth Annual Report, 1897, 334–43.

25. Garfield may have been the designer of the commission's stationery, which said that the panel "stands for a rational solution of the most important economic problem before the people of Michigan" and that, among other things, the "unparalleled beauty of our state" was at stake. Much of the destruction of the original forest of Michigan, among the finest in the world, was "inexcusable waste," the stationery said.

26. See Dempsey, *Ruin and Recovery*, 55.

27. *Journal of the House of Representatives,* May 28, 1901, 2378.

28. An Act for the Establishment of a Public Domain Commission, 1909 Mich. Pub. Acts 280.

29. Transactions of the Michigan Sportsman's Association for the Protection of Fish, Game, and Birds, 4th Annual Session, January 21–23, 1879.

30. See Dempsey, *Ruin and Recovery*, 41.

31. Quoted ibid., 42.

32. Ibid., 43.

33. Ibid.

34. Ibid., 141.

35. Air Pollution Control Act, 1965 Mich. Pub. Acts 348. The clean water bond act was subsequently repealed.

36. "History of the Michigan Environmental Protection Act," account by Joan Wolfe, August 1970.

37. Ibid.

38. Letter to Thomas J. Anderson, March 6, 1970, State Archives of Michigan.

39. Michigan Environmental Protection Act, 1970 Mich. Pub. Acts 129.

40. "Environmental Citizen Suits: Three Years' Experience under the Michigan Environmental Protection Act," *Ecology Law Quarterly* 4, no. 1 (Winter 1974): 7–8.

41. Now incorporated into the Natural Resources and Environmental Protection Act, 1994 Mich. Pub. Acts 451, and codified at Mich. Comp. Laws § 324.311, §§ 324.30501–15, and §§ 324.32301–15, respectively.

42. Now incorporated into the Natural Resources and Environmental Protection Act, 1994 Mich. Pub. Acts 451, and codified at Mich. Comp. Laws §§ 324.30101–13 and §§ 324.30301–23, respectively.

43. William R. Rustem et al., Public Sector Consultants, Inc., *Michigan's Environment and Relative Risk: Michigan Relative Risk Analysis Project,* 1992.

44. See Dempsey, *Ruin and Recovery*, 268.

45. Michigan Society of Planning Officials, *Patterns on the Land: Our Choices, Our Future* (Rochester: Michigan Society of Planning Officials, 1995).

46. See Dempsey, *Ruin and Recovery*, 281.

47. "State's Farmers Try to Save Space from Hungry Developers," *Detroit Free Press,* February 26, 2000.

48. "Unchecked Sprawl Throws Region into Uncertain Future," *Detroit News,* January 2, 2000.

49. Michigan Land Use Leadership Council, "Michigan's Land, Michigan's Future," http://www.michiganlanduse.org/finalreport.htm.

EIGHT

Ronald J. Bretz

170 YEARS OF A
BALANCING ACT

A Brief History of Criminal Justice in Michigan

Michigan wrote its first constitution in 1835. In the years since then, the criminal justice system has changed dramatically in some respects and very little in others. In terms of substantive criminal law—that is, criminal offenses and their elements—Michigan is still very dependent on the common law, just as it was in 1835. In the area of sentencing and punishment, Michigan has experienced some major changes, particularly in the last twenty-five years.

As for the human component of the system—the judges, prosecutors, and defense counsel—changes have involved mostly growth as the population has expanded and moved throughout the two peninsulas. One concern is that the system of appointment of counsel for indigent defendants has not progressed as far as many believe it should have. Finally, whereas Michigan was once a leader in providing rights to the accused that often either exceeded or anticipated the federal constitutional rights of the accused recognized by the U.S. Supreme Court, in recent years the Michigan Supreme Court has curtailed many of those rights. As the state has matured, the courts and the legislature have dealt with the single most difficult issue in criminal justice: balancing the need to deter crime and maintain order and the need to protect the rights of those accused of crime.

Substantive Criminal Law

During its territorial days, Michigan criminal law consisted primarily of the English common law supplemented by the Northwest Ordinance of 1787. Statutes from other territories and states, predominantly Indiana and Massachusetts, were adopted for use during the territorial period but later rejected after statehood. The only constant was the common law.[1]

The three judges of the territorial Michigan Supreme Court disagreed as to exactly what law made up the common law. Judge Augustus B. Woodward argued that the common law consisted of the written and unwritten law of England before September 3, 1189, the date of the coronation of Richard I, Coeur de Lion. Judge William Woodbridge believed it was the common law of 1776 unaffected by statutes, and Judge Solomon Sibley held that the English statutes in effect in 1776 could be part of the common law, as well.[2]

This disagreement on the source of the common law led to some difficulty in administering the laws in the new territory of Michigan. Judge Woodward complained about the confusion and called for a codified system of laws for Michigan. He pointed to the Ohio legislature's work as a model. Woodward envisioned a "comprehensive code that would displace the common law, rather than piecemeal codes that would subsist with it."[3]

Woodward's campaign fell short. The last major territorial code passed in 1820 consisted of only 119 laws, of which many were simply restatements of earlier statutes and others were supreme court rules of procedure. Woodward's quest for a comprehensive code was an extremely difficult undertaking, and it met much resistance, particularly from members of the bar.[4]

Michigan's longest-serving chief executive was territorial governor Lewis Cass (1813–31). Cass did not support Woodward's campaign for comprehensive codification and spoke against the adoption of "too many laws."[5] Among other reasons, Cass feared that an overabundance of codified laws would interfere with property rights. As a result, when Michigan attained statehood in 1837, it had a number of statutes, but they were secondary to the main source of law: the common law.[6]

Judge Woodward's vision has yet to be realized, particularly with regard to the criminal law. The first penal code was published in 1846, and it is the basis for the current Michigan Penal Code. That code was revised and republished as the Penal Code of 1931, but that revision "simply codified, consolidated and repeated the provisions of the initial code of 1846."[7] Michigan's current penal code has been described as "little more than a list of offenses with ranges of punishment."[8]

The above description of the penal code is apt. With a few limited exceptions, Michigan's statutes generally do not define the listed offenses.[9] As a result, the courts have had to supply the definitions. Consistent with Michigan's historical reliance on common law, the courts have looked to common law for the elements of the statutory crimes. This reliance is also consistent with the Michigan constitution, which provides that the common law is to remain in effect until it is "changed, amended or repealed."[10] Finally, the legislature has explicitly made it a felony to commit "any indictable offense at the common law, for the punishment of which no provision is expressly made by statute."[11]

Although the Michigan statutes make at least an attempt to define some offenses, there is even less statutory language on general criminal law principles and defenses.[12] The courts have had to rely on common law to define such concepts as the meaning of an act, causation, accomplice liability, intoxication, self-defense, and entrapment.[13] As a result of these perceived inadequacies in Michigan's statutory criminal law, there have been two very serious attempts to adopt a comprehensive criminal code envisioned by Judge Woodward. In 1964, two years after the publication of the American Law Institute's Model Penal Code, a committee initiated by the State Bar of Michigan drafted a Proposed Michigan Revised Criminal Code.[14] The proposed code was intended to replace the Michigan Penal Code with a truly comprehensive set of statutes independent of the common law. Although the Michigan House of Representatives passed the code, it failed in the Michigan Senate.[15]

A second attempt to replace the state penal code occurred in 1979, when another state bar committee published the Michigan Second Revised Criminal Code. The second proposed code was introduced in the House of Representatives in 1982 but died at the end of the legislative session.[16] As a result, Michigan's substantive criminal law is in the same general state as it was in 1846: a list of crimes and punishments without much explication.

This is not to say that the substantive criminal law has not changed with the times. It has. For example, the Michigan legislature in 1974 enacted the Criminal Sexual Conduct Act. This comprehensive set of statutes was the first in the country to fully define all sexual offenses and to discard the sexist anachronisms of common-law rape.[17] For example, the Michigan act barred evidence of the rape complainant's past sexual experiences except in limited circumstances, expanded the crime of rape to include male victims, and eliminated both the spousal exemption and the resistance requirement.[18]

In other efforts to keep up with criminal behavior in the late twentieth century, Michigan enacted a comprehensive controlled substances act in 1971 and completely replaced it in 1978.[19] The state legislature also enacted specific retail fraud statutes in 1988.[20]

Punishment

In the early territorial days, maintaining law and order was primarily a function of the military. Territorial punishments ranged from public flogging to death. Debtors were imprisoned. The earliest prisons were blockhouses or dungeons maintained at military forts.[21] Eventually, Michigan got into the prison construction business, building the first state prison at Jackson in 1838. That prison admitted its first prisoner in January 1839.[22]

The state prison at Jackson continued to expand until 1924, when a new prison was built north of Jackson. Designed to house more than five thousand inmates, it became the world's largest walled prison. By 1934, the last of the prisoners were moved from the old to the new prison.[23] The new prison became the State Prison of Southern Michigan and, after extensive renovations, reopened in 1997 as the Southern Michigan Correctional Facility.[24]

The second correctional facility in Michigan, the Detroit House of Correction, was built near Detroit in 1860. It was designed as a workhouse so that prisoners confined there could be gainfully employed. In 1867, women prisoners who had been committed to Jackson were moved to the Detroit House of Correction. For the next one hundred years, all women prisoners were committed to that facility.[25] In the late twentieth century, the Detroit House of Correction was closed. Currently, women prisoners are housed in three locations: the Scott Correctional Facility, the Western Wayne Correctional Facility, and Camp Brighton.[26]

In the beginning, youthful offenders also were committed to the state prison at Jackson. In 1851, it was reported that "five or six boys" were incarcerated at Jackson.[27] The youngest of these boys was reportedly only eleven years old.[28] By 1855, prison inspectors found five boys under fifteen and twenty-nine boys between fifteen and twenty years of age at Jackson. Many called for a "less disgraceful and withering punishment" for these juveniles.[29] Consequently, the legislature in 1855 authorized a House of Correction for Juvenile Offenders. The house was built in Lansing and admitted its first juvenile prisoners in 1856.[30]

In 1877, the state opened a state reformatory at Ionia. The goal of the legislature in authorizing the reformatory was to house young men, particularly first offenders. That goal was not achieved until 1937, when the Department of Corrections initiated a classification system that allowed for the segregation of all juvenile first offenders.[31] The Michigan Reformatory at Ionia was closed in 2001. At the time, it was the oldest physical plant still in use.[32]

As of 1970, there were four prisons operating in Michigan: the State Prison of Southern Michigan, opened in 1839; the Michigan Reformatory, opened in 1877; Marquette Branch Prison, opened in 1889; and the Handlon Correctional Facility, opened in 1958 as the Michigan Training Unit.[33] Three more prisons were opened in the 1970s, followed by an explosion of prison building from 1980 to 2002 during which the state opened thirty-nine new prisons.[34] The prison population increased from 9,079 in 1970 to 48,929 in 2003. The population of Michigan during that same time grew from approximately 8,875,000 to 9,990,000.[35]

There are a number of reasons offered for this remarkable growth in the prison population. First, from 1978 to 2002, the Michigan Controlled Substances Act provided for severe mandatory minimum sentences earning Michigan the distinction of having "the harshest mandatory sentences in the nation."[36] Possession of drugs like cocaine or heroin carried minimum sentences of ten years for 50 to 225 grams, twenty years for 225 to 650 grams, and life without parole for more than 650 grams.[37]

Second, there has been a drastic change in the parole process in Michigan, one that has had the effect of keeping people in prison longer than before. According to the Citizen's Alliance for Prisons and Public Spending (CAPPS), in 1992, the state radically changed the makeup of its parole board and its parole policies. The board itself went from a panel of corrections professionals to one made up of political appointees. As a result, parole rates (the percentage of prisoners granted parole when first eligible) dropped from 68 percent to 48 percent, many more parolees were returned to prison for technical violations and kept in prison for longer periods, prisoners with parolable life sentences were regularly denied parole, and even those granted parole were given release dates months into the future. As a result, in 2003, nearly 35 percent of Michigan prisoners were serving sentences past the first parole eligibility date. In 1991, by contrast, only 16.5 percent of prisoners were not paroled on their earliest release dates.[38]

Michigan instituted parole and probation as alternative punishments some years after the introduction of the first state prison. The state was considered a pioneer in the use of a parole system.[39] In 1885, the governor appointed an advisory board on "pardons, commutation of sentences and 'conditional licenses to go at large.'"[40] Probation first was authorized by statute in 1903 but was not used widely until the adoption of the Uniform Probation Act of 1913.[41]

Sentencing law also has seen a great deal of change, particularly in the last few decades of the twentieth century. In 1857, the legislature authorized the first "good-time" statute. This law was designed to reward prisoners for good behavior by permitting an earlier release from prison.[42] Time off for good behavior could be earned by all prison inmates who someday would be eligible for release. But, in 1978, a voter referendum severely limited the good-time law. Proposal B, as it was then known, denied good time to all inmates convicted of a number of enumerated violent offenses. In 1987, this rule was extended to prisoners convicted of any offense committed on or after April 1, 1987.[43]

In 1982, the legislature instituted a new type of good-time reductions with a system of disciplinary credits. Although this new procedure also involved a reduction in the prison sentence based on good behavior, it was much less generous to the prisoner than the previous good-time law.[44] Since the adoption of legislative sentencing guidelines in 1999, Michigan has had a so-called truth-in-sentencing law that requires all inmates to serve their judicially imposed minimum sentence without any early release based on good behavior.[45]

Traditionally, the trial judge in Michigan had a great deal of discretion in determining what sentence the offender would serve. With rare exceptions, the legislature gave the judge broad discretion in fashioning a sentence within statutory limits.[46] A 1902 amendment to the Michigan constitution of 1850 first authorized the use of indeterminate sentences.[47] Under this scheme, the judge committed the offender to the Department of Corrections for both a minimum and a maximum sentence. The parole board then reviewed the prisoner and his or circumstances just before the expiration of the minimum term to determine whether the prisoner safely could be released on parole.[48] In 1972, the Michigan Supreme Court limited the sentencing judge's discretion slightly by mandating that the minimum sentence could be no more than two-thirds of the maximum sentence. The court found this rule was necessary to give the parole board a reasonable opportunity to exercise its discretion.[49]

A new era of sentencing began in the 1980s in response to concerns about disparity in sentencing.[50] In 1983, the Michigan Supreme Court for the first time permitted appellate review of sentencing. The court held that an appellate court could reverse a sentence if it "shocked the conscience" of the appellate court.[51] In 1990, the court refined the rule to permit appellate reversal of a sentence if it was disproportionate to the offense and the offender.[52] The Michigan Supreme Court also introduced sentencing guidelines in 1984.[53] These first guidelines were based on then-current sentencing practices and recommended a minimum sentence range predicated on the seriousness of the crime and the involvement and background of the offender. The guidelines were updated in 1988 and then replaced by legislative guidelines in 1999.[54]

A discussion of the history of sentencing in Michigan would not be complete without a mention of the death penalty. Michigan was the first government in the English-speaking world to abolish the death penalty by statute.[55] It did so in 1846. Michigan also has a constitutional ban on the death penalty.[56]

Juvenile Offenders

In the nineteenth century, children very rarely were convicted of serious felonies. Those few who were often had their convictions reversed.[57] Following the lead of Illinois, which set up the first juvenile courts in 1899, the Michigan legislature attempted to create its first court for juveniles in 1905. That statute very quickly was held unconstitutional and replaced by a new law in 1907, which set up a juvenile division of the probate court.[58] The act was amended in 1915 to permit the trial in adult court of juveniles over the age of fourteen who were charged with felonies. In 1923, the legislature explicitly permitted the juvenile court to waive jurisdiction over juveniles fifteen years and older who were charged with felonies.[59]

In waiving jurisdiction over the juvenile, the juvenile court judge had to decide that the resources of the juvenile system were inadequate to deal with this particular offender. More particularly, the judge had to find either that the juvenile would not be amenable to treatment in the juvenile system or that the juvenile would be a danger to the public when released from juvenile custody.[60] The key feature of the waiver system was the discretion vested in the juvenile court judge to decide whether to try the fifteen- or sixteen-year-old juvenile as an adult.

The judicial-discretion waiver was the exclusive means for trying a juvenile as an adult from the inception of the law in 1923 until 1988. At that time, the legislature amended the juvenile code as well as the code of criminal procedure. The effect of these amendments was to erode the discretion of the judges. Under the amended provisions, if the juvenile was at least fifteen years old and charged with a serious felony, the prosecutor was given the discretion to decide whether the trial would be in juvenile or adult court. If the trial was in adult court, the judge still retained discretion to sentence the offender either to juvenile probation or to an adult sentence.[61] This procedure became known as "automatic waiver."[62]

The statute was amended again in 1996. First, the amended statute lowered the age for waiver to fourteen. It also removed discretion over some offenses from the prosecutor to the legislature itself. For certain violent felonies, the statute requires that the juvenile be tried and sentenced as an adult; neither the court nor the prosecutor has discretion to choose otherwise.[63] Finally, the amended statute for the first time allows a child of any age to be tried and sentenced as an adult, although the proceedings are to take place in juvenile court. However, if the child is under fourteen, the judge has discretion to sentence the convicted juvenile to juvenile probation, the adult corrections system, or a blended sentence that defers the issue of adult punishment until later.[64]

Based on the statutory amendments, the Oakland County prosecutor in 1997 charged an eleven-year-old boy, Nathaniel Abraham, with first-degree murder. Believed to be the youngest person ever charged and convicted as an adult in a modern democratic society, Abraham's case received international attention.[65] Following the trial, the judge opted to sentence Abraham to punishment in the juvenile system.[66]

The System

Michigan had an organized court system before it became a state. In territorial days, there was one supreme court governed by three judges.[67] The court was supposed to hold quarterly sessions in each county. However, it held sessions only in Detroit because of the difficulty of travel.[68] Eventually, each judge sat in one of the three circuits.[69] In 1815, the first county courts were established. These courts consisted of one chief justice and two associates. Sessions were held twice a year. The courts' jurisdiction included the power to try all offenses that were not capital and to hear appeals from the decisions of justices of the peace.[70]

The county courts were abolished in 1833 and replaced by district courts. The first district court was established in Detroit to hear criminal matters. In 1846, the district courts were abolished and once again became county courts. In 1850, the state was divided into eight judicial circuits, which, in 1897, were increased to forty. Circuit judges were elected to six-year terms and had complete jurisdiction as to that county. In 1857, the supreme court, then consisting of one chief judge and three associate judges, began holding its sessions in Lansing. In 1903, the court expanded to include eight justices.[71] Currently, the court consists of seven justices.

As the court system became established, so did the office of the county prosecutor. The first prosecutor's office was created in 1818, during the territorial period:

> That there shall be in each of the counties of the said territory, a prosecuting attorney to be appointed and commissioned by the Governor, whose duty it shall be to prosecute and defend in the court for that county for which they will be respectively appointed, all suits, whether for or against said territory: and who shall receive such compensation for their services, as the county commissioners of the respective counties shall from time to time deem proper and determine to be paid quarterly out of the treasuries of each county respectively.[72]

Originally the governor appointed prosecutors for their respective counties. These prosecutors also received compensation for their services out of the treasury of each county. In 1850, the prosecutor became an elected office with a two-year term. Under the 1963 constitution, this act was amended to allow for four-year terms.[73]

The Right to Counsel

Michigan historically has been a leader in protecting the rights of those accused of crimes. As early as 1820, Michigan provided by statute for the appointment of counsel at public expense for those accused of crimes.[74] The right to counsel for the accused was contained in Michigan's first constitution[75] and continues today.[76] The supreme court held for a number of years that the statute providing for appointed counsel was permissive. Although the constitution guaranteed the right of the accused to have an attorney, the trial court was not required to appoint one at public expense.[77] Although not required to, trial courts did utilize the statute: in an 1883 case, for example, the supreme court noted that the defendant had an attorney appointed to represent him.[78] However, the court remained steadfast in its interpretation of the statute: criminal defendants had no *right* to counsel at the public's expense.

This all changed on June 4, 1947, when the supreme court adopted a rule providing that indigent criminal defendants had a right to counsel appointed at public expense.[79] This rule made Michigan "a forerunner in the advancement of the principle that an indigent defendant is entitled to have counsel appointed to conduct his defense at the expense of the people."[80] The U.S. Supreme Court did not require the states to provide appointed counsel until the landmark case of *Gideon v. Wainwright* in 1963.[81] The state of Michigan, through its attorney general at the time, Frank Kelley, joined twenty-one other states in an amicus curiae brief encouraging the court to recognize a right to counsel for all indigents charged with felonies.

The Michigan constitution of 1963 also granted convicted persons the right to appeal to the newly created court of appeals. As originally enacted, article I, section 20, provided: "In every criminal prosecution, the accused shall have the right . . . to have an appeal as a matter of right; and as provided by law, when the trial court so orders, to have such reasonable assistance as may be necessary to perfect and prosecute an appeal."[82] Under U.S. Supreme Court precedent, the right to appeal carried with it the right to appointment of appellate counsel for indigents.[83] Once again, Michigan explicitly had provided a constitutional right to counsel on appeal before it was required to do so by the U.S. Supreme Court.

The right to appeal was limited significantly by a voter initiative in 1994. In that year, voters passed a proposal to amend the constitution to eliminate the right to appeal for all those defendants who pleaded guilty.[84] As a result, article I, section 20, was amended to add the following language: "except as provided by law an appeal by an accused who pleads guilty or nolo contendere shall be by leave of the court."[85]

Defendants who plead guilty or nolo contendere can appeal to the court of appeals only by leave of the court: the issue that has not been resolved is whether indigent defendants are entitled to the appointment of counsel to prepare an application for leave to appeal. The Michigan Supreme Court held that there is no state or federal constitutional right to counsel in these circumstances.[86] The U.S. Court of Appeals for the Sixth Circuit however, held in 2003 that Michigan's practice of denying appointment of counsel to prepare petitions for appeal for indigents who plead guilty or nolo contendere was a denial of due process.[87] In 2004, the U.S. Supreme Court reversed the decision of the Court of Appeals on a procedural issue. Although the Supreme Court did not express an opinion on the counsel issue, the decision had the effect of erasing the lower courts' decisions finding a right to counsel.[88]

Historically, lawyers appointed to represent indigents either at trial or on appeal were private practitioners who agreed to accept whatever fee the court offered. There generally was no guarantee that the appointed lawyer would be an experienced criminal defense practitioner. The 1960s saw a national movement toward the creation of public defender offices. These offices were staffed with attorneys who did nothing but represent criminal defendants and who typically developed an expertise in defense work.

Although Michigan was one of the first states in the country to authorize the appointment and compensation of defense counsel for indigents accused of crimes,[89] it was ranked forty-ninth in the nation in a 2001 survey of state funding for court-appointed defense counsel.[90] In 2004, only six of Michigan's eighty-three counties had trial-level public defender offices: Wayne, Kent, Washtenaw, Bay, Alpena, and Chippewa,[91] the first of which came into existence in the late 1960s. There is also a statewide public defender office for appeals, the State Appellate Defender.

Beyond these relatively few public defender offices, private attorneys and law firms assume the responsibility for most of the indigent cases. The state does not set a fee schedule to pay public defenders or court-appointed counsel for trial court work, and the burden of compensation falls on the counties individually.[92] Michigan is one of only four states that require the counties to bear the entire cost of court-appointed defense counsel at the trial level.[93]

As a result, a recent president of the State Bar of Michigan has described the current system of compensation for court-appointed defense counsel as an embarrassment:

> The reality is that the burden of indigent criminal defense in
> Michigan largely falls on the backs of a few lawyers who often
> work at outdated and indefensible rates of pay. It is these over-
> worked and underpaid lawyers who define the criminal defense
> system in Michigan, since the indigency rate among criminal de-
> fendants in Michigan courts, as elsewhere, has been close to 90
> percent for many years.[94]

The Exclusionary Rule and Other Constitutional Protections

Certainly one of the most controversial procedural rules in the criminal justice arena is the exclusionary rule. The concept is well-known: if the government violates a suspect's rights in obtaining evidence, the government is prohibited from using that evidence against that suspect in court. The U.S. Supreme Court created the rule in the 1914 case of *United States v. Weeks* in order to deter the government from violating the Fourth Amendment's search and seizure restrictions.[95] However, the Court applied the rule only to federal courts. The Court did not order state courts to observe the exclusionary rule until 1957.[96]

Michigan did not wait for the U.S. Supreme Court to impose the exclusionary rule on the states. In 1919, the Michigan Supreme Court became the first state after the *Weeks* decision to adopt an exclusionary rule.[97] In the Prohibition-era case of *People v. Marxhausen,* the police and other officials entered the defendant's home with a search warrant and without permission of the defendant who was not at home during the time.[98] The police discovered a number of bottles of liquor and seized them. At his trial for illegal possession of intoxicating liquor, the trial court dismissed the charge and ordered the liquor returned to the defendant. Relying on *Weeks,* the Michigan Supreme Court upheld the trial court's actions because the police had violated the prohibition on unreasonable searches and seizures under both the Michigan and federal constitutions.[99]

In 1933, the state supreme court upheld the trial court's exclusion of a firearm seized during an illegal search. The court's ruling resulted in the dismissal of firearms possession charges against two defendants.[100] The legislature responded by proposing a constitutional amendment to bar the exclusion from evidence of "any firearm, rifle, pistol, revolver, automatic pistol, machine gun, bomb, bomb shell, explosive, blackjack, slingshot, billy, metallic knuckles, gas-ejecting device, or any other dangerous weapon or thing, seized by any peace officer outside the curtilage of any dwelling house in this state."[101] The proposal was ratified in 1936. In 1952, the provision was amended to include "any narcotic drug or drugs," and the final list became a permanent part of the Michigan constitution.[102]

From the ratification of the 1936 amendment until the decision in *Mapp v. Ohio,*[103] in 1961, the Michigan Supreme Court refused to suppress any of the listed items even when the court found the items had been seized in violation of the constitution.[104] After *Mapp,* however, the court acknowledged the supremacy of federal law. The court now views the Michigan constitutional limitation on the exclusionary rule as a prohibition on the Michigan courts from extending the exclusionary rule beyond the scope required by the U.S. Supreme Court under the Fourth Amendment.[105]

The idea that a state supreme court can interpret the state constitution to set standards of protection for its citizens that are higher than those of similar provisions in the federal Constitution is well accepted. In Michigan, there have been a number of cases in which the state supreme court decided that the state constitution provided greater rights than its federal counterpart. For example, whereas the U.S. Supreme Court has held that drunk-driving checklanes do not violate the Fourth Amendment,[106] the Michigan Supreme Court has held that these police stops do violate the corresponding Michigan constitutional provision.[107] Similarly, although the failure of the police to inform an in-custody suspect of a lawyer's attempts to contact him prior to interrogation does not violate the Fifth Amendment,[108] it does violate the corresponding Michigan constitutional provision.[109]

The list of examples used to be much longer. Since about 1990, however, the Michigan Supreme Court has overturned a number of other decisions that had interpreted the Michigan constitution as providing individuals greater protections from police power. In 1975, for example, the court had found that police use of electronic eavesdropping with the consent of one of the participants was a "search" under the state constitution.[110] In doing so, the court rejected U.S. Supreme Court authority to the contrary.[111] Subsequently, in 1991, the Michigan court overruled its earlier decision because there was not a "compelling reason" to impose a rule different than the federal Constitution.[112]

Similarly, in 1997, the Michigan Supreme Court had held that the smell of marijuana alone is not sufficient for a police officer to form probable cause that marijuana currently is present.[113] That decision was overruled by the same court just three years later.[114] The latter court cited U.S. Supreme Court decisions from 1932 and 1948 in which the Court had found that odor alone (whiskey and opium) could indeed lead to probable cause.[115]

In 2004, the Michigan Supreme Court overruled two thirty-year-old precedents in reinterpreting the Michigan constitution. In a double jeopardy case, the court held that its earlier decision giving Michigan residents greater protection from double jeopardy was incorrect. The court instead adopted the federal constitutional rule as interpreted by the U.S. Supreme Court.[116] In the second case, the Michigan Supreme Court revisited its 1973 decision giving a suspect in custody the right to counsel at all pretrial identification proceedings.[117] In the 2004 case, the court adopted the U.S. Supreme Court's interpretation that counsel is required only for lineups held after formal charges have been filed.[118] Finally, in 2004, the court for the first time adopted the U.S. Supreme Court's good-faith exception to the exclusionary rule.[119] This exception permits the state to use illegally seized evidence if, at the time of the seizure, the police reasonably relied on a defective warrant issued by a magistrate.

Rights of Crime Victims

Michigan also has been a forerunner in the area of crime victim's rights. In 1985, the Michigan legislature passed the Crime Victim's Rights Act.[120] Three years later, the state amended its constitution to add a section on the rights of crime vitims.[121] Both the statute and the constitutional provision were designed to enumerate the rights of victims of crimes and to ensure that the victims receive adequate restitution.[122]

The victim's rights statute is quite lengthy and detailed, but the constitutional provision is more concise. It lists the following rights:

> The right to be treated with fairness and respect for their dignity and privacy throughout the criminal justice process.
>
> The right to timely disposition of the case following arrest of the accused.
>
> The right to be reasonably protected from the accused throughout the criminal justice process.
>
> The right to notification of court proceedings.
>
> The right to attend trial and all other court proceedings the accused has the right to attend.
>
> The right to confer with the prosecution.
>
> The right to make a statement to the court at sentencing.
>
> The right to restitution.
>
> The right to information about the conviction, sentence, imprisonment, and release of the accused.[123]

No one seriously questions the government's right to control crime and to punish offenders. Beyond that, there is little consensus on how to carry out this governmental duty. The conflict is as old as the law itself. The criminal law serves the essential purpose of imposing punishment on wrongdoers, but there are different philosophies of punishment. Some believe punishment should serve utilitarian purposes, such as deterrence of crime and rehabilitation of the offender. Others believe that the purpose of punishment is retribution: we punish the offender because it is deserved.[124] In the modern criminal justice system, both philosophies play a role, although, as Michigan history shows, time and politics tend to shift the emphasis back and forth.

In Michigan, as in most other states, the administration of the criminal justice system has involved a balancing act. The politicians in the courts and legislature who set criminal justice policy have oscillated between a concern for fairness and protection for those accused and convicted of crimes and a concern for the victims of crime and their perceived need for retribution.

Changing political attitudes over time have dramatically affected the criminal justice system. Although political inaction in the legislature has kept most of the 170-year-old, common-law-based penal code intact, political pressure has brought about the piecemeal updating of that penal code with a number of new crimes. The elected state supreme court has issued inconsistent interpretations of the substantive law as its membership has changed with election cycles and gubernatorial appointments. Finally, the courts, the legislature, and the voters have combined to modify the procedural and administrative facets of the criminal justice system.

Because the control and management of the criminal justice system is a function of government, it is inevitable that policies will change as governments change. The Michigan criminal justice system has undergone many changes and likely will continue to do so. However, future decision makers should heed the words of Ben Franklin: "All human situations have their inconveniences. We feel those of the present but neither see nor feel those of the future; and hence we often make troublesome changes without amendment, and frequently for the worse."[125]

Notes

The author would like to thank Melissa Armbrister and Tim Innes for their invaluable assistance in the preparation of this chapter.

1. Richard P. Cole, "Law and Community in the New Nation: Three Visions for Michigan, 1788–1831," *Southern California Interdisciplinary Law Journal* 4 (Winter 1995): 161, 230–31; William Wirt Blume, "Criminal Procedure on the American Frontier: A Study of the Statutes and Court Records of Michigan Territory," *Michigan Law Review* 57, no. 2 (December 1958): 195.

2. Blume, "Criminal Procedure on the American Frontier," 245–46.

3. Cole, "Law and Community in the New Nation," 207.

4. Ibid.

5. Ibid., 228.

6. Ibid., 230.

7. Jerold H. Israel, "The Process of Penal Law Reform" *Wayne Law Review* 14, no. 3 (Summer 1968): 769, 773–74.

8. Alan Saltzman, "The Proposed Revision of the Michigan Penal Code: A Rejection of Judicially Developed Principles of Justice in the Grading of Homicide," *University of Detroit Journal of Urban Law* 60, no. 4 (Summer 1983): 507, 511.

9. See, for example, 2002 Mich. Pub. Acts 2650, Michigan's Criminal Sexual Conduct Act, codified at Mich. Comp. Laws §§ 750.520a–l, a series of statutes that list and define most sexual assault offenses. However, as Saltzman points out, even these statutes are incomplete with regard to the mens rea, or mental element, of some of the offenses. Saltzman, "Proposed Revision of the Michigan Penal Code," 511n36.

10. Mich. const. of 1963, art. III, § 7.

11. An Act to revise, consolidate, codify and add to the statutes relating to crimes . . . , 1954 Mich. Pub. Acts 79, codified at Mich. Comp. Laws § 750.505.

12. Saltzman, "Proposed Revision of the Michigan Penal Code," 512–13.

13. Ibid.

14. Israel, "Process of Penal Law Reform," 773.

15. Saltzman, "Proposed Revision of the Michigan Penal Code," 508n4.

16. Ibid.

17. An Act to revise, consolidate, codify and add to the statutes relating to crimes . . . , 1974 Mich. Pub. Acts 1025, codified at Mich. Comp. Laws §§ 750.520 et seq.; Note, "Focusing on the Offender's Forceful Conduct: A Proposal for the Redefinition of Rape Laws," *George Washington Law Review* 56 (January 1998): 399.

18. 1974 Mich. Pub. Acts 1025, codified at Mich. Comp. Laws §§ 750.520 et seq.

19. Controlled Substance Act of 1971, 1971 Mich. Pub. Acts 608 (repealed), formerly codified at Mich. Comp. Laws §§ 335.301 et seq.; Public Health Code, 1978 Mich. Pub. Acts 865, codified at Mich. Comp. Laws § 333.7401.

20. An Act to revise, consolidate, codify and add to the statutes relating to crimes . . . , 1988 Mich. Pub. Acts 34, codified at Mich. Comp. Laws § 750.356c–d.

21. Willis Frederick Dunbar, *Michigan through the Centuries* (New York: Lewis Historical Publishing, 1955), 605.

22. Ibid., 606.

23. Ibid., 608.

24. Michigan Department of Corrections (MDOC), "Southern Michigan Correctional Facility," http://www.michigan.gov/corrections/1,1607,7-119-1381_1385-5357--,00.html.

25. Dunbar, *Michigan through the Centuries*, 607.

26. Michigan Department of Corrections, 2003 Statistical Report, 123, 125.

27. Dennis Thavenet, "'Wild Young 'uns' in Their Midst': The Beginnings of Reformatory Education in Michigan," *Michigan History* 60 (Fall 1976): 240, 241.

28. Ibid.

29. Ibid., 242.

30. Ibid., 248.

31. Dunbar, *Michigan through the Centuries,* 607.

32. Michigan Department of Corrections, 2001 Annual Report, 49 (note that the report said the facility was closed only temporarily; a recent *Detroit News* article pegged the cost of the job at $19 million).

33. Ibid.

34. Ibid.

35. Michigan Department of Corrections, 2001 Statistical Report, 110.

36. Families against Mandatory Minimums, http://www.famm.org/si_sent_by _state_michigan.htm.

37. Public Health Code, 1978 Mich. Pub. Acts 976, codified at Mich. Comp. Laws § 333.7403, amended by 2002 Mich. Pub. Acts Nos. 655 and 710. The statute was substantially amended in 2002, eliminating the life sentence without parole and restoring judicial discretion.

38. CAPPS: Citizens Alliance on Prisons and Public Spending, "The High Cost of Denying Parole: An Analysis of Prisoners Eligible for Release," http://www.capps-mi .org/pdfdocs/fulldatareport.pdf.

39. Dunbar, *Michigan through the Centuries,* 611.

40. Ibid.

41. Ibid., 611–12.

42. Ibid., 611.

43. See Lowe v. Dept. of Corr., 206 Mich. App. 128, 131–33, 521 N.W.2d 336, 337–38 (1994).

44. Ibid., 133, 521 N.W.2d 337.

45. Justin Brooks, "The Politics of Prisons," *Michigan Bar Journal* 77 (February 1998): 154; Sheila Robertson Deming, "Michigan's Sentencing Guidelines," *Michigan Bar Journal* 79 (June 2000): 652.

46. For example, the statutory penalty for first-degree murder is a mandatory sentence of life in prison with no parole. Michigan Penal Code, 1931 Mich. Pub. Acts 688, codified at Mich. Comp. Laws § 750.316. Note: The provision making this offense nonparolable was added later by An Act to revise, consolidate, codify and add to the statutes relating to crimes . . . , 1953 Mich. Pub. Acts 34, codified at Mich. Comp. Laws § 791.234(4).

47. Mich. const. of 1850, art. IV, § 47. The current constitution contains the same provision as article IV, § 45: "The legislature may provide for indeterminate sentences as punishment for crime and for the detention and release of persons imprisoned or detained under such sentences." Mich. const. of 1963, art. IV, § 45.

48. Dunbar, *Michigan through the Centuries,* 611.

49. People v. Tanner, 387 Mich. 683, 687–89, 199 N.W.2d 202, 203–4 (1972).

50. Deming, "Michigan's Sentencing Guidelines," 652.

51. People v. Coles, 417 Mich. 523, 339 N.W.2d 440 (1983).

52. People v. Milbourn, 435 Mich. 630, 461 N.W.2d 1 (1990).

53. Admin. Order 1984-1, 418 Mich. lxxx (1984).

54. Deming, "Michigan's Sentencing Guidelines," 652–53.

55. Eugene Wanger, "Historical Reflections on Michigan's Abolition of the Death Penalty," *Thomas M. Cooley Law Review* 23 (Michaelmas 1996): 755.

56. Mich. const. of 1963, art. IV, § 46.

57. Frank E. Vandevoort and William E. Ladd, "The Worst of All Possible Worlds: Michigan's Juvenile Justice System and the International Standards for the Treatment of Children," *University of Detroit Mercy Law Review* 78 (Winter 2001): 203, 208.

58. Ibid., 215–18; People v. McFarlin, 389 Mich. 557, 208 N.W.2d 504 (1973); An act to regulate the treatment and control of dependent, neglected and delinquent children, 1907 Mich. Pub. Acts 463, and An act to define, and regulate the treatment and control of delinquent children, 1907 Mich. Pub. Acts 42.

59. Vandevoort and Ladd, "Worst of All Possible Worlds," 218.

60. Probate Code of 1939, 1939 Mich. Pub. Acts 558, codified at Mich. Comp. Laws §§ 712a.1–4; People v. Dunbar, 423 Mich. 380, 385–86, 377 N.W.2d 262, 263–64 (1985).

61. Vandevoort and Ladd, "Worst of All Possible Worlds," 224; Judgment and Sentence, 1927 Mich. Pub. Acts 322, codified at Mich. Comp. Laws § 769.1.

62. Vandevoort and Ladd, "Worst of All Possible Worlds," 225.

63. Ibid., 227–28.

64. Ibid.

65. Infoplease, "Nathaniel Abraham," http://www.infoplease.com/ipa/A0781581.html.

66. CNN.com, "Michigan Judge Sentences Boy Killer to Juvenile Detention," http://archives.cnn.com/2000/US/01/13/abraham.sentencing.03/.

67. W. L. Jenks, "Judicial System of Michigan under Governors and Judges," *Michigan Law Review* 18, no. 1 (November 1919): 20.

68. Blume, "Criminal Procedure on the American Frontier," 238.

69. Jenks, "Judicial System of Michigan," 18.

70. Ibid., 24–25.

71. Blume, "Criminal Procedure on the American Frontier," 545–46.

72. Act Concerning the Attorney General and Prosecuting Attorneys, 1 Laws of the Territory of Michigan, § 1 (1818).

73. Mich. const. of 1963, art. VII, § 4.

74. An act regulating proceedings in criminal cases, Territorial Laws Michigan, vol. 1 (1820), 589, 590.

75. Mich. const. of 1835, art. I, § 10.

76. Mich. const. of 1963, art. I, § 20.

77. People v. Williams, 225 Mich. 133, 195 N.W. 818 (1923); In re Elliott, 315 Mich. 662, 24 N.W.2d 528 (1946).

78. People v. Murray, 52 Mich. 288, 17 N.W. 843 (1883).

79. Criminal Procedure—Arraignment and Sentencing, Michigan Court Rules Annotated Rule 35-A (adopted June 4, 1947; effective September 1, 1947).

80. People v. LaMarr, 1 Mich. App. 389, 393, 136 N.W.2d 708, 709 (1965).

81. Gideon v. Wainwright, 372 U.S. 335 (1963). In 1972, however, the Michigan Supreme Court adopted the federal constitutional rule announced in *Argersinger v. Hamlin,* 407 U.S. 25 (1972), limiting the right to counsel in misdemeanor cases to

those defendants who could actually be incarcerated as a result of their misdemeanor conviction. People v. Studaker, 387 Mich. 698, 199 N.W.2d 177 (1972). See also Mich. Court Rule 6.610(D)(2):

> (2) An indigent defendant has a right to an appointed attorney whenever
> (a) the offense charged requires on conviction a minimum term in jail, or
> (b) the court determines that it might sentence the defendant to jail.
> If an indigent defendant is without an attorney and has not waived the
> right to an appointed attorney, the court may not sentence the defendant to jail.

82. Mich. const. of 1963, art. I, § 20.

83. Douglas v. California, 372 U.S. 353 (1964).

84. Note, "Limiting Michigan's Guilty and Nolo Contendere Appeals," *University of Detroit Mercy Law Review* 73 (Spring 1996): 431.

85. Ibid.

86. People v. Bulger, 462 Mich. 495, 614 N.W.2d 103 (2000).

87. Tesmer v. Granholm, 333 F.3d 683 (2003).

88. Kowalski v. Tesmer, 543 U.S. 125 (2004).

89. An act regulating proceedings in criminal cases, Territorial Laws Michigan, vol. 1 (1820), 595, § 22.

90. Bruce Neckers, "It's a Crime: Michigan's System of Compensation for Criminal Defense of the Indigent Is Inadequate," *Michigan Bar Journal* 81 (January 2002): 8.

91. Michigan Council on Crime and Delinquency, "Model Plan for Public Defense Services in Michigan," http://www. abanet.org/legalservices/downloads/sclaid/indigentdefense/mi-modelplan.pdf, 4.

92. Neckers, "It's a Crime," 8.

93. Michigan Council on Crime and Delinquency, "Model Plan," 5.

94. Neckers, "It's a Crime," 8.

95. Weeks v. U.S., 232 U.S. 383 (1914).

96. Mapp v. Ohio, 352 U.S. 432 (1961).

97. U.S. Dept. of Justice, Office of Legal Policy, *Report to the Attorney General on the Search and Seizure Exclusionary Rule* ([Washington, D.C.]: [Supt. of Docs., U.S. G.P.O., distributor, 1988]), 5–18.

98. People v. Marxhausen, 204 Mich. 559, 171 N.W. 557 (1919).

99. Ibid., 561–67, 171 N.W. 557–59. The court based its holding on both the Fourth Amendment to the U.S. Constitution and the parallel provision in the Michigan constitution. Mich. const. of 1908, art. II, § 10.

100. People v. Stein, 256 Mich. 610, 251 N.W. 788 (1933).

101. 1935 Joint Resolution No. 2, Unreasonable searches and seizures; admission of evidence of firearms seized outside of dwelling house, 1935 Mich. Pub. Acts 468.

102. Mich. const. of 1963, art. I, § 11.

103. Mapp v. Ohio, 352 U.S. 432 (1961).

104. See, e.g., People v. Gonzales, 356 Mich. 247, 97 N.W.2d16 (1959); People v. Winkle, 358 Mich. 551, 100 N.W.2d 309 (1961).

105. People v. Pennington, 383 Mich. 611, 178 N.W.2d 471 (1970); People v. Moore, 391 Mich. 426, 216 N.W.2d 770 (1974).

106. Michigan v. Sitz, 496 U.S. 444 (1990).

107. Sitz v. Dep't. of State Police, 443 Mich. 744, 506 N.W.2d 209 (1993).

108. Moran v. Burbine, 475 U.S. 412 (1986).

109. People v. Bender, 452 Mich. 594, 551 N.W.2d 71 (1996).

110. People v. Beavers, 393 Mich. 554, 227 N.W.2d 511 (1975).

111. U.S. v. White, 401 U.S. 745 (1971). See also a discussion of these cases in Alan Saltzman, "The Michigan Supreme Court's Abdication of Authority over Criminal Prosecutions," *University of Detroit Mercy Law Review* 80 (Spring 2003): 281, 286–87.

112. People v. Collins, 438 Mich. 8, 475 N.W.2d 684 (1991).

113. People v. Taylor, 454 Mich. 580, 464 N.W.2d 24 (1997).

114. People v. Kazmierczak, 461 Mich. 411, 605 N.W.2d 667 (2000).

115. Taylor v. U.S., 286 U.S. 1 (1932); Johnson v. U.S., 333 U.S. 10 (1948).

116. People v. Nutt, 469 Mich. 565, 677 N.W.2d 1 (2004), *overruling* People v. White, 390 Mich. 245, 212 N.W.2d 222 (1973).

117. People v. Anderson, 389 Mich. 155, 205 N.W.2d 461 (1973).

118. U.S. v. Wade, 388 U.S. 218 (1967); Kirby v. Illinois, 406 U.S. 682 (1972).

119. People v. Goldston, 467 Mich. 939, 655 N.W.2d 232 (2004).

120. Order of restitution generally, as condition of parole, revocation of probation or parole, 1985 Mich. Pub. Acts 185, codified at Mich. Comp. Laws, § 780.766.

121. Mich. const. of 1963, art. I, § 24.

122. People v. Peters, 449 Mich. 515, 537 N.W.2d 160 (1995).

123. Mich. const. of 1963, art. I, § 24.

124. See Joshua Dressler, *Understanding Criminal Law* (New York: Matthew Bender, 2001), 13–23.

125. Benjamin Franklin, *The Works of Benjamin Franklin* (New York: G. P. Putnam's Sons, 1904), 176.

NINE

Paul Finkelman

THE PROMISE OF EQUALITY AND THE LIMITS OF LAW

From the Civil War to World War II

Legislative enactments serve a variety of functions in society. Most obviously, they are designed to tell people within a community how to behave and to provide sanctions for those who misbehave. Laws also make available services and opportunities for people within a community. Furthermore, laws tell the community—and indeed the larger world—what a society thinks of itself, what it believes in, and what it stands for. Finally, in reflecting a society's aspirations, laws are educational tools. They instruct citizens, immigrants, and visitors about the nature of a society. The history of civil rights laws and litigation in Michigan, from the end of the Civil War to the end of World War II, reflects all of these aspects of legislation.

This essay does not examine developments beyond World War II, in part because that period signaled a new era in civil rights at the state and national levels. Shortly after the war, decisions by the U.S. Supreme Court and legislation passed by Congress led to a nationalization of civil rights. It also signaled a new age in Michigan, as the state adopted a new civil rights act in 1948. That year, governor-elect G. Mennan "Soapy" Williams promised to implement the recommendations of the President's Commission on Civil Rights with the "'immediate creation' of a state commission that he [Williams] would assign the responsibility of developing a legislative and educational program 'to eliminate discrimination throughout the state,' including discrimination in employment."[1] Shortly after taking office, Williams appointed the Governor's Advisory Committee on Civil Rights, which set Michigan on the road to new legislation and new constitutional provisions to secure civil rights for all residents of the state. These changes ultimately included the state's Fair Employment Practices Act in 1955[2] and new civil rights provisions in the 1963 state constitution.[3] These changes in Michigan law were part of a new postwar dynamic in the state and the nation. But, as the rest of this chapter demonstrates, the expansion of civil rights in the mid-twentieth century was also consistent with Michigan's earlier history and its nineteenth-century commitment to civil rights.

The history of Michigan's law and legislation on race, in many ways, is quite remarkable. As Roy Finkenbine has set out in greater detail in this book, even before the Civil War Michigan provided legal protections to African Americans that they could not find elsewhere in the Midwest. After the Civil War, Michigan's legislators and courts marched steadily forward to expand civil rights and to protect basic liberties for all residents of the state. The enforcement of these laws, however, never matched the aspirations of their makers, but the repeated attempts by the legislature to create equality in the state are a significant legacy. The failure of these laws to achieve the goals of equality, on the other hand, illustrates the limitations of law, by itself, in changing social mores. Racism in Michigan could not be eradicated easily or immediately through legislation, prosecution, or civil lawsuits. On the other hand, the persistent efforts of the Michigan legislature led to greater equality and greater opportunity for African Americans than they had in most other states. The laws, even if not always successfully enforced or implemented, provided blacks in Michigan with useful tools as they and their white allies struggled for greater equality in the century after slavery came to an end.

Striving for Equality in Midcentury Michigan

On the eve of the Civil War, Michigan offered freedom to African Americans and some limited legal protections.[4] Slavery had been illegal since the territorial period, and the constitutions of 1835 and 1850 emphatically supported this position. Under federal law, fugitive slaves could be seized and removed from the state, but slave catchers coming to antebellum Michigan risked the hostility of a population, mostly of Yankee origin, that was deeply opposed to human bondage. Fugitive slaves or free blacks who were able to reach Michigan were relatively secure from capture. Michigan's location in the north made it virtually impossible to remove blacks, fugitive or free, because the nearest slave states—Virginia and Kentucky—were hundreds of miles away. Moreover, fugitive slaves living in Detroit found a hospitable community of free blacks and white abolitionists in nearby Canada.[5] If slave catchers searched for runaway slaves in Detroit, the fugitives from the South knew they could easily and quickly cross the Detroit River to a land where liberty was protected—ironically, from the American perspective—by the sovereignty of Queen Victoria. Furthermore, some whites in Michigan were willing to protect fugitive slaves, even at the risk of being sued under the federal fugitive slave acts of 1793 and 1850.[6] Some white abolitionists and many African Americans in the state were willing to take even greater risks to secure black freedom simply because they found slavery so morally wrong and so dangerous to the liberty of all Americans. For example, in 1833, a crowd of black rescuers severely beat Sheriff John M. Wilson, of Wayne County, when he unsuccessfully tried to prevent the removal of a fugitive slave from his custody.[7] In 1847, a mob in Marshall, Michigan, rescued a fugitive slave in the famous Crosswhite case, and Zachariah Chandler, who later served in the U.S. Senate, paid the fines imposed by a federal court on the rescuers.[8]

This popular revulsion toward slave catching had a direct impact on legislation and helped create Michigan's personal liberty law of 1855. This law banned the use of the state's jails to house captured fugitive slaves and prohibited state and local officials from participating in the capture, incarceration, or return of fugitive slaves.[9] In addition to protecting fugitives, Michigan was more welcoming to black migrants—fugitive or free—than other states in the region. Unlike the states of the lower Midwest, which had laws requiring black migrants to register with local officials, after statehood Michigan did not attempt to limit black migration or to require any sort of registration system for African Americans entering the state.[10] Once in Michigan, blacks were free to compete in the marketplace, to enter most professions, and to own real estate. They built churches and other social institutions in which their leaders openly campaigned against slavery while working toward a community where African Americans could prosper.

Public education was available to blacks, though not necessarily on an integrated basis. State laws did not require segregation or prohibit integration: local control of schools led to integration in some places in Michigan, while segregated schools emerged in other places, most significantly

Detroit. Like most other northern states, Michigan prohibited blacks from voting, although the implementation of this ban was not always certain. Ignoring the fact that the constitution limited suffrage to whites, Michigan blacks voted in the 1844 presidential election because neither party was willing to "challenge [them] on the ground of color."[11] Throughout the rest of the decade, blacks voted openly in Cass County, as well.[12] Although they were excluded from voting for members of the local and state governments and for members of Congress, property-owning black men were allowed to vote on bond issues for schools and on other tax referenda after 1855.[13]

Despite these successes, antebellum blacks hardly found full equality in Michigan. Following federal law, the state excluded blacks from the militia.[14] Except for voting for members of elected school boards after 1855, blacks could not legally vote in Michigan. Although some blacks voted in defiance of the constitution, most of the time and in most elections, they did not. Because jury service was tied to the franchise, blacks never served on juries. Although some schools were integrated, especially in rural areas, many were not. Most important, Detroit not only maintained separate schools but also lacked an elected school board, thus depriving blacks in that city of the one legal vehicle for voting: blacks in rural Cass County could vote for the school board, but blacks in Detroit could not.[15] On the social level, there were no state laws protecting black access to public accommodations, and the Michigan courts were not sympathetic to the claims of aggrieved black consumers.[16] Like all of the South and much of the North, Michigan prohibited blacks from marrying whites.

Michigan was more tolerant of blacks than were other midwestern states, but at midcentury the state was not ready to accept black equality. In 1850, Michigan adopted a new constitution, which continued to limit voting to whites. However, the convention recognized that some people in the state wanted a more expansive franchise. Thus, the ratification ballot provided a separate proposal to allow black suffrage. Although the main constitution was adopted, the provision for equal suffrage was soundly defeated.[17] Thus, when the Republicans swept the state, helping to send Lincoln to the White House, blacks in Michigan had significant legal and economic rights but lacked political and social equality.

Civil Rights in Postwar Michigan

Although clearly unequal citizens, blacks in Civil War–era Michigan could hope for a reasonably better future, when they might have more rights.

Even before the Civil War, Free Soil activism and Republican success in Michigan offered the promise of greater civil rights for blacks. The failure of the electorate to accept the black suffrage provision of the 1850 constitution, while ratifying the rest of the document, can be seen in a positive light. Although 32,026 voters opposed black suffrage, 12,840 voters—more than a quarter of the electorate—supported it. More significant, the very fact that the convention sent this measure to the voters suggests the growing importance of racial egalitarianism in the state. Support for black rights improved in the mid-1850s with the formation of the Republican Party. The leaders of this new party "officially committed themselves to the welfare of black citizens."[18]

In November 1854, the new party won victories throughout the state, and when the victorious Republicans took office in 1855 they controlled the state government. Once in power, the Republicans moved to eliminate racial discrimination and to protect black freedom. In 1855, as noted above, the state government allowed blacks to vote in school board elections. This partial enfranchisement was accomplished without a constitutional amendment because it came through a change in the state's school laws, not in its fundamental law on voting. That same year, the legislature passed a strong personal liberty law to protect free blacks and fugitive slaves from the long arm of the federal government and the fugitive slave law of 1850. During the Civil War, Michigan was deeply committed to the Union cause, which, by the end of the war, had come to support an end to slavery and the expansion of black freedom. As discussed below, Republican control of the state legislature after the war led to early enactments of civil rights legislation. Similarly, Republican control of the Michigan Supreme Court led to a new jurisprudence of freedom.

The first postwar assault on race discrimination came through litigation and the decisions of the state's highest court. Their newly won freedom inspired some blacks in Michigan to challenge the ban on their right to vote in general elections. In 1866, the Michigan Supreme Court reviewed the conviction of William Dean, a man of mixed racial ancestry, who had voted in Nankin Township, which is on the western end of Wayne County, in what is today Westland, Michigan. That Dean was allowed to vote in the first place suggests the emerging changes in the regulation of race in Michigan. Dean was of mixed ancestry and was probably a descendant of Europeans and Indians. He was, however, clearly at least partially of African ancestry. When he tried to cast his ballot, election officials challenged him on racial grounds. He asserted that he was a mixture of white and Indian and that men of such backgrounds could vote in the state. Because of his African ancestry, it would have been a simple matter to refuse his vote.

At least some election officials in Wayne County did not have the energy or desire to prevent a determined African American from voting. After the election, however, the Wayne County prosecuting attorney, who was a Democrat, brought charges against Dean for illegal voting.[19] The prosecution appears to have been both racially and politically motivated. Democrats at this time were hostile to black equality and civil rights. At the national level, Democrats opposed the Civil Rights Act of 1866, the creation of the Freedmen's Bureau, and the adoption of the Fourteenth Amendment. Wherever they could vote, blacks were overwhelmingly Republicans. Thus, it is hardly surprising that Democratic Party leaders in Wayne County would seek to prosecute a black for illegal voting.

The legal issues in this case were unclear. The Michigan constitution of 1850, which was in force at this time, limited the franchise to "white" men. Dean's lawyers asked the trial judge for three different charges on the issue of race and voting. First, they asked the judge to inform the jury that Dean had a right to vote if the jurors found Dean to be more than one-half white. The lawyers also asked for a charge to the jurors to find for Dean if he was only one-sixteenth black. Finally, the lawyers asked the trial judge to charge the jury to acquit Dean if the jurors believed he was mostly white, part Indian, and had "a trace only, or portion of negro or African blood in his veins," making him "a legal elector, as a person of 'Indian descent,' under the constitution, if they believed, from the same evidence, that he had all the other requisite qualifications."[20] In other words, Dean's lawyers asked for a variety of definitions of white, starting with the most expansive definition—more than half white—and ending with the least expansive—mostly white with only "a trace" of black ancestry. The judge, however, refused to give any of these instructions, and, after his conviction, Dean appealed to the Michigan Supreme Court.

In his majority opinion, Justice James V. Campbell hinted that this prosecution had been brought to settle the issue of mixed-race voters in the state. Campbell noted that if the court ruled in Dean's favor because he was "not more than one-sixteenth of African blood," then there would be no reason to consider his larger point—that if he were simply "less than one-half of African blood"—he would be "white" within the meaning of the 1850 constitution. Although Campbell noted that a decision on the one-sixteenth quantum would "dispose of this case," he did not want to do this because "the case is evidentially designed to obtain a ruling upon the general subject, in order the settle position of persons of mixed blood under our constitution."[21]

Justice Campbell stated that there had never been a "generally prevalent legal meaning which can be regarded as having become so attached to the word 'white,' as to have been of any governing weight in its adoption." He proudly noted that Michigan had "never sanctioned the discreditable penal enactments which put black men in the category of suspected criminals under bonds for good behavior, as was done in the [Michigan] territory" and other midwestern states. Nor had the state "attempted to make color a test of veracity in the witness box." More significantly, Campbell claimed that in his state "there has been no serious difference between the privileges of any of our inhabitants, in matters of mere private concern." He noted with regret that color was used for "political distinctions," despite "strong efforts to eradicate them." Campbell wrote, however, that these distinctions were solely among those "who could be classed as white or not white" and that no one in Michigan had ever "advanced the absurd notion that a preponderance of mixed blood, on one side or the other of any given standard has the remotest bearing upon personal fitness or unfitness to possess political privileges." Campbell asserted there was no "philosophical" basis for racial distinctions and claimed that "the recognition of slavery . . . created and confirmed the feeling which has so jealously separated the white race into the privileged and dominant people in this country." Campbell did not deny that the "right of the people to determine the qualification of electors" was "undisputed," but he was unwilling to extend the limitation on voting any further than was absolutely required by the language of the constitution. He also asserted the right of the courts to interpret this language because "the term 'white' has no ascertained and technically accurate legal meaning."[22]

After discussing various cases, mostly from Ohio, he asked: "If a man is not made white by a mere predominance of white blood, then the question arises: where is the line to be drawn, and how is the distinction to be ascertained?" Rules for suffrage had to be "uniform as far as possible." Color would not work, because he noted "there are white men as dark as mulattoes, and there are pure blooded albino Africans as white as the white Saxons."[23] The only interpretation that made sense was one of ancestry: "persons are white within the meaning of our constitution, in whom white blood so far preponderates that they have less than one-fourth of African blood."[24]

Chief Justice George Martin dissented from the court's opinion, while agreeing with the decision to overturn Dean's conviction. Martin argued that a "preponderance" of white blood made someone white: the rule should be that if someone was more than half white, the person was white. This was more expansive a position than the rest of the court was prepared to take. In taking this position, Martin denounced the "racial science" of the prosecution, which had offered the testimony of a medical doctor who claimed that the shape of Dean's nose proved he was not white. Martin was disgusted with the timidity of his fellow justices, who were unwilling to take the more liberal stand on race. He mocked the majority opinion, declaring that, under "the rule my brethren have established," the constitution should be "amended with all speed, so as to authorize the election or appointment of nose pullers or nose inspectors, to attend the election polls in every township and ward of the state, to prevent illegal voting."[25]

Despite Chief Justice Martin's anger that the decision was not expansive enough, this ruling overturned Dean's conviction and led to the enfranchisement of some men in Michigan who were of mixed ancestry. Not every mixed-race voter was allowed to vote, and subsequent litigation was necessary before a number of men in Wayne County, a Democratic stronghold, were registered.[26] The Democrats in Wayne County did not want to register more potential Republican voters if they could avoid doing so, and they did not want to support a more racially fair and more egalitarian society. But, despite this hostility to its decision, the supreme court had moved the state closer to racial equality. More important, all the judges had denounced racism and the absurdity of the emerging racial science of the period.

At this time, the Republican-controlled legislature remained deeply committed to black equality and civil rights. In the wake of the decision in *Dean,* the legislature moved to protect black rights. Perhaps the firm position of the court and its enormously respected jurists, including Thomas Cooley, emboldened the Republicans in the legislature and in the state constitutional convention.

In 1867, the Republicans totally dominated a state constitutional convention, holding three-quarters of the delegates to the Lansing Convention.[27] This majority rewrote the Michigan constitution and submitted it to the voters. Reflecting the now deeply held views of the Republican Party, the proposed constitution eliminated all racial discrimination in voting. It also contained controversial clauses prohibiting alcohol, authorizing local and municipal aid to railroads, and raising salaries for public officials. The Republican Party supported the constitution, and Republican candidates swept state offices that year. But the electorate emphatically rejected this new constitution. The meaning of this rejection is subject to different interpretations. Traditionally, scholars have argued that "the constitution was defeated primarily because of the suffrage question."[28] However, this interpretation ignores the significant role of the Michigan legislature in extending black civil rights in this period. Between 1865 and 1869, Michigan easily ratified the three Civil War amendments to the federal Constitution, which led to black suffrage on the same basis as white suffrage. In 1870, the electorate endorsed a change in the Michigan constitution that more sweepingly eliminated *all* racial discrimination in the fundamental compact of the state.

The 1867 constitution went down to defeat by a vote of 110,582 to 71,729. The suffrage issue surely led to Democratic opposition to the new constitution. But that accounted for, at most, a third of the electorate. The constitution was, in fact, defeated by Republicans. Oddly enough, the Republican Party controlled the state throughout this period and elected a governor, even as the Constitution was defeated. In a careful analysis of this contest, Martin Hershock concludes that the suffrage issue did not defeat the constitution. He points instead to the strong opposition of Republicans to subsidies for railroads, to prohibition, and to wage raises for the legislature. Republican leaders had no doubt about the general popularity of black suffrage. William Howard, the chairman of the state party, enthusiastically supported the new constitution, declaring his belief that the party would not support any candidate "who turns his back on this fundamental issue" of black suffrage.[29] If Howard's understanding of his party was correct, then perhaps the whole analysis of this vote should be turned inside out. It may be that the Republicans used black suffrage, which was popular among the rank and file, to garner support for the less popular aid to railroads and salary provisions for state officeholders. In other words, it may not be that suffrage undermined the constitution but that black suffrage was not strong enough to overcome deeper opposition to other parts of the constitution. This analysis is supported by the actions of the Republicans at the convention. They might have put the black suffrage clause on the ballot as a separate item—as they did with the controversial prohibition clause—allowing the electorate to ratify the new constitution without having to accept black equality. At the convention, the Republican majority, by a vote of 50 to 16, decisively voted down a proposal to submit black suffrage to the electorate as a separate provision.[30] In some ways, black suffrage at this time may be seen as an early version of what later became known as "waving the bloody shirt."[31] Republicans in Michigan were so committed to black suffrage and black civil rights that they were certain the issue could carry the constitution despite other provisions—such as those involving railroads—that lacked strong support within the party. Despite the defeat of the 1867 constitution, this analysis is supported by the statutes, constitutional changes, and court cases dealing with race in the period from 1867 to 1885.

In 1867, the Michigan legislature ratified the Fourteenth Amendment. The proposed amendment had been sent to the state in June 1866, but the legislature did not sit that year—thus no action could be taken until January 1867, when the state ratified the amendment with great speed and almost no debate. On January 7, Governor Henry Crapo sent a copy of the amendment to the state Senate. On January 9, the amendment was introduced, and, by a vote of 25 to 1, the state Senate ratified it on January 15. The next day, by a vote of 71 to 15, the Michigan House of Representatives ratified the Fourteenth Amendment.[32] This speedy and overwhelming vote for ratification indicates the level of support for black rights among Republicans in the state legislature. The vote in the Senate shows that even some Michigan Democrats, who might have been ambivalent or hostile to black rights, supported this fundamental change to the U.S. Constitution.

Just a few months after it ratified the Fourteenth Amendment, the Republican majority in the legislature turned to the issue of school segregation and adopted a general school law that prohibited segregation in public education in Michigan. The law was unambiguous, declaring, "All residents of any district shall have an equal right to attend any school therein."[33] The state was now fully committed to ending segregation in its public schools. Although some antebellum schools had been integrated by local boards, integration—or at least an end to segregation—was now the official policy of the state. At the time of the bill's passage, most of the state's schools were integrated, and only a few cities, such as Detroit and Jackson, appear to have had segregated schools.[34] Most of the districts in the state readily complied with the law, and throughout Michigan blacks attended school with whites. The one exception was the city of Detroit, which had the largest black population in the state. Detroit officials argued that the law could not affect their school system because the city had an independent school charter. In 1869, the legislature responded by repealing part of the Detroit school charter so that there could be no doubt that the statute applied to Detroit.[35]

This legislative change is significant because it demonstrates continued support for the integration of Detroit schools in the legislature. However, as set out by the supreme court in *Workman v. Board of Education of Detroit,* this new law was probably unnecessary.[36] In 1868, Joseph Workman sued to force the Detroit schools to admit his child on the same basis as white children. The Detroit school board argued that the 1867 law did not apply to the Detroit schools because the Detroit schools had been established independently of the general school laws. In addition, the school board claimed that racism within the city made it impossible to comply with the law.

The school board's lawyer argued that "there exists among a large majority of the white population of Detroit a strong prejudice or animosity against colored people, which is largely translated to the children in the schools, and that this feeling would engender quarrels and contention if colored children were admitted to the white schools."[37] This sort of argument presaged the claims of white southern leaders in the 1950s and 1960s, such as the public officials in Arkansas who tried to close the Little Rock public schools rather than integrate them. In the wake of the Civil War, in which more than two hundred thousand African Americans, including members of the First Michigan Colored Regiment, had fought for the Union cause, such blatant appeals to racism must have shocked the Republican-dominated Michigan Supreme Court.[38]

In May 1869, the state supreme court emphatically endorsed the constitutionality of the 1867 integration statute and found it fully applicable to the city of Detroit. Speaking for the court, Chief Justice Thomas M. Cooley dismissed the idea that any lawyer could argue that the law did not mandate integration.

> It cannot be seriously urged that with this provision in force, the school board may make regulations which would exclude any resident of the district from any of its schools, because of race or color, or religious belief or personal peculiarities. It is too plain for argument that an equal right to all the schools, irrespective of such distinctions, was meant to be established.[39]

The only legal issue for Cooley and his brethren was whether Detroit was exempt from the 1867 statute. The court found that the city was not exempt and thus had to integrate its schools.

In 1869, the issue of black suffrage once again arose in the state. Congress had passed the Fifteenth Amendment and sent it on to the states. In March, the legislature ratified the amendment despite harsh protests from Democrats. Republican legislators must have felt confident they could support black suffrage only a year after the state had rejected the proposed constitution that included black suffrage. Republicans were not worried that they would be defeated if they supported the amendment.

Following this vote, the Republicans in the legislature passed and sent on to the electorate a series of amendments to the state constitution. Rather than rewriting the whole document, they now introduced the controversial provisions of the proposed 1867 constitution as separate constitutional amendments. By the time these amendments went before the people of Michigan, the Fifteenth Amendment had been ratified and blacks had the right to vote on the same basis as whites. Democrats nevertheless opposed the provision because it went beyond suffrage. Indeed, the proposed amendment entirely eliminated the word "white" from the constitution and, thus, eradicated all racially based limitations in the fundamental law of Michigan, allowing blacks to vote, hold office, serve on juries, and serve in the militia. Fifty-two percent of those voting in the referendum supported black suffrage. In the same referendum, the voters defeated amendments to allow municipal aid to railroads and higher salaries for people in state government.[40] This vote reinforces the interpretation that these issues, not black suffrage, caused the defeat of the proposed 1867 constitution.

The addition of this amendment to the state constitution, combined with the three Civil War amendments to the U.S. Constitution, eliminated—at least formally—almost all racial discrimination from Michigan law. The ban on interracial marriage, created by statute decades before the Civil War, however, still remained on the books. Moreover, officials in some parts of the state were unenthusiastic or even uncooperative about enforcing the requirement that schools be integrated. Although the Michigan constitution and legislature had eliminated all formal racial distinctions except the ban on interracial marriage, the end of state-sponsored inequality did not guarantee an end to discrimination. Governmental entities no longer could discriminate, but private individuals, businesses, and corporations were not prohibited from discriminating against people on the basis of race. Furthermore, the legislature understood the dangers of private violence against blacks. During this period, Michigan's citizens read about the reign of barbarism in the South as white terrorists intimidated and lynched blacks and white Unionists. Thus, Michigan's Republican legislature continued to refine the state's laws to fight racism.

In January 1871, the state adopted a new revised code that contained a provision that made it a criminal offense for anyone to use a "disguise . . .

with intent to obstruct the due execution of the law, or with intent to intimidate, hinder, or interrupt any officer or any other person in the legal performance of his duty, or the exercise of his rights under the Constitution and laws of the State."[41] This law appears to have been on the books since before the Civil War, although the purpose of the statute at that time would have been to prevent criminals, or their friends and allies, from interfering with or intimidating law enforcement officers in the normal course of their duties. But in 1871, the law took on a new meaning. As early as 1868, there had been a small amount of Ku Klux Klan activity in the state. The Klan was not powerful at that time and was not terrorizing black or white citizens. Nevertheless, the legislature had taken action to prevent white terrorists from inflicting violence and intimidation on the people of Michigan.

On April 15, 1871, the legislature adopted a mandatory school attendance law for all children ages eight through fourteen.[42] Two days later, the state emphatically prohibited segregation in its public schools, placing itself at the cutting edge of equality. The new law left nothing to the imagination of local school officials who might not favor equality. The law declared: "All persons, residents of any school district, and five years of age, shall have an equal right to attend any school therein; and no separate school or department shall be kept for any persons on account of race or color."[43] Schooling on an integrated basis was now both available to and mandatory for all of Michigan's children.

Michigan Responds to the Jim Crow Era

By the end of Reconstruction, Michigan had integrated its schools and eliminated racial terminology in its constitution. Blacks were free to attend school with whites; black men could vote, serve in the militia, and be called for jury duty on the same basis as white men. One part of the state code still reflected antebellum notions of race. Like many other states, Michigan still banned interracial marriage.[44] In 1883, this changed, as Michigan repealed its ban on such marriages and retroactively legitimized all interracial unions that had already taken place in the state. What once had been the most volatile issue regarding race and law suddenly and without much fanfare had disappeared in Michigan.

The context in which this law was enacted illustrates the direction of civil rights in Michigan and its marked contrast to the direction the American South and the U.S. Supreme Court were taking. The same year that

Michigan allowed interracial marriage, the Supreme Court upheld the conviction of an interracial couple in Alabama. Tony Pace and Mary Jane Cox had not attempted to marry in Alabama because, as an interracial couple, they knew this was impossible and illegal. Nor did they even share a home together. Nevertheless, they were lovers, and their visitations led to a prosecution for interracial fornication. Under Alabama law, interracial fornication carried a greater penalty than same-race fornication. Furthermore, because Alabama prohibited interracial marriage, couples like Pace and Cox could not avoid the antifornication laws through marriage. Pace appealed his conviction to the U.S. Supreme Court, arguing that the differential sentence, as well as the antimiscegenation law, violated the equal protection clause of the Fourteenth Amendment. In *Pace v. Alabama,* the U.S. Supreme Court upheld this conviction and gave its indirect blessing to bans on interracial marriage.[45] Thus, at the very time that the southern states were vigorously prohibiting interracial marriage and sex and the Supreme Court was supporting this development, Michigan headed in a quite different direction.

With the adoption of the 1883 law, Michigan had eliminated all forms of state-sanctioned racial discrimination. Whites, blacks, and Indians were now formally equal in the state. Private discrimination remained legal, however, at least under state law. The federal Civil Rights Act of 1875 had prohibited a great deal of private discrimination, and thus legislators in Michigan may not have felt any need to legislate in this area.

Under the federal law, most public accommodations, such as hotels, restaurants, and theaters, could not discriminate on the basis of race. Many restaurants in Detroit apparently complied with the 1875 act, although some did not. In 1882, for example, the Fisk Jubilee Singers were denied accommodations at a downtown hotel.[46] In 1883, however, the year that Michigan repealed its ban on interracial marriage, the U.S. Supreme Court, in the *Civil Rights Cases,* struck down the federal Civil Rights Act of 1875.[47] The Court narrowly construed the Fourteenth Amendment to apply only to "state action" and held that Congress lacked any power to regulate private action. The Court refused even to consider that the Thirteenth Amendment, which banned slavery and involuntary servitude, might also restrict private discrimination. The Court's decision left the regulation of civil rights entirely in the hands of the states.

Southern states took advantage of this decision to begin a war on black rights through the creation of segregation laws. In the next quarter century, the South segregated almost every public and private institution, and the U.S. Supreme Court acquiesced to almost all of these laws. Michigan responded to the U.S. Supreme Court's decision in the *Civil Rights Cases* by passing its own legislation to prohibit racial discrimination. In May 1885, the legislature passed "An Act to protect all citizens in their civil rights."[48] The law was introduced by a Representative Robinson J. Dickson, a Republican from Cass County, which had the second-largest black population of any county in the state and the largest percentage of blacks in the state.[49] In commenting on the bill, the *Detroit Evening News* reported that blacks throughout the state complained that they could not get service at restaurants or obtain lodging at hotels. Interviews with hotel managers confirmed this, as the paper noted that most innkeepers were "more or less opposed to giving colored men, save in exceptional cases, the accommodations" that they offered to the white "travelling public."[50] With sweeping simplicity and enormous economy of language, the legislature, in three short sections, sought to end private discrimination in the state.

The law declared that all persons "within the jurisdiction" of Michigan were "entitled to the full and equal accommodations, advantages, facilities, and privileges of inns, restaurants, eating-houses, barber shops, public conveyances on land and water, theaters, and all other places of public accommodation and amusement."[51] The law provided fines of $100 and up to thirty days in jail for anyone who violated the law.[52] The law also provided similar fines and punishments for "any officer or other person charged with any duty in the selection or summoning of jurors" who excluded potential grand jurors or petit jurors on the basis of race.[53] With the passage of the law, Michigan seemed to have created a society in which race did not matter, at least in the public sphere.

The Michigan Civil Rights Act of 1885, although a huge step forward in race relations, did not guarantee equality. The law provided no mechanism for enforcement, short of a prosecution. In those parts of Michigan where the Republican Party was in power, enforcement might be easy. The party was still committed to racial equality, and, though few in number, Michigan's black voters were overwhelmingly loyal to the party of Lincoln, which was also the party of such stalwart supporters of black rights as Senators Jacob Howard and Zachariah Chandler. But in those parts of the state where Republicans were not in power, enforcement of the Civil Rights Act might be uncertain or nonexistent. Most important, the large and growing population of blacks in Detroit could not expect vigorous enforcement of the new law from the Democrats who controlled Wayne County and who were generally hostile to black rights.

Without the aid of a prosecutor, blacks had to turn to private lawsuits to secure integration. The Civil Rights Act did not explicitly provide for private suits, but such suits were rooted in the act, on the theory that a violation of the criminal law surely also constitutes an actionable civil wrong. Private lawsuits, however, are a cumbersome way to vindicate the civil rights of a significant number of people and to require private plaintiffs to bear the cost of law enforcement.

Compliance with the law was mixed. Some restaurants and hotels accepted black patrons, but others did not. In 1888, a black physician in Detroit, W. H. Haynes, sued the white owner of a restaurant, Fred Soup, who would not serve him. Eight of the jurors voted to support Haynes, but, with a deadlocked panel, the judge intervened to find in favor of Soup. The Wayne County judge ruled that Soup's establishment was not a public place within the meaning of the statute because it was unlicensed and part of his boardinghouse, In reaching this conclusion the judge distinguished Soup's restaurant from freestanding eating establishments, thus removing it from the scope of the statutory language that barred segregation in "inns, restaurants, [and] eating houses." The judge also declared the entire provision on public accommodations in the Michigan Civil Rights Act to be unconstitutional.[54] The case was not appealed, perhaps because the fact that Soup's establishment was unlicensed or that it was a "boardinghouse" rather than an inn or a restaurant undermined any appeal.

Instead, Haynes's attorney, D. Augustus Straker, took on another case, one involving William W. Ferguson, a college-educated black businessman in the city. In August 1889, the owner of Gies' European Restaurant refused to seat Ferguson and M. F. Walker, a catcher for a Syracuse, New York, baseball team, in his main dining room. He offered them a table in the bar area, where they could order from the main dining room menu. Gies even offered to put linens on the table in the bar, just as he would in the main dining room. However, Gies emphatically told Ferguson, "We cannot serve colored people right at those certain tables. . . . We cannot serve you at these tables. If you will sit over at the next table in the other row, I will see that you are served there all right, the same as any other person will be."[55]

Ferguson and Walker then left the restaurant and subsequently sued for damages. The case seemed ready-made to secure the enforcement of the state's Civil Rights Act. Gies did not deny that he segregated patrons and readily admitted he did so because they were black. Moreover, there was no doubt that Gies's establishment, unlike Fred Soup's boardinghouse, was a licensed restaurant open to the public. Indeed, the fact that Gies served blacks in the "saloon section" of the restaurant but not the main dining room underscores the public nature of the business.

At the trial, circuit judge George Gartner told the jury that "all citizens under the law have the same rights and privileges, and are entitled to the same immunities;—it makes no difference whether white or colored." Gartner's charge denounced discrimination and the nation's racist past. He asserted that the "reasoning of Chief Justice Taney in his opinion in the *Dred Scott Case* is now largely and almost universally regarded as fallacious and contrary to the principles of law then claimed to exist" and that the "fifteenth amendment placed the colored citizen upon an equal footing in all respects with the white citizen." He noted that many states had adopted laws "to modify and overcome the prejudices entertained by many of the white race against the colored race, and to place the latter upon an equal footing with the former, with the same rights and privileges." This, he instructed, was the "object" and the "purpose" of Michigan's civil rights act of 1885.[56]

This charge should have led to a verdict for Ferguson. However, Gartner did not stop with this forceful support of equality. Instead he told the jury that, although Gies could not practice "unjust discrimination," it was permissible for him to "reserve certain portions of his business for ladies, and other portions for gentlemen, while he may also reserve other portions for his regular patrons or borders." Similarly, Gartner told the jury, the restaurant might "reserve certain tables for white men, and others where colored men would be served, provided there was no unjust discrimination." Gartner stated that "full and equal accommodations" did not mean "identical accommodations, but by it is meant substantially the same accommodation." He asserted that a patron at a restaurant had "no more right to insist upon sitting at a particular table than a guest at a hotel has the right to demand a particular room, as long as the accommodations offered are substantially equal."[57]

This charge came close to articulating the separate but equal standard that the U.S. Supreme Court endorsed a few years later in *Plessy v. Ferguson*.[58] But the Michigan trial judge did not even state that there needed to be equality in the facilities. Gies admitted that the tables and other aspects of service in the saloon area were not equal to those in the other part of his restaurant. And Judge Gartner said that this was unnecessary. To pass muster under Michigan's civil rights law, Judge Gartner told the jury, the service had only to be "substantially the same." Not surprisingly, the jury found for Gies. On the basis of this charge to the jury, Ferguson took his case to the Michigan Supreme Court.

The Michigan Supreme Court emphatically and unanimously over-turned the verdict. Justice Allen B. Morse offered an extraordinary denun-ciation of racism and prejudice. The opinion certainly reflected the age in which Morse lived, an age in which even the most egalitarian whites prob-ably did not *truly* believe that the races were equal. As the extensive quota-tions below show, Morse implied that being black was similar to having a birth defect or "deformity," and he paternalistically rejected treating peo-ple differently on that basis. Despite its paternalism and latent racism, Morse's opinion was a profound rejection of segregation and race prejudice.

Morse began his opinion by explaining that the "fault" in Gartner's "in-struction is that it permits a discrimination on account of color alone which cannot be made under law with any justice." Restaurant owners might be free to make rules for other types of customers,

> [b]ut in Michigan there must be and is an absolute, unconditional equality of white and colored men before the law. The white man can have no rights or privileges under the law that are denied to the black man. Socially people may do as they please within the law, and whites may associate together, as may blacks, and exclude whom they please from their dwellings and private grounds; but there can be no separation in public places between people on account of their color alone which the law will sanction.[59]

Six years after *Gies,* in *Plessy v. Ferguson,* the U.S. Supreme Court cited *Roberts v. City of Boston,* an antebellum case allowing segregated schools, to bolster its support for the separate but equal doctrine.[60] Judge Gartner had cited this case to support his decision that Gies did not have to seat black patrons next to white patrons. But, the Michigan Supreme Court would have none of this. The court noted that the *Roberts* case "was made in the *ante bellum* days, before the colored man was a citizen, and when, in nearly one-half of the Union, he was but a chattel. It cannot now serve as a prece-dent."[61] In an extraordinary affirmation of racial equality, the Michigan court asserted that the *Roberts* case was

> [b]ut a reminder of the injustice and prejudice of the time in which it was delivered. The negro [*sic*] is now, by the Constitution of the United States, given full citizenship with the white man, and all the

rights and privileges of citizenship attend him wherever he goes. Whatever right a white man has in a public place, the black man has also, because of such citizenship.[62]

After quoting almost in its entirety the Michigan Civil Rights Act of 1885, Justice Morse declared that the 1885 act

> exemplifies the changed feeling of our people towards the African race and places the colored man upon a perfect equality with all others, before the law in this state. Under it, no line can be drawn in the streets, public parks, or public buildings upon one side of which the black man must stop and stay, while the white man may enjoy the other side, or both sides, at his will and pleasure; nor can such a line of separation be drawn in any of the public places or conveyances in this act.[63]

Morse held that, under the common law, white men had always had "a remedy against any unjust discrimination to the citizen in all public places" and that since the adoption of the Civil War Amendments, and especially after the passage of the Michigan Civil Rights Act, "the colored man, under the law of this state, was entitled to the same rights and privileges in public places as the white man, and must be treated the same there; and that his right of action for any injuries arising from an unjust discrimination against him is just as perfect and sacred in the courts as that of any other citizen."[64]

Emphatically denouncing racism, Justice Morse declared that "any discrimination founded upon the race or color of the citizen is unjust and cruel [and] can have no sanction in the law of this state."[65] Morse believed that this sort of discrimination, which could be found in other states, "taints justice."[66] Morse then went on to demolish the racist notion that God had made blacks inferior to whites, stating that such ideas were founded on reasoning that "does not commend itself either to the heart or judgment."[67]

As he wrote this opinion, Morse probably reflected on his own life. As a young man, he had served in the 16th Michigan and lost an arm storming Missionary Ridge. Thus, he understood the cost of equality, declaring

> The humane and enlightened judgment of our people has decided—although it cost blood and treasure to do so—that the

negro [*sic*] is a man; a freeman; a citizen; and entitled to equal
rights before the law with the white man. This decision was a just
one. Because it was divinely ordained that the skin of one man
should not be as white as that of another furnishes no more reason that he should have less rights and privileges under the law
than if he had been born white, but cross-eyed, or otherwise de-
formed. The law, as I understand it, will never permit color or misfortune that God has fastened upon a man from his birth, to be
punished by the law. . . . The law is tender, rather than harsh, toward all infirmity; and if to be born black is a misfortune, then the
law should lessen, rather than increase, the burden of the black
man's life.[68]

This section of the opinion certainly smacked of paternalism—the
comparison of blackness to a deformity reflects the racism of the age. At
the same time, however, it also reflects the social reality of the age. Most
whites *treated* blacks as if their race was, at best, a birth defect: they looked
at the condition of African Americans and realized that the circumstances
of their birth and the life chances they had were unfortunate. But, again,
despite the racism of the opinion, Morse's conclusion was anything but
racist. Although recognizing "the prejudice against association in public
places with the negro, which does exist, to some extent in all communities," he emphatically asserted that "it is not for the courts to cater to or
temporize with a prejudice which is not only not humane, but unreasonable." Thus, Morse declared, he could never "deny to any man any rights
and privileges that belong in law to any other man, simply because the
Creator colored him differently from others, or made him less handsome
than his fellows,—for something that he could not help in the first instance, or ever afterwards remove by the best of life and human conduct."[69]
This portion of the opinion anticipates, to a large degree, the modern idea
that distinctions cannot be made on the basis of immutable characteristics.
    Morse concluded by reaffirming the principle that "all men are equal be-
fore the law."[70] He accepted the idea that any person "may draw his social
line as closely as he chooses at home, or in other private places, but he cannot in a public place carry the privacy of his home with him, or ask that
people not as good or great as he is shall step aside when he appears."[71] Citing the state's civil rights act and its school laws, Morse asserted that "all citizens who conform to the law have the same rights to such places, without
regard to race, color, or condition of birth."[72] Thus, he ordered a new trial.

In *Gies,* the Michigan Supreme Court offered one of the most emphatically egalitarian opinions of the century. The court placed Michigan in the vanguard of jurisdictions offering legal protection for black civil rights. Unfortunately, the decision gave Ferguson only the right to a new trial and did not guarantee him a fair judgment. That was left to a jury, which on re-trial awarded him only token damages.[73] This outcome illustrates the gap between legal rights and the political realities of racism in Detroit, where juries were overwhelmingly white and made up of people, usually Democrats, unsympathetic to civil rights.

In 1893, the Michigan legislature once again intervened to create a level playing field for African Americans. The Michigan Civil Rights Act of 1885 dealt with businesses and public accommodations. But, in the early 1890s, a new form of business discrimination began to appear in the field of life insurance.

In the 1880s, the self-taught statistician Frederick L. Hoffman began to research the relationship between race and health, and, in 1892, he published an article implying that blacks never should be insured at the same premium as whites because of their high mortality rate.[74] By this time, most major insurance companies either refused to sell to blacks or sold to them at premiums higher than those they changed to whites. In 1893, Michigan attempted to stop this practice. The act prohibited any life insurance company doing business in the state from making "any distinction or discrimination between white persons and colored persons, wholly or partially of African descent, as to the premiums or rates charged for policies." Any company not following this law could be fined $500 for each violation, and officers of the company issuing such policies could be fined from $50 to $500 and sentenced to up to a year in jail.

Six years later, Michigan again amended its marriage law. The new provision had nothing to do with race—it regulated health. However, this new amendment was added to the section of the law that previously had been amended in 1883 to allow interracial marriage. In amending this section, the legislature took the opportunity to reaffirm the 1883 law legalizing interracial marriages and to reconfirm the validity of all interracial unions in the state that had taken place before 1883. This reaffirmation of interracial marriage was probably legally unnecessary, but by doing so Michigan placed itself squarely on the equality side of the great divide in the nation over race. In this period, the South was moving to segregate everything it could and to disfranchise blacks as much as possible, and the U.S. Supreme Court was readily giving its blessing. Michigan, on the other hand, was passing new civil rights legislation in the 1890s and reaffirming its commitment to equality.

The Promise and the Failure of Law

At the turn of the twentieth century, Michigan's legal system was enormously protective of black rights, and the state continued to pass civil rights laws until midcentury. In 1929, for example, Michigan responded to the revitalization of the Ku Klux Klan with an antimask law aimed directly at the Klan.[75] In 1937, at the behest of Charles C. Diggs, a black state senator, the legislature strengthened the existing Civil Rights Act, making it applicable to "inns, hotels, restaurants, eating houses, barber shops, billiard parlors, stores, public conveyances on land and water, theaters, motion picture houses, public educational institutions, in elevators, on escalators, in all methods of air transportation and all other places of public accommodation, amusement, and recreation, where refreshments are or may hereafter be served."[76] After the passage of this law, there were some arrests and prosecutions for refusal to serve blacks.[77] An act of 1941 prohibited discrimination in civil service hiring.[78] These laws culminated with the Michigan Fair Employment Practices Act of 1955.[79]

Yet, despite these laws, race relations in Michigan became much worse in the twentieth century. Some of this was due to changing demographics. Between 1870 and 1910, the state's black population grew from 11,849 to 17,115. By contrast, the white population went from 1,167,282 to 2,785,247. After 1910, however, the black population grew dramatically, to 60,082 in 1920 and to 169,453 in 1930. This huge growth in the black population, much of it in Wayne County, led to a white backlash.[80] Complicating the black population growth was a change in the makeup of the white population. The descendants of the Yankees and New Englanders who had settled the state in the nineteenth century were still the most politically and economically powerful group in the state, but new immigrants, from eastern and southern Europe, as well as from Appalachia, flooded into the state. In the 1920s, a revitalized Ku Klux Klan appealed to white Protestants, fearful of European immigrants and southern blacks. In Detroit, the Klan had attracted some thirty-five thousand members by the middle of the decade.[81] Meanwhile, at the national level, the Supreme Court had turned its back on blacks, as had both national political parties. Although Michigan maintained some of its heritage as a racially egalitarian state, the pressures of immigration, migration, and national trends in law led to a diminution of support for racial equality.

Private decision makers, especially real estate agents, brokers, and developers, along with some public officials, severely limited housing options for blacks, leading to rigid residential segregation.[82] The state supreme court still supported civil rights, in some contexts,[83] but upheld the legality under state law of restrictive covenants in housing in 1922, and again in 1947, and of discriminatory practices by real estate brokers and agents in 1963.[84]

Perhaps the best example of the tension between law and reality in Michigan is the case of Ossian Sweet. By the early 1920s, blacks in Detroit had been ghettoized by a combination of private business practices—such as restrictive covenants, the refusal of banks to give loans to blacks for homes in some neighborhoods, and the refusal of real estate agents to show houses to blacks in white neighborhoods—and public policies that kept blacks out of some Detroit neighborhoods as well as suburbs like Grosse Pointe and Dearborn. In 1925, Dr. Ossian Sweet, a successful black physician, purchased a house in an all-white neighborhood in Detroit.[85] The seller charged Sweet a third more than a white would have paid for the property and then self-financed the sale at an exorbitant 18 percent interest rate. But "there was no way the Sweets were going to get a bank loan. They had to take what they could get."[86] Housing discrimination put successful African Americans at the mercy of those few whites willing to sell them a house and left most other blacks crammed into increasingly overcrowded and depressed neighborhoods. Legislation, at least before the civil rights revolution that began in the late 1940s, was unable to deal with this sort of discrimination.

Although an individual private actor—the person who sold Sweet his home—might break with the unwritten racial rules, other private actors often were unwilling to accept the result. In late summer of 1925, a mob attacked Sweet's home. Sweet and his friends defended the home, and in the process a white was killed. Eleven people—Sweet, his wife, his two brothers, and friends who had come to help him—were indicted for murder. In May 1926, a jury of twelve white men concluded that, in Michigan, black men had a right to defend their homes from enraged mobs of whites. Despite the prejudice and racism in the city, despite the rise of the Ku Klux Klan in the North in this period, fundamental justice prevailed.

Sweet's acquittal did not lead to racial harmony, nor did it open up Detroit's housing market to blacks. Instead, the case symbolizes the complexity of race and law in Michigan. Formally, legal equality reigned, but private discrimination in housing and employment left blacks ghettoized and often underemployed. Court decisions respected private property and upheld restrictive covenants. But, in Sweet's case, the jury also respected private property and affirmed Sweet's right to defend his home from the mob. This surely distinguished Michigan from much of the nation—in many states, the mob would have lynched Sweet for killing a white or even for moving into a white neighborhood. The attack on Sweet's house, his indictment for defending his home, and the deplorable housing and employment options for blacks, especially in Detroit, show that law and legal traditions of Michigan could not easily eradicate racism and hatred. The outcome of the Sweet case and the existence of civil rights legislation, on the other hand, show that equality and racial fairness were still embedded in Michigan's legal culture. On a good day—such as the day the jury acquitted Henry Sweet for helping defend his brother's house— this culture allowed the rule of law to overcome hatred and prejudice.

Notes

I thank the following friends and colleagues for their unselfish advice and assistance in the writing of this chapter. I owe a special debt to Judge Avern Cohn for his encouragement and assistance in writing this chapter. In addition I thank Dan Bell, Martin J. Hershock, Marc W. Kruman, Melanie Nelson, Carol Pettit, Stephanie J. Wilhelm, the staff at the Walter P. Reuther Library, Wayne State University, the staff at the University of Michigan Law Library, and the staff at the University of Tulsa Law Library. Some of the research for this article was supported by a travel grant from the Bentley Historical Library at the University of Michigan. I thank William K. Wallach and the staff of the Bentley Historical Library for their help on this project.

1. Sidney Fine, *Expanding the Frontiers of Civil Rights: Michigan, 1948–1968* (Detroit: Wayne State University Press, 2000), 26.

2. An Act to promote and protect the welfare of the people of this state by prevention and elimination of discriminatory employment practices . . . , 1955 Mich. Pub. Acts 411. See also Preston P. Le Breton and Betty L. Le Breton, "The Michigan State Fair Employment Practices Act," *University of Detroit Law Journal* 34 (January 1957): 337.

3. Mich. const. of 1963, art. 1, § 2; ibid., art. V, § 29. See also the chapter by Frank Ravitch in this volume.

4. See generally Avern Cohn, "Constitutional Interpretation and Judicial Treatment of Blacks in Michigan before 1870," *Detroit College of Law Review* (Winter 1986): 1121–30.

5. Carter G. Woodson, *A Century of Negro Migration* (Washington, D.C.: Association for the Study of Negro Life and History, 1918), 35–36.

6. See, e.g., Giltner v. Gorham, 10 F. Cas. 424 (C.C.D. Mich. 1848) (No. 5,453). This was a successful suit brought by a slave owner to recover the value of fugitive slaves whom he had recaptured but who subsequently had been freed by antislavery whites. This is also known as the "Crosswhite Case."

7. David Katzman, *Before the Ghetto: Black Detroit in the Nineteenth Century* (Urbana: University of Illinois Press, 1973), 10.

8. John H. Yzenbaard, "The Crosswhite Case," *Michigan History* 53 (Summer 1969): 131–43; Willis F. Dunbar and George S. May, *Michigan: A History of the Wolverine State*, 3d ed. (Grand Rapids: William B. Eerdmans Publishing, 1995), 304–5 and 310; Giltner v. Gorham, 10 F. Cas. 424 (C.C.D. Mich. 1848) (No. 5,453).

9. An Act to Protect the rights and liberties of the inhabitants of this State, 1855 Mich. Pub. Acts 413.

10. For a discussion of Ohio's laws, see Paul Finkelman, "Race, Slavery, and Law in Antebellum Ohio," in *The History of Ohio Law*, ed. Michael Les Benedict and John F. Winkler (Athens: Ohio University Press, 2004), 2:748–81.

11. Katzman, *Before the Ghetto*, 33, citing Michigan, Senate, *Documents*, No. 15 (1845), 11.

12. Katzman, *Before the Ghetto*, 33.

13. 1855 Mich. Pub. Acts 44–45, 413–16; see Katzman, *Before the Ghetto*, 35.

14. Cohn, "Constitutional Interpretation and Judicial Treatment of Blacks," 1123.

15. Katzman, *Before the Ghetto*, 35.

16. Day v. Owen, 5 Mich. 520 (1858) (court denied relief to a black who sued a ship owner when the ship captain refused to let him pay for cabin service and use a cabin on the ship).

17. Francis Newton Thorpe, *The Federal and State Constitutions, Colonial Charters, and Other Organic Laws of the States, Territories, and Colonies Now or Heretofore Forming the United States of America* (Washington, D.C.: Government Printing Office, 1909), 4:1974

18. Katzman, *Before the Ghetto*, 175.

19. People v. Dean, 14 Mich. 406, 426 (1866).

20. Ibid., 427.

21. Ibid., 414.

22. Ibid., 416–17 (emphasis in original).

23. Ibid., 422–23.

24. Ibid., 425.

25. Ibid., 438–39.

26. Katzman, *Before the Ghetto*, 36.

27. Martin J. Hershock, *The Paradox of Progress: Economic Change, Individual Enterprise, and Political Culture in Michigan, 1837–1878* (Athens: Ohio University Press, 2003), 200.

28. George Blackburn, "Quickening Government in a Developing State," in *Radical Republicans in the North: State Politics During Reconstruction*, ed. James C. Mohr (Baltimore: Johns Hopkins University Press, 1976), 126. See also Katzman, *Before the Ghetto*, 36–37.

29. William Howard, quoted in Hershock, *Paradox of Progress*, 202.

30. *Journal of the Constitutional Convention of the State of Michigan* (Lansing, Mich.: J. A. Kerr, 1867), 702–3, 845–47.

31. During Reconstruction, this phrase was used to describe attempts to shore up support in the North by reminding voters of atrocities committed against Unionists and blacks by white Democrats in the South.

32. Caroline W. Thrun, "School Segregation in Michigan," *Michigan History* 38 (March 1954): 19–21.

33. Of Primary Schools, 1867 Mich. Pub. Acts 43.

34. People ex rel. Workman v. Bd. of Educ. of Detroit, 18 Mich. 400 (1869).

35. An act relative to the free public schools of Detroit, 1869 Mich. Pub. Acts 71.

36. People ex rel. Workman v. Board of Education of Detroit, 18 Mich. 400 (1869).

37. Ibid., 407.

38. Organized in Michigan in July 1863, the unit was renamed the 102d U.S. Colored Infantry in early 1864. See Katzman, *Before the Ghetto,* 48.

39. Ibid.

40. Hershock, *Paradox of Progress,* 207.

41. "Offenses against Public Justice," chap. 247, sec. 19, *The Compiled Law of the State of Michigan* (Lansing: W. S. George, 1872), 2:2109.

42. An Act to compel children to attend school, 1871 Mich. Pub. Acts 251–52.

43. An Act to amend sections sixteen . . . amending an act to establish graded and high school . . . , 1871 Mich. Pub. Acts 274.

44. An Act to amend . . . laws . . . relative to marriage, 1883 Mich. Pub. Acts 16.

45. Pace v. Alabama, 106 U.S. 583 (1883). For the background of this case, see Peter Wallenstein, *Tell the Court I Love My Wife: Race, Marriage, and Law—An American History* (New York: Palgrave, 2002), 110–14.

46. Katzman, *Before the Ghetto,* 94.

47. U.S. v. Stanley (The Civil Rights Cases), 109 U.S. 3 (1883).

48. An Act to protect all citizens in their civil rights, 1885 Mich. Pub. Acts 131 (hereafter, Michigan Civil Rights Act of 1885).

49. Joseph E. McMahon, "The Michigan Civil Rights Act, 1885, 1964" (unpublished paper, Bentley Historical Library, University of Michigan, Ann Arbor, 1976), 27.

50. *Detroit Evening News,* February 10, 1885, 3, quoted in McMahon, "Michigan Civil Rights Act," 13.

51. Michigan Civil Rights Act of 1885, § 1, 131–32.

52. Ibid., § 2, 132.

53. Ibid., § 3, 132.

54. Katzman, *Before the Ghetto,* 95; Michigan Civil Rights Act of 1885.

55. Ferguson v. Gies, 82 Mich. 358, 360, 46 N.W. 718 (1890).

56. Ibid., 361.

57. Ibid., 362.

58. Plessy v. Ferguson, 163 U.S. 537 (1896). The Ferguson in this case was a white judge in Louisiana and not related to the plaintiff in *Gies.*

59. Gies, 82 Mich. at 363.

60. Roberts v. City of Boston, 59 Mass. (5 Cush.) 198 (1850).

61. Gies, 82 Mich. at 364.

62. Ibid.

63. Ibid., 364–65.

64. Ibid., 365.

65. Ibid.

66. Ibid., 366.

67. Ibid.

68. Ibid., 366–67.

69. Ibid., 367.

70. Ibid.

71. Ibid., 368.

72. Ibid.

73. Katzman, *Before the Ghetto*, 95–96.

74. The article was later incorporated into Frederick K. Hoffman, *Race Traits and Tendencies of the American Negro* (1896; repr., Clark, N.J.: Lawbook Exchange, 2004).

75. An Act to protect all citizens in their civil rights, *Compiled Laws of the State of Michigan 1929* (Lansing: Franklin DeKleine, 1930), ch. 16809–10.

76. An Act to amend . . . "An act . . . relating to crimes . . . ." 1937 Mich. Pub. Acts 185.

77. Richard W. Thomas, *Life for Us Is What We Make It: Building Black Community in Detroit, 1915–1945* (Bloomington: Indiana University Press, 1992), 129.

78. County Civil Service Act, 1941 Mich. Pub. Acts 711.

79. An Act to promote and protect the welfare of the people of this state by prevention or elimination of discriminatory employment practices and policies based upon race, color, religion, national origin or ancestry; to create a state fair employment practices commission, defining its functions, powers and duties; and for other purposes, 1955 Mich. Pub. Acts 411. On the history of the passage of this act and the modern period of race relations in Michigan, see Fine, *Expanding the Frontiers of Civil Rights*.

80. Detroit's black community grew even more dramatically, from about 6,000 in 1910 to about 40,000 in 1920 and to around 120,000 by 1930. Katzman, *Before the Ghetto*, 207.

81. Kevin Boyle, *Arc of Justice: A Saga of Race, Civil Rights, and Murder in the Jazz Age* (New York: Henry Holt, 2004), 8.

82. As late as 1962, the official position of real estate brokers in the state was that "certain of our peoples are not yet prepared to accept all racial, creedal and ethnic groups as social intimates or as neighbors living in close proximity." Michigan Real Estate Association, *Statement of Policy and Code of Ethics* (Lansing: Michigan Real Estate Association, 1962), 2, pamphlet in Detroit Committee on Community Relations Papers, box 26, file 8, Walter P. Reuther Library of Labor and Urban Affairs, Wayne State University, Detroit.

83. See Bolden v. Grand River Operating Corp., 239 Mich. 318, 214 N.W. 241 (1927).

84. Parmalee v. Morris, 218 Mich. 625, 188 N.W. 330 (1922); Sipes v. McGhee, 316 Mich. 614, 25 N.W.2d 638 (1947); McKibbon v. Michigan Corp. and Sec. Comm'n, 369 Mich. 69, 119 N.W.2d 557 (1963).

85. Ironically, the seller of this house was a man of mixed racial ancestry who was passing for white. Boyle, *Arc of Justice*, 146.

86. Ibid.

TEN

Elizabeth Faue

"METHODS OF MYSTICISM" AND THE INDUSTRIAL ORDER

Labor Law in Michigan, 1868–1940

The day has passed when methods of mysticism can be
employed for the purpose of defeating the legal rights of trades
unions.

—*John Scannell*[1]

In his book, *Working Class Justice,* labor lawyer Maurice Sugar addressed
one of the chief obstacles to labor organization and collective bargaining
of his age—the labor injunction. Starting with the 1898 state supreme court
decision in *Beck v. Railway Teamsters' Protective Union,* Michigan workers
faced a barrage of court-ordered restrictions that cast the boycott as an infringement on the rights to free commerce, held even nonviolent picketing
to be illegal, and often charged individual participants in strikes with criminal intimidation. By seeking labor injunctions as a remedy in equity courts,
businesses relied on a system that granted striking workers few protections. Equity courts provided great advantages for employers, allowing
them to replace costly trials and expensive investigation with the relatively
loose standards of proof that prevailed at injunction hearings. At the same
time, hearings on labor injunctions neglected or skirted now widely accepted
rights for labor defendants. For these reasons, the labor injunction became
the target that ranked at the top of organized labor's political priorities in
the decades between the great labor struggles of the 1870s and the passage
of federal and state labor relations laws.[2]

The judge-made law of the labor injunction was only one aspect of
labor laws that invoked the police powers of the state to maintain public

order, protect the common welfare, and ensure economic rights. Although labor injunctions caught the eye of contemporary observers, labor laws covered a broad range of conditions stemming from the expansion of mass production in industry and the growth of the labor force. Harassment and intimidation of workers, dangerous working conditions, union incorporation, maximum working hours, workers' compensation, and labor mediation became the subjects of laws both nationally and in the state of Michigan. By 1940, state and federal laws had expanded economic rights and civil protections to individual workers and ensured the growth and stability of the labor movement.

In many ways, the history of labor law mirrors the general changes in American law, legal practice, and the court system since Reconstruction. Landmark Supreme Court decisions in the Progressive Era and under the New Deal treated the labor question directly, invoking new protections for workers and creating precedents for the expansion of federal authority in some areas and reinstating restrictive legal boundaries for legislative and economic action in others. The emergence of laws to protect employees at the workplace—to regulate hours, workplace safety, the employment of women and children, and employers' liability—served the public beyond organized labor. Moreover, protective laws required the expansion of the state apparatus in ways that challenged the voluntarism of both labor and capital. Michigan's factory acts constituted a second way to improve the condition of the working class in the context of increasingly hostile workplace relations.[3]

Throughout the period, it was primarily local ordinances, state statutes, and political practices that set the parameters within which organized labor and labor reformers operated. Local police, state militia, and private detectives were of primary importance in limiting and breaking labor organization and protests, and local courts were responsible for enforcing employer injunctions. In this way, local and state laws were more important than federal ones in determining the outcome of strikes and the efficacy of protective labor laws.[4] State laws limiting political expression, vagrancy statutes, and local ordinances criminalizing disorderly conduct, trespassing, and property damage were the ways in which local businesses and employer associations were able to restrict and even bar labor organization. Employer influence in local government and in the courts was effective, but also locally variable. By the 1930s, the balance between workers and employers, unions and businesses, shifted visibly to open up new arenas and strategies for labor action. This change was paralleled by increasing emphasis on federal laws and executive orders to set the conditions of workplace relations.

The Security of Individual Rights

Between 1867 and 1940, Michigan's state legislature and courts were responsible for the creation of a body of statutory laws, local ordinances, and judicial practices that regulated employment and governed private labor relations. Ordinary criminal law regarding disorderly conduct, destruction of property, and physical violence; state statutes regarding conspiracy to restrain trade and employment; and laws that restrained political expression, such as criminal syndicalism laws, red flag laws, and loyalty oaths, were effective tools in controlling labor's power and constraining popular protests against employers. Police and state militia, prosecuting attorneys, and state and local courts intervened in labor conflicts and issued injunctive remedies that hindered labor organization in the state. Court challenges to labor injunctions and employment laws further shaped the context of labor relations. Some of the earliest labor laws in Michigan, however, supported workers' claims. They enforced mechanics' liens against debtors, guarded against worker intimidation and "molestation," and protected "political purity" by forbidding employers from firing or threatening to fire workers in an effort to influence elections.[5]

The economic depression that began in 1873 significantly altered the relative calm of labor relations in the state. Public outcry against the so-called tramp problem inspired the state legislature and local municipalities to pass new laws regarding vagrancy and migrant labor. In Detroit, as historian John Schneider has shown, arrests for vagrancy and other misdemeanors, such as being drunken and disorderly, were on the rise. The continued in-migration of homeless men and women led the city council to pass an even stricter vagrancy ordinance the following year.[6]

The year 1877 was marked by more than an increase in vagrants in Michigan's largest city. Across the state, there were outbreaks of labor violence on the railroads, a product of the depression and of the willingness of railroads to use the crisis to drastically reduce their payroll through layoffs and wage cuts. Nationwide labor conflicts began that summer, starting with the disturbance on the Baltimore & Ohio Railroad. Locally, the struggle between railroads and the engineers, trainmen, and conductors who worked the lines had been ongoing since the late 1860s. Michigan was the home of the first railroad labor organization—the Brotherhood of Locomotive Engineers—and the scene of frequent railroad strife. The railroad brother-hoods had not flinched from confronting employers, and they often were fined for disobeying state statutes prohibiting the destruction of railroad property. Still, railroad companies believed that the strike funds available made it possible for trainmen to pay the costs of striking with little or no risk to themselves.[7] While strikers intimidated and threatened those run-ning the lines, there were no state laws that "could be applied to that evil." Strikers often were charged with only trespass or assault and battery. The engineers, a legislator argued, "had a large fund for self-protection and ag-gressive operations and the fines with which these offenses are punished would be paid and the violence would go on till their ends were attained."[8]

In January 1877, disturbances on the Grand Trunk Railroad in Michigan led to mob violence. The 3d Regiment of the state militia was called out to protect the lines in Port Huron. A large crowd there "blew off" the engine and stopped the local train from running; one protester was arrested be-fore the crowd dispersed. Nearby, in Sarnia and Belleville, Ontario, a gath-ering crowd at the railroad station was more threatening. Protesters, in-cluding several former employees, destroyed an engine. The provincial government sent the 49th Rifle Regulars to protect the rail lines. The troops at first could do little to quell the crowd. As it was later reported, "The sudden but effectual disabling of one locomotive seemed to greatly enrage the mob, who now resorted to several acts of personal violence" with "occasional brandishing of revolvers and the hurling of car bolts out the engine." Only with difficulty were the troops able to disperse the crowd. Despite the relatively limited damage in Michigan, there were rea-sons to fear additional trouble on the railroads, come summer.[9]

In this context, the Michigan state legislature considered a law spon-sored by F. A. Baker, a lawyer and state representative from Detroit. The proposed act sought to prohibit intimidation of workers, destruction of property, and any conspiracy that might keep companies, especially rail-roads, from operating regularly during labor disputes. Although section three explicitly exempted workers who "voluntarily" quit employment, "whether by concert of action or otherwise," from the provisions of the law, Baker's bill was meant to discourage strikes and collective protests. The law, known as Public Act 11 of 1877, passed by substantial margins in both the state House and Senate, was signed into law on February 14, 1877, and was scheduled to take effect on August 21, 1887.[10]

With the onset of a national railroad strike in July, Michigan communities prepared for the worst. The Detroit Board of Trade formed a protective association that could be mobilized to suppress unruly crowds, and the city hired three hundred special policemen in anticipation of violence against the railroads. Tramps became the target of police work, and forty persons were arrested for vagrancy during the strike. Vagrancy arrests in 1877–78 doubled the number of the previous year. As the *Free Press* reported, "The whole moral and physical force of the community must be brought to bear promptly and effectively in checking and preventing any spread of the evil and in meting out deserved punishment to the violations of the law and of the public peace." When the Michigan Central Railroad was struck, however, there was surprisingly little violence, even though the Baker Conspiracy Law, designed for just such a contingency, was not yet in force.[11]

Although labor advocates protested that Michigan's conspiracy law was "a constant menace to organized workingmen,"[12] the act remained dormant for nearly a decade. An emerging labor movement began to take shape and to create new political pressures to change state laws concerning labor. Under the leadership of radical labor reformers and trade unionists, such as Greenbacker Richard Trevellick and anarchist Joseph Labadie, the Knights of Labor (Knights, KOL) made significant progress in organizing workers across the state of Michigan. Starting with the first locals organized in Detroit in 1878, the Knights brought more than twenty-five thousand Michigan workers under the workingmen's banner. These membership gains were reflected in bargaining power with employers and political clout, as workingmen's candidates won elections and access to the political system. By 1886, the KOL and labor advocates held thirty-six seats in the state legislature and won many other local offices.[13]

With this political representation came an aggressive new agenda in the state legislature. Repealing the Baker Conspiracy Law was foremost on the list, but organized opposition delayed the effort. Beyond this demand, labor's political agenda at both local and state levels placed a high priority on the workings of labor law, the police, and the court. Of secondary importance was the passage of protective labor legislation that limited the work of women and children and attempted to safeguard workers. In 1883, 1885, and 1897, labor representatives supported statutes that allowed for the incorporation of the Knights of Labor, trade and labor societies, and labor associations.[14] They also supported the passage of mine safety and inspection laws, statutes regulating women's working conditions and prohibiting convict labor, and several compulsory education laws that were to serve as a brake on the employment of children. Two of the most important achievements were the creation of a Bureau of Labor and Industrial Statistics in 1883 and the passage in 1885 of a law defining a legal day's work as ten hours. Finally, labor advocates supported a law creating a state court of mediation and arbitration.[15]

As with most protective legislation, these labor laws required the cooperation and diligence of state government to oversee their operation. Workingmen's advocates could prod state legislators to enact laws but could not necessarily prevail upon the executive branch to ensure compliance. For this reason, laws often remained unenforced. Child labor was a case in point. Determined employers and needy families could find ways to circumvent rules concerning children's employment and compulsory school attendance. Despite the creation of a state court of arbitration in 1889, to cite another example, the court held no hearings until 1897, when reform governor Hazen Pingree appointed members to the long-inactive agency. Factory inspection laws worked only if inspectors were appointed and paid, and, even then, a shortage of inspectors assured that worker safety and women's and children's labor laws were routinely violated.

The passage of laws concerning labor unions, employment, and labor relations did, however, create a new field of legal practice. Employers, workers, and unions needed experienced lawyers to define workplace rights, set standards for working-class justice, and give voice to demands within and outside the workplace. Individual workers required the services of lawyers to oversee labor cases under laws that varied from state vagrancy statutes and city ordinances to new state laws protecting labor unions. In 1886, Henry Haigh, a local attorney and labor reformer, published a primer called *A Plain Statement of the Laws Relating to Labor,* which referenced Michigan state statutes.[16] The handbook covered the broad sweep of laws involving the rights and duties of employers and workers. Haigh explained customs and contracts of employment, mechanics' lien laws, laws regarding strikes and boycotts, and the prohibition of conspiracy in labor actions. Stirred by debates among the Knights of Labor, Haigh advocated state arbitration as a reasonable remedy for the conflict between employer and workers. Arbitration, he wrote, "enables disinterested parties, whose judgements are not warped, whose minds are unbiased, and who may, without prejudice, study all sides of the problem and determine with clearness as to what in fairness can be done, to adjust the differences without interrupting business, engendering hatred, or precipitating conflict which may end in want, riot, or bloodshed." Haigh further proposed ways in which arbitration might be administered.[17]

Labor's legal efforts took place in a context of enhanced employer power and organization, an often contradictory state supreme court, and the growing conservatism of the judiciary and the state legislature in matters of property rights, individual welfare, and the state's police power. Under Thomas Cooley, the Michigan Supreme Court offered a contradictory and ambiguous opinion of labor legislation. The Cooley court was, for many, the voice of Jacksonian moderation, harboring suspicion toward organized capital and organized labor alike.[18] Labor law in Michigan drew on a common-law legacy in its specific prohibition of economic conspiracy and economic coercion, with little regard for the vulnerability of individual workers in a capitalist system. The courts recognized the right of workers to organize unions and to quit work if their employer did not meet their terms; but the law did not sanction concerted action in many other contexts. The most reliable way to assure that workers had rights was the political ability to influence and shape police practices and the local judiciary. Finally, working-class juries came to play an important role in maintaining some claim to collective action.[19]

No Human or Divine Law

The growth of the Knights of Labor and trade unions in the 1880s meant that the chief obstacles against labor organization were the relative economic power of employers and the existing legal framework of conspiracy law. In Michigan, that meant the Baker Conspiracy Law, which remained in force despite the efforts of working-class advocates in the state legislature to repeal it. As the Knights of Labor began to challenge employers across the state, many labor activists were apprehensive about the uses to which the Baker law could be put. During prolonged labor struggles in 1885 and 1886, these concerns seemed justified. Both in the Saginaw Valley lumber strike of that year and in conflicts that followed, the Baker law and police interventions suggested that the existing legal framework undermined labor organization.

The 1885 Saginaw Valley strike illustrated the ability of the conspiracy law to intimidate and even to curtail labor organization and the willingness of state and local authorities to go beyond labor law in protecting private property during labor disputes. Prior to 1885, the Knights of Labor had organized energetically among workers in the Saginaw Valley. Native-born and immigrant, skilled craftsmen and unskilled laborers, the workers in Bay City, Saginaw, and elsewhere took the opportunity to improve their working conditions seriously. Above all, the passage of the ten-hour law in 1885, championed by labor reformer, trade unionist, and state legislator Thomas Barry, promised an end to employer abuses. Workers believed that the law went into force once the legislature had passed it. The delayed effective date and the efforts of employers to circumvent the law through contracts requiring eleven-hour days or by wage concessions led Saginaw Valley workers to strike in July of 1885. Workers at ninety sawmills and forty salt mines stopped work in this massive protest.[20]

Representative Barry and *Labor Vindicator* editor D. C. Blinn went to Saginaw to support the strike. At the same time, they were anxious to restrain striking workers from destroying any property or doing any personal violence. Barry, as a labor paper later reported, "counseled them to keep sober and commit no violence." Moreover, he took pains to violate "no human or divine law" and, instead, placed himself in danger by defending one obstinate mill owner from the wrath of the crowd.[21] Despite the lack of property destruction, the strike was the occasion of the first use of state militia against strikers in Michigan and the first time a state governor deputized Pinkerton agents hired by a private firm.[22] Barry and Blinn were charged under the provisions of the Baker Conspiracy Law with "willfully and maliciously" and "by means of intimidation" closing the sawmills. When Barry went on trial months later in Saginaw, he was acquitted of the charges, but the strike already had been lost. Barry later faced a civil suit, which found him liable for damages incurred during the strike.[23] Working-class juries acquitted labor defendants of conspiracy charges, but they later were held responsible for civil damages. The lesson was not lost on conservative politicians or on the new employer associations that organized around the turn of the century.[24]

In the aftermath of the Barry trial, labor sympathizers in the state legislature made the first of many coordinated efforts to repeal the Baker Conspiracy Law. As during Barry's trial, labor advocates focused on the inequalities between workers and their employers, inequalities that the law only magnified. According to the Knights' *Labor Leaf*, the law was designed "to terrorize and punish those misguided men who sought to preserve their lives and liberty, to support their families, and to enjoy the private property which they should be enabled to earn by their industry and frugality."[25] The law's author, however, charged that "[n]o legislation should be adopted the tendency of which would be to place the business of the country in the hands, or under the control, of irresponsible bodies, unknown to the law, and representative of no one but themselves."[26] It was,

Baker argued, the goal of working-class radicals to repeal the law, because that law was "an obstacle to their illegal purposes." The Baker law was repealed by the legislature in Public Act 23 of 1891. It was the last significant political victory for organized labor for many years.[27]

In the years after 1891, organized labor lacked the political and economic clout needed either to imagine or to enact a more positive legislative agenda. Moreover, like the national American Federation of Labor, the craft unionist Michigan Federation invested less in state solutions to labor problems than in labor organization as the means to improve skilled workers' wages and conditions. Such voluntarism in labor's political strategy did not preclude supporting state laws to protect those who lacked the economic and political power to bargain with employers, namely women and children. Other issues of concern were work safety, employer liability, and workers' compensation, which were increasingly the objects of state action in the Progressive Era.[28] Protective legislation in these areas was less subject to judicial reversal. As historian Melvyn Urofsky has shown, although courts were ambivalent about labor organization, they generally supported the regulation of conditions of employment, particularly when it involved women, child labor, and hazardous occupations.[29] In Michigan, as elsewhere, the interest of the state in protecting women was shown in a series of laws that were governed by both moral and practical considerations. Maximum-hour laws were designed to protect working women's health, strength, and future motherhood. For moral reasons, employers were required to enclose staircases to protect women from men's gaze; they were to provide seats, separate dressing rooms, and toilets for women employees and to shield them from objectionable language. A 1907 law summarized the prohibitions; women were not to work in places where liquor was sold or where "life, limb, health or morals [were] endangered."[30] When employers challenged these laws, the Michigan Supreme Court upheld the right of the state to protect workers, to inspect workplaces, and to restrict the working hours, conditions, and employment of women and children.[31] Among the victories of progressive labor reform was the passage of a workers' compensation act, later modified in 1919.[32]

Government by Injunction?

Despite gains in labor legislation that regulated entry into the labor force and working conditions in the most dangerous trades, workers found themselves increasingly constrained by new local ordinances and state

statutes governing the use of and conduct in public spaces. Early precedents in the federal courts that restrained strikes against railroads under
government trusteeship or concerned the obstruction of federal mails set
the patterns for local and state courts to issue injunctions against union-led
strikes and boycotts. Locally, the refusal of the Brotherhood of Locomotive Engineers, a union with origins in Michigan, to haul freight for a boy-
cotted railroad set the stage for the first round of court actions against
labor. In *Toledo, Ann Arbor & Northern Michigan Railroad v. Pennsylvania
Company,* Justice William Howard Taft, writing for the U.S. Circuit Court,
issued an injunction against the brotherhood and its president, P. M.
Arthur, on the basis of their violation of the Interstate Commerce Act.
The notoriety of this case and of others, such as the *In re Debs* decision,
inspired a wave of labor injunctions in Michigan and nationally.[33]

The first important labor injunction in Michigan was tested in *Beck v.
Railway Teamsters' Protective Union* in the state supreme court in 1898. Cited
in many subsequent decisions, the *Beck* ruling imposed a broad interpretation of the economic rights of employers and a correspondingly restrictive
definition of the rights of workers to strike and boycott an employer. In
effect, *Beck* declared peaceful picketing to be an unlawful violation of the
rights of employers and workers. Although the decision endorsed the free
association of workers in labor unions, it declared most collective action
by unions to be an infringement of individual liberty through economic
coercion. Bypassing the need for conspiracy law, *Beck* struck at the heart of
labor by defining all picketing as coercive.[34]

Beck was followed by a barrage of labor injunctions issued by local and
state courts. When they had the resources, labor unions challenged these
injunctions in court. These challenges led to a string of court decisions that
upheld temporary restraining orders and issued contempt citations against
workers and unions that failed to obey. As Joseph Harrison wrote, "The
broad reach of the labor injunction offered in *Beck* gained definition in
Foundry Co., Ludwig, In re Hamlyn, and *In re Langell.* Each decision further
narrowed the scope of activity open to a defendant union or a union member following the issuance of an injunction."[35]

As a legal remedy for employers, the labor injunction surpassed earlier
doctrines of criminal conspiracy and supplemented the widespread use of
disorderly conduct charges and antipicketing ordinances to restrict, if not
ban, labor organization. Injunctions offered businesses relief from the an-
noyance and intimidation of striking workers and the damaging effects of
public boycotts of their products, as well as insulation from public opinion.

The process of obtaining labor injunctions allowed employers to cast their striking employees as threats to public order and to put business failures and the high costs of living squarely at the door of labor unions. The chief advantage of the labor injunction, however, was that it placed questions of worker rights outside the reach of jury trials under criminal and civil law and put it before judges whose sympathies, if not entirely predictable, were predominantly conservative. Belief in the sanctity of property rights and the limited use of state action underwrote the judicial predisposition to grant injunctions to employers in labor conflicts.[36]

There were a limited number of legal and political options for labor organizations. They could contest injunctions in the courts, a course of action that elicited little success. In addition, they could and did campaign to reform the judiciary and to force conservative, business-oriented judges from the bench. Business, too, had a stake in the process of electing and appointing judges, and labor met with limited success in its efforts to keep employer-friendly judges from the court.[37] Still, only laws that exempted labor from antitrust action or that prohibited or restrained the use of the injunction could remedy labor's legal disadvantages. The passage of antitrust law reform held out some hope of exempting labor from court-issued injunctions and antitrust actions, but employers contested such measures in Congress, the state legislature, and the courts. By 1913, when the Commission on Industrial Relations put together its controversial report on labor conflict, the labor injunction—even more than the use of state militia and private police forces—had become the major obstacle to the peaceful conduct of labor relations. Court-issued injunctions disrupted the process of collective bargaining and undermined the fragile fabric of industrial democracy. They threatened the free speech and individual rights of workers on the one hand and the government's legitimacy as an impartial arbiter on the other. The suppression of these rights in the courts thus fueled working-class discontent and weakened workers' attachment to and belief in the law. As the Commission on Industrial Relations wrote, "Such injunctions have in many cases inflicted grievous injury upon workmen engaged in disputes with their employers, and their interests have been seriously prejudiced by the denial of jury trial, which every criminal is afforded, and by trial before the judges against whom the contempt was alleged."[38]

The commission's hearings had extended to investigating local labor conflicts. It heard testimony on a strike that raged in copper mines in Michigan's Upper Peninsula. More than sixteen thousand copper miners had gone out on strike against mine owners. Under the leadership of the

Western Federation of Miners, the workers held their strike against private police and military intervention. Special state laws and ordinances gave private police the right to carry concealed weapons, and the state legislature passed a law that covered the costs of defending companies against strikes. In the interim, the mining companies relied on more than twenty-six hundred militia men and seventeen hundred special deputies to control the striking miners. During the strike, there were seven hundred arrests for violating court orders and disturbing the peace. Although a local judge tried to dismiss a temporary restraining order, the state supreme court upheld it in a landmark case that seemed only to confirm the court's commitment to restrict and even to break labor unions.[39]

Working-Class Justice

The widespread use of labor injunctions had a chilling effect on labor organization. As historian Michael Willrich has written, "The sweeping language of some labor injunctions, posted like royal decrees at work sites and in neighborhoods, imposed judge-made criminal codes on entire communities of workers in Chicago and other cities."[40] So, too, in Detroit and other communities in Michigan, labor unions saw injunctions intimidate workers from joining unions and participating in strikes. In 1916, even the large and relatively powerful printers' local in Detroit confronted organized legal opposition. Conducting a strike for union recognition, the local faced a barrage of charges ranging from disorderly conduct to violations of a sweeping labor injunction. Not only firms but the Employers' Association of Detroit stood aligned against workers' rights.[41]

Like other major cities, Detroit witnessed the rapid increase of labor conflict in the years preceding World War I. This new insurgency mobilized thousands of workers and increased the political power and visibility of organized labor. Progressive reformers passed important new state labor laws, including a modified workers' compensation law, an act that sought to exempt unions from state antitrust actions, and a statute that prohibited sex discrimination in pay.[42] The vibrancy of the labor revival, however, provoked employer responses in the courts and in the state legislature. Labor injunctions continued to be issued at every turn. For these reasons, the Detroit Federation of Labor, its constituent unions, and other labor organizations in the state conducted a petition campaign against labor injunctions. When the petition campaign failed, labor organizations turned to direct actions against employers, choosing openly to violate labor injunctions and to contest their convictions in court. Such tactics led local and state courts to temper their actions against unions, and, in one case, labor's aggressive stance allowed striking waitresses the time they needed to force an employer to the bargaining table.[43]

An increase in strikes and labor actions during and after the war led to state efforts to contain labor organization and protest. During the war, factories in large cities were the subject of extensive government surveillance. In 1918, the city of Detroit passed a war work ordinance, which required workers to register to obtain a work permit. The system, which saw little use in the waning days of the war, had been designed to keep track of workers, to regulate employment, and to restrict mobility.[44] Nationally, the Espionage and Sedition Acts served to dampen labor organization, as did the government offensive against the Industrial Workers of the World. In Michigan, federal efforts were echoed by state statutes that prohibited the waving of red flags and forbade the advocacy of any form of militant political or trade organization.[45]

The most significant among these laws was Public Act 255 of 1919, an antisyndicalism statute that made illegal not just violent acts and property destruction but political advocacy and organization. "Without a doubt," the *Detroit Labor News* argued, "it [was] the most vicious piece of legislation ever put over upon a suffering and abused working class." It seemed directed at the burgeoning labor organization in the state. As with the creation of a state constabulary, "[t]he intent of this law [was] not only to single out for punishment the so-called 'reds,' but to crush all labor organizations whenever they dare claim the goods of which they have been robbed."[46] The law brought a wave of arrests. Some labor organizers faced local jail on misdemeanor charges; others were put up on federal charges; and still others precipitously were deported in the hysteria that followed the war. Workers were arrested for holding meetings, vagrancy, distributing anarchist literature, and belonging to the Communist Party. Some sixty-two men and women were placed in custody "in anticipation" of protests on International Labor Day in 1920.[47] A few years later, a meeting of Communists in Bridgman, Michigan, led to the arrest and trial of several organizers under the criminal syndicalism act and to public outcry against the violation of individual civil liberties.[48]

By the mid-1920s, the strength of labor had been tested in labor injunctions and during a postwar political reaction that created new restrictions on working-class political organization and on the ability of labor unions to organize. Despite the passage of the Clayton Antitrust Act with provisions exempting labor from antitrust suits, a record number of labor injunctions were issued during the decade. Furthermore, organized labor's protection under the Clayton Act proved short-lived. The landmark case *Duplex Printing v. Deering* (1921), which had originated in a Michigan challenge, struck down labor exemptions as unconstitutional. Even protective labor legislation for women suffered a setback, and state minimum wage laws for women were undermined by the Supreme Court decision in *Adkins v. Children's Hospital* (1925). Conservative reaction found representation in a state legislature that was overwhelmingly Republican for most of the decade. No new labor protections were passed after 1919, and there was no effort to reform the court system to restrain the wave of injunctions. The direct action campaign in Detroit had little impact in other areas of the state.[49]

An embattled labor movement developed a network of lawyers whose practice, while not exclusively dedicated to conflicts between employers and workers, was predominantly working-class in clientele and labor-oriented in focus. In Michigan, Maurice Sugar, who would become a major legal counsel for the emerging automobile workers' union, led others in learning to use legal procedure to gain rights that otherwise eluded workers. Central to Sugar's success as a labor lawyer was his mastery of the technical aspects of the law. As biographer Christopher Johnson noted, Sugar used procedural errors, employing the prosecution's mistakes as a weapon against the class bias inherent in the judicial system. It was in procedure, Sugar wrote, that "the substance of democracy is preserved."[50] The sheer number of court-issued labor injunctions gave Sugar experience in combating the minute details and intricate requirements of the law. Injunction law gave the advantage to the employer; confronting the substance of any injunction, given this advantage, was difficult, if not impossible. Instead, as Sugar wrote in his unpublished autobiography, "[e]very bill of complaint, every restraining order, every summons, every service, was scrutinized minutely, dissected carefully in the search for a legal objection" upon which to ground a plea for dismissal or to delay an injunction long enough to allow workers to win labor disputes.[51] As Sugar argued, "I felt that the legal cards were stacked against labor, so I concentrated on the means of preventing those cards from being played."[52] Sugar's tactics relied on the same means by which employers had long defeated strikes. Time, often the enemy of striking workers, was less threatening when used to postpone judgment.

Sugar's legal tactics influenced a generation of labor lawyers, including Lee Pressman, who became lead attorney for the Congress of Industrial

Organizations. Throughout the later 1930s, they turned to Sugar to create new legal tactics and strategies to enlarge the available area for labor legal action. Labor law, a lay interest for many progressive legal scholars, became a major field of study in the course of the Depression decade. Instituted not just in the production of legal casebooks but in the development of curriculum at state law schools, labor law took on even greater importance with the emergence of labor law reform and the rapid growth of the labor movement during the 1930s.

Law and Order versus the New Deal Order

The upsurge of worker organization during the Great Depression brought opportunities for the labor movement to mobilize politically to overturn restrictive laws. In particular, the labor injunction became the target of new federal legislation. The struggle to reform the judiciary and to restrict the use of labor injunctions ended when Congress passed the Norris–La Guardia Act in 1932. The act outlawed contracts that prohibited workers from joining unions and extended protection to labor unions against antitrust cases, private damage suits, and court-issued labor injunctions.[53] As part of President Franklin Delano Roosevelt's New Deal reform, labor's congressional allies sponsored legislation that guaranteed the right of workers to join unions and to bargain collectively—the National Industrial Recovery Act of 1933 and the far-more-sweeping National Labor Relations Act of 1935. These political victories proved to be the key to organizing workers in mass production industries and even in service, clerical, and sales work.[54]

Despite Democratic breakthroughs in the state legislature and government in 1932 and again in 1936, Michigan remained a predominantly Republican political stronghold. Many local political officials and state court judges were committed to the industrial and political status quo. Conservatives introduced a measure against labor's actions with the Spolansky Act of 1931. The law had as its ostensive purpose the registration of immigrants and naturalized citizens in Michigan. It implicitly threatened the deportation of dissenting workers. Although organized labor supported the bill, restrictions on the employment of resident aliens and its possible use against dissidents brought together an alliance of conservative and radical organizations against its implementation. The American Civil Liberties Union was able to secure a permanent injunction against it.[55] The Spolansky Act, however, was only one of a series of laws meant to dampen working-class organization and political dissent generally. In 1931 and 1935, for example, a Republican-dominated state legislature passed laws that required teachers and other educators to take an oath supporting the state constitution.[56]

Employers and conservative groups saw growing labor militancy and, in particular, the wave of sit-down strikes that began in 1935 as a threat to property rights and to law and order. The increasing incidence of farm and labor protests led to a revival of the criminal syndicalism law. Passed in 1935, the updated version of the statute declared that anyone who "advocates, aids, or takes any active part in the overthrow by force or violence of the government of the United States and/or of any state" was guilty of a felony. It may have been a sign of changing political fortunes that section two added, "Nothing in this act shall be construed to prohibit or abridge the lawful right of free speech, liberty of the press or in any manner interfere with the right of peaceful picketing or striking in industrial controversies." Despite this caveat, labor advocates saw the criminal syndicalism statute as a threat to worker organization. In 1933, Maurice Sugar appealed the 1922 indictments of communists in the Bridgman case and won dismissal of the charges. Along with others, he fought the use of the syndicalism statute against farm and labor protests throughout the state. Buttressed by local ordinances that prohibited public assembly and public distribution of flyers, however, local law enforcement still willingly quelled mass protests like the Ford Hunger March.[57] Direct action remained, as in earlier decades, one of the few options against punitive laws.

The new restrictions on political speech and organization, like those of earlier decades, stood in opposition to an emerging consensus on individual civil liberties.[58] Federal legislation, such as the National Industrial Recovery Act and the Wagner Act, offered implicit and explicit guarantees of workers' rights to organize and bargain collectively.[59] The election of former Detroit mayor Frank Murphy to the Michigan governorship in 1936 signaled the beginning of a more labor-friendly state government. Labor unions hoped to forestall court-issued injunctions or at least their enforcement by local authorities. Furthermore, new federal labor relations agencies opened the door for widespread organization of unorganized industrial and service workers. A freer legal and political environment made it possible to challenge the automobile industry, which held a stranglehold over labor organization in Michigan in such open-shop bastions as Detroit and Flint.

Labor's weapon of choice in 1937 was the sit-down strike. The pervasive use of labor injunctions against picketing, the importation of replacement

workers, and police intervention had prevented labor unions from organizing either mass production industries or retail and service trades. The
sit-down strike became a force to equalize the discrepancy in power between workers and employers. It stopped the machinery of the workplace
and of the court system, even as it allowed workers to assert property
rights in their jobs. The public show of the sit-down strikes fueled worker
organization throughout the state. Union survival, however, required unprecedented vigilance, and the public was greeted not only with the first
dramatic wave of labor protests but subsequent protests at other automobile plants, as well as in workshops, factories, restaurants, and department
stores.

Labor's success was met by a fierce backlash among voters in Michigan
that seemingly repudiated the progress that unions had made. Among the
first victims of revived conservatism was Governor Frank Murphy, who
had kept the state's National Guard units from interfering with sit-down
strikes in Flint and Detroit.[60] Murphy's ambitious plan for a state-level
"little New Deal" met with substantial Republican opposition in the state
legislature. In particular, a state labor relations bill, which lawyers represent-
ing both employer and labor interests had drafted at Murphy's request,
failed to draw the required legislative support. Both Republican senators
and Democratic representatives found reasons to oppose the bill. Moreover, the growth of labor conflict and especially the violence that seemed
to attend sit-down strikes proved problematic. As a later court decision intoned, "No one who lived through the period can ignore the terror which
this lawless labor technique imposed not only upon the automotive industry and its non-union employees . . . but upon all employers of labor in
Michigan."[61] Only a tougher stance toward labor, conservatives argued,
would create a lasting labor peace. Branded as a governor weak on crime
and sympathetic to the radical labor movement, Murphy was defeated in
his bid for reelection in 1938.[62]

Under the new Republican governor, Frank Fitzgerald, the Michigan
state legislature passed a law extending legal protections to labor unions
but also significantly curtailing their actions. In 1939, the State Act for Compulsory Arbitration and Mediation created new machinery to address
changes in labor relations in the state's workplaces. Seen as a balance for
the open provisions of the federal labor relations act, Michigan's law invoked penalties against labor violence, instituted a cooling-off period for
strikes, and prohibited sit-down strikes. It also created a state labor mediation board to oversee disputes and, in a significant concession, banned dis-

crimination against union membership in the workplace. Although the law seemed unusually harsh, it was comparable to other state labor laws introduced in 1939 and prefigured the restrictions of the Taft-Hartley Act of 1947.[63]

The ambivalent outcome of the struggle over labor legislation and the implementation of a state labor law restricting unions did not halt further worker organization. Indeed, two important court decisions in 1940 suggested that liberalization of federal labor law under the Wagner Act preempted the state-level restrictions. Long a virulently antiunion employer, Ford Motor Company had prohibited leafleting of workers both on and near its premises, a ban that led to violence during the 1937 organizing campaign. A National Labor Relations Board hearing found Ford's aggressive tactics to be unfair labor practices. The company had been supported in its efforts by local Dearborn police who refused to intervene at the plant or to stop the security men from attacking picketers. At the local level, justice of the peace Lila Neuenfeld found that a long-standing ordinance outlawing leafleting at the Rouge plant was invalid, paving the way for the successful organization of the company.[64] The case was followed by a U.S. Circuit Court decision in *NLRB v. Ford Motor Co.*, in which the court ruled that Ford was guilty of unfair labor practices. The decision, although it charged Ford to remedy its practices, also allowed the company leeway in continuing to press its own case with workers. In 1941, in the wake of these decisions, Ford signed union contracts with the United Auto Workers. Federal laws led to changes in labor relations that even local police forces and state legislation could not undermine.[65]

Federalizing Labor Law

As in other American states, labor law in Michigan has a long, complicated, and paradoxical history. In its origins in the Republican-dominated politics of the nineteenth century, the labor legislation that empowered and restrained labor organization and workers' rights in Michigan flowed from concern over the public interest, belief in the sanctity of property rights, and adherence to the doctrine of limited governance and restricted police powers for the state. These beliefs were challenged and reshaped in the half century from the labor wars of the 1870s to the emergence of a federal regulatory state in the 1930s. At first, common-law concepts of conspiracy and freedom to contract aided conservative legislators and judges in proscribing the collective action, both economic and political, of labor organizations and individual workers. The risks that mass production industry and the powers of corporate employers brought to Michigan workers guided new strategies aimed at protecting the most vulnerable workers—primarily women and children—and restraining the collective actions of workers in bargaining, protest, and political action. New beliefs about government powers, the character and use of the law, and the challenges faced by workers brought a new industrial relations regime, codified by federal law and regulated by public agencies.

The most significant change over these decades remained not in the control and regulation of labor relations so much as in the mechanism by which it occurred and the level of government that became dominant in arbitrating, mediating, and deciding labor relations. By the end of the 1930s, the federal government, not local municipalities and state legislatures, had become the major force in shaping workplace relations and conditions at all levels. Although certain sectors remained outside the purview of the National Labor Relations Board, the majority of workers in private sector employment had the option of seeking redress from federal authorities. There were no guarantees, as workers and unions began to learn in 1947 with the passage of the Taft-Hartley Act, that the federal government would remain a neutral and even prolabor force in union organization and bargaining; but local judges no longer ruled over the process as they did in the heyday of labor injunctions. The one arena in which labor law remained undefined was public employment. Local, state, and federal employees had to wait more than twenty years for the reform of labor law and a similar opportunity to replace "methods of mysticism" with the logic of government regulation.

Notes

1. John Scannell, secretary of the Michigan Federation of Labor, "Injunctions in Industrial Disputes," Labor Injunctions, uncatalogued manuscripts file, Joseph A. Labadie Collection, Hatcher Graduate Library, University of Michigan, Ann Arbor.

2. See, e.g., John Philip Frey, *The Labor Injunction: An Exposition of Government by Judicial Conscience and Its Menace* (Cincinnati: n.p., [1923?]). On labor's political priorities, see William E. Forbath, *Law and the Shaping of the American Labor Movement* (Cambridge, Mass.: Harvard University Press, 1989); Julie Greene, *Pure and Simple Politics: The American Federation of Labor and Political Activism, 1881–1917* (Cambridge: Cambridge University Press, 1998); William G. Ross, *A Muted Fury: Populists, Progressives, and Labor Unions Confront the Courts, 1890–1937* (Princeton, N.J.: Princeton University Press, 1994).

3. Carl Eugene Parry, "Labor Legislation of Michigan" (Ph.D. diss., University of Michigan, 1909); Ward Sager, *Legislation Affecting Workers* (Ann Arbor: Department of Vocational Education, University of Michigan, 1944).

4. See Edwin E. Witte, *The Government in Labor Disputes* (New York: McGraw-Hill, 1932); Thomas Ralph Clark, *Defending Rights: Law, Labor Politics, and the State in California, 1890–1925* (Detroit: Wayne State University Press, 2002).

5. Parry, "Labor Legislation," 1–27. See also Molestation Act, 1867 Mich. Pub. Acts; An act to maintain political purity, 1877 Mich. Pub. Acts 205.

6. John C. Schneider, *Detroit and the Problem of Order, 1830–1880: A Geography of Crime, Riot, and Policing* (Lincoln: University of Nebraska Press, 1980), 109. See also Margaret C. Barrett, "'Trifling with the Liberty of Men': Tramps, Vagrants, and Michigan's Disorderly Persons Act, 1865–1903" (master's thesis, Wayne State University, 1995).

7. See Parry, "Labor Legislation," 10–14, 280–89; Schneider, *Detroit and the Problem of Order,* 104–16; Robert V. Bruce, *1877: Year of Violence* (Indianapolis: Bobbs-Merrill, 1959).

8. House Memorial on the Bill, *House Journal* (1887), 204, quoted in Parry, "Labor Legislation," 281.

9. *Detroit News,* January 2–5, 1877; *Correspondence Respecting the Disturbance on the Line of the Grand Trunk Railway, January 1st, 1877* (Ottawa: McLean, Roger, 1877), quote at 5.

10. Parry, "Labor Legislation," 11–14.

11. *Detroit Free Press,* July 24, 1877, quoted in Schneider, *Detroit and the Problem of Order,* 109; Steve Babson, Ron Alpern, Dave Elsila, and John Revitte, *Working Detroit* (Detroit: Wayne State University Press, 1986), 10.

12. *Detroit Labor Leaf,* January 26, 1887.

13. Doris B. McLaughlin, *Michigan Labor: A Brief History from 1818 to the Present* (Ann Arbor: Institute of Labor and Industrial Relations, University of Michigan–Wayne State University, 1970), 19–49; Richard Oestreicher, *Solidarity and Fragmentation: Working People and Class Consciousness in Detroit, 1875–1900* (Urbana: University of Illinois Press, 1986); Carlotta Anderson, *All-American Anarchist: Joseph A. Labadie and the Labor Movement* (Detroit: Wayne State University Press, 1998), 23–35, 47–159.

14. See Parry, "Labor Legislation," 18–19, on labor's political agenda. See An Act to provide for the incorporation of local assemblies of the Knights of Labor of North America, 1883 Mich. Pub. Acts 171; An Act to provide for the incorporation of societies to promote the interests of trade and labor associations, 1885 Mich. Pub. Acts 163; and An Act to provide for the incorporation of labor associations, 1897 Mich. Pub. Acts 15, for incorporation statutes.

15. Parry, "Labor Legislation," 54–85, 267–70. The State Court of Mediation and Arbitration was created in An Act to provide for the amicable adjustment of grievances and disputes that may arise between employers and employes, 1889 Mich. Pub. Acts 359.

16. Henry A. Haigh, *A Plain Statement of the Laws Relating to Labor* (Detroit: Co-operative Publishing, 1886). See also Thomas S. Cogley, *The Law of Strikes, Lockouts and Labor Organizations* (Washington, D.C.: W. H. Lowdermilk, 1894); Morgan E.

Dowling, *The Wage Workers' Remedy* (Detroit: J. F. Erby, 1894); Frederic J. Stimson, *Labor and Its Relations to the Law* (New York: Charles Scribners' Sons, 1895), among others.

17. Haigh, *Plain Statement*, 23.

18. See Jeffrey Sklansky, *The Soul's Economy: Market Society and Selfhood in American Thought, 1820–1920* (Chapel Hill: University of North Carolina Press, 2002), 205–24.

19. Brown v. Stoerkel, 74 Mich. 269, 41 N.W. 921 (1889); Beck v. Ry. Teamsters' Protective Union, 118 Mich. 497, 517, 77 N.W. 13, 21 (1898); Joseph S. Harrison, "Labor Law and the Michigan Supreme Court, 1890–1930" (master's thesis, Wayne State University, 1980), 9–11.

20. For accounts of the strike, see Michigan, Bureau of Labor and Industrial Statistics, *Third Annual Report* (Lansing, Mich.: Bureau of Labor and Industrial Statistics, 1887), 92–134; Jeremy W. Kilar, *Michigan's Lumbertowns: Lumbermen and Laborers in Saginaw, Bay City, and Muskegon, 1870–1905* (Detroit: Wayne State University Press, 1990), 212–49; Anderson, *All-American Anarchist*, 112–13.

21. *Detroit Labor Leaf,* January 27, 1886.

22. F. Clever Bald, *Michigan in Four Centuries: Line Drawings by William Thomas Woodward* (New York: Harper and Bros., 1954), 297; George N. Fuller, ed., *Michigan: A Centennial History of the State and Its People* (Chicago: Lewis Publishing, 1939), 2:273.

23. Webber v. Barry, 66 Mich. 127, 130–31; 33 N.W. 289, 291–92 (1887).

24. *Detroit Labor Leaf,* January 13, 20, 27, 1886; *Detroit News,* January 8, 13, 14, 22, 23, 1886.

25. *Detroit Labor Leaf,* January 26, 1887.

26. House Memorial, quoted in Parry, "Labor Legislation," 284.

27. Parry, "Labor Legislation," 284; *Detroit Free Press,* March 5, 6, 1891. On the repeal, see Anderson, *All-American Anarchist*, 163, 171.

28. Parry, "Labor Legislation," 54–259.

29. Melvin I. Urofsky, "State Courts and Protective Legislation during the Progressive Era: A Reevaluation," *Journal of American History* 72 (June 1985): 63–91.

30. State laws regarding women's employment are discussed in Parry, "Labor Legislation," 143, 234–38. See also Michigan, *Laws Relating to Labor* (Lansing, Mich.: Wynkoop, Hutterbeck, and Crawford, 1913); Sager, *Legislation Affecting Workers*, 181.

31. The Blowers' Law, which regulated conditions in the polished metals industry, was unsuccessfully challenged in People v. Smith, 108 Mich. 527, 66 N.W. 382 (1896). On the challenge to the women's hour law, see Withey v. Bloem, 163 Mich. 419, 128 N.W. 913 (1910). For the national picture, see Julie Novkov, *Constituting Workers, Protecting Women: Gender, Law, and Labor in the Progressive Era and the New Deal Years* (Ann Arbor: University of Michigan Press, 2001).

32. Betty W. Allie, "History of Workmen's Compensation in Michigan," *Michigan History Magazine* 30, no. 2 (April–June 1946): 317–50; Robert D. Hatfield, "Labor's Input and Response to Michigan's Work Safety and Disability Compensation Laws, 1870s–1943," seminar paper, Wayne State University, 1991. See also John Fabian Witt,

The Accidental Republic: Crippled Workmen, Destitute Widows, and the Remaking of American Law (Cambridge, Mass.: Harvard University Press, 2004).

33. Toledo, Ann Arbor & Northern Michigan Ry. Co. v. Pennsylvania Co., 54 F. 730 (C.C.N.D. Ohio 1893), discussed in Michigan, Bureau of Labor and Industrial Statistics, *Eleventh Annual Report* (Lansing, Mich.: Bureau of Labor and Industrial Statistics, 1894), 389–418; In re Debs, 158 U.S. 564 (1895).

34. Beck v. Ry. Teamsters' Protective Union, 118 Mich. 497, 77 N.W. 13 (1898), is discussed in Maurice Sugar, *Working Class Justice: A Popular Treatise on the Law of Injunctions in Labor Disputes* (Detroit: Detroit Federation of Labor, [1916]). See also Harrison, "Labor Law and the Michigan Supreme Court," 9–10, 12–14; Thomas A. Klug, "The Roots of the Open Shop: Employers, Trade Unions, and Craft Labor Markets in Detroit, 1859–1907" (Ph.D. diss., Wayne State University, 1993), 820–23.

35. Harrison, "Labor Law," 18. See Enterprise Foundry Co. v. Iron Molders' Union of North America, Local No. 186, 149 Mich. 31, 112 N.W. 685 (1907); Ideal Mfg. Co. v. Ludwig, 149 Mich. 133, 112 N.W. 723 (1907); In re Hamlyn, 149 Mich. 699, 113 N.W. 20 (1907); In re Langell, 178 Mich. 305, 144 N.W. 841 (1914).

36. Witte, *Government in Labor Disputes*, has the most exhaustive inventory of injunction abuse.

37. See *American Federationist* 6, no. 2 (April 1899): 44; *Detroit Labor News*, May 23, 1919; Klug, "Roots of the Open Shop," 827, for examples of election campaigns to unseat judges.

38. U.S. Commission on Industrial Relations, *Final Report* (Washington, D.C.: Government Printing Office, 1916), quoted in Sugar, *Working Class Justice*, 30.

39. Baltic Mining Co. v. Houghton Circuit Judge, 177 Mich. 632, 144 N.W. 209 (1913). See also William A. Sullivan, "The 1913 Revolt of the Michigan Copper Miners," *Michigan History* 43, no. 3 (1959): 294–314; William Beck, "Labor and Order during the 1913 Copper Strike," *Michigan History* 54, no. 4 (1970): 275–92; Larry Lankton, *Cradle to Grave: Life, Work, and Death at the Lake Superior Copper Mines* (New York: Oxford University Press, 1991), 219–43.

40. Michael Willrich, *City of Courts: Socializing Justice in Progressive Era Chicago* (Cambridge: Cambridge University Press, 2003), 42.

41. Christopher H. Johnson, *Maurice Sugar: Law, Labor, and the Left in Detroit, 1912–1950* (Detroit: Wayne State University Press, 1988), 54–61.

42. An Act to amend section six of act number 329 of the session laws of 1905, 1917 Mich. Pub. Acts 346–47; An Act to prohibit discrimination as between sex in the payment of wages of males and females engaged in the manufacture or production of any article, 1919 Mich. Pub. Acts 427–28.

43. Jacob Hall, "Detroit Labor's Postwar Anti-Injunction Campaign," seminar paper, Wayne State University, 2004.

44. Thomas Klug, "Employers' Strategies in the Detroit Labor Market, 1900–1929," in *On the Line: Essays in the History of Auto Work,* ed. Nelson Lichtenstein and Stephen Meyer (Urbana: University of Illinois Press, 1989), 59–63.

45. *Detroit News*, March 2, 1912; May 3, 1913; An Act to prohibit the display of a red flag, 1919 Mich. Pub. Acts 179; An Act defining the crime of criminal syndicalism, 1919 Mich. Pub. Acts 452.

46. "What Michigan Legislature Did—Also Whom," *Detroit Labor News,* May 9, 1919, 7; "Michigan, My Michigan," *Detroit Labor News,* September 26, 1919, 3.

47. For arrest cases, see *Detroit News,* July 7, 14, 24, 1919; April 15, 30, 1920; May 1, 2, 4, 1920. See also Agnes Inglis, "The Acheff Case," April 26, 1920, uncatalogued manuscripts file, Labadie Collection; *Danger! Stop! Warning! Shall These Two Men Be Railroaded to the Penitentiary?* [flyer, 1919], criminal syndicalism vertical file, Labadie Collection.

48. Labor Defense Council, *The Burns and Daugherty's Attack upon Labor and Liberty. Defend Your Liberty!* (Chicago: Labor Defense Council, [1925?]); People v. Foster (1923), unreported; People v. Ruthenberg, 229 Mich. 315, 201 N.W. 358 (1924).

49. On Michigan's connection to the *Duplex Printing* case, see McLaughlin, *Michigan Labor,* 73; Duplex Printing Press Co. v. Deering, 254 U.S. 443 (1921); Adkins v. Children's Hosp. of the Dist. of Columbia, 261 U.S. 525 (1923).

50. Maurice Sugar, unpublished autobiography, quoted in Johnson, *Maurice Sugar,* 103.

51. Ibid.

52. Ibid.

53. See George I. Lovell, *Legislative Deferrals: Statutory Ambiguity, Judicial Power, and American Democracy* (Cambridge: Cambridge University Press, 2003), 161–216.

54. A good introduction is Melvyn Dubofsky, *The State and Labor in Modern America* (Chapel Hill: University of North Carolina Press, 1994), 107–67.

55. Thomas A. Klug, "Labor Market Politics in Detroit: The Curious Case of the 'Spolansky Act' of 1931," *Michigan Historical Review* 14 (Spring 1988): 1–32.

56. 1931 Mich. Pub. Acts, No. 19, which amended An Act to provide a system of public instruction, 1927 Mich. Pub. Acts 602–766; An Act to require all teachers, instructors, and professors . . . to take and subscribe an oath or affirmation to support the Constitution of the United States, 1935 Mich. Pub. Acts 34–35.

57. An Act to promote respect for the constitution, laws and institutions of this state and the United States, 1935 Mich. Pub. Acts 266; Eldridge Foster Dowell, *A History of Criminal Syndicalism in the United States* (Baltimore: Johns Hopkins Press, 1939), 134–37.

58. See Geoffrey D. Berman, "A New Deal for Free Speech: Free Speech and the Labor Movement in the 1930s," *Virginia Law Review* 80, no.1 (1994): 291–322; Carl Swidorski, "The Courts, the Labor Movement, and the Struggle for Freedom of Expression and Association, 1919–1940," *Labor History* 45 (February 2004): 61–84; Gilbert J. Gall, "'Rights Which Have Meaning': Reconceiving Labor Liberty in the 1940s," *Labor History* 39 (August 1998): 273–90; Theodore J. St. Antoine, "Justice Frank Murphy and American Labor Law," *Michigan Law Review* 100 (June 2002): 1900–1926.

59. See Christopher L. Tomlins, *The State and the Unions: Labor Relations, Law, and the Organized Labor Movement in America, 1880–1960* (Cambridge: Cambridge University Press, 1985), 99–243, for an introduction.

60. Sidney Fine, "Frank Murphy, Law and Order, and Labor Relations in Michigan, 1937," in *Union Power and Public Policy,* ed. David Lipsky (Ithaca, N.Y.: New York State School of Industrial and Labor Relations, Cornell University, 1975), 1–23; Sid-

ney Fine, *Frank Murphy: The New Deal Years* (Chicago: University of Chicago Press, 1979), 289–325.

61. Quote is from NLRB v. Ford Motor Co., 114 F.2d 905 (6th Cir. 1940).

62. See James Wolfinger, "The Strange Career of Frank Murphy: Conservatives, State-Level Politics, and the End of the New Deal," *Historian* 65 (Winter 2002): 377–402; Fine, *Frank Murphy,* 491–528.

63. An Act to promote respect for the constitution, laws and institutions of this state and the United States, 1935 Mich. Pub. Acts 266.

64. City of Dearborn v. Rolland J. Thomas, No. 70589 (October 31, 1940).

65. NLRB v. Ford Motor Co., 114 F.2d 905 (6th Cir. 1940). See also Babson, Alpern, Elsila, and Revitte, *Working Detroit,* 109–10; John Barnard, *American Vanguard: The United Auto Workers during the Reuther Years, 1935–1970* (Detroit: Wayne State University Press, 2004), 104–8, 153–64.

ELEVEN

Liette Gidlow

THE MICHIGAN WOMEN'S COMMISSION AND THE STRUGGLE AGAINST SEX DISCRIMINATION IN THE 1970S

In its annual report for 1973–74, the Michigan Women's Commission (MWC) concluded that more than two thousand of the state's statutes explicitly differentiated between women and men. The commission, an executive body charged with "directing attention to critical problems confronting women as wives, mothers, homemakers, and workers," identified and articulated women's issues, documented cases of sex discrimination, and pursued remedial action through networking, legislative lobbying, and the courts. The commission took up a broad range of women's issues, including equal access to unemployment insurance, expansion of minimum wage laws to occupations filled predominantly by women, pay equity, occupational safety, equal access to public accommodations, equal access to credit, educational equity, criminal sexual conduct, abortion, gender bias in the courts, and the underrepresentation of women on the bench. By the early 1970s, the Michigan Women's Commission had emerged as an important force for sex equity in Michigan law.[1]

The MWC became a powerful proponent of feminist legal reform in the state, but it did not start out as one. The commission evolved over a decade from an organization so weak that its very existence turned upon the outcome of gubernatorial elections into an institution firmly established and permanently housed in the Michigan Civil Rights Commission. Commissioners learned early that their efforts were most effective when they worked in coalition with others—for example, with labor women of the United Auto Workers for pay equity and with rape crisis professionals and feminist lawyers for reform of the state's rape law. Still, the MWC found that activity by the Michigan electorate, the state government, and the federal courts could stymie or supersede its work. The successes and failures of the Michigan Women's Commission show how sometimes reform in one state precipitated reform in others and how, at other times, progress for women at the state level depended upon progress at the federal level, whether in Congress or in the federal courts.

The MWC in the 1960s and 1970s

The Michigan Women's Commission was formed as the state-level counterpart to President John F. Kennedy's Commission on the Status of Women (PCSW). The presidential commission, established by executive order in December 1961, was the brainchild of women labor activists including Katherine Ellickson, assistant director of the Social Insurance Department of the AFL-CIO, and Esther Peterson, formerly of the Amalgamated Clothing Workers and the new head of the Women's Bureau in the U.S. Department of Labor. The PCSW was charged with evaluating the economic, social, and political progress of American women and making recommendations on key topics such as social insurance and tax laws, protective labor legislation, political and civil rights, property rights, and access to services such as child care and continuing education. Early in its history, the PCSW encouraged each state to form its own commission to investigate how state laws and policies shaped the quality of women's lives.[2]

Michigan was, in fact, the first state to form such a commission. In the summer of 1962, Democratic governor John B. Swainson established the Governor's Commission on the Status of Women. The state commission explicitly patterned its agenda and organization on that of the federal commission and decided to focus on many of the same issues, including social and labor legislation, educational opportunities, and political and civil rights.[3]

This quick start might suggest that the Michigan commission enjoyed enthusiastic support in its early years, but that was not the case. Between 1962 and 1968, the commission was unstable, bereft of resources, and often ineffective. The first commission, appointed in August 1962, found itself prematurely terminated when Governor Swainson lost his bid for reelection in November of the same year. Swainson's successor, Republican George Romney, established a new commission in 1963 and again in 1967; for two years in between, though, its authorization lapsed as the governor and the state legislature battled over whether it should be reestablished by executive order or by statute. Each commission was given an expansive charge but few resources with which to fulfill its responsibilities. The first commission's annual budget totaled a mere $200. Commissioners served without pay or reimbursement of expenses and had to solicit donations for the office supplies needed to support basic operations.[4]

During this period, the membership of the commission—by necessity, women who had enough personal resources to devote time to a demanding volunteer enterprise—was mostly drawn from the ranks of the state's middle-class and elite women, especially clubwomen, businesswomen, and academics. Their activities often reflected a conservative political outlook. Echoing President Kennedy's charge to the PCSW, the state commission made clear that its goal was not to take women from the home but to "develop recommendations for services which will enable women to continue their traditional activities within the home while making a maximum contribution to their communities, the state and the nation." In keeping with the prefeminist practice of the period, commission members frequently signed reports using their husbands' names—as Mrs. John Finegan or Mrs. Wilber Brucker Jr., for example. Although the commission took up many issues important to women—such as the need for a state minimum wage, continuing education for older women, and the underrepresentation of women in municipal, county, and state government positions—they often attributed the problems they found not to unequal opportunity or discrimination but to a lack of women's interest or daring, as when the 1965 report noted the low numbers of women serving as officers in political party organizations and urged that "women overcome reluctance or apathy or lack of knowledge."[5]

The commission gained a stable institutional base when it was established by statute in 1968, and, increasingly, its membership, activities, and recommendations reflected the growing feminist movement of the period. Public Act 1 of 1968, introduced in bill form by state senator Lorraine Beebe, of Dearborn (who four years later would serve as commission chair), established the Michigan Women's Commission and charged it with "stimulat[ing] and encourag[ing]" the study of "the status of women in this state" and recommending "methods of overcoming discrimination against women in public and private employment and political and civil rights." In the next five years, the MWC developed into an effective feminist voice and a permanent advocate for women's interests in Lansing. In 1991, the commission, along with a number of other state agencies charged with civil rights advocacy, was placed under the auspices of the Michigan Civil Rights Commission.[6]

As the commission became better institutionalized, its membership became more diverse. By 1972, the MWC had its own budget allocation, ending the need for members to ask the governor's office for permission every time they needed to make an expenditure or solicit help from the steno pool. Although academics and businesswomen continued to serve on the commission in substantial numbers, in the early 1970s the commission's membership grew more economically, racially, and ethnically diverse. Members became more middle-class, bringing to their work on the commission a broader range of life experience. A Boy Scout den mother replaced a Junior Leaguer, and the commission added a factory worker and an artist as well as lawyers, a Head Start administrator, and a professional lobbyist. By the mid-1970s, the MWC's membership also regularly included African American, Latina, and Native American women, and the agency published on issues of particular concern to ethnic women.[7]

In the same period, the MWC began to adopt feminist methods and to make connections to feminist networks. In 1970, the commission sponsored its first "Speak Out" to solicit input from representatives of women's groups in the state and the general public on the "inequalities [women] have suffered because of their sex" and how the commission could more effectively represent and serve them. The commission's follow-up work after the meeting helped to build the attendees into a network by continuing to communicate with them as legislation in their areas of interest came up in Lansing. Over time, a number of commission members formed strong ties to national and international women's agencies and organizations, including the Women's Bureau of the U.S. Department of Labor, the International Association of Commissions on the Status of Women, and the National Organization for Women.[8]

The feminist transformation of the commission became most apparent in the choice of issues it began to address. As early as 1970, the commission took up issues such as the federal Equal Rights Amendment and access to family planning and abortion services. A few years later, it promoted broad civil rights reform by supporting the Elliott-Larsen Civil Rights Act of

1976, which prohibited discrimination on the basis of sex in housing, employment, education, and public accommodations. The MWC also pursued civil rights reform by working on legislation focused on affirmative action in higher education, discrimination in the issuance of credit, the use of gender-neutral language in state law, housing discrimination, domestic violence, and sexual harassment. The commission promoted legislative reforms by initiating bills in cooperation with legislators and legislative staff, testifying before legislative committees, lobbying at the state House of Representatives, and working with state agencies to develop regulatory law and encourage enforcement. The commission counted among its achievements the passage of legislation banning insurance discrimination on the basis of sex and marital status in 1976 and a 1978 law creating a state domestic violence prevention and treatment board and offering services to victims and their dependent children.[9]

Among the many issues it addressed, the Michigan Women's Commission had a special concern for sex equity in law. In addition to its legislative lobbying, it sponsored conferences to investigate the need for statutory change and made special efforts to reach out to women and inform them of their rights. In 1974, the commission sponsored a daylong series of talks and workshops on women and the law and lined up speakers with national reputations, including Sylvia Roberts, chair of the American Bar Association's Committee on Rights for Women and the plaintiff's attorney in the landmark sex discrimination case *Weeks v. Southern Bell Telephone and Telegraph Co.,* the case that defined the scope of a "bona fide occupational qualification" and held that an employer could take sex into account only if it could prove that all or substantially all women could not perform the job efficiently and safely. The conference offered workshops on a full range of legal issues of interest to women, including laws on marriage, divorce, child custody, educational access, mental health, welfare rights, and rape.[10]

The commission likewise reached out to inform women of their legal rights, not only through an extensive press operation and by routinely supplying the state's public libraries with packets on commission activities but also by issuing specialized pamphlets. The commission's most widely circulated brochure outlined in laypersons' language legal issues of everyday concern to women—their husbands' legal responsibilities to support their families, the legal grounds for divorce, married women's property rights, eligibility for Social Security, the legality of abortion, and equal pay at the workplace, among others. Beginning in 1969, the commission put out about thirty thousand copies of the brochure each year and updated it regularly.

The changing name of the brochure reflected clearly the feminist change under way at the agency. In 1969, the commission titled the brochure *Laws of Special Interest to Women in Michigan;* in 1974, the revised piece was called *Know Your Rights as a Woman.*[11]

The MWC also commented from time to time on judicial decisions and called on the courts to promote sex equity. The commission's response to the much-watched U.S. Supreme Court ruling in *General Electric v. Gilbert* was especially strong. In 1976, the Court held that an employer-based disability insurance plan that excluded income protection for time lost from work due to pregnancy did not violate the sex discrimination prohibitions of Title VII of the 1964 Civil Rights Act because the employer did not intend to discriminate against women. The commission, joining a chorus of protest from women's groups, "voice[d] its dismay" at the Court's action and passed a resolution urging it to reconsider the standard in future cases and calling upon state legislatures and Congress to pass corrective legislation.[12]

Although the commission in the early 1970s addressed a wide range of issues of concern to women, its efforts to reform the law in three areas stand out. In 1972, the commission helped to pass an ambitious equal pay law. Between 1969 and 1972, it spearheaded a campaign to reform access to abortion. In 1974, it helped lead a movement to revise laws pertaining to rape. In each of these areas, the MWC was a key player in the effort to make Michigan's laws more equitable for women. Some of these efforts were highly successful; others were not, their effectiveness constrained by or dependent upon the actions of other policymaking bodies.

The "Best, Broadest" Equal Pay Law in the Nation

The Michigan Women's Commission had long agitated for improvement in the state's laws requiring that women and men be paid the same wages for performing similar work. In 1972, the commission's efforts paid off. Touted at the time of its passage by commission member and labor activist Myra Wolfgang as the "best, broadest equal pay for equal work law in the nation," the Equal Pay for Equal Work Act failed to narrow the wage gap between the sexes. The life and death of Michigan's pay equity statute shows some of the limits of the commission's effectiveness—and, indeed, of the effectiveness of legislative reform in improving the circumstances of the state's women.[13]

Responding to studies that showed that women on average earned fifty-nine cents for every dollar earned by men, in the spring of 1962, a year in advance of the passage of similar legislation at the federal level, Michigan joined twenty-one states in enacting an equal pay law. The product of efforts by activists from the state Department of Labor, the Women's Bureau of the U.S. Department of Labor, Michigan State University's Labor and Industrial Relations Center, and the Michigan Federation of Business and Professional Women's Clubs, Public Act No. 37 made it a misdemeanor for an employer to "discriminate in any way in the payment of wages as between sexes who are similarly employed."[14]

From its earliest days, the commission identified equal pay as an important issue and showed concern about the implementation of the 1962 law. That year, the Labor and Social Legislation Committee of Governor Swainson's first, short-lived commission complained about the enforcement mechanism in the law that required individuals to file criminal charges against their employers to seek redress. The commission pointed out that "[f]acilities for inspecting and insuring that [the] 'equal pay' law and similar legislation are put into effect are not available." As early as 1964, the commission recommended that enforcement be placed in the hands of state regulators and that the Michigan Department of Labor assume responsibility for investigating and resolving complaints.[15]

"[V]iolations of the equal pay law are . . . rampant," commission chair Bette Finegan complained at a meeting of the commission in late 1970. By 1971, pay equity had become the "number one priority item" on the commission's agenda. Finegan, a clubwoman and onetime member of the Republican Party's state central committee, and Myra Wolfgang, a former international vice president of the Hotel Employees and Restaurant Employees Union (HERE) and a familiar face in restaurant and hotel workers' organizing efforts in downtown Detroit, took the lead on this issue, Wolfgang bringing to the table considerable experience in union campaigns to equalize pay scales between women and men. In part because of the efforts of the commission, which "actively supported" the equal pay bill as it made its way through the legislature, in July 1971 Republican governor William G. Milliken signed the bill into law. It was considered an especially good pay equity law because it applied to all women workers between the ages of eighteen and sixty-five and covered employees of very small businesses and other job classifications who were exempt from the federal law. "[T]his new law," the governor remarked at the signing ceremony, "is a significant step forward in guaranteeing to the women of this state the same opportunities for choosing their own life style that men now possess."[16]

A step forward perhaps, but not as significant a step as the law's supporters had hoped. Certainly, there were some instances in which women used the law to win equitable pay. In 1972, twenty-two-year-old University of Michigan student Ellen Christensen filed a complaint with the Michigan Civil Rights Commission against Harper Hospital, where she worked as a nurse's aide, arguing that nurses' aides and orderlies performed the same work but that the aides were paid less. Later certified as a class action suit on behalf of Christensen and 234 other women, the hospital settled for $365,102 and agreed to equalize the pay scale between the two occupational classifications. Although the pay disparity at Harper was not revealed, differentials at other Detroit-area hospitals at the time ranged from forty-two cents an hour at Detroit Osteopathic Hospital to sixty-five cents an hour at Hutzel Hospital.[17]

The Michigan Department of Labor, however, lacked the resources to enforce the law systematically. Even before the law took effect, John Thodis, chief deputy director of the state Department of Labor, warned MWC members that enforcement would be limited by both the small number of state inspectors available and the state legislature's failure to provide new funds for implementation. The department, he promised the MWC in an October 1971 hearing, would "enforce the new legislation with all vigor possible," but that vigor would "be limited to seventeen people who do other things as well"—that is, the seventeen state inspectors who already were responsible for enforcing the state's minimum wage and migrant labor laws. Under those circumstances, Thodis believed, "there is no way [this] department can give the broad enforcement that the bill needs."[18]

As early as 1973, the MWC realized that other barriers also prevented the law from effectively raising women's pay. Unequal opportunities for employment and, in particular, occupational segregation by sex meant that men and women often did not perform obviously similar work, making the law difficult to apply to a vast range of job classifications. The commission's Task Force on Women and Employment soon concluded that "[a] comprehensive program to eliminate sex stereotyping" in employment was necessary if the equal pay law was to work. Unsatisfied with the practical effect of the law, the commission complained: "Equal pay for equal work and equality of opportunity in employment must become a reality rather than just State laws."[19]

The issue did not go away. The commission showed a continuing concern for the matter, pointing out, for example, in the 1987–88 report of its

Economic Equity Task Force that "[i]n 1980 women earned only 64 cents for every dollar earned by men" and that this figure had barely budged in thirty years. A 1987 study published jointly by a group that included the Michigan Women's Commission and Democratic lieutenant governor Martha Griffiths concluded that there were still "wide differences in male and female earnings for full-time workers in most occupations." Women "dominate[d]" the work force in sales and service occupations and earned about half the amount earned by men similarly employed. Even professional women, they found, were not exempt: white women doctors earned about two-thirds as much as their male counterparts.[20]

Indeed, the issue still has not gone away, and the latest data show that the situation has grown worse. A recent study based on census data from 2000, data that correct for women's movement in and out of the work force during child-bearing years that earlier researchers had blamed for wage disparities, showed that Michigan women employed full-time and year-round made sixty-seven cents for every dollar earned by men, considerably worse than the national average of seventy-three cents and a disparity that ranked Michigan among the three worst states in the nation. In southeast Michigan, the figures were even grimmer: in some counties, including Lapeer, Livingston, and Monroe, women earned fifty-nine cents for every dollar earned by men—exactly the level of the national figures that first sparked interest in the pay equity issue in the early 1960s. The optimistic headlines of thirty years ago have been replaced with bleak ones; now, the message is that "Michigan [is] among [the] worst in equal pay for women."[21]

In short, despite the efforts of the Michigan Women's Commission and others, the equal pay problem continues to defy solution. The MWC remains interested in the issue, but the prospects for solving the problem are dim. A bill that would amend the Elliott-Larson Civil Rights Act and define an employer's failure to give equal pay for comparable work as a civil rights violation has been stalled in the Michigan legislature since its introduction in 2003. Occupations continue to be segregated by sex, and broad-scale economic transformations further complicate the problem. Manufacturing jobs remain some of the best-paying jobs in the state, and three-fourths of those are still held by men. As the manufacturing sector continues to contract, women are finding that their access to these good-paying jobs shrinks as well. The "best, broadest" equal pay law in the nation, it turns out, failed to fulfill its early promise.

Abortion Rights

On the issue of abortion rights, the work of the MWC likewise produced mixed results. The commission succeeded in putting the issue on the public agenda in Michigan, but, despite repeated attempts and a nasty lawsuit in the state supreme court, it failed to achieve greater access to abortion for the state's women. On this issue, action by the U.S. Supreme Court achieved what state-level reformers in Michigan could not.

Until the mid-nineteenth century, common law in the United States governed access to abortion and generally allowed termination of a pregnancy until quickening, the point at which the mother could begin to feel the fetus move. In the middle of the century, doctors began to call for a ban on the procedure by midwives, arguing that it was often dangerous for women and that, when an abortion was absolutely necessary, it should be performed by a doctor. The Michigan legislature criminalized abortion, outlining punishments for doctors who performed them, in 1846. By the early twentieth century, reformers had succeeded in establishing legal bans on abortion in every state.[22]

The prohibitions, of course, did not mean that abortions ceased. Indeed, in the first few decades of the twentieth century, abortions seem to have been widely available. Through about the 1930s, midwives and doctors in private practice frequently performed the procedures despite the bans while communities and law enforcement officials who regarded abortions as unsavory but often necessary looked the other way. In some areas, doctors performed abortions under the cover of state laws that carved out exceptions if the doctor deemed that the procedure was justified on "therapeutic" grounds.[23]

In the 1940s, hospitals began to perform more abortions, giving the procedure greater visibility, subjecting it to more public scrutiny, and, ironically, reducing access. Operating under broad interpretations of state laws that allowed "medical exceptions" to the ban when the mother's life was threatened, hospitals formed oversight committees, bureaucratizing the process to control access to the procedure, ensure standards, and deflect criticism. These boards evaluated patients requesting abortions on a case-by-case basis and decided which women could get them. Frequently, applications by women who were white and middle-class or elite were approved; women of color and women who could not afford to pay the fees that, by the early 1970s, ran between $600 and $800 often were turned away. These women, in turn, were much more likely to die from botched procedures performed by illegal providers and, when permitted to receive a hospital abortion, were much more likely also to be sterilized, with or without their consent, to punish them for their sexual transgressions and prevent them from getting into such a predicament again. By some estimates, in the 1960s illegal abortions resulted in the deaths of some five to ten thousand women per year.[24]

Pressure for change came from physicians who saw the human toll that resulted from illegal abortions, civil-liberties-minded lawyers who wanted to carve out a zone of privacy around the body, prosecutors uncomfortable with bringing charges against doctors, and, by the late 1960s, women who saw reproductive rights as a feminist issue and a matter of personal dignity and autonomy. "Convinced that the right of a woman to determine her own reproductive life" was "a basic human right," the Michigan Women's Commission took a stand. In 1969, the same year in which the national organization of Planned Parenthood took a position supporting repeal of antiabortion laws, the commission adopted a resolution calling for repeal of the state's laws penalizing physicians who performed abortions. The movement was fueled in part by the case of Pleasant Ridge gynecologist Dr. Jesse Ketchum, against whom Oakland County prosecutor Thomas Plunkett filed charges for allegedly agreeing to perform an abortion on an undercover state policewoman at a Southfield, Michigan, motel. Plunkett brought the charges reluctantly, stating publicly that he was "in full favor of repeal of the present abortion law." The MWC channeled its energy into working for passage of a bill pending before a state Senate committee sponsored by Senator John McCauley (D-Wyandotte) that would have removed criminal penalties against licensed doctors performing abortions. Commission chair Bette Finegan summed up the views of the members: "[A] woman has the right to personal privacy. . . . [W]hether or not she has an abortion should be a matter between her and her doctor."[25]

The commission's views proved controversial, and Michigan was not among the seventeen states that legalized or decriminalized abortion before the U.S. Supreme Court's *Roe v. Wade* decision in 1973. Repeated attempts in the state legislature to reform Michigan's abortion laws went down to defeat. By 1970, reform supporters had formed the Michigan Organization for the Repeal of Abortion Laws (MORAL) to work for change, but yet another reform bill was defeated in the state Senate in May of that year.[26]

Frustrated by these defeats in the legislature, the commission vowed to take revenge at the ballot box and resolved to work to defeat the senators who had voted against reform. "[B]y their failure to liberalize the abortion law," these legislators had "left thousands of Michigan women, the poor and the nonwhite, with no choice except to have an unwanted child." Angrily, commission women charged that the Senate had failed "to fulfill its obligation to the women of Michigan" and resolved to "work toward electing senators who will effectively recognize the needs of women in the state." The resolution expressed their frustration but proved to be poor politics, as state Senate members who were targeted by the MWC noted pointedly that they funded the commission's work through the budget of the governor's executive office. Commission friend and state senator Lorraine Beebe backpedaled and tried to undo the political damage, arguing that punitive action at the ballot box was uncalled for and urging voters to judge senators by their overall voting records. Reverting to a focus on the issue, the MWC soon "reaffirmed" its support for abortion law repeal and testified at ten public hearings on the matter in 1970 and 1971.[27]

Stymied by the legislative deadlock, reform advocates turned the next year to a state referendum to achieve liberalization. If ratified, the referendum would have allowed doctors working in licensed facilities to perform abortions through the twentieth week of gestation. The MWC joined forces with the Michigan Referendum Committee, a new coalition of seventy-five proreform organizations, including the American College of Obstetrics and Gynecology, the Michigan Council of Churches, and the American Bar Association, to gather signatures to place the referendum on the ballot and to work for passage. After an unsuccessful attempt by prolife organizations to get the Michigan Supreme Court to remove the question from the ballot, the election took place on November 7, 1972, and the referendum was soundly defeated.[28]

Roe achieved what state reformers in Michigan could not. On January 22, 1973, the U.S. Supreme Court extended the finding of a constitutional right to privacy in its 1965 decision on contraception, *Griswold v. Connecticut,* to first-trimester abortions. A complex decision, *Roe* balanced the interests of the mother, the fetus, and the state in each trimester of pregnancy. Guided by the judgment of a physician, the woman's right to privacy prevailed over competing interests in the first trimester, while the state's interest in protecting potential human life prevailed in the third. The Michigan Women's Commission, long an advocate for women's right to choose, was well satisfied with the Court's action in *Roe*. As the commission put it in a 1974 resolution on the first anniversary of the Court's decision, the rights articulated in *Roe* needed to be assured so that "the long-standing evil of criminal abortion practices shall not return to haunt the lives of Michigan women."[29]

The right to have an abortion has been contested in Michigan, as else-where, in the years since the Court's decision. A 1988 state referendum, opposed by the MWC, ended Medicaid funding for abortions until 1991, when the state supreme court found that the state constitution's equal pro-tection clause offered "greater protection than its federal counterpart" and invalidated the referendum. That same year, the legislature passed the Parental Rights Restoration Act, which delegated to probate court judges the decision whether a minor girl may get an abortion without parental consent. The MWC remained a participant in the policymaking process but found that its power was constrained by the dynamic interplay of pol-icy decisions rendered by the state's voters, the Michigan legislature, and state and federal courts.[30]

Model Rape Law Reform

In its efforts to revise the state's laws on rape, the Michigan Women's Commission, working in coalition with other groups, achieved a degree of success that had eluded it on pay equity and abortion rights. The rape law revision in 1974 truly initiated a national wave of reform, modernized the definition of the crime, and humanized the legal process for victims. Dubbed "the most sweeping rape law reform in the country," the new Michigan statute, many scholars agree, served as a model for other states. Indeed, in the two decades after the new statute took effect in Michigan, every other state enacted some type of rape law reform, many borrowing elements of the new Michigan law. The Michigan Women's Commission played a critical role in this process of reform. Working under the auspices of the Michigan Women's Task Force on Rape formed in early 1973, com-mission members collaborated with feminist lawyers, members of the Lansing chapter of the National Organization for Women, professionals from rape crisis centers across the state, and other activists to develop a con-sensus for change, recommend provisions of the new law, and lobby for passage.[31]

Prior to these statutory changes, rape in Michigan, as elsewhere, was conceived of as a crime rooted in desire in which women often were treated as though they were complicit in the act. By law rape could be per-petrated only by a male against a female; was limited to criminal acts in-volving vaginal penetration; required that the perpetrator use physical force; and required the victim to offer her "utmost resistance" from "the inception to the close" of the assault. Up to this point, the 1906 case *People v. Murphy* still held: lacking the resistance factor, the act was " not rape." The requirement of resistance was distinctive to rape prosecutions: a person held up at gunpoint, for example, did not have to show "resistance" to prove in a court of law that a robbery had been committed.[32]

The new Michigan law addressed each of these defects, above all by treating rape as a crime of violence in which the perpetrator intends to dominate, brutalize, and degrade the victim. Public Act 266, signed into law by Governor Milliken on August 12, 1974, extended protection to men as well as to women; broadened the definition of the criminal act to include sex crimes that did not involve vaginal penetration; broadened the definition of "force" beyond simple physical force; and no longer required that the victim resist. No longer men, but "persons," could commit the crime or be victims of it. The crime was no longer termed rape but rather "criminal sexual conduct," a category that included "sexual contact" as well as other types of sexual penetration. "Force" was redefined as "force or coercion" and included not only physically overcoming the victim but also threatening physical force or coercion, causing personal injury to the victim, or knowing or having reason to know that the victim was mentally incapacitated or physically helpless. Finally, the law explicitly stated that the "victim need not resist" his or her perpetrator.[33]

Public Act 266 offered further reforms to the state's rape law. It differentiated four degrees of criminal sexual conduct, ranging from a first-degree felony for violent cases of sexual penetration to a fourth-degree misdemeanor for some cases of sexual contact. It established mandatory minimum sentences for persons convicted of a second or subsequent offense. It also established the possibility of criminal prosecution for marital rape in cases in which the couple was living apart and one spouse had sued for a legal separation or divorce. The law also offered several more protections for victims. It specified that "the testimony of a victim need not be corroborated in prosecutions"; it instituted rape shield provisions that put tight limits on the admissibility of evidence regarding a victim's prior sexual history; and it permitted the victim's and defendant's names to be withheld during proceedings at the request of counsel.[34]

At least four studies have concluded that the Michigan law significantly changed the prosecution of rape in Michigan. These studies used a range of methodologies, from time series data comparing the numbers of arrests and convictions before and after implementation of the law, to comparisons between states, to interviews of criminal justice officials to determine their views of whether and how change resulted from the reform. The most comprehensive study to date, by Professors Cassia Spohn and Julie Horney at the Department of Criminal Justice at the University of Nebraska, concluded that the number of rapes reported, indictments, convictions, and incarcerations in Detroit increased in the years following implementation of the new law and that prosecutors, armed with the new rules of evidence and the new rape shield provision, became more likely to prosecute.[35]

In the years after passage, the Michigan Women's Commission witnessed several unsuccessful challenges to the new law. State appellate courts found on at least two occasions that the law's rape shield provisions did not violate a defendant's Sixth Amendment right to confront his or her accuser. The commission continued to support refinements in the statute, such as the 1989 law that barred a defendant from filing a civil action against a plaintiff while criminal proceedings were still ongoing. The next year, the commission supported the bill that became Public Act 191, which required persons convicted of criminal sexual conduct to submit to blood and saliva tests.[36]

The Michigan Women's Commission celebrated the 1974 criminal sexual conduct statute as one of its greatest accomplishments, and with good reason. The changes in the definition of the crime and standards of evidence made a substantial impact on women's lives in the state by making the crime easier to prosecute and by establishing clearly that the victim was not responsible for her own victimization. The spread of the Michigan reforms to other jurisdictions has benefited many thousands of American women in the same way.

The work of the commission on these three issues shows the MWC at its most effective and at its least. On the issue of rape law, the coalition of which the commission was a vital part launched a wave of legal reform so sweeping that Michigan's approach to the prosecution of sex crimes became practically a national standard. On the issue of abortion, the commission never succeeded in expanding access to the procedure; although other states liberalized their abortion laws in the early 1970s, only the U.S. Supreme Court was able to achieve that goal for Michigan women. On the issue of pay equity, progress at both the state and the federal level has been slow and thwarted by issues beyond the effective reach of either—the decline in manufacturing jobs, the growth of the service sector, and the persistent segregation of occupations by sex.

Its record showed both successes and failures, but in the early 1970s, the Michigan Women's Commission came into its own. A small, struggling, and transient organization at its inception in the early 1960s, the commission's development in the late 1960s reflected the growing women's movement around it. Despite its limitations, by the early 1970s the commission had become an important proponent of sex equity, achieving significant improvements in Michigan law and influencing reform efforts in other states as well. At a minimum, the commission's permanent presence assured, for the first time in Michigan's history, that women would be formally and consistently represented in the state's public affairs.

Notes

1. Michigan Women's Commission, *Women's Program for 1973–1974* [c. 1973], 5, Records of the Michigan Women's Commission (hereafter "MWC Records"), RG 77–78, State Archives, Lansing, Michigan; Michigan Women's Commission Act, 1968 Mich. Pub. Acts 1, § 2.

2. Katherine Pollak Ellickson, "The President's Commission on the Status of Women: Its Formation, Functioning, and Contribution" (unpublished paper, photocopy provided by Ohio State University Libraries, 1976), 2–3; President's Commission on the Status of Women, *American Women* (Washington, D.C.: Government Printing Office, 1963), 7. On the roles of labor feminists in stimulating the women's movement of the 1960s and 1970s, see Dorothy Sue Cobble, *The Other Women's Movement: Workplace Justice and Social Rights in Modern America* (Princeton, N.J.: Princeton University Press, 2004).

3. *Current Status* [newsletter of the President's Commission on the Status of Women], November 1962, 10, reel 1, Papers of the U.S. Commission on the Status of Women, Robert E. Lester, project coordinator (Bethesda, Md.: University Publications of America, 2001). For an overview of the MWC's early work, see Sidney Fine, *Expanding the Frontiers of Civil Rights: Michigan, 1948–1968* (Detroit: Wayne State University Press, 2000), 271–78.

4. Irma Liverance, *Michigan Status of Women Commission Report,* 1967, 1, MWC Records.

5. Governor's Commission on the Status of Women, *Progress Report* [1962], 1, MWC Records; Executive Order 10980, 1961, reprinted in President's Commission on the Status of Women, *American Women,* 1963, 76; *[Report of the] Governor's Commission on the Status of Women,* 1965, 17, MWC Records.

6. Michigan Women's Commission Act, 1968 Mich. Pub. Acts 1, §§ 3a, 3c. Executive Reorganization Order No. 1991–20. On institutionalization as part of the "life cycle" of a social movement, see Sidney Tarrow, *Power in Movement: Social Movements and Contentious Politics,* 2d ed. (Cambridge: Cambridge University Press, 1998), 147–50.

7. *Detroit Free Press,* January 1, 1972, MWC Records; pamphlet, "Michigan Women's Commission" [c. 1975], MWC Records; "Mujeres Unidas de Michigan,"

Michigan Women [newsletter published by the MWC], May 1977, vol. 1, no. 4, MWC Records.

8. MWC, *Annual Report, 1970–1971,* 4–5, MWC Records; Bette Finegan to William G. Milliken, September 28, 1971, MWC Records; MWC, *Annual Report, 1970–1971,* 5, MWC Records; press release, Office of the Governor, July 13, 1972, MWC Records.

9. MWC, *Annual Report, 1970–1971,* 1, MWC Records; MWC, *Michigan Women's Commission, 1975–1976,* 17–18, MWC Records; MWC, *Equality: Women's Program, 1973–1974* (n.p., 1975), 6; MWC, *Michigan Women's Commission, 1975–1976,* 16–17, 5; MWC, *Bienniel* [sic] *Report, 1977–1979,* 18, 16;.

10. Press release, MWC, November 26, 1974, MWC Records; Weeks v. Southern Bell Telephone and Telegraph Company, 408 F.2d 235 (1967); conference program, MWC, "Equality: Women and the Law," 1974, MWC Records.

11. Bette Finegan and Mrs. Neil E. Warren, "Michigan Women's Commission Annual Report, A Report of Action, 1970–1971," 1971, 4, MWC Records; State Department of the Attorney General and Department of Civil Rights, "Know Your Rights as a Woman" [c. 1974], MWC Records.

News about the MWC appeared in the *Detroit Free Press,* May 7, 1965; *Royal Oak Daily Tribune,* July 1969; *Pontiac Press,* September 12, 1969, B-6; *Mining Journal,* September 12, 1969; *Detroit News,* June 28, 1970; *Detroit Free Press,* May 18, 1972; and elsewhere. Copies of these and other news clippings can be found in the MWC Records.

12. General Electric Co. v. Gilbert, 429 U.S. 125 (1976); MWC, *Michigan Women's Commission, 1975–1976,* 1977, 14–15, MWC Records.

13. *Detroit Free Press,* January 1, 1972, MWC Records.

14. Michigan Penal Code, Act. No. 378 of 1931 Mich. Pub. Acts, as amended, quoted in pamphlet, Michigan Department of Labor, "Laws and Recommendations on the Employment of Women in Michigan" [c. 1970], MWC Records.

15. Governor's Commission on the Status of Women, "Progress Report," 1962, 5, MWC Records; Governor's Commission on the Status of Women, Report, October 28, 1964, 13, MWC Records.

16. *Detroit News,* November 22, 1970; *Traverse City Record-Eagle,* July 29, 1971; and *Detroit Free Press,* January 1, 1972, all in MWC Records.

17. *Detroit Free Press* [c. August 1972], MWC Records.

18. *Detroit Free Press,* October 21, 1971, MWC Records.

19. MWC, *Women's Program for 1973–1974* (n.p., c. 1973), 9, MWC Records.

20. MWC, *1987–1988 Biennial Report* (n.p., c. 1989), 4; Rosemary Sarri et al., *Women in Michigan: A Statistical Portrait* (n.p., published jointly by the Michigan Women's Commission, Lt. Governor Martha Griffiths, the Michigan Equal Employment and Business Opportunity Council, and the Institute for Social Research at the University of Michigan, 1987), 3.

21. Institute for Women's Policy Research, *The Status of Women in the States,* 2002, cited on http://www.aflcio.org/issuespolitics/women/equalpay/eqp_stat.cfm, accessed on July 28, 2004; *Detroit News,* September 19, 2002, cited on http://www.detnews.com/2002/census/0209/19/a01-591546.htm, accessed on July 27, 2004.

22. Jennifer Nelson, *Women of Color and the Reproductive Rights Movement* (New York: New York University Press, 2003), 7–8; *Detroit News,* March 19, 1970, MWC

Records. For a broad overview, see James C. Mohr, *Abortion in America: The Origins and Evolution of National Policy, 1800–1900* (New York: Oxford University Press, 1979).

23. Linda Gordon, *The Moral Property of Women: A History of Birth Control Politics in America* (Urbana: University of Illinois Press, 2002), 299–300.

24. Nelson, *Women of Color and the Reproductive Rights Movement*, 8–10, 191n4.

25. *Detroit News*, November 21, 1969, March 19, 1970, MWC Records.

26. Gordon, *Moral Property of Women*, 300; *Detroit News*, November 21, 1969, March 19, 1970, *Flint Journal*, June 14, 1970, all in MWC Records.

27. *Flint Journal*, June 14, 1970; Bette Finegan and Mrs. Neil E. Warren, "Michigan Women's Commission Annual Report, A Report of Action, 1970–1971," 1971, 7, both in MWC Records.

28. Clipping [*Detroit News?*], n.d., MWC Records.

29. Griswold v. Connecticut, 381 U.S. 479 (1965); Judith A. Baer, ed., *Historical and Multicultural Encyclopedia of Women's Reproductive Rights in the United States* (Westport, Conn.: Greenwood, 2002), xv; MWC, *Equality: Women's Program, 1973–1974* (n.p., 1975), 22.

30. Doe v. Dir. of Dept. of Soc. Servs., 187 Mich. App. 493, 468 N.W.2d 862 (1991); Barbara Hinkson Craig and David M. O'Brien, *Abortion and American Politics* (Chatham, N.J.: Chatham House Publishers, 1993), 349, 361n50; Lawrence M. Friedman, *American Law in the Twentieth Century* (New Haven, Conn.: Yale University Press, 2002), 535. See also Suellyn Scarnecchia and Julie Kunce Field, "Judging Girls: Decision Making in Parental Consent to Abortion Cases," *Michigan Journal of Gender and Law* 3, no. 1 (1995): 75–123.

31. Cassia Spohn and Julie Horney, *Rape Law Reform: A Grassroots Revolution and its Impact* (New York: Plenum Press, 1992), 29, 36, 17; Audrey Z. Martini and Micahel C. Ziolkowski, "Understanding Michigan's Criminal Sexual Conduct Statute" (n.p., 1977), 1; photo, signing of S.B. 1207 into law [1974], MWC Records.

32. People v. Murphy, 145 Mich. 524, 109 N.W. 524 (1906); MWC, *Equality: Women's Program, 1973–1974* (n.p., 1975), 26.

33. Criminal Sexual Conduct Statute, Act. No. 266, 1974 Mich. Pub. Acts, quotes at sec. 520b(1), 520c(1), 520b(1)f, 520i.

34. Ibid., quote at sec. 520h.

35. Spohn and Horney, *Rape Law Reform*, 86–92. See ibid., 29–30, for a literature review.

36. People v. Dawsey, 76 Mich. App. 741, 746, 257 N.W.2d 236, 237 (1977); People v. Hackett, 421 Mich. 338, 356, 365 N.W.2d 120, 128 (1984); Spohn and Horney, *Rape Law Reform*, 28; MWC, *1989–1990 Biennial Report* (n.p., c. 1991), 15.

TWELVE

Byron D. Cooper

LEGAL EDUCATION
IN MICHIGAN

In the autumn of 1843, nineteen-year-old Thomas M. Cooley arrived in Adrian, Michigan, with the intention of continuing the legal education he had already begun in the office of an attorney in Palmyra, New York. Soon after his arrival in Adrian, Cooley entered an apprenticeship with another attorney, and, in 1846, he was admitted to the bar of Michigan.[1] Cooley's legal education was typical for the times.

During the territorial period prior to Michigan's statehood in 1837, admission to the practice of law generally required an examination before territorial judges and certification by an attorney that the applicant had studied the law for a specified period that varied from three to four years.[2] A similar provision was enacted into the first state code.[3] Although the practice fell into disuse during the twentieth century, apprenticeship remained a method of acquiring a license to practice law until the legislature eliminated it in 1949.[4]

At the time Cooley was admitted to the bar, antilawyer sentiment throughout much of the United States was leading to what Roscoe Pound called the deprofessionalization of the practice of law.[5] The delegates to the 1850 constitutional convention in Indiana, for example, adopted a provision that "[e]very person of good moral character, being a voter, shall be entitled to admission to practice law in all Courts of justice."[6] This section, approved by the voters, was not repealed until 1933.[7]

In the same year as the Indiana convention, a similar proposal was made in the Michigan constitutional convention.[8] Although the provision had strong support and was twice approved by the delegates, it ultimately was modified merely to permit suitors to appear on their own behalf.[9] So some kind of training remained necessary for admission to the Michigan bar. In the decades following statehood, these methods had mixed results. Thomas Cooley later wrote of this period: "Michigan had its full share of lawyers, many of whom were well trained in their profession, and would be a credit to it anywhere. Others were untrained, unlettered, and unkempt, and their vulgarity and insolence would be tolerated nowhere but in the woods."[10]

Apprenticeship training, whatever its virtues, perpetuated the racial and gender biases of the bar. African Americans found apprenticeships not readily available to them.[11] One theme in the history of legal education in Michigan has been the efforts of administrators and faculty in institutional programs to promote diversity in the bar by making legal education widely available to students regardless of gender, race, and, at times, wealth and even talent.

When Augustus B. Woodward, chief judge of the Territory of Michigan, drew up the 1817 act to create what later became the University of Michigan, he included in what he called the Catholepistemiad several didaxiim (or departments), one of which—Ethica—was to study philosophy, political science, and law.[12] Despite repeated requests from the state legislature and from members of the bar, the Law Department of the University of Michigan was not established until March 1859, when the university regents appointed as law professors Michigan Supreme Court Justice James V. Campbell, Detroit lawyer Charles I. Walker, and Thomas Cooley, who by then had practiced law and served as official reporter for the state supreme court.[13] Campbell was named dean, and Cooley was named secretary. Because Cooley was the only member of the faculty who moved to Ann Arbor, he gradually assumed the role of dean and eventually was given that title.[14]

Admission standards for the new school were extremely modest. Students had to be of good moral character and, after 1860, at least eighteen years of age.[15] Through the 1870s, the university president and regents repeatedly recommended entrance examinations for the law school, but Cooley merely responded by noting that the faculty had observed steady improvements in the prelaw preparation of the students. From the beginning, the student body was diversified in terms of geographic origins.[16] Apparently without comment, the school admitted Gabriel Hargo, its first African American student, in 1868.[17] Sarah Killgore, its first woman student, was admitted in 1870 and became the first woman admitted to the Michigan bar. When she moved with her husband to Indiana in 1875, however, she was unable to practice law because she could not vote.[18]

In teaching such a diverse group of students, the first faculty members relied on the lecture method, with no assigned texts. Cooley seldom addressed the law of any specific jurisdiction and spoke chiefly about the common law in general.[19] After Christopher Columbus Langdell inaugurated his case method of instruction at Harvard in 1870, law schools around the country began to follow the Harvard method. Students read court decisions instead of secondary texts and developed their own analytical skills under the guidance of the faculty, who, in most classes, assumed the role of Socrates in teaching by asking questions. But the faculty at Michigan remained committed to the use of lectures and recitations based on textbooks. In 1877, even the university president expressed concern that because of all the attention being given to methods of legal training, the law school should take care to retain its high reputation.[20]

Paul Carrington is surely correct in interpreting Cooley's commitment to the teaching methods then in use at Michigan as a reflection of his hostility to the creation of an intellectual meritocracy.[21] But if Michigan's students were passive vessels, they often were storm tossed. All students were required to produce a thesis of forty folios and to undergo examinations or quizzes at the end or start of each class to assess what they had just learned. According to Cooley, this examination was accompanied "by explanations, by remarks additional to what had been said before, by the citation of illustrative cases, and by responses to such questions as the students felt inclined to ask."[22] A surviving account of these daily examinations by a member of the class of 1883 is reminiscent of accounts of students in classes taught by the most demanding Socratic teacher.[23]

Throughout the nineteenth century, faculty at the law school put special emphasis on exercises that required students to apply in practice settings the legal doctrine learned in lectures or from texts. The first class lecture for students was given on October 4, 1859, and nine days later the first moot court was held, with Cooley as judge. During the first year, students participated in twenty-two moot courts, over which either Cooley or Walker presided. Students drafted pleadings and briefs, analyzed cases, and argued before the judge, who issued an opinion. Michigan eventually acquired a reputation as a "practical" school because of the range of exercises employed.[24]

From the beginning, the regents determined that Michigan should be a national law school and advertised its program in Chicago, New York, Cincinnati, St. Louis, and Washington, D.C. Indeed, twenty-six out of ninety students in the first class were from states other than Michigan, and the proportion of out-of-state students grew to around 60 percent throughout most of the nineteenth century.[25] Such diversity poses problems with regard to the teaching of practical applications based on state law. If the local jurisdiction is used for class exercises, the class or the school as a whole runs the risk of being branded as teaching only local law. The Michigan faculty addressed this issue in a number of ways, including the creation of club courts for a variety of states. In the 1914–15 school year, property students required to draft conveyancing documents were permitted to choose the state in which to place the problem.[26] Graduates of such a program may have had little to fear in competition with students from a pure case method school.

For the law school as a whole, however, the fact that all students could choose to pursue a legal career through an apprenticeship rather than at a law school limited the establishment of high standards for admission or for graduation.[27] In 1895, dean-elect Harry B. Hutchins called on the state legislature to eliminate apprenticeships as a means for admission to the bar, arguing that educational opportunities are "at the door of the rich and poor alike" and that a poorly equipped bar or judiciary imposed great and needless expense on litigants and the public alike.[28] But change was to come slowly.

Michigan got a competitor in 1889, but one that doubtless caused little concern in Ann Arbor. The Sprague Correspondence School of Law was established in Detroit by William Cyrus Sprague, a young man who had graduated from the Cincinnati Law School in 1883 and had practiced law in Ohio, Minnesota, and Michigan. He published a number of abridged editions of Blackstone's *Commentaries,* which all Sprague students were required to buy, as well as a variety of manuals and several periodicals, including the *Law Student's Helper* and *American Legal News.* By 1894, Sprague claimed that his law school offered fifty-six classes to some sixteen hundred enrolled students and that the *Helper* had more than five thousand paid subscribers.[29]

The Sprague School may have provided at least some training to people who aspired to become lawyers but lacked the resources or mobility to enroll in a law school or to serve an apprenticeship. Antoinette Leach was an early Sprague alumna. She lived in Sullivan, Indiana, and finished her course at the Sprague School in 1893.[30] When she applied to the Indiana circuit court for admission to practice law, the court found that, not being a voter, she should be denied admission. She appealed to the Indiana Supreme Court and prevailed: the court ruled for the first time that women, although not entitled to vote, were eligible for admission to the bar in Indiana.[31]

The Sprague School continued operations at least until World War I and, from reports published in the *Law Student's Helper,* seems always to have been interested in the efforts of women seeking to be admitted to the bars of every state. It is impossible to determine whether this concern arose from principle or from a marketing strategy.

Neither the University of Michigan nor the Sprague School could meet the needs of apprentices working in law offices in Detroit, who apparently wanted live instruction but could not afford to live in Ann Arbor. About thirty-five of them had formed the Cooley Law Club, primarily for social purposes, but some members were interested in the possibility of establishing an evening law school in Detroit. They contacted the secretary of the Chicago College of Law, an institution similar to what they hoped to establish. He recommended that they get the assistance of a real lawyer, preferably a scholarly one. The group turned to Floyd R. Mechem, a Detroit lawyer who was well known for his 1889 treatise on the law of agency. Mechem agreed to become the first dean and an instructor in the new school. An agreement to create the Detroit College of Law (DCL) was signed on December 7, 1891. Classes, held only in the evening, began on January 2, 1892, and, in all, sixty-one students registered during the first year.[32]

The first announcement issued by DCL stated that the "college opens its doors to all classes, without regard to sex, color or citizenship."[33] In 1893, Lizzie J. McSweeney, a member of the first graduating class, became the first woman to receive a degree from Detroit College of Law.[34] That class also included an African American student, whose name is unknown; he apparently did not graduate. The first African American to graduate was Walter H. Stowers, of the class of 1895,[35] and the first African American woman lawyer in Michigan was Grace Costavas Murphy, who graduated from DCL in 1923.[36]

Although Mechem remained at Detroit College of Law for less than a year, his commitment to the new school was strong. He taught classes there until he became a full-time teacher at the University of Michigan in November 1892. In 1893, he published the first casebook edited by University of Michigan faculty.[37] At least in his courses at Michigan, he taught strictly by the case method—the students briefed cases in a format that they still are urged to employ a century later.[38] Mechem's methods reflected Michigan's gradual shift toward the case method.

In an important study published by the Carnegie Foundation for the Advancement of Teaching in 1921, Alfred Z. Reed maintained that the case method of study was inappropriate for part-time schools because its success depends on "abundant outside preparation."[39] Indeed, the earliest DCL catalogs suggest a heavy reliance on textbooks, but it seems likely that Mechem influenced teaching methods there. In the late 1890s, Dean Philip Van Zile and faculty member Jasper Gates each published two casebooks with the West Publishing Company, enabling DCL to join the likes of Harvard, Columbia, and Michigan as only the tenth law school in the country whose faculty had published casebooks—an astonishing achievement for a school with a part-time dean and faculty.[40] Detroit College of Law also implemented a strong practical component, including moot courts, simulated trials, and case clubs, and took advantage of its location in a large city to require students to visit some of the twenty courts in session and, from time to time, to brief cases pending there.[41]

In the first bar examination administered by the new Michigan Board of Law Examiners in 1896, all 32 DCL graduates were successful, and news of this achievement circulated widely. By 1910, DCL had 235 students drawn from nineteen states and taught by twenty-six faculty members, all part-time. For the 1910–11 school year, DCL inaugurated a part-time day school in which classes were taught in the late afternoon to permit practitioners to continue as instructors. The first full-time dean was employed in 1916, but full-time faculty were not hired until 1937.[42]

By 1915, DCL's facilities had become a problem, and, not for the last time, the school sought an affiliation with an organization that could provide assistance. For a few years, DCL had been using space in a building owned by the Young Men's Christian Association (YMCA). The YMCA was interested in adding a law school to its educational program and could offer not only physical facilities but also support services, including financial management and promotion of the school. Detroit College of Law had been incorporated in 1893 by the five original law clerks, and control of the school had passed to fathers of two of the original owners. Under the oversight of the interim dean, John C. Bills, control of DCL was transferred to the YMCA on August 12, 1915. The YMCA was to have complete control over financial management of the school, but the college maintained its corporate name and control over academic programs.[43]

Affiliation with the YMCA seemed to bring new vitality to DCL. By the mid-1920s, enrollment exceeded seven hundred students. As part of the YMCA, the students and faculty at DCL had full access to its facilities, which were used for athletic competitions as well as social events. Such activities, held in the 1920s and, to a lesser degree, the 1930s, were useful not only in building ties among students but also in providing them with access to alumni mentors. A member of the class of 1930 later said that when he graduated from DCL, he knew "practically every graduate in the school before me and those who were in school with me."[44]

Not every prospective law student in Michigan was satisfied with the choice of either the University of Michigan or Detroit College of Law. Alumni of the Detroit college operated by the Jesuits repeatedly requested that the college establish a law school so that graduates could attend a Catholic law school. At the time, there was considerable interest among Jesuit colleges in developing programs that could rival those at secular institutions. Georgetown had established a law school in 1870, and Creighton University in Omaha had brought Jesuit legal education to the Midwest in 1904.[45] In 1911, Detroit College became the University of Detroit after a reorganization and the establishment of a school of engineering. A law school followed shortly thereafter, and the first classes were held on October 1, 1912.[46]

Just as DCL had turned to the Chicago College of Law for advice, the president of the University of Detroit sought counsel not from another law school in the state but from the dean at Creighton's new law school, who responded with extensive advice on law school administration. He pointed out that the "University of Michigan maintains a very good Moot Court and it is important that you offer instruction in this practical phase of the law."[47]

There was little that was distinctively Catholic about the new law school. There were no courses on canon law, natural law jurisprudence, or the legal philosophy of St. Thomas Aquinas. Being Catholic was not a requirement for admission, and there is no evidence that Catholics were preferred. One of the few reflections of the religious affiliation of the school was a series of lectures given by the new university president, Father William F. Dooley, S. J., as described by a student in 1915: "[T]his humble and retiring man has found time to conduct classes in the Law Department, to instruct students in Legal Ethics."[48]

From the first, the school had both a day and an evening division. The school's bulletin made clear that instruction would be by lectures, text-books, or cases.[49] All students were required to prepare a thesis and to en-roll in a variety of programs involving moot court and trial court practice, brief-making, procedures for common forms of action, equity practice, and the preparation of chattel mortgages and conditional sales contracts.[50]

For the most part, the law schools in Detroit fared well during the 1920s. The first class at the University of Detroit in 1912 comprised 28 students. Enrollments steadily grew, and, by 1926, there were 255 students. The growth of DCL had been even more spectacular, rising to 735 students by that same year.[51]

Developments during the 1920s were even more significant at the University of Michigan than they were at either Detroit school, but not because of enrollments. By that time, the University of Michigan had limited en-rollment to 571 students in an attempt to control class size.[52] UM faculty had a long and distinguished pattern of scholarship and publication.[53] The conception of the role of law school faculty was changing; as UM Dean Harry B. Hutchins wrote in 1908, the law teacher has a duty, beyond the demands of teaching, to make permanent contributions to the store of legal knowledge.[54] By 1920, the university was very much in need of new facilities for the law school, especially the law library. The need for new fa-cilities and for research support was more than sufficiently addressed by the funds provided by an 1882 alumnus of the law school, William W. Cook, whose gifts provided both the magnificent buildings that make up the Law Quadrangle and an endowment to support research.[55]

Despite the large increase in enrollments in the 1920s at DCL, substan-tial dissension there produced what one student called "the great schism."[56] Allan Campbell, a prominent attorney who had graduated from DCL in 1901, taught at the University of Detroit from 1914 to 1923 and began teach-ing at DCL in 1925. In 1921, he was elected to the Detroit Board of Educa-tion, where he eventually became president. He was one of the leaders of an initiative in 1926 to transfer control of DCL from the YMCA to the Board of Education. Campbell believed "that the school will fare better under public administration by the Detroit school board than under the more or less financially restricted supervision of the Y. M. C. A."[57] When that effort failed, Campbell and four other DCL faculty members, including John C. Bills, the interim dean who had overseen the transfer of DCL to the YMCA, petitioned the school board in 1927 to create a new law school. Campbell rallied lawyers in Detroit to support the proposal. Opposition within the board of education was led by Dr. John S. Hall, who told newspaper reporters that the city did not need more law schools or more lawyers and that "[i]t is rumored that Mr. Campbell will be dean of the new school."[58] In fact, the school board was struggling at the time to keep up with the exploding metropolitan population and had nearly nine thousand elementary school children on half-day schedules because of shortages of facilities. Campbell and his supporters maintained that the proposed law school would be self-supporting.[59] It was true at the time that, although the need for new elementary and secondary school facilities had become urgent, funding was not a serious problem.[60] In June, the resolution creating the Detroit City Law School passed, and the new school opened on September 15, 1927, with Campbell as dean and his law partner Arthur Neef, who also had taught at DCL, as secretary. Campbell had a career at his law firm until, on January 1, 1930, he was appointed state circuit court judge. In fact, his career kept him so occupied that most of the administrative work fell to Neef.

The new school offered only evening classes. Campbell made some effort to lure students away from DCL, but few apparently went, some because they did not want to change to an evening program.[61] The size of the first class was unexpectedly large—265 students, although 30 dropped out during the year because of job demands. Of the 265 students, 150 had transferred from other law schools, so, in June, 1928, there was a small graduating class.[62] Of the 230 students in the 1928–29 class, 27 were women.[63] For the 1927–28 academic year, the tuition at Detroit City Law School was $110 for residents and $150 for nonresidents; at DCL, it was $115; at the University of Michigan, it was $118 for resident men, $109 for resident women, and $20 more for nonresidents; and at the University of Detroit, it was $191.[64]

In the 1930s, deteriorating economic conditions affected all law schools in Michigan, although none as seriously as some schools in other states. The executors of the Cook funds at the University of Michigan decided to go ahead with construction of the last building in the Law Quadrangle "as a measure of unemployment relief."[65] Detroit College of Law had planned the construction of a new building in the early 1930s; after some delay, construction began in 1935, and the building opened in fall 1937.[66]

The chief concern of the three law schools in Detroit in the 1930s, however, was to get accreditation from the American Bar Association (ABA). In 1923, the ABA had begun issuing lists of approved schools, one of which, its "A list," included the University of Michigan. As the ABA developed accreditation standards, there emerged a strong bias against part-time schools, proprietary schools, evening schools, schools with no full-time faculty, and schools affiliated with the YMCA.[67] Heated debates occurred at ABA meetings over the standards and the extent to which they were forcing all schools to fit the same mold, regardless of the impact on those who could not afford to go to traditional law schools.[68] The University of Detroit obtained accreditation fairly easily in 1933. The Association of American Law Schools (AALS) had been established in 1900 to ensure high standards among law schools through its membership requirements. The University of Michigan had been a charter member of the AALS, and, in 1934, the University of Detroit became the second school in Michigan accepted as a member. Despite funding limitations, Detroit City Law School met the ABA's requirements over a period of three years by creating three full-time faculty positions in 1935, by expanding its library to the required seven thousand volumes, and by moving to larger facilities in 1936.[69] The school received provisional accreditation in 1937, whereupon it was integrated into Wayne University, which had been created when the Detroit school board's higher education programs were brought together in 1933. Arthur Neef was appointed dean.[70] The addition of day classes in the fall of 1937 led to full accreditation in 1939.[71] After the school was fully accredited, some alumni thought the school should discontinue the evening program because the prestigious Eastern schools did not have part-time programs, but Neef was adamantly opposed. He maintained that the chief purpose of the school was to provide an education for those who had to earn their own way; the more affluent could go elsewhere if they chose.[72]

Detroit College of Law encountered significant difficulties in its efforts to receive ABA accreditation. Despite the construction of a stunning new building, the hiring of four full-time faculty members, and the implementation of full-time day classes and a postgraduate program in 1937–38, DCL encountered resistance in the ABA to accreditation. After the DCL board of trustees was reorganized in 1939 by adding DCL alumni to the YMCA directors, the ABA granted accreditation in 1941. The YMCA recognized the importance of membership in the AALS, which was very uncomfortable with YMCA control, and agreed to transfer all of the stock to the trustees of the law school for $1, along with the building and forgiveness of a $50,000 debt. Because the building had been owned by the YMCA, the YMCA retained a future interest in it if DCL ever went out of business as an independent law school, at which time all the school's assets or liabilities would go to the YMCA.[73] In 1946, both Wayne University's law school (formerly Detroit City Law School) and DCL were approved for membership in the AALS.

Every law school is differently situated, depending on its mission, its competition, its source and level of funding, the strengths of the faculty, and many other factors. The Wayne University Law School was fortunate to have Neef as its chief administrator and, after 1937, its dean. Neef seems to have made few major speeches and to have been involved in few national controversies. At the end of his career, it was said of him: "He is the invisible man. [Beyond his circle of friends and the academic community,] he is at best a shadowy presence, a face in the crowd, a wisp of smoke. Nobody knows his name. Yet few men anywhere have had such a profound influence upon the formation of a major university[.]"[74] Neef realized early in his tenure that the caliber of the law school ultimately depended on the strength of the university. He devoted as much time—and probably considerably more—to the university as he did to the law school. He handled many critical initiatives with the state legislature; he advised the university's presidents; he oversaw property acquisitions, some of which were called Neef's Follies at the time, that permitted the eventual expansion and consolidation of the university's programs. In addition to being the law school dean, he became secretary to the board of governors, provost of the university, and university vice president. "Art Neef's fingerprints are all over the gargantuan educational complex that is Wayne State University."[75] It is surely a sign of Neef's brilliance that the *last* major project he undertook, after getting funding for so many university buildings and projects, was a new law school complex finished in 1966, just before he retired.

The military effort in World War II reduced student enrollments at all schools. At the end of the war, the surge in enrollments was felt at all schools, but the peak years varied by school. In 1948, the University of Michigan had 1,057 students; in 1950, the University of Detroit had 632 students, and DCL had 481; Wayne made an effort, because of its limited capacity, to hold down enrollments by rejecting nonresidents but nevertheless had 504 students in 1954.[76]

The 1950s proved to be good years for the public law schools. For the University of Michigan, the 1950s were one of the school's "golden ages."[77] The faculty explored new areas of the law, such as atomic energy, while strengthening its contributions to such traditional areas as tax law.[78] The university did not, however, prevail in one of its historical strengths, the teaching of practice and procedure. It had developed the so-called Michigan plan, which reallocated the traditional content of procedural courses and included a practice laboratory, in which students conducted trials according to the law of the jurisdictions in which they intended to practice.[79]

This approach was dramatically overwhelmed by a new casebook edited by Richard H. Field and Benjamin Kaplan of the Harvard Law School, who federalized the civil procedure course and determined the content of procedure courses "for the modern era."[80]

At Wayne University's law school, the 1950s were profitable years, during which the law school began its highly successful graduate programs in tax and labor law.[81] But the most important development was the shift of control over the university from the Detroit Board of Education to the state in 1956.[82] Wayne University became Wayne State University. A former president later said that Neef was the strategist and campaign manager for this project.[83]

The 1950s were more difficult for the private law schools that were dependent on tuition revenue. At DCL, enrollments fell from 481 students in 1950 to 246 in 1954, apparently creating a financial crisis.[84] The problem must have resulted, at least in part, from DCL's decision to raise admission standards regarding prelaw credentials effective in the 1952–53 school year.[85]

The environment was not auspicious for substantial increases in academic standards at tuition-dependent schools. In 1954, the University of Detroit hired a young priest, Father David C. Bayne, S.J., who became acting dean. Father Bayne's intention was to make the University of Detroit the "finest law school in the United States." He established very high standards for both admission and graduation. He attempted to eliminate the evening program, which he believed did not attract students with sufficiently good credentials. He participated in student recruitment and was, no doubt, behind the alumni effort to create a dormitory called the Inn of St. Ives for out-of-state students. The effects of Father Bayne's program were immediate. In 1957, all University of Detroit graduates passed the Michigan bar examination; the school's bar passage rate was first in Michigan in 1958 and again in 1959. But the impact of such high standards was devastating to enrollment levels. By 1959, there were fewer than one hundred students enrolled in the school. The university president, his patience running out, prepared a report in 1959 stating that it was not essential that every student pass the bar examination on the first attempt and that many successful judges and lawyers had taken the bar examination twice. The president also maintained that the evening program was essential to the university's mission to serve metropolitan Detroit, including those who must earn their way through law school.[86] In 1960, Father Bayne, who never had been made permanent dean, left and eventually joined the faculty of the University of Iowa.

The 1960s brought significant changes in legal education, perhaps nowhere more so than in Michigan. The law schools in Michigan, which had been remarkably open to student diversity, had been very slow to appreciate faculty diversity. Elizabeth Gallagher, hired as a librarian at DCL in 1948 and made a full professor in the late 1960s, was perhaps the first woman to be named to a Michigan law school faculty.[87] In 1958, Wayne's law school became the first in the state to hire an African American law professor, followed by DCL and the University of Michigan in 1970 and by the University of Detroit in 1972.[88] Harry Edwards, the first African American law professor at the University of Michigan, later recalled the importance to students of his presence on the faculty. Shortly after he began teaching at Michigan, members of the Black Law Students Association met with him and stated that they did not want him to be on picket lines; they wanted him to be a role model, as good as any professor in the school.[89]

Student and faculty idealism—and a 1965 change in the Michigan court rules to permit supervised law students to appear in court[90]—led to the expansion of the modest existing clinical programs at the state's law schools. Schools expanded their internship and externship programs as well. At Wayne State, committed students and attorneys from the Detroit Chapter of the National Lawyers Guild established the Free Legal Aid Clinic to aid indigent residents of Detroit.[91] The most ambitious program was that at the University of Detroit, which received a grant of $242,000 from the Office of Economic Opportunity to fund a clinic with research, curricular, and publication components.[92] As initial programs settled down to sustainable levels, law schools continued to expand and explore new approaches to clinical education.

In 1973, a new law school held its first classes in Lansing. Thomas E. Brennan, the chief justice of the Michigan Supreme Court, believed that the demand for legal education exceeded the space available at existing law schools and, furthermore, that too many applicants were turned away from law schools by excessive admission standards, producing an elitist legal profession. The Thomas M. Cooley Law School was incorporated in 1972 with Brennan as its president.[93] From an entering class of seventy-six students in 1973, Cooley grew in three decades to more than two thousand students, making it the largest law school in the United States.

In its admissions decisions, Cooley has rejected exclusive reliance on aptitude test scores and undergraduate grades in favor of much broader range of criteria, including such factors as job history, career potential, graduate degrees, military service, and recommendations from practitioners.[94] The size of Cooley's class has permitted the school to build impressive buildings for the library and for faculty and organizational offices. In 2002, Cooley opened a satellite campus at Oakland University and, in 2003, another one in Grand Rapids. Throughout its history, Cooley has encountered problems with the ABA accreditation process, first with its Lansing program and more recently with its satellite programs.[95]

Economic considerations in the 1990s led the two private schools in Detroit to achieve greater efficiency and strengthening of academic programs through merger and affiliation. The University of Detroit consolidated its programs with those of Mercy College in 1990, creating the University of Detroit Mercy.

By the early 1990s, DCL once again needed to expand its facilities to handle increased enrollments and to meet ABA accreditation requirements. After considering Michigan State University (MSU), Lawrence Technological University, and Oakland University, the trustees decided that an affiliation with MSU would best serve its long-term goals.[96] Michigan State University's presidents and boards of trustees had been interested in forming a law school since at least the 1960s. In 1966, the school had submitted a request to the state legislature, which was unsuccessful.[97] Dennis Archer, the mayor of Detroit, and David Adamany, the president of Wayne State University, objected forcefully to DCL's proposed affiliation with MSU. Mayor Archer offered to sell at least $15 million in revenue bonds to keep DCL in the city. Adamany claimed that a DCL-MSU law school never would be a truly private law school and that, by receiving tax support, it would weaken Wayne.[98] Nevertheless, DCL affiliated with MSU in 1995, and, by 1997, a new building had been built on MSU's campus in East Lansing. The name, after several permutations, finally was changed to the Michigan State University College of Law by the MSU board of trustees on April 14, 2004. The school remains financially independent and has its own governance structure, including some MSU administrators who also are law school board members.[99] The affiliation has given the law school opportunities for many dual-degree programs and a greater emphasis on scholarship.[100] In 2003, the school entered into a partnership with Grand Valley State University to offer graduate programs in taxation and business administration, offering some courses in both Grand Rapids and East Lansing and some through remote video feeds.[101] The school's old home, the subject of a settlement with the YMCA in 1996, is now under Detroit's Comerica Park.

A former owner of the Detroit Tigers and the founder of Domino's Pizza, Thomas S. Monaghan sold his interest in the latter for a reported $1 billion in 1998. He decided to use $50 million to create a law school to study and teach the law from a Roman Catholic point of view. He found an experienced dean in Bernard Dobranski, then dean of the Catholic University of America law school and former dean of the University of Detroit Mercy School of Law, and, in 2000, they opened the school, named Ave Maria School of Law and located in Ann Arbor.

Ave Maria certainly developed a distinctive mission founded both on professional training and on Catholic doctrine as expressed through sacred tradition and the teaching authority of the Church. The school requires all students to take courses in moral foundations of the law, in jurisprudence, and in law, ethics, and public policy. Ave Maria faculty are asked to address moral issues in all courses and, when appropriate, to explore them through the teachings of the Catholic Church or other religious traditions. Dean Dobranski has written that "we have yet to find a course where something from the tradition is not appropriate and relevant."[102]

To compete with schools like Notre Dame and the University of Chicago, Ave Maria has established a generous scholarship program through which about 70 percent of the students receive scholarships ranging from 50 to 100 percent of tuition costs.[103] By 2004, the school had an enrollment of two hundred students drawn from forty-three states with degrees from more than one hundred colleges and universities. The ABA seems very satisfied with the Ave Maria program. In 2003, the first graduating class at Ave Maria scored the highest passing rate on the Michigan bar examination.[104]

Legal education in the last three decades has been undergoing substantial changes. The early success of applying economic analysis to legal issues led to efforts to apply nearly every other academic discipline to the study of law. Cutting-edge scholarship came to be interdisciplinary, leading George Priest, of Yale, to predict that the "law-school curriculum will come to consist of graduate courses in applied economics, social theory, and political science."[105] By the early 1990s, fully a third of the faculty at the University of Michigan had interdisciplinary interests and several had Ph.D.s in other disciplines or joint appointments with other departments in the university.[106] Because the Socratic method is far too time-consuming for teaching theory, it appears that the lecture method may be returning.[107] This trend toward theory was attacked perhaps most aggressively by Harry Edwards—by then a judge of the U.S. Court of Appeals—in the pages of the *Michigan Law Review* in 1992.[108]

The University of Michigan Law School's commitment to racial diversity in admissions led to a lawsuit that resulted in a decision by the U.S.

Supreme Court in 2003 that racial classifications are constitutional "only if they are narrowly tailored to further compelling government interests."[109] In *Grutter v. Bollinger,* the Court held that the law school did indeed have a compelling interest in maintaining a diverse student body, an interest that lies "at the heart of the Law School's proper institutional mission."[110] The Supreme Court saw the law school's mission as facilitating "cross-racial understanding," maintaining "the fabric of society," and training the nation's leaders.[111]

All of Michigan's law schools, to a large degree, have had distinctive missions. National trends and accreditation standards have narrowed the scope within which those schools have been able to experiment. Rejected models still have something to offer: the learning of skills through apprenticeship, the civility and camaraderie engendered by smaller schools, the experimentation with methods of simulating practice at Michigan, and even the Sprague Correspondence School's experience with distance education. In few fields of education is it as difficult to anticipate the future as it is in legal education.

Notes

The author gratefully acknowledges the generous assistance of the archivists at the Bentley Historical Library of the University of Michigan, the Special Collections of the University of Detroit Mercy Libraries, and the Wayne State University Archives, as well as the law library staffs of the Ave Maria School of Law, the Michigan State University College of Law, the Thomas M. Cooley Law School, and the University of Detroit Mercy School of Law. He has benefited much from the assistance of Dorothy Finnegan of the College of William and Mary and Nickolas Kyser of the University of Detroit Mercy, as well as his research assistant, M. Scott Martin, UDM Class of 2006.

1. Lewis G. Vander Velde, "Thomas McIntyre Cooley," in *Michigan and the Cleveland Era,* ed. Earl D. Babst and Lewis G. Vander Velde (Ann Arbor: University of Michigan Press, 1948), 78.

2. Elizabeth Gaspar Brown, "The Bar on a Frontier: Wayne County, 1796–1836," *American Journal of Legal History* 14 (April 1970): 136–48.

3. Revised Statutes of the State of Michigan, §§ 12–14 (1838).

4. Act of June 15, 1949, 1949 Mich. Pub. Acts 614 (codified, as amended, at Michigan Compiled Laws § 601.53).

5. Roscoe Pound, *The Lawyer from Antiquity to Modern Times* (St. Paul: West, 1953), 223–42.

6. Indiana const. of 1851, art. VII, § 21.

7. Joint Resolution of March 8, 1933, 1933 Ind. Acts 1257. Some analysts believed that no person "of good moral character" could apply for bar admission without

some legal training. See James J. Robinson, "Admission to the Bar as Provided for in the Indiana Constitutional Convention of 1850–1851," *Indiana Law Journal* 1 (April 1926): 209–17; Bernard C. Gavit, "Legal Education and Admission to the Bar," *Indiana Law Journal* 6 (November 1930): 67–91.

8. *Report of the Proceedings and Debates in the Convention to Revise the Constitution of the State of Michigan 1850* (Lansing: R. W. Ingals, 1850), 812.

9. *Journal of the Constitutional Convention of the State of Michigan 1850* (Lansing: R. W. Ingals, 1850), 389, 395; Mich. const. of 1850, art. VI, § 24.

10. Thomas McIntyre Cooley, *Michigan: A History of Governments* (Boston: Houghton, Mifflin, 1885), 248.

11. Edward J. Littlejohn and Donald L. Hobson, "Black Lawyers, Law Practice, and Bar Associations—1844 to 1970: A Michigan History," *Wayne Law Review* 33, no. 5 (1987): 1629.

12. Frank B. Woodford, *Mr. Jefferson's Disciple: A Life of Justice Woodward* (East Lansing: Michigan State, 1953), 158–59. James V. Campbell, later a colleague of Cooley's in the University of Michigan Law Department and on the Michigan Supreme Court, described Woodward's terminology as "neither Greek, Latin nor English . . . a piece of language run mad." Ibid., 160.

13. Elizabeth Gaspar Brown, *Legal Education at Michigan, 1859–1959* (Ann Arbor: University of Michigan Law School, 1959), 3–16; Henry Wade Rogers, "Law School of the University of Michigan," *Green Bag* 1 (1889): 199–203.

14. Brown, *Legal Education at Michigan, 1859–1959*, 31–39.

15. Summarized ibid., 716.

16. See table ibid., 687–93.

17. Elizabeth Gaspar Brown, "The Initial Admission of Negro Students to the University of Michigan," *Michigan Quarterly Review* 2 (Fall 1963): 233.

18. "Michigan's First Woman Lawyer," *Michigan Bar Journal* 63 (June 1984): 448.

19. See Gordon Gray Young Student Notebook, 1863–1864; James D. Bryson Notebook, 1867–1868, Bentley Historical Library, University of Michigan, Ann Arbor.

20. Quoted in Brown, *Legal Education at Michigan, 1859–1959*, 191.

21. Paul D. Carrington, *Stewards of Democracy: Law as a Public Profession* (Boulder, Colo.: Westview, 1999), 7–45.

22. Quoted in Brown, *Legal Education at Michigan, 1859–1959*, 183.

23. Ibid., 192–93.

24. Ibid., 226.

25. See table ibid., 694–95.

26. Ibid., 110, 196, 197, 230, 234, 675.

27. This concern was expressed by several Michigan faculty: see, e.g., Henry Wade Rogers, "Law Schools and Legal Education," *American Law Register* 36 (June 1888): 341; Jerome C. Knowlton, "Embarassments [*sic*] to Legal Education," *Michigan Law Journal* 1 (February 1892): 12.

28. H. B. Hutchins, "Legal Education: Its Relation to the People and the State," *Michigan Law Journal* 4 (May 1895): 152, 149.

29. *Law Student's Helper* 1 (August 1893): 225; ibid., 2 (January 1894): 5.

30. "A Plucky Indiana Woman," *Law Student's Helper* 1 (June 1893): 135. Although it contains no mention of her connection with the Sprague School, the best account of Leach's career is Vivian Sue Shields and Suzanne Melanie Buchko, "Antoinette Dakin Leach: A Woman before the Bar," *Valparaiso University Law Review* 28 (Summer 1994): 1189.

31. In re Leach, 134 Ind. 665, 34 N.E. 641 (1893).

32. Gwenn Bashara Samuel, *The First Hundred Years Are the Hardest: A Centennial History of the Detroit College of Law* (Detroit: Detroit College of Law, 1993), 1–5.

33. Ibid., 9.

34. Ibid., 14.

35. Edward J. Littlejohn, "African American Lawyers and the Detroit College of Law: 1892–1970," ibid., 27–29.

36. Littlejohn and Hobson, "Black Lawyers, Law Practice, and Bar Associations," 1673.

37. See list in Douglas W. Lind, "An Economic Analysis of Early Casebook Publishing," *Law Library Journal* 6 (Winter 2004): 113. Lind omits Marshall D. Ewell's *Cases on Domestic Relations* (Boston: Little, Brown, 1891). Ewell was a "non-resident lecturer" at Michigan from 1890 to 1896. The casebook is a revision of a work that Ewell published in 1876, perhaps in preparation for his teaching at Union College of Law in Chicago in 1877. The 1891 casebook was actually prepared for and used by students in the school of law at Columbia, although apparently Ewell did not teach there. In 1892, Ewell founded the Kent College of Law in Chicago, which merged in 1900 with the Chicago College of Law, becoming the Chicago-Kent College of Law.

38. See Harry Leith Goodbread Student Notebook, 1897–1898, Bentley Historical Library, University of Michigan, Ann Arbor.

39. Alfred Z. Reed, *Training for the Public Profession of Law* (New York: Carnegie Foundation, 1921), 412.

40. Based on data in Lind, "Economic Analysis of Early Casebook Publishing."

41. Samuel, *First Hundred Years Are the Hardest,* 16, 40–41, 59.

42. Ibid., 17–18, 26, 50, 53.

43. A long-needed account of YMCA law schools is Dorothy E. Finnegan, "Raising and Leveling the Bar: Standards, Access, and the YMCA in the Field of Evening Law Schools, 1890–1940" (paper presented at the annual meeting of the Association for the Study of Higher Education, Portland, Ore., November 2003).

44. Interview with Gwen Bashara Samuel, quoted in Samuel, *First Hundred Years Are the Hardest,* 60.

45. Gilbert J. Garraghan, *The Jesuits of the Middle United States* (New York: America Press, 1938), 3:480.

46. Herman J. Muller, *The University of Detroit 1877–1977: A Centennial History* (Detroit: University of Detroit, 1976), 79, 88.

47. Paul L. Martin to William F. Dooley, June 26, 1912, School of Law Historical Papers, vol. 1 (1912–22), Special Collections, University of Detroit Mercy Libraries.

48. "Senior Law Class," *Tamarack* [published by students of the University of Detroit] (June 1915): 32.

49. University of Detroit, *Announcement of the College of Law, 1912–1913* (Detroit: University of Detroit, 1912), 8.

50. University of Detroit, *Announcement of Law School 1913–1914* (Detroit: University of Detroit, 1913), 16–22.

51. Alfred Z. Reed, *Present-Day Law Schools in the United States and Canada* (New York: Carnegie Foundation, 1928), 456.

52. Brown, *Legal Education at Michigan, 1859–1959,* 701.

53. Elizabeth Gaspar Brown, "The Law School of the University of Michigan: 1895–1984: An Intellectual History," *University of Michigan Journal of Law Reform* 18 (Winter 1985): 342–44.

54. H. B. Hutchins, "The Law Teacher: His Functions and Responsibilities," *Columbia Law Review* 8 (May 1908): 369.

55. Kathryn Horste, *The Michigan Law Quadrangle: Architecture and Origins* (Ann Arbor: University of Michigan Press, 1997), 31–67; Brown, *Legal Education at Michigan, 1859–1959,* 305–26.

56. Arthur W. Brown, "Senior Class History," *Forum* [published by the senior class of DCL] (1928): 59.

57. James R. Irwin, "Chapter VIII: A History of the Detroit City Law School (Now the Wayne University Law School)," 182, Arthur Neef Biography File, 4N-G-2-7, University Archives, Wayne State University, Detroit (draft of a chapter of an Ed.D. dissertation on the history of Wayne University sent to Neef on May 21, 1951, and containing corrections by him).

58. "Law School Intrigue Scored by Dr. Hall," Law School File—Clippings, Undated to 1965, University Archives, Wayne State University, Detroit.

59. See clippings from various newspapers in F&M File, Burton Historical Collection, Detroit Public Library.

60. Jeffrey Mirel, *The Rise and Fall of an Urban School System: Detroit, 1907–81,* 2d ed. (Ann Arbor: University of Michigan Press, 1999), 65.

61. Samuel, *First Hundred Years Are the Hardest,* 104–5.

62. Irwin, "Chapter VIII," 185.

63. Clarence M. Burton and Agnes Burton, *History of Wayne County and the City of Detroit, Michigan* (Chicago: S. J. Clarke Publishing, 1930), 1:796.

64. Reed, *Present-Day Law Schools,* 455–57.

65. "Start $1,500,000 U. of M. Building at Ann Arbor," *Michigan Manufacturer and Financial Record,* April 4, 1931, 9.

66. Samuel, *First Hundred Years Are the Hardest,* 90–91.

67. Robert Stevens, *Law School: Legal Education in America from the 1850s to the 1980s* (Chapel Hill: University of North Carolina Press, 1983), 172–204.

68. Susan K. Boyd, *The ABA's First Section: Assuring a Qualified Bar* ([Chicago]: American Bar Association, 1993), 26.

69. Leslie L. Hanawalt, *A Place of Light: The History of Wayne State University* (Detroit: Wayne State University Press, 1968), 282–83.

70. "Law School Recognized by Bar Association," *Detroit Collegian,* January 14, 1937; "Law School Integrated into Wayne University," *Detroit Collegian,* March 10, 1937; "Board Names Arthur Neef Dean of Law School," *Detroit Collegian,* April 16, 1937.

71. Hanawalt, *Place of Light,* 478n4.

72. "From Art Hagan," [evidently a retirement tribute, undated], Arthur Neef Biography File, University Archives, Wayne State University, Detroit.

73. Samuel, *First Hundred Years Are the Hardest,* 122–23.

74. "From Art Hagan."

75. Ibid.

76. See "Law School Registration" in annual volumes of the *Journal of Legal Education,* beginning with 1 (1948): 300; Hanawalt, *Place of Light,* 284.

77. James J. White, "Letter to Judge Harry Edwards," *Michigan Law Review* 91 (August 1993): 2117.

78. Brown, "Law School of the University of Michigan," 348–53.

79. Charles W. Joiner, "Teaching Civil Procedure: The Michigan Plan," *Journal of Legal Education* 5, no. 4 (1953): 464–71.

80. Mary Brigid McManamon, "The History of the Civil Procedure Course: A Study in Evolving Pedagogy," *Arizona State Law Journal* 30 (Summer 1998): 435.

81. Hanawalt, *Place of Light,* 284–85.

82. Ibid., 415.

83. George E. Gullen Jr., "Arthur F. Neef: June 9, 1899: August 29, 1978," Arthur Neef Biography File, University Archives, Wayne State University, Detroit.

84. John S. Abbott, who was a professor from 1954 onward and eventually dean, later told Gwen Bashara Samuel that, in 1959, the school was insolvent and unable to pay its debts; the situation eased only with the increased enrollments in the 1960s. Samuel, *First Hundred Years Are the Hardest,* 117. It seems likely that Abbott's recollection of the timing is wrong. From the low in 1954, the school's enrollment climbed steadily to 538 in 1959 and continued to rise in the 1960s.

85. Ibid., 121.

86. School of Law, Historical Papers File, Special Collections, University of Detroit Mercy Libraries.

87. Based on a comparative analysis of the AALS *Directory* from 1948 to 1970.

88. Littlejohn and Hobson, "Black Lawyers, Law Practice, and Bar Associations," 1677.

89. Harry T. Edwards, "Symposium: Race and the Judiciary," *Yale Law and Policy Review* 20, no. 2 (2002): 328.

90. "Rule 921. Legal Aid Clinics," 376 Mich. xli (1965).

91. "WSU Law Students, Attorneys Open Free Legal Aid Clinic," *Legal Advertiser,* December 2, 1965.

92. Norman L. Miller and James C. Daggitt, "The Urban Law Program of the University of Detroit School of Law," *California Law Review* 54 (May 1966): 1009; John W. McAuliffe, "The Urban Law Program of the University of Detroit," *Journal of Legal Education* 20, no. 1 (1967): 83.

93. Thomas E. Brennan, "To envision what is not, *but can be,*" *Benchmark* [publication of Thomas M. Cooley Law School], Trinity Term, 1998.

94. "New Admissions Procedure Announced," *Pillar* [publication of Thomas M. Cooley Law School], December 1977.

95. See, e.g., "Accreditation—A Special Report," *Benchmark,* Hilary Term, 1982; "Cooley Law School Sues Bar Association over Lack of Accreditation," *Grand Rapids Press,* March 31, 2004.

96. "Resolution of the Trustees of the Detroit College of Law" [adopted February 21, 1995], *Amicus: Magazine of the Detroit College of Law,* Spring 1995, 3.

97. "This Matter of a Third Law School," *Grand Rapids Press,* February 28, 1966; Leo Zainea, "Seek Quick Approval of Law School Request," *Michigan State News,* August 18, 1966.

98. "Legislators Review Law School's Plans for a Move," *Detroit Free Press,* February 8, 1995.

99. "Michigan State University Law School Name Change Reflects Integration, Collaboration," *Ascribe Newswire,* April 16, 2004 (Nexis).

100. See David Thomas, "The Role of Scholarship," *Amicus: Magazine of Michigan State University–Detroit College of Law,* Winter 2000, 7–11.

101. "Grand Valley Says It Aims to Fill Void, Not Compete," *Grand Rapids Press,* May 26, 2003.

102. Bernard Dobranski, "New Lawyers for a New Century—Legal Excellence and Moral Clarity: The Founding of Ave Maria School of Law," *University of Toledo Law Review* 36 (Fall 2004): 60–61.

103. "Monaghan's Dream Matures," *Detroit News,* May 18, 2003. Ave Maria claims to be the most heavily tuition-discounted law school in the country. Dobranski, "New Lawyers for a New Century," 62.

104. "Ave Maria Is Best in State on Bar Exam," *Detroit News,* November 9, 2003.

105. George L. Priest, "Social Science Theory and Legal Education: The Law School as University," *Journal of Legal Education* 33, no. 3 (1983): 441.

106. James J. White, "Letter to Harry Edwards," *Michigan Law Review* 91 (August 1993): 2177.

107. Ibid., 2179.

108. Harry T. Edwards, "The Growing Disjunction between Legal Education and the Legal Profession," *Michigan Law Review* 91 (October 1992): 34.

109. Grutter v. Bollinger, 539 U.S. 306, 326 (2003).

110. Ibid., 329.

111. Ibid., 330–32.

CONTRIBUTORS

RONALD J. BRETZ is professor of law at Thomas M. Cooley Law School in Lansing, Michigan, where he teaches criminal law and criminal procedure and is chair of the Criminal Law Department. He earned a B.A. (with honors) at Michigan State University (1973) and a J.D. at Wayne State University Law School (1976). He has written a number of articles in legal journals reviewing criminal law decisions of the Michigan appellate courts. He also has written and lectured on the use of scientific evidence in criminal cases.

PAUL D. CARRINGTON is professor of Law at Duke University. He has taught law since 1957, and at the University of Michigan from 1965 to 1978. He is the author of *Stewards of Democracy* and *Spreading America's Word*, works recounting the deeds and misdeeds of American lawyers in which Michigan Supreme Court justice Thomas Cooley is a prominent figure. His most recent works are two edited volumes: *Reforming the Supreme Court: Term Limits for Justices* (with Roger Cramton) and *Law and Class in America: Trends since the Cold War* (with Trina Jones). He has been active in judicial law reform efforts, particularly with regard to the jurisdiction of appellate courts, the rules of civil litigation, and the selection and tenure of judges in state courts. From 1985 to 1992, he served as reporter to the committee of the Judicial Conference of the United States advising the Supreme Court on changes in the Federal Rules of Civil Procedure.

DAVID CHARDAVOYNE is a lawyer practicing in Farmington Hills, Michigan. He received his B.A. from the University of Michigan and his J.D. (*magna cum laude*) from Wayne State University Law School, where he is an adjunct faculty member. He also serves as an adjunct professor at the University of Detroit Mercy School of Law. His book, *A Hanging in Detroit: Stephen Gifford Simmons and the Last Execution under Michigan Law*, was named a Michigan Notable Book for 2004 by the Library of Michigan Foundation. He is a member of the board of trustees of the Historical Society for the U.S. District Court for the Eastern District of Michigan and is a frequent contributor to the society's journal, the *Court Legacy*, as well as to the annual survey of Michigan law published by the *Wayne Law Review.*

BYRON D. COOPER is director of the Kresge Law Library at the University of Detroit Mercy School of Law, where he has taught property law, English legal history, and other subjects. He earned A.B., M.S., J.D., and M.L.S. degrees from Indiana University in Bloomington. He has published articles and given presentations on librarianship, legal history, and property law. He is past chair of the Michigan Library Consortium and the Conference of Law Libraries of the Association of Jesuit Colleges and Universities and is currently honorary correspondent in Michigan for the Selden Society, which is devoted to the study of English legal history.

DAVID DEMPSEY currently serves as Great Lakes policy adviser for Clean Water Action and is a policy consultant to the Michigan Environmental Council. He served as environmental adviser to Michigan governor James J. Blanchard from 1983 to 1989. President Clinton appointed him to serve on the Great Lakes Fishery Commission in 1994, where he served until 2001. Michigan governor Jennifer Granholm appointed him to the Michigan Natural Resources Trust Fund board in November 2003. Now a resident of St. Paul, Minnesota, Dempsey was born in Michigan and spent most of his life there. He is the author of two books on the environment: *Ruin and Recovery: Michigan's Rise as a Conservation Leader* and *On the Brink: The Great Lakes in the 21st Century,* the recipient of a 2004 Award of Merit from the Historical Society of Michigan and a Michigan Notable Book for 2005. Recently, Dempsey authored a biography of William G. Milliken, Michigan's longest-serving governor and a champion of the environment (forthcoming, 2006).

ELIZABETH FAUE is professor of history at Wayne State University. She earned her doctorate at the University of Minnesota and she was Susan B. Anthony Post-Doctoral Fellow in Women's Studies at the University of Rochester. She joined the faculty at Wayne State University in 1990. Faue is the author of *Community of Suffering and Struggle: Women, Men, and the Labor Movement in Minneapolis, 1915–1945* (1991), *Writing the Wrongs: Eva Valesh and the Rise of Labor Journalism* (2002), and numerous articles on labor, gender, and politics. From 1991 to 2003, Faue served as coordinator of the North American Labor History Conference. She currently is at work on two books—one on the American welfare state and the other a study of loyalty and allegiance in national crises in the twentieth-century United States.

PAUL FINKELMAN is the President William McKinley Professor of Law and Public Policy and Senior Fellow in the Government Law Center at Albany

Law School. He received his B.A. from Syracuse University in 1971 and his M.A. (1972) and Ph.D. (1976) from the University of Chicago. He is the author or editor of more than twenty books and more than one hundred articles and book chapters. He is the author of *Slavery and the Founders: Race and Liberty in the Age of Jefferson* and *Defending Slavery: Proslavery Thought in the Old South*, and the coauthor of *A March of Liberty: A Constitutional History of the United States*.

ROY E. FINKENBINE is professor of history and director of the Black Abolitionist Archives at the University of Detroit Mercy. A specialist on African American involvement in the transatlantic antislavery movement, he is the coeditor of the five-volume *Black Abolitionist Papers, 1830–1865* and *Witness for Freedom: African American Voices on Race, Slavery, and Emancipation* and the author of "Boston's Black Churches: Institutional Centers of the Antislavery Movement," in *Courage and Conscience: Black and White Abolitionists in Boston*. He is also the editor of *Sources of the African American Past*.

LIETTE GIDLOW is associate professor of history at Bowling Green State University. She received her A.B. from the University of Chicago and her doctorate from Cornell University. She is the author of *The Big Vote: Gender, Consumer Culture, and the Politics of Exclusion, 1890s–1920s* (2004) and numerous articles about politics, gender, and citizenship. She is at work on a history of television advertising in presidential campaigns from the 1950s to the present day.

MARTIN J. HERSHOCK is associate professor of history and chair of the Department of Social Sciences at the University of Michigan–Dearborn. He is the author of *The Paradox of Progress: Economic Change, Individual Enterprise, and Political Culture in Michigan, 1837–1878*, which received an Award of Merit from the Historical Society of Michigan in 2004, and of a number of articles on nineteenth-century Michigan history. A lifelong resident of Michigan, Hershock resides in Canton with his wife Kathy and daughters Rebecca and Rachel.

JOHN W. QUIST is associate professor of history at Shippensburg University. He received his Ph.D. from the University of Michigan and is the author of *Restless Visionaries: The Social Roots of Antebellum Reform in Alabama and Michigan*.

FRANK S. RAVITCH is professor of law at the Michigan State University College of Law where he teaches courses in constitutional law, law and religion, professional responsibility, and torts. He is the author of *Law and Religion,*

A Reader: Concepts, Cases, and Theory; Employment Discrimination Law (with Pamela Sumners and Janis McDonald); and *School Prayer and Discrimination: The Civil Rights of Religious Minorities and Dissenters.* He is currently working on *Masters of Illusion: The Supreme Court and the Religion Clause* and on a treatise with Scott Idelman and the late Boris Bittker, *Religion and the State in American Law,* which is supported by a grant from the Lilly Endowment. In 2001, Professor Ravitch was named a Fulbright Scholar and served on the Faculty of Law at Doshisha University in Kyoto, Japan, where he taught U.S. constitutional law and law and religion and engaged in research. More recently, Professor Ravitch wrote an amicus brief to the U.S. Supreme Court on behalf of the Interfaith Alliance and the Horace Mann League in support of the petition for writ of certiorari in *Chandler v. Siegelman,* a school prayer case from Alabama. He regularly speaks on topics related to church-state and civil rights law to a wide range of national and local organizations and as a media expert. He lives in Haslett, Mich., with his wife Jamie and daughters Elysha and Ariana.

INDEX

Endnotes are indicated by the letter n and note number following the page number(s).